CW01375966

'A GREAT EFFUSION OF BLOOD'?
INTERPRETING MEDIEVAL VIOLENCE

'A GREAT EFFUSION OF BLOOD'?

Interpreting Medieval Violence

Edited by

Mark D. Meyerson

Daniel Thiery

Oren Falk

UNIVERSITY OF TORONTO PRESS
Toronto Buffalo London

© University of Toronto Press Incorporated 2004
Toronto Buffalo London
Printed in Canada

ISBN 0-8020-8774-4

∞

Printed on acid-free paper

Library and Archives Canada Cataloguing in Publication

A great effusion of blood? : interpreting medieval
violence / [edited by] Mark D. Meyerson, Daniel Thiery, Oren Falk.

Includes bibliographical references.
ISBN 0-8020-8774-4

1. Violence – Europe – History. 2. Violence in literature – History.
3. Civilization, Medieval. I. Meyerson, Mark Douglas, 1957–
II. Thiery, Daniel III. Falk, Oren, 1969–

HN380.V5G74 2004   303.6'094'0902   C2004-903265-8

'Violence, the Queen's Body, and the Medieval Body Politic' by John Carmi Parsons
was first published in *'The man of many devices, who wandered full many ways...':
Festschrift in Honor of Janos M. Bak*, edited by Balaza Nagy and Marcell Sebok
(Budapest: CEU Press, 1999).

University of Toronto Press acknowledges the financial assistance to its publishing
program of the Canada Council for the Arts and the Ontario Arts Council.

University of Toronto Press acknowledges the financial support for its publishing
activities of the Government of Canada through the Book Publishing Industry
Development Program (BPIDP).

Contents

Contributors vii

Abbreviations viii

Introduction 3
MARK D. MEYERSON, DANIEL THIERY, and OREN FALK

PART I: VIOLENCE AND IDENTITY FORMATION

1 Violence and the Making of Wiglaf 19
   JOHN M. HILL

2 Defending Their Masters' Honour: Slaves as Violent Offenders in Fifteenth-Century Valencia 34
   DEBRA BLUMENTHAL

3 The Murder of Pau de Sant Martí: Jews, *Conversos*, and the Feud in Fifteenth-Century Valencia 57
   MARK D. MEYERSON

4 Violence and the Sacred City: London, Gower, and the Rising of 1381 79
   EVE SALISBURY

5 Bystanders and Hearsayers First: Reassessing the Role of the Audience in Duelling 98
   OREN FALK

6 Scottish National Heroes and the Limits of Violence 131
ANNE MCKIM

PART II: VIOLENCE AND THE TESTAMENT OF THE BODY

7 Seeing the Gendering of Violence: Female and Male Martyrs in the *South English Legendary* 147
BETH CRACHIOLO

8 Violence or Cruelty? An Intercultural Perspective 164
DANIEL BARAZ

9 Body as Champion of Church Authority and Sacred Place: The Murder of Thomas Becket 190
DAWN MARIE HAYES

10 Chaucer's *Clerk's Tale*: Interrogating 'Virtue' through Violence 216
M.C. BODDEN

11 Violence, the Queen's Body, and the Medieval Body Politic 241
JOHN CARMI PARSONS

12 Violence in the Early Robin Hood Poems 268
RICHARD FIRTH GREEN

13 Canon Laws regarding Female Military Commanders up to the Time of Gratian: Some Texts and Their Historical Contexts 287
DAVID HAY

Conclusion 315
MARK D. MEYERSON, DANIEL THIERY, and OREN FALK

Contributors

Oren Falk, Assistant Professor of History, Cornell University

Mark D. Meyerson, Associate Professor of History, University of Toronto

Daniel Thiery, Assistant Professor of History, Iona College

Daniel Baraz, Postdoctoral Fellow in the School of Business Administration, Hebrew University of Jerusalem

Debra Blumenthal, Assistant Professor of History, University of California Santa Barbara

M. C. Bodden, Associate Professor of English, Marquette University

Beth Crachiolo, Assistant Professor of English, Berea College

Richard Firth Green, Humanities Distinguished Professor of English, Ohio State University

David Hay, Assistant Professor of History, University of Lethbridge

Dawn Marie Hayes, Assistant Professor of European History, Montclair State University

John M. Hill, Professor of English, United States Naval Academy

Anne McKim, Senior Lecturer of English, University of Waikato

John Carmi Parsons, Lecturer and Postdoctoral Fellow in Medieval Studies, Southern Methodist University

Eve Salisbury, Assistant Professor of English, Western Michigan University

Abbreviations

ACA	Arxiu de la Corona d'Aragó
APPV	Archivo de Protocolos del Patriarca de Valencia
ARV	Archivo del Reino de Valencia / Arxiu del Regne de València
BAV	Biblioteca Apostolica Vaticana (Vatican City)
BL	British Library (London)
BN	Bibliotheque Nationale (Paris)
CCCM	Corpus Christianorum, continuatio medievalis
CCSL	Corpus Christianorum scriptorum Latinorum
CSEL	Corpus scriptorum ecclesiasticorum Latinorum
EETS	Early English Text Society
ÍF	Íslenzk fornrit
KLNM	*Kulturhistorisk leksikon for nordisk middelalder*
MGH	Monumenta Germaniae historica
AA	Auctores antiquissimi
LdL	Libelli de lite imperatorum et pontificum
NGL	*Norges gamle Love indtil 1387*
PG	Patrologia Graeca (ed. J.-P. Migne)
PL	Patrologia Latina (ed. J.-P. Migne)
PO	Patrologia orientalis
RHF	Recueil des historiens des Gaules et de la France
MS(S)	manuscript(s)
n.s.	new series
o.s.	original series
s.s.	supplementary series

'A GREAT EFFUSION OF BLOOD'?

Introduction

MARK D. MEYERSON, DANIEL THIERY, and OREN FALK

'A great effusion of blood' was the shorthand often used throughout medieval Europe to describe the effects of immoderate interpersonal violence. Scribes working in criminal courts, for example, employed this phrase when recording the accusations which plaintiffs levelled against individuals who had allegedly assaulted them or their loved ones. Revelling in descriptions of battles, bloodbaths, and mayhem, medieval chroniclers lionized the heroes and demonized the villains responsible for such effusions of blood. *Effusio*, which in classical Latin had meant simply a 'pouring forth,' came to mean in the Middle Ages primarily a 'shedding of blood'; in the vernaculars, too, derivatives like *effusioun* (in the example of Middle English) became indissolubly paired with *blood*.[1] Yet how much substance, red or otherwise, is there really to these sanguinary turns of phrase? Since judicial scribes' succinct renderings of the perpetration of violence were based on the mere accusations of plaintiffs, the modern interpreter of court records is often left guessing whether such great outpourings of blood actually took place or, in those cases in which the authorities indeed saw the wounds of live victims or the corpses of dead ones, whether the accused had resorted to violence in the manner and for the reasons declared by the plaintiff. Similarly, literary renderings of violence raise questions of the dramatic effect that authors intended to elicit and of the audiences' horizons of expectations: did descriptions of bloodletting shock audiences, titillate them, or leave them unmoved?

The questions arising from the appearance and deployment of one loaded phrase hint at the great complexity of the problem treated in one way or another by the essays in the present volume: the interpretation of violence in medieval society and culture. The problem is complex because it entails coming to grips, implicitly or explicitly, with multiple views: the views of modern scholars regarding the psychology and comportment of medieval people; the views of medieval persons themselves regarding the violence of which they were the perpetrators or the victims; the views of medieval writers who deployed descriptions of violent acts in their texts to achieve a particular effect; and the views of medieval readers, the audience for these accounts of violence, whether enacted or threatened, human or divine.

Students of medieval culture have evinced a growing interest in the phenomenon of violence in recent years. Most of the essays in the present collection in fact originated in the conference 'Violence in Medieval Society' organized by the Centre for Medieval Studies at the University of Toronto in 1998. Other collections have also appeared reflecting this trend in medieval studies.[2] The fascination with violence in the Middle Ages stems, to a significant degree, from the post-modern challenge to the master narrative of the history of the West, which links western progress, rationality, and the civilizing process to the rise of orderly nation-states. Living in a post-modern era of fragmenting states, ethnic and sexual violence, and fiercely fought culture wars has moved medievalists increasingly to focus on the violence involved in the process of state formation and on the people excluded and the voices silenced in the rise of western culture. Whereas an earlier generation of historians tended to view medieval violence as a primitive and anarchic force of social dissolution, gradually superseded in the course of historical progress,[3] violence is now seen not merely as characteristic of a safely medieval and barbaric past but as integral to the historical processes that have brought us to our present condition, as foundational to what we have become. A violent Middle Ages, with its repressive states, persecuting majorities, and patriarchal structures is 'darkly familiar, the analogue of a negatively construed modern West.'[4] In this light, the sociopolitical order of the Middle Ages appears as the direct precursor of modernity, the modernity which has produced the Holocaust and which, therefore, may not differ as much from earlier periods as Zygmunt Bauman has suggested.[5]

Yet this conception of a violent Middle Ages, highlighting repressive institutions, persecuting mentalities, and patriarchy, privileges violence on a vertical plane, usually 'top-down' violence: that of the state against its subjects, of Christians against Muslims and Jews, of orthodox Catholics against heretics, of rural lords and urban oligarchs against peasants and the urban poor, and of men against women.[6] (Of course, the violence of the lower classes against their superiors, in the form of spectacular rebellion or canny resistance and evasion, also receives attention.) Often excluded from the new, and sometimes teleological, master narrative of repression and persecution[7] is violence on a horizontal plane, i.e., intragroup violence: violence among Jews, among Muslims, among poor Christians, among women, and so on.

It is precisely the phenomenon of horizontal, intragroup violence that raises the most challenging questions as to what distinguishes us from medieval people.

For insofar as intergroup or international violence is concerned, the ethnic nationalism and international conflicts of the twentieth century more easily lead us to the uncomfortable conclusion that only our higher level of bureaucratic and technological sophistication separates us from – or perhaps makes us more barbaric than – our medieval ancestors.[8] As for intragroup violence, consideration of the modern social norms and assumptions that proscribe, pathologize, and curb violence within states or within ethnic groups may well lead us to the opposite conclusion: that the behaviours and emotions of medieval people, as evinced in their propensity for violence, really did differ significantly from our own.

The acceptance of such a conclusion need not involve exaggerating the alterity of the Middle Ages and viewing the ideas and conduct of medieval people as bizarre and grotesque; nor does it imply complete agreement with the thesis of Norbert Elias on 'the civilizing process.'[9] Few scholars today would subscribe to Elias's notion that the development of a court society and the taming of the European nobility, especially from the end of the Middle Ages, effected a change in norms and a reduction of violence throughout society. Medievalists in particular have criticized his characterization of medieval people as irrational, given to extreme emotions, and uncontrollably violent. They have also questioned his almost exclusive emphasis on the lay aristocracy, his assumption that new aristocratic mores necessarily percolated down to or were aped by the lower classes, and his relative neglect of the latter and the church in his treatment of the ideological and social changes essential to the civilizing process.[10]

Yet, however medievalists and others have criticized and qualified the work of Elias, it is difficult to avoid concluding that medieval people used and understood violence differently, and that what separates us from our medieval forebears is not just the greater efficacy of modern states in controlling and suppressing violence but, more importantly, fundamental modifications in mentality and behaviour. Nowadays, for example, no mainstream work of art can afford to show graphic depictions of violence with the same casual candour with which medieval hagiographers presented roasting saints and impaled martyrs. Similarly, according to anthropologists, verbal insults were deemed an acceptable means of disgracing a rival among the highly competitive townsmen of late twentieth-century Andalusia, but physical assaults were socially proscribed – a marked departure from the behavioural norms of their medieval and early modern ancestors.[11]

Indeed, most inhabitants of the nation-states of the modern industrialized West regard the violence perpetrated on their own streets or depicted on the movie screens of their theatres as aberrant, antisocial, pathological behaviour. Only in certain instances of ethnic and political conflict, or on the fringes of the artistic world, do some individuals or groups ignore the social codes pathologizing physical violence.[12] By contrast, in medieval society, as some scholars much influenced by the work of anthropologists have concluded, violence was integral to the processes through which social status was contested and affirmed and economic resources allocated within communities, essential to the creation and maintenance of social order. For medieval people violence was, in other words, normative social practice, a form of social discourse utilized not just by kings, knights, inquisitors, and mobs to oppress and abuse others, but by artisans and peasants, men and women of whatever religion, to lay claim to honour and integrity, and to establish and defend a place for themselves and their families in local society.[13]

The essays in this collection seem to indicate that violence or the threat thereof was omnipresent in the Middle Ages, influencing in some way the thoughts and conduct of everyone: informing political action and discourse; contributing to the gendering of social behaviour; shaping language and textual production; framing and strengthening national, communal, and religious identities; and structuring relations between church and state, or master and slave. If violence was so integral to the social and textual strategies of medieval people, one might well ask why there was not more bloodshed, more 'effusions of blood.' After all, medieval states were notoriously inefficient and judicial and police institutions of only limited efficacy. Yet interpersonal relations and community life did not so frequently degenerate into bloody anarchy. Medieval texts tend to glory in the gore and to telescope history, omitting the long lulls between violent eruptions. Yet, on closer inspection, even many of these texts – the stuff of medieval studies – reveal that violence was not an expression of the irrationality and extreme emotions of medieval people but a product of their rationality, a behaviour well understood and strategically deployed. Precisely because violent behaviour was normative, medieval people could efficiently draw upon private and public resources to limit it. The ability to control violence in a violent world is one of the more striking manifestations of the resourcefulness of medieval people.

The essays in this volume have been organized into two groups: 'Violence and Identity Formation' and 'Violence and the Testament of the Body.' Although other categorizations are certainly possible – for the articles collected here afford a diversity of approaches to the basic problem of interpreting medieval violence – these broad groupings serve to highlight both the social utility of violence and the grounding of the medieval imagination in the physicality of violent acts. In their various ways, all of these essays negotiate the tensions between violence as historical fact and as a mode of representation.

The essays in the first group all treat, in some way, the relationship between violence and the creation and consolidation of individual and group identity. If, as has been suggested above, violence was normative, an accepted form of social discourse, then it is not surprising that violence, actual and textual, was elemental to self and group definition. In investigating how violence both shaped and was shaped by individual, familial, religious, civic, and national identities – i.e., how individuals and groups responded to or enacted violence – these essays substantiate the assertion of Charles Phythian-Adams that the structure of a society can be best apprehended when 'it *seems* in peril of collapse and thus *theoretically* at its most ineffectual.'[14]

In socially or politically stratified societies, acts of violence can become the means through which an individual advances beyond his or her inherited status. Prowess most often transcends pedigree in times of crisis, be it Cincinnatus leaving his plough to lead Rome or a farmer's son crawling up the beaches of Normandy. Employing anthropological and psychological theories in an analysis of the Anglo-Saxon poem *Beowulf*, John Hill contends that the 'violent, hand-searing assistance' which Wiglaf renders against the dragon elevates his status from mere retainer to that of kinsman and heir to the throne. Wiglaf, whose kinship to Beowulf is too remote for any passive inheritance of great honour, actively appropriates the highly honoured position of 'adopted kinsman' through violence. From the commencement of the fight to its fatal conclusion, the ennobling power of violence is revealed. Wiglaf's identity progresses beyond the status of 'loyal subject' to the more elevated level of 'noble heir.' Yet, the scars on Wiglaf's hand are a permanent reminder of the means through which his new status has been achieved: a reminder that violence can subjugate and deform as much as it can elevate and transform.

Not all acts of violence elevate the status of their participants. In those societies where the law severely limited the agency and real power of unfree individuals, violence was a means more of confirming subjection than of establishing integrity and autonomy. By focusing on individual agency and the relative power of those implicated in acts of violence, one can discern whether the autonomy of a particular individual is truly present, or only illusory. Mediterranean slavery has been romantically depicted as a benign socializing mechanism through which slaves became fully integrated members of their masters' houses. Responding to this optimistic depiction of slavery by Jacques Heers, Debra Blumenthal's investigation of the registers of the *Justicia Criminal* in fifteenth-century Valencia shows that the dishonourable status of slaves both facilitated and resulted from acts of violence in which their masters compelled them to participate. The base status of slaves made them prime vehicles for violently dishonouring the rivals of their masters and also for deflecting any consequent punishment by the central authority away from those who actually gained from the slaves' deeds. Although masters increased their own honour through the possession of slaves as well as the employment of them in struggles with their peers, the personal status of the slaves was not enhanced. It is ironic that at the very moment when the slaves appear most dynamic in the records – as during these acts of violence – they are not transcending but rather reinforcing their identity as objectified instruments for controlling the ebb and flow of honour.

Compared to that of slave revolts, the violence of Valencian slaves during these interpersonal conflicts never threatened to diminish the power of their masters or to transcend the customs and duties of a subjugated individual. Slaves defended their masters' honour as slaves, not as family members.

Still, among free persons, as the anthropologist Jacob Black Michaud has contended, familial identity is a powerful component in the enactment, perpetuation, and control of violence. Violence tests the bonds of kinship and reveals how such bonds intertwine with other social networks.[15] Religious affiliation is usually considered to have been the most important form of classification in the pre-modern world, and affixed to each religion – at least by many in the West – are certain stereotypical attitudes to violence, from active Muslim militancy to crusading Christian oppression to passive Jewish victimization. In Mark Meyerson's 'thick description' of a murder case from late medieval Valencia, kinship proves to be more potent than orthodox religious ties as factions composed of Jews and *conversos* (baptized Jews) actively participate in the social discourse of the blood feud. Rival families expressed their honour publicly through ritualistic, yet sometimes quite sanguinary, acts of violence against other Jewish and *converso* families. During a feud between two families, the community would mentally register each violent encounter as honourable for one family and dishonourable for the other. Thus, for Jews of fifteenth-century Valencia, family identity and prestige were determined by the Jewish and *converso* communities together, but the standards by which these communities judged did not remain static. As kinship and blood ties were enervated in the late fifteenth century, *conversos* and Jews increasingly emphasized the duties of religious observance more than the duties of kinship. External religious affiliation and public practice became more crucial aspects of honour than conduct in the blood feud.

Religious ideology has often become enmeshed in the formation of other, more profane group identities, such as those of nationalists, knights, rebels, and revolutionaries. The appropriation of religious status often empowers such groups to employ violence under the veil of divine will. As they slowly rose to social and economic prominence in the late Middle Ages, towns legitimated their status as autonomous entities through religious pageantry and processions that both united the town and juxtaposed it with outlying communities. In the poem *Vox clamantis*, the sacredness of civic identity colours John Gower's attitude towards the violence of the Rising of 1381. For Gower, a cleric and a citizen of London, violence is only acceptable when wielded on behalf of the sacred – in this instance, the city of London made sacred on the feast of Corpus Christi. Eve Salisbury, with the support of Rene Girard's theory of sacrifice,[16] shows that Gower denounces the illegitimate 'polluting' violence of the rebels, as well as the London citizens' massacre of the resident Flemish, while praising the licit, sacrificial violence of the mayor of London, an 'urban saint' who saves the sacred city from the external threat of Tyler's 'pagan' pollution. Violence fashions the identities of individuals and groups by shrouding them in sacred legitimacy which is polarized against the pollution of the 'other.' Like the citizens of sixteenth-century Lyon, each participant group in the Rising of 1381 claims divine sanction for its cause and attempts through violence to prevent pollution by oppressive royal advisors, treasonous rebels, or economically subversive foreigners.[17] For Gower, only the mayor of London can claim to have truly defended the city's sacred identity and thus to have enacted divine vengeance upon those who had polluted the feastday of God's sacred body and murdered his holy servants.

Like Gower's writing, the Norse sagas and the chronicles of Scotland evince the 'perspectival' nature of violence. Whether a certain action should be deemed 'violent' is often contested by the victimizer, victim, and observers, but it is the latter two who have marked advantages in this contest.[18] Wiglaf and the mayor of London could not simply conclude on their own that their belligerence was heroic or ennobling; their conduct was evaluated by others who witnessed their feats of fury. Through his analysis of duels in medieval Scandinavia, Oren Falk illuminates the importance of witnesses to all types of violence involving formal structure and signification. According to Falk, bystanders are 'to a great extent the interpreters, enunciators, and indeed authors of unfolding events.' While duelling Norseman hack and slash at each other, playing their role as warriors to the fullest, the onlookers manage numerous parts as passive witnesses, agitated directors, willing substitutes, intervening editors, and hearsay-spouting reviewers. Indeed, as soon as two individuals agree to engage in combat, they relinquish control over their identities to the crowd of onlookers who not only grade the fighting but also, on occasion, goad the fighters to assume aggressive postures which they might be reluctant to take. This enactment of violence for the sake of satisfying the demands of bloodthirsty witnesses leads Falk to comment, 'we ought to be thinking not of witnesses to a fight, then, but of fighters to a witness.'

While spectators certainly loomed large in contestations over the merits of violent deeds, no group possessed as much clout as the victims – an axiom that proves even more true when discussing international, rather than interpersonal, conflict. As victims of international aggression, the Scottish chroniclers depict the actions of Edward I at the siege of Berwick in 1296 as exploits of illegitimate aggression, transgressing the limits of chivalrous conduct. Conversely, the lowly William Wallace, like Wiglaf, transcends the status of even royal figures, such as Robert the Bruce, through superiority in acts of legitimate violence. In an analogous manner, the chronicles of Scotland forged a national identity upon the commemoration of acts of chivalry, an ethos that legitimized and sacralized many aspects of violence. This alliance between chivalry and Scottish national identity secured the moral high ground from which Scottish chroniclers could hurl insults upon the English who resided in the immoral plains below. In other words, through the depiction of England as a nation of violent, impious offenders and the Scottish as strict adherents to the limits of socially acceptable, chivalric aggression, the chroniclers transform writing into a symbolic practice, 'a form of violence in its own right.' Words and deeds are intertwined in the formation of a national identity that always borders on but never crosses the contemporary limits of violence.

Though violence usually has a primary political and social significance, the site at which it is made palpable is typically the individual human body. Bodies are subjected to different forms and degrees of harmful force in order to define them, restrain them, coerce or manipulate their actions. They are trained, armed, and honed into weapons of domination, assertiveness, or resistance. They are displayed, hidden, disguised, or re-presented to bear witness to the power and importance of violence. The essays in the second part of this collection all explore facets of such processes, tracing the 'personal' in 'interpersonal' violence. Not surprisingly, perhaps, many of the bodies studied here are female: their gendered marginality accentuates the brute mechanics of violence in their social interactions.

Throughout the Middle Ages, the bodies of martyrs are noteworthy as sites for enacting, negotiating, and representing violence. Almost by definition, martyrs require that horrific physical harm be inflicted on them: the failure of torture to break the martyr's resolve testifies to God's power and to his confessor's fidelity. Yet the specific ways in which hagiographers manipulate this basic formula allow them to deploy violence against their saintly subjects in infinite variation. Beth Crachiolo's essay inspects a gendering agenda evident in one popular thirteenth-century English anthology, which invites its readers to visualize female martyrs' bodies subjected to graphic torture, but draws the readerly gaze away from the bodies of their male counterparts. Martyred men are typically ecclesiastical officials; they model 'Christian steadfastness and action,' verbally contradicting those who physically persecute them; their deaths help propel a grand narrative of church history. Women, on the other hand, are usually only characterized as virgins; 'models of steadfastness and *reaction*,' their afflicted bodies are the passive objects of action and vision: they serve merely as illustrations to the grand narrative. Crachiolo's reading applies feminist insights to both the male persecutors the text depicts and to its authors and audience, whom 'a gory form of entertainment' socialized simultaneously in Christian piety and in what Catharine MacKinnon has identified as the eroticization of women's subordination. Crachiolo's analysis of English hagiography thus concurs with what other feminist medievalists, like Kathryn Gravdal or Brigitte Cazelles, have shown for neighbouring literatures.[19]

The gouged eyes, mangled limbs, and charred flesh of martyrs also play a key role in Daniel Baraz's wide-ranging essay. Starting with a seemingly straightforward and empirical definition of *violence* as 'application of physical force against an individual or against a group of people,' Baraz proceeds to probe shifting perceptions of violence by juxtaposing them to a category of *cruelty*. Whereas the former can be arranged along a continuum from slight to severe, the latter turns out to be a distinct and inflexible classification, related to the upper end of the severity scale. More importantly, cruelty is a category tied to human (rather than divine) criteria; it is a label inherently evaluative and political in application; and it is a unique product of high medieval European culture. Baraz arrives at these startling conclusions through an intercultural examination of the way similar violent acts are treated in different periods and places: he compares early medieval accounts of Viking raids with later rewritings, superimposes tales of Mongol atrocity over late antique descriptions of the Vandal conquest, and contrasts Latin martyrdom narratives with oriental cognates. While Eastern Christian passions tend to deny that a martyr felt any pain, claim that he welcomed it, or even suggest that he deserved it for his sins, similar texts in the West focus instead on castigating the persecutors' cruelty and anticipating their deserts. Baraz suggests that the conceptual category of cruelty came to the fore in the high Middle Ages as a strategy in the war of attrition between church reformers and lay authorities. Emphasizing the depravity inherent in excessive violence was a way of placing secular potentates at a moral disadvantage while elevating the ethical status of ecclesiastics, tacitly assimilated to the persecuted martyrs.

Where Crachiolo and Baraz look broadly at martyrdom accounts as a genre, Dawn Hayes and M.C. Bodden each examine the workings of violence in a specific martyr's story. Their analyses have implications no less multifaceted and far-reaching, however, for being anchored in individual cases. Hayes takes as her object of scrutiny one of the most celebrated political martyrdoms of the Middle Ages, Thomas Becket's assassination in Canterbury Cathedral. Her reading of this familiar event is innovative, however, in applying the exegete's fine scalpel to Becket's corpse: she meticulously peels away multiple levels of typological meaning applied to the archbishop's murder by contemporaries. The precise location where Thomas fell, the part of his body which the assassin's sword struck, the date and time on which the crime was committed – all these details conspire (or are made to conspire by the authors of his *vitae*) to anoint Becket with a sacrificial sanctity. Rather than contaminate the hallowed ground it spills on, his blood dyes it a regal purple, consecrating the church for whose integrity he fought. Paradoxically, his Girardian scapegoating redeems even his adversary, Henry II: having wrought the archbishop's murder, the English king became able to do penance for it and be reconciled with the church. Finally, Becket's blood (preserved as a relic) also carries his sanctity forward in time and distributes it in space, casting the benediction of his sacrifice even over future generations.

René Girard's sacrificial paradigm likewise informs M.C. Bodden's reading of Chaucer's *Clerk's Tale*, a transposition of hagiography into the conventions of romance.[20] The suffering that Walter inflicts on Griselda, Bodden suggests, is patterned after the probative and purgative torments God has his martyrs endure. Chaucer is wary of this patterning, however, calling into question the merit of extending it by allegoresis to interpersonal relations: there is a 'difference between what can be asked by God of a human being and what can be asked by a human being from another human being.' The *Tale* emphasizes Griselda's countenance, her *chiere*, as the liminal battlefield between her private interiority and her husband's dominion over her; it also stresses Walter's drawn-out programme, extending her suffering over many years. These emphases paint Walter as an arbitrary tyrant, concerned with manifesting hidden truth through spectacular torture (*à la* Michel Foucault and Elaine Scarry),[21] rather than as a benevolent patriarch, testing his creature's faith for her own good. Walter appears as just another abusive husband, seeking to break and colonize his spouse's autonomy. By embedding the *Tale* within multiple levels of commentary, Bodden argues, Chaucer refuses to let it 'glorify the cultural domination over women'; his narrative is rather 'a cultural backlash,' an *avant la lettre* feminist charter.

Griselda also appears briefly in John Parsons's essay. He evokes her as a 'peasant girl stripped of humble garb and clothed at her wedding in rich attire,' then deprived again of her regalia and sent away in nothing but a shift, which equivocally conceals (yet reveals) her nakedness. But Parsons refuses to see Griselda, or any other of the ladies who put on or take off clothes in his paper, as a passive victim of male gazes, immolated for the good of church, kingdom, or the institution of patriarchy. In his reading, degrees of undress become signals in a code that self-willed royal consorts could aggressively wield (even if male writers depicting their contentious actions could also inflect it, and audiences could interpret it freely for themselves). A complex cultural discourse emerges, 'accessible to all levels of medieval society' from official royal chronicler to folktale *raconteur*, centred on the display of aristocratic women's bodies. Manipulating this display might allow a lady some degree of agency, but it could also link her with her lord's never-trustworthy – and occasionally violent – subjects. 'The ruler's control of his wife's body thus signifies control of his domains'; challenging the one might lead a lord to re-examine the other, improving performance of his public duties, but it might also align an insubordinate woman with the disorderly margins, exciting violence from 'those not normally associated in governance.' Parsons thus offers a nuanced reading of queens' carnivalesque public performances, documenting how the display of the literal underpinnings of royal rule – the consort's body, incarnating political alliances and producing heirs – might also unleash misrule and resistance.

Seldom in the medieval tradition is the unruly threat of those who would not be ruled more patent than in the Robin Hood cycle, the topic of Richard Green's essay. The medieval Robin (as J.C. Holt, Stephen Knight, and others have reiterated)[22] is nothing like his jolly modern-day namesake, the generous athlete of the greenwood; he is a rough-and-tumble outlaw, rather given to shooting his adversaries in the back. Significantly, Robin's enemies typically hold office (or collaborate) with the king's bureaucracy. For Green, outlaw characters embody a folk yearning to defy centralizing late medieval statehood, slowly consolidating that form of coercive authority Foucault described as based on the 'spectacular' punitive logic manifested in a centrally erected scaffold. The merry men, in contrast, embody a community-based form of coercion, which Green dubs 'an "occlusive" economy of punishment.' This type of authority depends on the ability to expel offenders, to efface their social being, to execute them at the edge of the wilderness and cast their bodies into the outer darkness. Although carnivalesque – a term Green pauses to weigh and refine – it would be erroneous to view occlusive popular governance as chaotic, he argues. 'The cynical brutality [of the early ballads] should be read as symptomatic of a clash between two penal regimes, the older occlusive regime that underlies the very institution of outlawry itself, and the newer spectacular regime represented by the Sheriff of Nottingham.' That such violence strikes us as cynical, brutal, and horrific – not rational, necessary, and sanitary – is testimony to the long-term ascendance of the spectacular (and later, the carceral) regime.[23]

The final essay in this volume likewise throws light on the long-term enforcement of elite value systems, to the point where infraction against them appears to violate natural taboos. David Hay's examination of canon lawyers' opposition to female participation in warfare revises historiographic commonplaces in several important ways. First, it supports the view of eleventh-century reform as a watershed in European cultural structuring, a period when opposition to female militancy was articulated and in some respects institutionalized, most famously in Gratian's *Decretum*. Hay's second major point, however, is that this position was in fact neither new nor univocal, but rather the outcome of a crescendo in a dispute over women's proper public role going back centuries: 'the early medieval tension between canonical theory (which had sought to restrict women's access to public authority) and military practices (in which women sometimes did exercise command) spread for a brief time into the realm of canon law itself.' Finally, a third major point emerging from Hay's tracing of the dispute is that actual women did play a not negligible role in medieval war-making, both before and after canonical opposition to their doing so was proclaimed. Hay thus joins a growing number of historians who detect traces of recurrent female participation in mutual killing, that greatest of all human industries, and who debunk the still pervasive stereotype of war as an exclusively masculine domain. In the course of doing so, Hay also illustrates (with deceptively casual ease) how a philologist's attentiveness to source filiation, a historian's awareness of specific political circumstances and social contexts, and an anthropologist's ear for native informants' terminological distinctions (such as between *bellator* and *dux*) can cooperate to piece together the cultural mosaic of a medieval puzzle.

* * *

We, the editors, want to thank the director and staff of the Centre for Medieval Studies at the University of Toronto for their generous assistance in the organization of the conference on medieval violence and in the production of the resultant volume. We are especially grateful to Ms Anna Burko for her fine and careful copyediting of the volume.

Notes

1 For the meaning of *effusio* in classical Latin, see Charlton T. Lewis and Charles Short, *A Latin Dictionary* (Oxford 1879, repr. 1993), s.v. For the medieval shift in meaning (doubtless influenced by the frequent collocation of *effusio* with *sanguinis*, but not dependent on it), see J.F. Niermeyer, *Mediae Latinitatis lexicon minus: Abbreviationes et index fontium*, ed. C. van De Kieft and G.S.M.M. Lake-Schoonebeek (Leiden and New York 1976), s.v. The further specialization of meaning in the vernaculars is illustrated by the *Middle English Dictionary*, which lists 'emission or flow (of blood)' as the primary sense of the noun *effusiōun* (s.v.). Nine examples of such usage are provided, compared to only three of the two additional senses – and even one of these further examples (from 15th-century parliamentary rolls), illustrating the sense 'dispersal, waste (of property),' reads: 'Well nygh infinite cost and effusion bothe of Good and Blood, that this land hath borne and suffered.'

2 See B.P. McGuire, ed., *War and Peace in the Middle Ages* (Copenhagen 1987); T.N. Bisson et al., 'The "Feudal Revolution,"' and the ensuing debate in *Past and Present* 142 (1994) to 155 (1997); Guy Halsall, ed., *Violence and Society in the Early Medieval West* (Woodbridge 1998); Donald J. Kagay and L.J. Andrew Villalon, eds, *The Final Argument: The Imprint of Violence on Society in Medieval and Early Modern Europe* (Woodbridge 1998); Anna Roberts, ed., *Violence against Women in Medieval Texts* (Gainesville 1998); Barbara H. Rosenwein, ed., *Anger's Past: The Social Uses of an Emotion in the Middle Ages* (Ithaca and London 1998); Donald J. Kagay and L.J. Andrew Villalon, eds, *The Circle of War in the Middle Ages: Essays on Medieval Military and Naval History* (Woodbridge 1999); Richard W. Kaeuper, ed., *Violence in Medieval Society* (Woodbridge 2000).

3 E.g., Johan Huizinga, *The Autumn of the Middle Ages*, trans. Rodney J. Payton and Ulrich Mammitzsch (Chicago 1996 [2nd Dutch ed. 1921]); Marc Bloch, *Feudal Society*, trans. L.A. Manyon, 2 vols (Chicago 1961 [1939]); and a number of the essays in *Violence and Civil Disorder in Italian Cities, 1200–1500*, ed. Lauro Martines (Berkeley and Los Angeles 1972).

4 Paul Freedman and Gabrielle M. Spiegel, 'Medievalisms Old and New: The Rediscovery of Alterity in North American Medieval Studies,' *American Historical Review* 103.3 (1998) 702.

5 Zygmunt Bauman, *Modernity and the Holocaust* (Cambridge 1988).

6 Among the most successful examples of such research are R.I. Moore, *The Formation of a Persecuting Society: Power and Deviance in Western Europe, 950–1250* (Oxford 1987); Robert Bartlett, *The Making of Europe: Conquest, Colonization, and Cultural Change, 950–1350* (Princeton 1993); and James B. Given, *Inquisition and Medieval Society: Power, Discipline, and Resistance in Languedoc* (Ithaca 1997).

7 For a cogent critique of some aspects of this master narrative, see David Nirenberg, *Communities of Violence: Persecution of Minorities in the Middle Ages* (Princeton 1996).

8 The distinction between *inter*- and *intra*-group violence can, of course, be rather blurry. E.g., the violence of the Nazis against German Jews, understood here as intergroup violence, could be seen alternatively as intragroup violence among Germans. The recent bloodshed in the former Yugoslavia, to take another example, could also be categorized as intragroup violence among Yugoslavians, but is probably best viewed as intergroup violence between Serbs, Croats, and Muslims.

9 Norbert Elias, *The Civilizing Process: The History of Manners* and *State Formation and Civilization*, trans. Edmund Jephcott, 2 vols (Oxford 1978–82 [1939]).

10 See, for instance, Barbara Rosenwein's thoughtful concluding essay, 'Controlling Paradigms,' in *Anger's Past*, 237–44. Jonathan Fletcher, *Violence and Civilization: An Introduction to the Work of Norbert Elias* (Cambridge 1997), offers an interesting gloss on and spirited defence of some of Elias's interpretations.

11 On late medieval Valencia, see the essays by Blumenthal and Meyerson in this volume, as well as an essay by the latter, '"Assaulting the House": Interpreting Christian, Muslim, and Jewish Violence in Late Medieval Valencia,' in *The Children of Abraham: Judaism, Christianity, and Islam in the Middle Ages*, ed. A. Dykman and M. Tacconi (University Park, PA, forthcoming). David Gilmore, *Aggression and Community: Paradoxes of Andalusian Culture* (New Haven 1987), offers an anthropological reading of modern practices. The contrast between medieval and modern norms is challenged by Falk, this volume.

12 An obvious example is the violence between Catholics and Protestants in Northern Ireland, on which see, e.g., Graham McFarlane, 'Violence in Rural Northern Ireland: Social Scientific Models, Folk Explanations, and Local Variation,' in *The Anthropology of Violence*, ed. David Riches (Oxford and New York 1986), 184–203; a

16 Introduction

    less known but no less telling example is the violence of Andalusians against migrant North African farm labourers in the province of Almería in January 2000.

13. See, e.g., William Ian Miller, *Bloodtaking and Peacemaking: Feud, Law, and Society in Saga Iceland* (Chicago 1990); Stephen D. White, 'Feuding and Peacemaking in the Touraine around the Year 1100,' *Traditio* 42 (1986) 195–263; idem, 'The Politics of Anger,' in *Anger's Past*, 127–52; and Mark D. Meyerson, *The Muslims of Valencia in the Age of Fernando and Isabel: Between Coexistence and Crusade* (Berkeley and Los Angeles 1991), ch. 6 ('Conflict and Solidarity in Mudejar Society').
14. Charles Phythian-Adams, 'Rituals of Personal Confrontation in Late Medieval England,' *Bulletin of the John Rylands Library* (1991) 67, our italics.
15. Jacob Black Michaud, *Cohesive Force: Feud in the Mediterranean and the Middle East* (New York 1975).
16. René Girard, *Violence and the Sacred*, trans. Patrick Gregory (Baltimore and London 1972).
17. Natalie Zemon Davis, 'The Rites of Violence,' in her *Society and Culture in Early Modern France* (Stanford 1975), 156.
18. William Ian Miller, *Humiliation and Other Essays on Honor, Social Discomfort, and Violence* (Ithaca and London 1993), 55. See also David Riches, 'The Phenomenon of Violence,' in *The Anthropology of Violence*, esp. 8–9.
19. Catharine A. MacKinnon, *Sexual Harassment of Working Women: A Case of Sex Discrimination*, with a foreword by Thomas I. Emerson (New Haven and London 1979), 221; Kathryn Gravdal, *Ravishing Maidens: Writing Rape in Medieval French Literature and Law* (Philadelphia 1991); Brigitte Cazelles, ed., *The Lady as Saint: A Collection of French Hagiographic Romances of the Thirteenth Century*, Middle Ages Series (Philadelphia 1991).
20. In addition to the essays by Hayes and Bodden, see Salisbury's adaptation of Girard's thesis, this volume.
21. Michel Foucault, *Discipline and Punish: The Birth of the Prison*, trans. Alan Sheridan (London and New York 1977). Elaine Scarry, *The Body in Pain: The Making and Unmaking of the World* (Oxford 1985). See also Green's essay, this volume.
22. See, e.g., R.H. Hilton, ed., *Peasants, Knights, and Heretics: Studies in Medieval English Social History*, Past and Present Publications (Cambridge 1976); J.C. Holt, *Robin Hood*, rev. ed. (New York 1989); Stephen Knight, *Robin Hood: A Complete Study of the English Outlaw* (Oxford 1994).
23. The typology Green suggests helps flesh out the process Peter Brown describes (*Society and the Holy in Late Antiquity* [Berkeley 1982], 322–5) as a shift from government by consensus to government by coercion; various contributors to *Disputes and Settlements: Law and Human Relations in the West*, ed. John Bossy, Past and Present Publications (Cambridge 1983), likewise discuss this process as the displacement of transactional dispute resolution by the rule of law.

PART I

VIOLENCE AND IDENTITY FORMATION

1 Violence and the Making of Wiglaf

JOHN M. HILL

In the last third of *Beowulf*, as Wiglaf rushes into combat to help his lord, Beowulf, against an ancient, fiery dragon, the extraordinary violence he faces is not in itself repugnant. We do not read the violent scenes in which Wiglaf acts alongside Beowulf, protected by Beowulf's iron shield, as nasty or brutish. Their activity is combat after all, even defensive warfare in their case (in that the dragon attacked devastatingly the night before); therefore, we can see their actions as a good kind of violence, the retributive and supportive violence of those who have been attacked, assuming we identify with Beowulf and Wiglaf against the dragon.

From their perspectives, violence involves justified revenge and protection of his people on Beowulf's part and admirable magnanimity on Wiglaf's; thus, violent, armed exertion here is honourable. The behaviour of the so-called cowards – Beowulf's ten retainers other than Wiglaf, all of whom, including Wiglaf, had been relieved of going into battle against the dragon – is other than honourable; indeed, one could say that their failure to help Beowulf in his time of need does violence to the magnanimous possibilities of the lord-retainer relationship. Wiglaf shows us the dimensions of that magnanimity (a free gift, in effect, because not obligated once Beowulf tells his retainers that the fight with the dragon is his alone) when he steps forward to join Beowulf. I will discuss aspects of that action below as part of Wiglaf's state of mind. But I want to move beyond seeing Wiglaf as mainly, for some readers even automatically, virtuous in his violent support of his noble lord. Rather I want to present that violence as more than a good. I will argue for it as a crucible within which Wiglaf acquires a new nobility and kinship identity; thus, I will approach violence here as a kind of warrior midwifery, combat induced. In this and in similar instances, such as in *The Battle of Maldon* and *The Battle of*

Brunanburh, violent warrior action is entirely justified in Anglo-Saxon heroic story. But only in *Beowulf* does that action significantly change the identity and status of the warrior involved.[1]

Initially, then, what is Wiglaf's status and identity? Most commentators on Wiglaf's violent, hand-searing assistance in the dragon fight see him as a model of the loyal retainer – this in pointed contrast to the ten cowardly (*tydre treowlogan*, line 2847a in Frederick Klaeber's *Beowulf* [3rd ed., Boston 1950]), turned-wit retainers Wiglaf castigates after the battle (lines 2864–91). His motivation and group standing are not analyzed beyond, say, a sense of urgency that triggers memories of obligations sealed in the gift hall.[2] Usually he is seen simply as doing the right thing, as a kinsman and loyal retainer or friend should – indeed, if we accept Rolf Bremmer's argument, as a war companion and sister's son should.[3] If Beowulf in fact is Wiglaf's mother's brother, then we have here another instance of the most tender of cross-group ties between warriors in the poem. However, that 'if' is a big one. Rolf Bremmer has to invent a sister for whom there is no evidence, either direct or implicit, and he has to assume a kinship tie the poet nowhere names in his treatment of Wiglaf and Beowulf. In fact, an initial close kinship of any sort is unlikely because of how the poet identifies Wiglaf and how Wiglaf speaks about Beowulf.

Because too much is usually assumed about Wiglaf – such as that he is a close kinsman to Beowulf, that he acts in an unthinking, idealistic way, and that he is much the same after his violent encounter as he was before (i.e., an exemplary, right-minded *retainer*) – we would do well first to assess whatever we can about Wiglaf's prior relationship with the Geats, doing so in terms of the vestigial, matrilineal kinship system reflected in the prominence of the sister's son–mother's brother tie among them. What the 'matrilineal' means here is that the Geats to some notable extent encourage inheritance down the mother's line and affectively value that line, rather than that they have a matriarchic organization. Proceeding first in this way should help us place Wiglaf socially and in a familial way in relationship to Beowulf and the Geats.

Initially Wiglaf speaks of Beowulf only as his lord and ring-giver. We should note that the poet identifies Wiglaf eight times, with high, half-line consistency, as Weohstan's son (beginning with *Weoxstanes sunu*, line 2602b), Weohstan being a Wægmunding who serves the Swedish king, Onela, in combat against Onela's rebellious nephews. Upon introducing Wiglaf the poet offers an extensive identification of him only as that son, a beloved shield warrior and man of the Scylfings, Ælfhere's kinsman. We should, furthermore, keep in mind that Wiglaf clearly does not behave automatically and that he does not consider his behaviour ethically transparent. In effect his boasts explain him at length in terms that both invoke and *modify* the kinds of traditional social forms and obligations that Peter Clemoes, among many others, emphasizes.[4]

Wiglaf begins by recalling the conventional agreements the retainers made with Beowulf in the mead hall (of martial services in exchange for gifts, of gifts for martial services); but then he separates himself from the group by noting that Beowulf chose them but 'gave me' these gifts (presumably shield and spear, lines 2638b–40). So far Wiglaf could be seen as simply refreshing the ancient, reciprocal ideal. However, he then notes the anomalous position in which the retainers find themselves: Beowulf has ordered that they stay out of the fight! Despite that order, he, Wiglaf, thinks the day has come when Beowulf could use the strength of good battle-warriors. At least for himself, God knows that he, Wiglaf, would rather burn beside his gold-giver than not act now. The heightened, personal intensity of this is not merely traditional. Nor does Wiglaf in this generous impulse of his – generous because not obligated, given Beowulf's earlier command to the retainers – call Beowulf his lord and kinsman. Indeed, although kin in some vague sense, we do not know how Wiglaf's old-father relates exactly to Beowulf's Geats. When we consider all of the above, then, we can also entertain the possibility that Wiglaf and his scenes are much more than idealized illustrations of kinship-minded, heroic action. Wiglaf's mixed family, his father's Wægmundings and Ælfhere's Scylfings or Swedes, connect somehow with Beowulf's Geats, perhaps through a marriage between Hreðel, Beowulf's maternal grandfather and foster-father, and a Wægmunding princess. While the poet says nothing of the kind, clearly Hreðel had a queen or queens who bore him three sons, one of whom is Hygelac, Beowulf's uncle and lord, and a daughter, she being Beowulf's mother. In these offspring an unmentioned queen is more palpably present than is an unmentioned sister.

One can even appropriately speculate here about ties through women in *Beowulf*. Especially in the world of these people, the Weder-Geats, rather than following the men simply we should follow the gifts and offers, which to a surprising extent means following the women. Note that Beowulf has already inherited everything he has – his lands, his wealth, his subkingship – from his mother's side of the family, she who, according to Hroðgar, was blessed in his birth (lines 945–6). Other than the honour of identification, Beowulf has nothing from his father, Ecgþeow. Indeed, after Hygelac's death in battle, the Geat kingdom itself is first offered to Beowulf by a young woman, the apparently very important Hygd, Hygelac's queen, who seems to prefer Beowulf over her own son, Heardred. Heardred is a sister's son to someone we only know as Hereric, obviously Hygd's brother, significantly mentioned when the poet first tells us of Heardred's death, line 2206 (as though to emphasize that Heardred is not just a Geat king but a sister's son also). Beowulf refuses Hygd's startling offer – startling because, up to this point, in matters of inheritance and succession we have been looking at male to male descent among the Danes and at named male to male ties regarding Beowulf, his maternal grandfather Hreðel, and his uncle and lord Hygelac (forgetting at times that those ties go through a woman: Beowulf's mother, Hygelac's sister, Hreðel's daughter). Moreover, as a sign of her great importance to him, Beowulf pointedly gives gifts to Hygd – the splendidly ornamented necklace Wealhþeow had, along with three graceful horses and bright saddles (lines 2172–5a). Excepting Grendel's mother, no other female in the poem receives gifts – the receiver of gifts being in an honoured and potentially powerful position.

That Beowulf gives Hygd the great necklace Wealhþeow gave him says something. When giving the necklace to Beowulf, Wealhþeow hoped that he would prosper in his strength and be kindred kind in his advice to her sons (*ond þyssum cnyhtum wes / lara liðe*, 1219b–20a, with *liðe* coming from the vocabulary of kinship amity rather than from the reciprocal, ethical vocabulary of the warband – although at poem's end it is just that kind of kinship amity the Geats extol in Beowulf when they say he was most kind to the people [*leodum liðost*, 3182a]).[5] By giving that necklace, in part signified by Wealhþeow's hope, Beowulf may now proffer such a role in relationship to Hygd and her offspring. In the event, Beowulf does decline Hygd's offer of the kingdom when she prefers him to her own son, Heardred. Here, in effect, she prefers an affine, a sister's son on her husband's side. We might otherwise expect her to favour her own son, thus emphasizing a matriline in relation to her brother (her son's *eam* or mother's brother). Instead she mediates this matter between her son and her *husband's* sister's son, choosing an exogamous matriline. Perhaps she does this because of Beowulf's enormous prowess – after all, he destroyed the warband Dæghrefn led fatefully against Hygelac. For his part, Beowulf prefers to support his maternal cousin, Heardred, nephew to Hygd's brother. In effect, we have two generations of sister's sons among the Geats. In doing what he does, Beowulf assumes a continuing, protective and secondary role toward Heardred, i.e., toward his mother's brother's son. In these events his father does not count – a father Hroðgar calls an 'old father' or grandfather anyway, a term (*ealdfæder* or *ær-fæder*) that just means 'ancestor' in *Beowulf*. When Beowulf does eventually inherit the kingdom it of course comes to him from his mother's side. Later, and through an unstated tie, Beowulf also receives rich Wægmunding lands, which he gives to Wiglaf (*wicstede weligne*, 2607a).

While not clear, it makes sense in the context of the comments above to suggest that the Wægmunding legacy has nothing much to do with Beowulf's father; rather, it may have come to him through a mother's mother, Hreðel's queen, Beowulf's maternal grandmother. A matriliny of sorts – with fathers relegated to a distant aside as ancestors (for Beowulf as well as for Wiglaf later) and with a mother interceding between heirs, especially between brother and son – seems apparent among the Geats. We have inheritance through one woman and the gift-receiving importance of another – status points that differentiate lines of influence among the Geats from what seems the case with both Swedes and Danes. The latter groups are organized through agnates, either father to son or brother to brother in matters of inheritance and succession, with the Swedes embroiled dynastically, given tensions between uncle and nephews (brother's sons). Residues of an ancient matriliny exist elsewhere in *Beowulf*, such as in the Hildeburh and Finn story, in matters of the sister's son–sister's brother tie – a tie that makes more sense matrilineally than it would in terms of patrilineal inheritance.[6] But nowhere in *Beowulf* is the matrilineal as prominent as it is among the Geats, whether regarding the mother's brother–sister's son tie or the roles of a young queen like Hygd – a point worked out in a somewhat different way by Stephen Glosecki.[7]

Beowulf gives those rich Wægmunding lands he inherited to Wiglaf, thus honouring Wiglaf's Wægmunding ancestry and reinvesting those possessions both in his young retainer and as a reinstated patrimony and folkright for that retainer (*þe he him ær forgeaf, / wicstede weligne Wægmundinga, / folcrihta gehwylc, swa his fæder ahte*, 2606b–8). If we think then of matrilineal relations for Beowulf among the Geats, Wiglaf is a kinsman *potentially* dear but somewhat removed, connected with Beowulf plausibly through the mother's mother's side. Again, Beowulf has received nothing from his father's side, which apparently does not count at all. With this in mind, we can now refocus our attention on Wiglaf's actions in the dragon fight and reassess the outcome. We can consider the ways in which kinship is built through reciprocity, loyalty, courage, and violence operating together here within a psychology of loaned gifts, energy, and response to unforeseen events and their consequences.

When he feels impelled to help Beowulf, who is suffering the dragon's heat, Wiglaf essentially departs from novice warrior status. The poet describes it in this way (2625b–7): *Þa wæs forma sið / geongan cempan, þæt he guðe ræs / mid his freodryhtne fremman sceolde* ['That was the first time that the young warrior had to endure and attend to the onslaught of battle with his noble lord']. While it is possible that Wiglaf has fought before, and that this fight is simply his first alongside Beowulf, calling Wiglaf a 'young warrior' places him in the youthful time of life (*geogoðfeorh*, 537) and distinguishes him from mature members of the warband (the *duguð*). At the least, he is a young warrior about to prove himself in the greatest battle of his young life.

Probably he has already gone through a warrior initiation ritual of some sort – anthropological reports on such rituals, while usually coming from clan-based peoples (the Anglo-Saxons did not form clans), note in common a socializing effect, a channeling of competitive aggression between the mixed cohorts of older and younger warriors. In this regard, Jeffrey A. Fadiman's *Oral History of Tribal Warfare: The Meru of Mt Kenya* offers a particularly detailed account.[8] After the time of initiation among the men and then a period of withdrawal from the general community (when the novice vows, say, not to return from the deprivations of the bush until some stated event occurs, such as the birthing of a male calf), the novice warrior will go into his first raid. There he will earn a praise name for whatever he does and will be known by that name or by one acquired later in his bachelor warrior career. Assuming he does something martially worthy, and thus does not earn an ironic praise name, he may then, should he decide to marry, display himself armed but otherwise naked at a ritual dance where adolescent girls will chant his praise name. After that dance ritual, he keeps his praise name forever and ordinarily acquires the appropriate parental permission to court one of the girls. Thus there is first an initiation into the world of men.

If anything like this existed in Anglo-Saxon warrior rituals, we might suggest that some such process has been capped in Wiglaf's case perhaps by Beowulf's bestowal upon him of the rich folkright Weohstan once enjoyed. The Meru period of boast and a withdrawal from the community might be paralleled or else reflected obliquely and later in Wiglaf's case by his singular, boast-filled movement away from the group of chosen retainers; then there is the battle and the new identity earned, which can lead to a new standing within the community. All of this in the Meru case reflects competition among warrior cohorts and an aggressive, although carefully socialized, sexual psychology.

Because violence and social rituals are never affairs that exist only at conscious political or social levels, Ariane Deluz and Suzette Heald, believing that psychological depths are also mobilized, have recently gathered essays together in an intriguing volume called *Anthropology and Psychoanalysis: An Encounter through Culture*. They hope to reinvigorate several engagements in the twentieth century between anthropology and psychoanalysis, engagements led originally by such pioneers as Geza Roheim, Margaret Mead, and Weston La Barre before being provisionally updated by such anthropologists as Melvin Spiro, Waud Kracke, Georges Devereux, and Ganath Obeyesekere.[9] Deluz's and Heald's special, quite contemporary interest is in the many ways in which the new, more subjective and reciprocally reflective, field work in actual cultural worlds resembles the analyst's engagement with a patient: both are dynamic, unpredictable journeys. Both kinds of encounters involve effort to understand an Other through interaction and dialogue. Thus Deluz and Heald emphasize voyaging through culture and through psychoanalysis, with psychoanalytical perspective being a way to engage anew with culture. For a coda to their volume, they have an analyst, R.H. Hook, comment on the anthropological material. In the course of remarking on manhood initiations involving circumcision rituals, Hook suggests that – while there is always some ambivalence or ambiguity in destructive violence, given the terrible linkage of death to life – at least among a people called the Gisu the power of the father is displaced onto ancestors and the oedipal crisis is resolved when the boy becomes a man and then marries.[10]

The parallel relevance of this summary to Wiglaf's situation is arresting. He already has an honoured relationship with his lord, Beowulf, and he is introduced as having both a father, a 'fore-father,' and some sort of tie to a Scylfing ancestor (the mysterious Ælfhere or 'army-elf'). This certainly reads like a displacement onto ancestors of some kind of identity and energy. Moreover, Wiglaf boasts emotionally about what he feels impelled to do, and why, in Beowulf's time of need; he then commits himself to battle alongside Beowulf, protected from dragon fire by Beowulf's iron shield. After the battle a physically tested and partially maimed Wiglaf – his hand has been severely burned – has a clear, new standing in the community and has earned powerful epithets of praise. What that maiming means psychologically one cannot easily say. Perhaps it forms part of an exchange for something gained, in line with the kinds of bodily exchanges in Germanic myth whereby Odin loses an eye while gaining wisdom and Tiu loses a hand in Fenris wolf's mouth while gaining juridical power.[11] And indeed Wiglaf's identity does change dramatically in relationship to both Beowulf and the Geats. We are now in a position to follow out that change.

The good retainer acts on his lord's behalf, presumably having internalized a disposition to do so in the course of accepting weapons and rings, stating what he will do, and drinking from the ritually proffered mead cup. That disposition, moreover, is something that violence or the threat of violence actuates psychologically (i.e., it refreshes the learned and previously reinforced disposition).[12] One's lord's needs become one's own, as in a sense one's energy and one's weapons become his loans now called in – a process central to the confirmed formation of a powerful warrior conscience. This would be an intensely aggressive conscience, even potentially a predatory one. That deeply forged rightfulness contains a sense of identity already, one that even supercedes blood kinship, as is the case to which Wiglaf's sword speaks eloquently. His father, Weohstan, received it along with much battle gear from Onela, having first taken both sword and gear from Onela's nephew, Eanmund, whom Weohstan slew on Onela's behalf in a dynastic feud within the Swedish royal house. Onela, the poet carefully tells us, does not blame Weohstan for that slaying (*þæt him Onela forgeaf, / his gædelinges guðgewædu, / fyrdsearo fuslic, no ymbe ða fæhðe spræc, / þeah ðe he his broðor bearn abredwade*, 2616b–19). Eanmund's remnant then seems to signify the 'kinship' of the sword (i.e., a constructed kinship or brotherhood, if you will, established through battle) as well as patrilineal descent. The sword by which Onela's retainer becomes more honoured than is Onela's rebellious nephew – that sword becomes Wiglaf's heirloom when Weohstan dies. This kind of social bonding and signifying is as much a part of the poem's world as is the revenge ethic itself and should not be confused, as many commentators have confused it, with the destructive aspects of that ethic.[13]

As a similar transaction occurs in Wiglaf's case, and as he in effect wields a bond of violence (the sword) on Beowulf's behalf, a dear kinship (in contrast to a close blood kinship) forms between Beowulf and Wiglaf. In effect the kinships of the hall, nobility, and courage come together through violent action, the outcome being something dear and initially unforeseen. We have either a newly fostered adoption or apparent right of inheritance and succession or both.[14] Crucially, however, we need to see that this new relationship, this 'ecstatic union' as Edward B. Irving, Jr, calls it, develops in the course of action – that Wiglaf is not given to us as Beowulf's close kinsman; rather, he becomes a special kinsman, the last of Beowulf's Wægmunding countrymen. The dragon fight does not display a static or otherwise typical relationship idealized. Something transactional occurs.

That centrally transactional process, of course, begins with exchange and honouring in the hall. Old English *lean* as gift or payment is our word 'loan.' Its basic Old English range is both as reward for service and as violent requital for injury or wrong committed. Thus gifts are loans looking for a return in service or gifts – an idea that has now become commonplace in the anthropology devoted to the study of primitive economies (from the conceptually groundbreaking work of Bronislaw Malinowski, Marcell Mauss, and Marshall Sahlins to the more subtle work of Marilyn Strathern).[15]

What the giver looks for, essentially, is some internalization of his needs as one's own. In a martial context this means violent requital on one's lord's behalf. Psychologically what seems to be involved for the novice warrior is precarious. He is borrowing energy and an obligation, so to speak. Out of that borrowing an aggressive, even punishing conscience can form on the lord's behalf, assuming some suitable internalization of needs has taken place. Psychologically considered, the right-minded retainer is not really his own man until he becomes a lord in his own right, and even then there are reciprocally honouring ties to ancestors and even to God (who rewards right doers).

In Wiglaf's case, the evidence for the making of kinship comes from the poet's gnomic, approving comments and from his language of kinship – beginning with *sib* but emphasizing Wiglaf's immediate family, that in effect he is no close kin of Beowulf's, and culminating in the constructed honorific, *sibæðelingas*, which appears just before the maxim that such should a warrior be, a kin-thane when needed (2707–9a): *ond hi hyne þa begen abroten hæfdon, / sibæðelingas; swylc sceolde secg wesan, / þegn at ðearfe!*). Also, we can turn to Wiglaf's boasts regarding what he intends to do, boasts emphasizing honour, gifts, and reciprocity in the hall, not kinship ties. He does turn the matter personally, however, when he addresses the other retainers Beowulf has brought along and speaks of Beowulf as 'our' lord but 'my' gold-giver. Although crucially presented in his first moment as feeling sorrow in response to his lord's fire-encompassed suffering, Wiglaf is not initially particularized further except as an image of right personhood, of mindfulness. Nevertheless, something new begins here: a kinship-forming model of magnanimous loyalty – not loyalty obligated – in one's lord's time of need, gloss his own actions however Wiglaf will.

Beginning with line 2675, when Wiglaf seeks safety with Beowulf, the poet says that he bravely carried on from behind his kinsman's shield (*under his mæges scyld / elne geeode*, 2675b–6a). Yet the poet has had Wiglaf, just prior to this heightened moment (2663–8), address Beowulf not as kin but as 'dear one.' Then Wiglaf urgently recommended that Beowulf in his suffering in fact recall those youthful vows Beowulf made never to let his fame decline (perhaps here obliquely responding to Beowulf's earlier, self-steeling remarks [2425–7, 2490–2509, 2511–15] about having often survived the rush of battle). In that remarkable speech, the poet has Wiglaf eloquently take Beowulf back to the great king's awesome youth, perhaps even to the energies of Beowulf's own initiation into tremendous manhood. Now Beowulf must, Wiglaf adds, defend his life with all his strength and with all the surge of pride that a rejuvenated warrior spirit and thoughts of great deeds can provide. In only a final half-line does Wiglaf say that he will fully support Beowulf (*Leofa Biowulf, læst eall tela, / swa ðu on geoguðfeore geara gecwæde, / þæt ðu ne alæte be ðe lifigendum / dom gedreosan; sceallt nu dædum rof, / æðeling anhydig, ealle maegene / feorh ealgian; ic ðe fullæstu*, 2663–8). Thus Wiglaf becomes the voice of warrior encouragement in dire extremity, although he himself has yet to confront and survive the cauldron of battle.

Aside from his intense, personal, and clearly magnanimous motivation, his kinship is still that of action, the kinship that puts a fully supporting and serving countryman in lethal harm's way: the battle kinship of the brave retainer. And so it remains through the course of deadly bite (for Beowulf) and charred hand (for Wiglaf) until Eanmund's remnant, that giant-forged sword Weohstan gave to Wiglaf, pierces the dragon's bellows. With the dragon's fire extinguished, Beowulf can deliver the killing thrust. Soon after this we are told that the fire-injured Wiglaf helped Beowulf, whom the poet calls at this moment either Wiglaf's kinsman or the great, powerful one (MS *mægenes*, 2698b). Perhaps scribe b does not understand the two characters as close blood kin, although soon they will be called these noble kinsmen in action who killed the dragon. An honorific plural, *sibæðelingas*, embraces them both as they mutually achieve a costly victory. However, the poet no sooner climactically acknowledges that new status as made kinsman than he moves to Wiglaf as thanely object. We are told that just as Wiglaf did, so should a warrior do, be a *thane* in his lord's time of need (*swylc sceolde secg wesan, / þegn æt ðearfe!*

2708b–2709a). Kinship and thaneship issues merge here in some way, as though being a warrior kin to a battle lord is being a thane and vice versa.

Still, in honorific terms Wiglaf has clearly progressed. He is now linked in action and identity with Beowulf as noble kinsman. When the old Beowulf begins to speak in his dying moments, aware of death's nearness, he pointedly notes that he would give his battle gear to a son now if he had been granted a son as his heir. He then comments on the ethical life he has led in his long rule of the Geats, perhaps doing so to impress the ethical upon Wiglaf. Then he asks for another service, directly calling Wiglaf beloved as he urges Wiglaf to retrieve some of the dragon's great treasure. That address completes the framework of deep endearments, from Wiglaf's *leofa Biowulf* (2663a) to Beowulf's *Wiglaf leofa* (2745a). In each case something is also urged: great, summoned strength and energy in the first case; a quick, energetic retrieval of treasure from the dragon's mound in the second – the latter so that Beowulf might scrutinize the ancient treasure he has won and hence resign himself more willingly to the loss of life and lordship.

When Wiglaf returns, laden with treasure, Beowulf thanks God for all of that treasure he can now leave to his people after his death. As an explicit acknowledgment of Wiglaf's new status in relationship to himself and the Geats he now urges in the imperative plural that Wiglaf must still attend to the people's needs (*fremmað gena / leoda þearfe*, 2800b–1a). He, Beowulf, can no longer do so. In urging Wiglaf's attentions to the needs of the Geats, Beowulf in effect would have Wiglaf become their ring-lord, distributing the great treasure that has now become Beowulf's man-price. But Beowulf has not yet passed on any of the war regalia of leadership. That occurs after he orders a mound built for himself. What he does next is give Wiglaf his great neck-ring, his gold-plated helmet, and his corselet. He urges Wiglaf to use them well (*het hyne brucan well*, 2812b).

What he means by these final gifts is clear enough in the gifts themselves and in his farewell: 'You are the last of our kind, the last of the Wægmundings.' By virtue of that connection, and to add to the folkright of Wiglaf's ancestral father, which he has already given to Wiglaf, Beowulf gives his battle gear – a warrior inheritance that parallels the sword and other gear Wiglaf received from Weohstan. Thus Beowulf becomes here something like a face-to-face father to Wiglaf, although the corselet may well be Hreðel's heirloom (as was the corselet Beowulf removed before the Grendel fight and which he wanted Hroðgar to send to Hygelac in the eventuality of his death). Beowulf is ever the fostered Geat, his mother's people having no obligations to Hroðgar, this despite Hroðgar's framing of Beowulf's arrival so long ago in the Grendel time as an implicit return for Hroðgar's settlement of a feud on Beowulf's father's behalf. Perhaps Beowulf would now, late in his life, materially tie Wiglaf to himself as though to a matrilineal group – to mother's father, Hreðel being Beowulf's maternal grandfather and originally fostering king, this before Hygelac, his maternal uncle, became Beowulf's lord. It is these Geats and their offspring – Hreðel, Hygelac, Hæðcyn, Herebeald, and Heardred – who are Beowulf's close kinsmen on his mother's side, with Heardred being his maternal uncle's young son. No doubt these are the ones he has in mind when he says that fate has swept away or else sped off all of his kinsmen. He will now follow after (*ealle wyrd forsweop* [or MS *speof*] *mine magas to metodsceafte, / eorlas on elne*, 2814b–16a). The kinship distinction here is pivotal: Beowulf says that 'you,' Wiglaf, are the last of our 'kind,' of the Wægmundings. But clearly Beowulf does not think of Wiglaf as the last of Beowulf's personal kinsmen (*mine magas*). Those have already gone, nobles in their valour, and now Beowulf will follow after. But before he goes he has in effect designated Wiglaf as his heir, urging him to use all of the war-gear he has given him, especially to use it well.

That injunction suggests pleasurable possession along with right-minded behaviour. Hroðgar uses the same phrase in his great gift-giving after the Grendel fight, a giving that involves some kind of attempt to adopt Beowulf and invite him to a leading place as possible successor. That invitation is also materially present in the very gifts Hroðgar gives, gifts expressing both Hroðgar's dynastic line (the corselet of Heorogar, Hroðgar's brother and predecessor as king) and his own role as battle king. Thus the phrase has formal significance beyond the mere bestowal of rewards for services rendered. Even the key verb can have such force. Wealhþeow uses *brucan* imperatively when she urges Hroðgar to enjoy his wealth and, should he die, to leave his kingdom to his sons (she worries that Hroðgar will adopt Beowulf and leave all to him). She also urges Beowulf to enjoy the great necklace she gives in her counter-giving and to be kind to her sons, her language there suggesting a kindred kindness, not the loyalty-inducing kindness of lordship (lines 1216–20a). And Beowulf has used the phrase earlier upon his return to Hygelac, when he passes on to Hygelac, in exactly the same order, the greatest of the gifts Hroðgar has given him (2155–62). Through that gesture and others, Beowulf earns the poet's unreserved praise for behaving as a kinsman (*mæg*) should, especially as a nephew deeply loyal. To have used that formal phrase when addressing Hygelac suggests that Beowulf understands it as part of a ritual handing on within a context of dear kinship and retainership, of ties to his maternal uncle and lord in Hygelac's case.

Thus Beowulf would honour and please Wiglaf and would instructively give war-band leadership to his now especially beloved Wiglaf, who soon will berate the cowards and call Beowulf his kinsman when telling how he could only help Beowulf a little. He could not save Beowulf's life, even though in the battle he rose to a level above his usual measure. Wiglaf now clearly thinks of himself as a kinsman, not just a much-honoured retainer – this even though he is still consistently referred to as Weohstan's son. He now assumes command, however, and says that Beowulf threw away his gifts to the men who showed their lack of valour. He dismisses them and their kindred, pronouncing their future of harried exile from their lands and joys. Although not a Weder-Geat, Wiglaf asserts leadership here by discrediting the cowards and becoming leader in the fulfillment of Beowulf's last will and testament. He leads a reformed group of Geats into the dragon's mound to plunder that treasure hoard with him. Both in action and in the epithets now applied to him, Wiglaf, while telling the remaining Geats what Beowulf told him to do, is marked with praise. Unlike the Meru warrior's, Wiglaf's name does not change; but his reputation and his relationship to the Geats do. To emphasize that change, the poet successively calls him 'battle-brave,' 'wise,' and then 'summoner of king's thanes' – a nearly thematic elevation to throne-worthiness. It is as battle-worthy (*hæle hildedior*, 3111a) that Wiglaf orders Geats who have property to supply wood and labour for the building of Beowulf's pyre; and it as *se snotra sunu Wihstanes* (3120), the wise son of Weohstan, that he chooses seven king's thanes to plunder the dragon's barrow with him (the power of choosing, of deciding, is a lord's and implies powers of assessment, wisdom). But all of this leadership and these new epithets of praise were anticipated when Wiglaf proclaimed the harder wisdom gained through violent support of his lord: death is better for any warrior than a turned-wit life. That is, death is better than the morally inverted intelligence of a life that flees, takes gifts, makes commitments, and then lacks moral judgment in the lord's time of need. This, Wiglaf's moment of clearest commitment to super-ego demands on his lord's behalf, is the crucial step in the making of dear kinship through mutually supportive violence.

After the Geats descend into the dragon's barrow, Wiglaf is named no more. He disappears into the collectivity of the Geat people as they prepare the funeral pyre and then the funeral mound. What has happened to Wiglaf? The poet's last words given to him prefaced the epithet 'wise.' The last words we hear from Wiglaf are delivered to Geatish property owners, those who own halls and thus can supply the wood for Beowulf's funeral pyre. Wiglaf says that fire shall now feed on the greatest of warriors, he who always survived the showers of iron, the storms of arrows and spears over the shield wall, the arrows fully aided by their feathered shafts (lines 3114b–19). No natural rain will either revive this great king or douse his funeral pyre, Wiglaf might say, although Beowulf survived the deadly showers of war often enough. In addition to his new leadership, this funeral poetry expresses Wiglaf's poetical powers, a third kind of wisdom, that of song alongside the wisdom gained from combat and the wisdom that informs his choice of good, noble retainers. His lines about showers of iron make him Beowulf's intellectual as well as military heir.

That he is the last of the Wægmundings may well matter now, given his disappearance into the collective actions of the Geats who mourn their great king (although in my opinion he is not erased, as Edward B. Irving would have it).[16] Scholars have long puzzled over just who the Geats were and what the poem prophesizes about them and their fate. Are they eventually wiped out by their enemies, as the messenger Wiglaf sends to the town seems to have feared? Or do they as a collectivity become Wægmundings eventually, following Wiglaf to his folkright, the rich lands of his father? We can hardly tell and certainly should not assume their annihilation. The poem for its part does not look ahead clearly. Instead it turns around upon its sad last scenes and leaves us with the mournful praise songs of these sons of nobles, grown now to twelve in number and undoubtedly including Wiglaf in that the praising epithet applied to him fifty-six lines before (*hildedior*) now applies to them all. In their constructions and mourning, indeed, in their constructive mourning they are all either people of the Weders or people of the Geats as they focus on these last, much approved, rites for their great king. Their final superlatives in praise of Beowulf elevate him to legendary standing, far above that of any ordinary thane, including their already praiseworthily recharacterized and socially ascendent leader, Wiglaf, Weohstan's son.

Notes

1 An expanded version of this essay, going off in the direction indicated here and involving a larger discussion of psychological issues, has been published as ch. 1 in my book *The Anglo-Saxon Warrior Ethic* (Gainesville 2000).
2 Peter Clemoes, *Interactions of Thought and Language in Old English Poetry* (Cambridge 1995), 413, thinks of Wiglaf as typifying for the poet true fidelity, personifying the type of the true retainer and kinsman. There is some sort of momentary rupture in the whole lord-retainer system for Clemoes, and Wiglaf here restores it.
3 See Rolf H. Bremmer, 'The Importance of Kinship: Uncle and Nephew in *Beowulf*,' *Amsterdamer Beiträge zur älteren Germanistik* 15 (1980) 21–38. Working by analogy with other warrior pairs in the poem – Sigemund and Fitela, Hygelac and Beowulf – with the first in each pair being the maternal uncle (an *eam*) to the younger warrior, Bremmer first argues interestingly that all sister's sons are warrior comrades for their maternal uncles. This suggests that Hnæf comes to visit his sister, Hildeburh, in the Finn episode with Hildeburh's son in his retinue. Given that Beowulf and Wiglaf form a close fighting pair, Bremmer then moves in the opposite direction, from cooperation to likely kinship tie: he supposes a sister for Beowulf and makes Wiglaf that sister's son. Of course the poet gives us no such configuration: Beowulf has no sister. Regarding Wiglaf generally, Edward B. Irving, Jr, *A*

32 John M. Hill

Reading of Beowulf (Philadelphia 1968) has set the latter-day norm for seeing the character less as an individual than as an idea of family ties.

4   Clemoes, *Interactions*. Clemoes would tie Beowulf and Wiglaf together as uncle and nephew in an exemplary relationship profoundly reenacted in the dragon fight.

5   For war-band vocabulary, see D.H. Green, *The Carolingian Lord: Semantic Studies on Four Old High German Words – Balder, Frô, Truhtin, Hêrro* (Cambridge 1965). The terms *liðe* and *gedefe* concern what is kind, fitting, and gentle. Tellingly, *gedefe* in *Beowulf* can be used ironically in warrior contexts, while *ungedefe* concerns the accidental slaughter of a kinsman (and lord) when Hæðcyn shoots Herebeald, his brother.

6   Marriage outside of the kinship group, exogamy, can have a number of effects. It can solidify the home group (marriage within tending to split groups), it is an opportunity to ally oneself economically and politically with another group, and it is a way to dispose of daughters. But the movement out of women has a compensatory return in the coming back of sister's sons for fosterage, which further ties the two groups together in this second generation. The sister's son has blood ties to both groups and can call on possible solidarity both in terms of his matriline and his patriline, although the immediate matriline, the mother's brother and his agnatic kin, seems more important. As a war-band tie, this might function affectively and materially in several ways: fostering incurs special debt and special feeling (for the fostered as well as for the son's father and his group); fostering does not raise quarrels as otherwise might occur between brothers or between uncles and brothers' sons (both being either sad or fractious issues in *Beowulf*); and the fostered son still has identification of some sort with his father, keeping the alliance and possible resource tie alive in the second generation.

7   Stephen Glosecki, '*Beowulf* and the Wills: Traces of Totemism?' *Philological Quarterly* 78 (1999) 14–47, a special issue on anthropological approaches to Old English literature, John Hill guest editor. In n. 2 of his essay, however, Glosecki adds that 'perhaps we should speak of "fratilateral" rather than agnatic or bilateral succession in proto-historic Germanic dynasties. [I suspect] that the prehistoric pattern was *cognatic* in the obsolete sense, i.e., "matrilineal," with mother intermediating between heirs, specifically between her bother and her son.' Glosecki later notes that while the poet's prosody might have him use *ealdfæder* for *fæder*, the 'distinction between father and grandfather is so minimal that the two terms, virtual synonyms, are metrically interchangeable' (n. 37). In matrilineages, male kin on the father's side are collapsed together, not carefully distinguished.

8   Jeffrey A. Fadiman, *An Oral History of Tribal Warfare: The Meru of Mt Kenya* (Athens, OH 1982), 75–122. See also Thomas M. Kiefer, *The Tausug: Violence and Law in a Philippine Moslem Society* (New York 1972), where support groups are highly flexible and changeable, and Klaus-Friedrich Koch, *War and Peace in Jalemo: The Management of Conflict in Highland New Guinea* (Cambridge, MA 1974).

9 Suzette Heald and Ariane Deluz, eds, *Anthropology and Psychoanalysis* (London 1994) give relevant citations in bibliography to their Introduction. However, to what they have we should add the following: Geza Roheim, *Australian Totemism* (London 1925); idem, *Magic and Schizophrenia* (Bloomington 1970); Weston La Barre, *The Ghost Dance: The Origins of Religion* (New York 1970); Waud H. Kracke, *Force and Persuasion: Leadership in Amazonian Society* (Chicago 1978); Sudhir Kakar, 'Stories from Indian Psychoanalysis: Context and Text,' in *Cultural Psychology: Essays on Comparative Human Development*, ed. James W. Stigler, Richard A. Schweder, and Gilbert Herdt (Cambridge 1990), 427–45.

10 R.H. Hook, 'Psychoanalysis as Content,' in Heald and Deluz, *Anthropology and Psychoanalysis*, 230–1.

11 In a comparative Indo-European context, Georges Dumézil comments on Tiu's loss of his hand in relation to Odin's loss of an eye and formulates what he calls the 'two mutilations, clearly symbolic ... which first create and later manifest the lasting quality of each of the gods, the paralyzing visionary and the chief of legal procedure.' See his *Gods of the Ancient Northmen*, trans. Einar Haugen (Berkeley 1973), 46.

12 For drinking the *ful*, see Helen Damico, *Beowulf's Wealhtheow and the Valkyrie Tradition* (Madison 1984), ch. 3, n. 38.

13 See, e.g., Martin Camargo, 'The Finn Episode and the Tragedy of Revenge in *Beowulf*,' *Studies in Philology* 78 (1981) 12–34; and Catherine A. Carsley, 'Reassessing Cultural Memory in *Beowulf*,' *Assays* 7 (1992) 31–41.

14 Edward B. Irving, Jr, 'Heroic Role-Models: Beowulf and Others,' in *Heroic Poetry in the Anglo-Saxon Period: Studies in Honor of Jess B. Bessinger, Jr*, ed. Helen Damico and John Leyerle (Kalamazoo 1993), 367–8: 'The two victors are now in ecstatic union, and the rejoicing poet joins them. In a way, we are invited to see them as no longer vaguely "kinsmen" but as the closest of family-members, father and son. Though Beowulf laments that he has no son to leave his war-gear to, when he is dying he, in fact, leaves it to Wiglaf in what looks faintly like an "adoption" scene. /¶ Will Wiglaf prove a rightful heir? Can he continue to imitate the great role-model he followed into the consuming flames?' By now Wiglaf has in fact been adopted, I will argue, but not as 'son,' rather as though he were a 'sister's son.' In this intense but figuratively familial sense Rolf Bremmer's suggestion that Wiglaf is in fact Beowulf's sister's son now has an emotive relevance.

15 Bronislaw Malinowski, *Argonauts of the Western Pacific* (New York 1961); Marcel Mauss, *The Gift: Forms and Functions of Exchange in Archaic Societies*, trans. Ian Cunnison (New York 1967); Marshall Sahlins, *Stone Age Economics* (New York 1972); Marilyn Strathern, *The Gender of the Gift: Problems with Women and Problems with Society in Melanesia* (Berkeley 1988).

16 Irving, 'Heroic Role-Models,' 367.

2 Defending Their Masters' Honour: Slaves as Violent Offenders in Fifteenth-Century Valencia

DEBRA BLUMENTHAL

Few historians have investigated the social and human dimensions of the institution of slavery in the later medieval period, particularly for the Iberian peninsula. The slave-holding of this period seems to be of a markedly different character from the rural slavery of the early Middle Ages or the plantation slavery of the modern period. Slave-holding in the later Middle Ages was predominantly urban, artisanal, and domestic. As a result, a number of scholars, most notably Jacques Heers, have tended to consider it a kinder, gentler form of slavery. As Stephen Bensch has noted, 'recent scholarship has looked upon urban slavery, at least in comparison to the massive brutality of the later transatlantic slave trade, as a rather benign institution, a form of forced social integration that brought Mediterranean peoples into close contact. The slave blocks of Venice and Genoa, and even Valencia and Mallorca have begun to take on the character of miniature Ellis Islands.'[1]

Bensch is referring here primarily to the work of Jacques Heers. In his pioneering study of the relations between masters, slaves, and servants in the medieval western Mediterranean, Heers argued that Greek, Tartar, and Circassian slaves imported from regions bordering the Black Sea were, like free female servants recruited from the immediate countryside, seamlessly integrated into their new urban surroundings. These predominantly white female slaves would eventually convert to Roman Catholicism, earn their freedom, and intermarry with members of the local population.[2] According to Heers's model, in the medieval Mediterranean world, the institution of slavery worked more towards the socialization than the subjugation of racially and culturally distinct peoples.

Although Heers's research is broad in scope, the bulk of his evidence (primarily notarial records and prescriptive texts) comes from Italy. His conclusions do not seem to reflect the realities of the Iberian peninsula in the later Middle

Ages. The fifteenth century was a watershed period for intercultural relations in the peninsula. The assimilation of *conversos*, or Jewish converts to Christianity, was of preeminent concern, leading to the establishment of the Spanish Inquisition and the ultimate expulsion of Jews from Spain in 1492. That year also marked the end of Muslim rule in the peninsula with the fall of the Nasrid sultanate of Granada – the conquest of which flooded the slave markets with Muslim captives.[3] With regard to the Iberian context, one can hardly assume that slaves were willing converts or that masters welcomed them, once baptized, into their households and communities with open arms.

Caution seems especially merited in the case of the kingdom of Valencia. A frontier society located near Islamic territories, the kingdom of Valencia also harboured *within* its borders a sizable free Muslim population whom Valencian Christians never completely trusted.[4] Confronted by an infidel enemy without as well as within, Christians viewed their slaves – many of whom were foreign Muslims captured in corsair activity – with ambivalence.

In addition, the composition of slave populations in fifteenth-century Valencia and Italian cities differed significantly with regard to both race and gender. While Heers's largely Italian-based evidence indicates an overwhelming preponderance of white females, the male-female ratio among slaves living in the kingdom of Valencia – where war and corsair activity continued to supply a significant portion of its slaves – was almost even, with, if anything, a slightly higher percentage of males.[5] The most obvious contrast, however, was the marked presence of black Africans. Portuguese exploration of the western coast of Africa brought increasing numbers of African slaves into the Iberian peninsula, who, in Valencia, comprised as much as 40 per cent of the slave population by the second half of the fifteenth century and would face distinct challenges with regard to their ultimate integration into Valencian society.[6] In the city and kingdom of Valencia, the religious, cultural, and (increasingly) racial boundaries separating slaves from their masters were not so easily erased, the path towards assimilation, manumission, and integration not so smooth.

* * *

On a summer afternoon towards the end of the fourteenth century, a Tartar slave named Miquel, 'induced by a malign spirit, the fear of God and of royal lordship put aside,' seized a knife and repeatedly stabbed his mistress in the back while she was kneading dough. His mistress dying instantly, Miquel – 'not content with the death he had caused to his mistress' – proceeded to attack his master, stabbing the tanner twice and with such force that the wounds were considered fatal.[7] Arrested by municipal authorities and asked why he had murdered his mistress and attacked his master, the neophyte Christian replied that he had done it because 'he was very angry and upset' upon learning that his master and mistress, whom he had served more than six years, had decided to sell him.[8]

Episodes like the one just related – instances of slaves rising up and brutally assaulting their masters – are exactly the sort of slave violence I expected to find in criminal court records dating from the late fourteenth and fifteenth centuries,[9] a period when the city of Valencia was not only well on its way towards becoming the Crown of Aragon's principal port and most populous city, but also boasted a diverse and burgeoning slave population. The formal charges laid against this Tartar slave as well as his confession and ultimate death sentence are all preserved in the records of the *Justicia Criminal* [criminal justice], the annually elected municipal official presiding over all criminal proceedings under the city of Valencia's jurisdiction. Yet in the fifteen volumes extant from the late fourteenth and fifteenth centuries, it is the only incident of its type encountered. One ought not to conclude from this, however, that other such incidents did not occur. Indeed, sensational acts of insurrection – a black male slave attacking his master with an unsheathed sword or a Tartar male slave trying to drown his master in a vat of wine – were habitually cited by masters as grounds for the nullification of contracts of manumission.[10] While such dramatic incidents of slave rebellion were recounted in the records of the civil magistrate of the city of Valencia, slave violence of a very different and less spectacular sort can be found in the records of the criminal justice.[11]

Most scholars studying criminal activity in the city of Valencia during this period have concentrated their efforts on examining formal briefs and depositions similar to those recounting the murder and assault perpetrated by the Tartar slave noted above.[12] Indeed, this seems only natural since these records – found in sections entitled *demandes* and *denunciacions* – are among the most comprehensive and detailed available. Less exploited, however, are the sections found at the front of the large tomes constituting the records of the criminal justice. More or less the equivalent of a police blotter, these sections entitled *clams, cedules,* and *letres* are a mixed bag of documents. Intermixed with the somewhat tedious setting of court dates, issuance of citations, and release of prisoners on bail bonds are reports of suspicious deaths and serious injuries as well as allegations of physical assault and verbal abuse. While *demandes* and *denunciacions* were formal written documents drawn up by professionals once a dispute had been brought to trial, *clams* and *cedules* were preliminary verbal complaints[13] or reports filed by court officials often only moments after an incident had occurred.[14] The injured party was given ten days within which to file a formal lawsuit; the failure to do so meant the automatic nullification of all charges. While in most cases it seems that the plaintiff would simply allow the ten-day period to lapse, others explicitly withdrew their charges.[15] Given the high costs of litigation and the alternative mechanisms for conflict resolution available, it seems that many of these disputes would be settled without the criminal justice's intervention. Hence, these incomplete and, at times, enigmatic entries registered as *clams* and *cedules* document incidents that otherwise would escape our notice, giving us a much broader perspective on social relations in the city of Valencia during the fifteenth century.

Indeed, it was only after leafing through these terse yet tantalizing entries that I discovered what seem to have been more 'typical' instances of slave violence. Slaves are surprisingly prominent in these records, and their appearance before the court of the criminal justice more often seems to have been the consequence of having acted as their masters' accomplices than as their adversaries. In the records of the criminal magistrate of the city of Valencia, slaves were charged most frequently not in violent acts perpetrated against their masters, but in acts of violence directed against their masters' enemies and, at least ostensibly, executed on their masters' behalf.

What ought we to make of these striking episodes of persons without honour[16] defending their master's honour by harassing, insulting, and even assaulting members of rival households? It could be argued that the participation of slaves in these disputes is the ultimate symbol of their integration. One could interpret their engagement in these feuds as evidence that slaves considered the battles of their masters as their own.[17] I would argue, however, for a different view. The fact that the slaves performing these functions were almost exclusively black males, is, in and of itself, highly suggestive, raising serious questions about whether these acts of violence executed on their master's behalf were truly symbolic of their integration.

Trying to determine the motives of slaves on the basis of these records is, at best, a tricky venture. Since the records were written largely from their masters' perspective the only thing that these records can tell us with any degree of certainty is how *masters* wished to view and interpret the actions of their slaves. While slave defendants were often described as acting 'on their master's orders' and, in most cases, criminal charges were filed jointly against both master and slave, urban authorities expressed no qualms about holding slaves liable for such crimes.[18] Indeed, I will show how in at least one instance, a slave ultimately was held solely responsible for an assault in which an entire band of armed men participated.

In examining the significance of these episodes in which slaves ostensibly defended their master's honour, I will proceed in the following manner. First, I will describe what exactly these slaves were doing, and then consider three interrelated questions: what motivated masters to entrust these tasks to their slaves? to what degree were slaves held accountable for their actions? and, by way of conclusion, what does this suggest about the relative place and function of slaves in their masters' households as well as within the broader community?

It is in the context of my interest in considering the relative integration of slaves in fifteenth-century Valencian society that I wish to examine the participation of slaves in feuds between households.

In fifteenth-century Valencian society, a slave, beyond being a source of labour, was a source of honour. Contemporaries viewed slaves as essential adornments for the household of any honourable man or woman *(de be)*. In 1450, a recently widowed noblewoman filed a petition before the civil magistrate of the city of Valencia requesting an allowance in excess of three hundred gold florins to sustain her and her household *(familia e servents)* during the mandatory one-year mourning period *(any de plor)* before she could recover her dowry. In her petition, Margarita demanded funds not only to help defray the expenses connected with her own physical sustenance, but to feed, clothe, and shelter two 'ladies' *(dones)*, a female servant, a squire, and one female slave. When the curator of her husband's estate objected, arguing that Margarita would be well enough served by a more modest household staff of two attendants (an elderly male servant and a female slave), the widow's advocate maintained that an entire retinue of household attendants was essential to the preservation of the widow's honour. For, he insisted, Margarita's husband, Johan Tolsa, had been 'a knight and landed gentry man who was accustomed to having a household well outfitted with squires, ladies, male and female slaves, and beasts of burden' such that his wife had been 'at all times well attended and served in the household.' Furthermore, the widow's advocate continued, Margarita herself was 'a woman of lineage.' When she contracted marriage with Johan Tolsa she possessed over fifty thousand sous in patrimony and did not live miserably but as a lady of honour and of lineage. Given the status, lineage, and patrimony of both Johan and Margarita, he concluded, it was clear, and one could not deny, that 'according to justice she should be given the said three hundred gold florins as they are very necessary to her.'[19] This view – that maintaining a 'suitable' number of slaves and servants was essential to maintaining one's status in the community – was not restricted to members of the nobility.[20] Indeed, a striking characteristic of fifteenth-century Valencian society is the extent to which slave-holding extended to individuals of a broad range of economic levels and social conditions. Nobles, urban professionals, and artisans all owned slaves.[21] Slave-mastership extended to men and women, members of the laity as well as members of the clergy, and – though subject to certain restrictions – Muslims and Jews as well as Christians. An important component of 'living honourably' in fifteenth-century Valencia was having a household 'well outfitted with squires, ladies, male and female slaves, and beasts of burden.'[22]

Yet beyond simply being external indexes of their masters' and mistresses' wealth and standing in the community, slaves, at times, were active participants in the often violent contests pitting household against household in pursuit of status and power.[23] In their peregrinations around the city, Valencian noblemen customarily were escorted by a male slave bearing a sword. In a suit filed in 1454 against a squire accused of assaulting a nobleman, the nobleman's wife insisted that her husband had done nothing to provoke the attack. For, whether travelling on horseback or on foot, she stressed that he carried 'no arms whatsoever with him.' Rather, 'as is customary among men of honour of the present city,' he had his male slave, who travelled in his company, carry his sword for him.[24] This noblewoman's description of how slaves bore their masters' swords, I would argue, can be seen as a metaphor for the more broadly conceived expectation that slaves should defend and protect their masters' honour. Consider, for example, the following entry taken from the aforementioned registers of the criminal justice. On 31 July 1464, a woman filed a verbal complaint against a nobleman and his black slave, alleging that 'today, after midday, said black slave, *on the orders of his master*, had beaten her with diverse blows rendering her completely bruised in her person.'[25]

Female as well as male slaves were expected to defend their master's honour. The female slave of a nobleman insulted the rival of her master's son by shouting at him in the street 'almost menacingly' from an upper-story window, 'you are not man enough to speak against the house of Francesch de Vilanova!'[26] A female slave belonging to a wool-comber also used her tongue as a sword in her master's defence in an incident reported in 1456. After charges of verbal assault had been filed jointly against both master and slave, the criminal magistrate ordered that Marta 'not utter words injurious to Johan de Valencia or to his wife,' whether in their presence or in their absence.[27]

Besides tongues and fists, slaves could employ everyday household objects as weapons in their efforts to dishonour and humiliate their masters' enemies.[28] In one instance, a shopkeeper complained that 'because of the dispute which is between him and Johan Vidal, priest,' an unspecified member of Vidal's household standing on his terrace, possibly a slave, dumped a bedpan full of animal and human excrement on him while he was standing in the street below.[29]

Literally fighting their master's battles was simply one more distasteful task which masters might entrust to their slaves. Just as they could be ordered to saw down trees, prune vineyards, and stoke the fires of their ovens, male slaves could be called upon to bludgeon, gash, and otherwise debase their master's enemies. In addition to doing the cooking, cleaning, and sewing, female slaves might be expected to contribute to the household economy by taunting, slandering, and verbally degrading their master's enemies.

In the examples we have outlined so far, slaves, their masters' henchmen, acted alone (went unaccompanied) in the perpetration of violence; in other instances, slaves simply joined the fray. In 1464 a farmer filed a verbal complaint against a group of men – including a black male slave – for assaulting his household. The farmer related how the previous evening, a farmer as well as a black male slave and a squire in the service of the nobleman Gizbert Valleriola had shown up at his home armed with crossbows 'and many other weapons.'[30] Similarly, in 1441, a harness-maker and his wife accused a rival (another harness-maker and his wife) of violating their truce agreement by directing a group of armed men, including their Moorish male slave named Mahomat, to attack their household. The harness-maker claimed that his rival had not only instigated the attack but also not so surreptitiously participated in it. The victims claimed that, during the course of the attack, the rival as well as his wife not only threw bars and sticks of wood at them from an upper-story window, but shouted down to the assailants words of encouragement such as 'Kill him!' 'Eliminate him!'[31]

Hence, while it was expressly the duty of *knightly* retainers (squires or *scuders*) to come to their masters' military aid when called upon,[32] in certain circumstances heads of households mobilized as many individuals as they could muster, including and perhaps even especially their slaves, when the situation demanded the humiliation as well as the physical castigation of their enemies. Whether they took the form of a surprise attack launched late on a Sunday evening or a highway ambush on a deserted stretch of road, these actions seem to have been aimed at catching an unarmed and unsuspecting enemy unawares. Slaves – in particular, lone black slaves – seem to have been stock figures in these rather unchivalric contests.

These attacks typically involved a diverse cast of characters, uniting sons, younger siblings, extended relatives, and assorted retainers in a common mission with domestic servants and slaves. Nevertheless, these were not bands of equals whose common experiences in combat forged bonds of solidarity that crossed boundaries of status, race, and religion. Not entirely fighting side by side, within these larger groups slaves were assigned a special function and given a distinctive role.[33]

In his account of the events of the reign of Alfonso the Magnanimous, court chaplain Melchior Miralles describes a highway ambush involving a black male slave. What is remarkable about Miralles's account of the 'very cruel' murder of the nobleman Jaumot Escrivà is that, although the black male slave was but one of several assailants, he is set off from the rest of the group by his mode of transit, his weaponry, and his actions.

On that particular late autumn afternoon, Escrivà (part of a hunting party that included two noblemen, their squires, and 'two or three others') was on his way home after a day's hunt. Riding well ahead of the rest of his companions, he was intercepted by a band of armed men who had been lying in wait for him in a heavily wooded portion of the road. Hardly a random assault by road bandits, the attack on Escrivà included the sons of several prominent

Valencians as well as one black male slave. Though they were all of one party, while his cohorts were 'astride fine horses' the black male slave travelled 'on foot.' When the attackers all burst out from their hiding place and attacked Escrivà with their lances, the black male slave remained behind, not participating in the initial assault. The slave was called upon only afterwards to perform the real bloody work, administering the death blow. Miralles states this fairly unequivocally: 'they had the black man slit his throat.'[34] A similar division of labour is discernible in Miralles's description of an attack against the gardener of a nunnery. Once again, while it was a free person of higher or equal standing to the victim – the provost (*paborde*) of the nunnery – who initiated the attack, it was a black male slave who finished it. Indeed, it was only after his master had grabbed the victim by the hair that the black male slave stepped in, seized the gardener's 'lance,'[35] and stabbed him with it between the shoulders. The slave thereupon turned around and gave the gardener's very pregnant wife a few strong whacks with the blunt end of the 'lance' for good measure. Emphasizing that it was the slave (and not his master) who dealt the mortal blow, Miralles noted that, some three weeks later, the gardener died as a result of the wound administered by the slave.[36]

Certainly, masters entrusted these tasks to their slaves because they were messy and unpleasant. Nevertheless, there seems to be more behind this tendency than an aversion to the cruder aspects of shedding blood. Considering these two anecdotes in conjunction, it would seem that masters had their slaves execute these attacks on their behalf for two other reasons: they were interested in wreaking especial dishonour on their enemies while at the same time displacing the blame from themselves.

Literally adding insult to injury, masters could compound the shame of an assault by entrusting the deed to a 'base' or 'vile' person.[37] Fifteenth-century Valencians could not conceive of anyone more 'base' or 'vile' than a black male slave.[38] In a dispute between siblings over their father's inheritance, one of the more peculiar accusations which Johana Blasquo levelled against her brother was that he had purchased a black male slave named Manyiques for the sole purpose of having him assassinate his siblings one by one, so that he, their father's sole living heir, would not have to share the inheritance with anyone. Johana maintained that her brother had specifically commissioned a black male slave to do the deed because he wished to vilify as well as eliminate his rivals. His alleged motive was stated more explicitly when Johana accused her brother of threatening her husband not just with murder but with an especially insulting and shameful death: being killed by 'the most contemptible black male slave in his household.'[39] Both of these accusations suggest that a master might seek the enhancement of his honour by entrusting the maiming, injuring, and dishonouring of his enemies to his slave. Indeed, by having the most marginal figure in society inflict the wound, the hierarchical inversion so integral to dishonour was made all the starker.

Turning now to a consideration of the degree to which slaves were held responsible for these crimes, one ought to keep in mind that the underlying conviction in these records is that slaves, though patently expected to do their master's bidding, had a choice in the matter and thus could be held accountable for their actions. It is interesting to note that in the aforementioned case of the black male slave allegedly purchased for the sole purpose of assassinating his master's rivals, the slave reportedly had refused to obey his master's orders. According to Johana's testimony, Manyiques was unwilling to be his master's hit man, with the result that her brother, 'seeing that the said black male slave did not wish to do this,' placed him in irons and put him in the stockade (*serra*).[40]

Although such willfulness on the part of a slave could irk or even antagonize his/her master, a slave's possession of free will occasionally could come in handy for masters seeking to deflect responsibility for a crime on to their slaves. While slaves did not possess a full juridical personality – they could not testify for or against their masters in a criminal court of law, nor could they ordinarily file charges against their masters[41] – they nevertheless retained criminal liability. The relevant statute in Valencia's legal code (*Furs de València*) states that although no corporal or pecuniary penalty could be imposed upon a slave by a court of law, 'this is understood to apply only with regard to a civil and not a criminal action.'[42] A slave could be charged and convicted in a criminal court of law. Indeed, while a master was held ultimately responsible for any business transactions effected by his/her slave,[43] with regard to the criminal acts committed by a slave, the issue of a master's liability was significantly more complex. To establish a master's liability, the court had to prove either that the slave had perpetrated the offence with the master's permission or that, given the opportunity, the master could have prevented the slave from committing the crime.[44] Masters could exploit this gray area surrounding their relative culpability for criminal acts committed by their slaves either by professing their ignorance and denying their roles as instigators to these attacks, or by bewailing their powerlessness and proclaiming their absolute inability to control the violent impulses of their slaves. Hence, perhaps an added motivation for masters to send their slaves on these violent errands was that, in doing so, they might shift responsibility for these crimes on to their slaves. The following example will show that just as slaves themselves were sold, bartered, and exchanged, a slave's crimes could similarly be disowned, disavowed, and repudiated by their masters.[45]

In late August, 1456, a band made up of at least twelve men, including a black male slave, was accused of ambushing a farmer's wife named Caterina. Caterina Gyronis, wife of farmer Martí Vidal, testified that 'for some time now' there had been a feud between her and the members of the Noguera household. Ostensibly in perpetuation of this feud, the previous Friday Caterina was attacked by a band of about a dozen armed men. In her formal complaint, Caterina identified as among her assailants Bernat Noguera's son, his brother-in-law, seven of Noguera's 'fellows,' and his black male slave named Jordi. It bears noting, however, that Caterina differentiated between the black male slave and the rest of her assailants, describing Noguera's son, brother-in-law, and seven fellows as 'all of one company such that if any one of them has a grudge and wishes to injure a person, it was their practice that they would all combine forces ... to assault houses, estates, and rural properties as well as to lay ambushes on the public roadways.'

Knowing that she had gone to the nearby suburb of Campanar and would be returning to Valencia later that evening, this gang of armed men lay in wait for Caterina in a secluded spot just off the royal highway. When they saw Caterina and the two young men escorting her approach – all three of them proceeding 'simply, not doing harm or damage to anybody' – the assembled company, 'armed with many diverse weapons,' emerged from their hiding place 'suddenly and with deadly intent.' Shouting 'Kill! Kill!' and with their swords and lances unsheathed, they charged onto the royal highway. Seeing this multitude of men barrelling straight towards them, Caterina's two young escorts immediately took flight, leaving her completely defenceless before this armed throng. Hit 'repeatedly about the head and face and all over her body,' Caterina also received stab wounds 'in the back and in the right leg.'[46]

There is a significant postscript to this case. For this assault against a defenceless farmer's wife in which allegedly over a dozen men participated, it was the lone black male slave, in the end, who was held solely accountable. Three days after she filed her oral complaint, the farmer's wife dropped the charges against each and every one of her assailants *except* the black male slave Jordi. In a rather bizarre turn of events, Caterina stated that she now wished to renounce her suit since 'she knew and it was certain that the injury or injuries done to her person had been and were committed by Jordi, the black slave of Bernat Noguera's father, for his own motives and at his own risk.'[47]

Holding a black male slave solely responsible for the assault seems a particularly convenient resolution to this dispute. Indeed, it seems to have been a compromise negotiated between the two parties in an effort to maintain both households' sense of honour. The demands of the injured party for vengeance and justice would be met inasmuch as someone was being held accountable. Moreover, this would be accomplished without Noguera really having to admit his culpability: he was incriminated only tangentially as the slave's master. Being able to lay blame on someone other than the two principals in the dispute – especially, I would argue, on someone as negligible and dispensable as a black male slave – perhaps made it easier for the feuding parties to come to some sort of truce. Presumably, Noguera would have provided some form of compensation to Caterina in order for her to agree to this settlement. This episode effectively demonstrates how slaves could be used as scapegoats, with masters deflecting onto them liability for crimes executed on their behalf and at their instigation.[48]

Certainly whether acting on their master's behalf or on their master's orders, slaves also acted in their own self interest. In his study of domestic servants in renaissance Venice, Dennis Romano points to similar incidents involving servants 'closing ranks' to defend their masters. Although Romano points to this as evidence that, to varying degrees, servants identified with and internalized the values of their masters, he also admits that public displays of loyalty and obedience were not always nor necessarily sincere. He stresses that, just as masters could adopt various tactics to deal with their slaves and servants, slaves and servants could be similarly calculating when it came to deciding how to behave towards their masters. While many guilelessly acted as their masters wished them to, others 'after having calculated the costs and potential benefits' only pretended to do so.[49] As the following example illustrates, this is something that was readily acknowledged, and indeed emphasized, in fifteenth-century Valencian sources. Not simply their masters' agents, slaves were often portrayed as shrewd and crafty individuals with motives of their own.

In a formal lawsuit (*demanda*) filed in 1441, a shepherd charged the son of a Valencian farmer and his black male slave with assault and battery. What is particularly striking about this case is that the black male slave was accused not only of joining in on the attack but of deceitfully provoking it, all under the guise of defending his master's honour. In a deposition filed before the criminal justice, the shepherd related how he had first encountered the slave one Sunday afternoon while he was grazing livestock near the 'Barranch de Torrent.' The slave struck up a conversation with him and even convinced him to share his lunch. The shepherd maintained that when he asked the slave if his master would mind it if he grazed his herd on his property, the slave responded enthusiastically, telling him that there was 'plenty of grass and that he should go there.' Trusting in the slave's assurances, the shepherd led his herd out to pasture on this farmer's property. When the slave reappeared shortly thereafter, the shepherd continued, he entrusted him with a quarter of a sheep and some cured meat – a 'gift' intended for the slave's master in recompense for use of his property. In the end, however, the shepherd maintained, he was poorly repaid for the generosity he had shown this slave. Not only did the slave keep the gifts intended for his master but, when his master's son returned home, the slave feigned ignorance when the shepherd was spotted grazing livestock on their property. Indeed, the shepherd charged, the slave encouraged and incited the son to forcibly eject him from their property. Eagerly joining in the ensuing attack, moreover, the black male slave 'came to the aid of his master' and attacked him with his *lança de Xerez*,[50] shouting 'injurious words,' and, finally, once the shepherd had fallen to the ground, holding him down while his master's son stabbed him (with the shepherd's own knife!) in the head and face.[51]

Although the shepherd stated that he held them both responsible for the attack, describing both the farmer's son and his slave as extremely arrogant (*superbios*) and notorious troublemakers, what is distinctive about this case is that the black male slave was accused of instigating as well as participating in an assault. In his deposition, the shepherd contended that the farmer's son, too, was a victim of the slave's deceit. The black male slave allegedly hoodwinked both the victim and his partner in crime. Exploiting his membership in his master's household, the slave was credited with mobilizing its forces in order to achieve his own ends. He managed to secure for himself lunch, a quarter of a sheep, and some cured meat, all the while portraying himself as the faithful defender of his master's honour, as his master saw his fields despoiled and became embroiled in a potentially costly legal battle.

Certainly one is tempted to accept the shepherd's story at face value and view this episode as an extraordinary example of 'slave agency' in late medieval Valencia. On the other hand, considered in conjunction with the cases just outlined, one must also admit the possibility that this 'haughty' black male slave, like the aforementioned Jordi, might simply have been a convenient scapegoat, facilitating the resolution of this dispute between farmer and shepherd by assuming responsibility for the assault.

In conclusion, while initially these episodes might seem to constitute strong evidence that slaves were fully integrated members of their master's households and thus bore their share of the burden of defending and maintaining their honour, further exploration of the sources reveals a much more complicated picture. Slaves were favoured agents in these assaults precisely because they were liminal figures. Masters could accept and deny responsibility for a slave's actions as they willed, either acknowledging them as the acts of a loyal dependent engaged in defending their honour or disavowing them as the acts of a devious and unruly other. Having their slaves (particularly their black male slaves) ridicule, assault, and batter their enemies – again *because* they were marginal figures – carried the added bonus of rendering the offence more degrading. Although the bonds that tied slaves to their masters were real, they were not indissoluble. While masters expected their slaves to love and obey them as well as come to their defence, they also viewed them with a significant amount of ambivalence and wished to retain the ability to do with them as they willed. Hence a slave's membership in a household was more provisional than permanent; the protection it conferred could, in the end, prove rather illusory. The

46 Debra Blumenthal

frustration slaves felt at this – frustration at their precarious and unstable position on the periphery of society – can be read in acts of violence similar to the one with which we began. A baptized Christian Tartar slave slaughters his mistress and brutally attacks his master, not in a dramatic attempt to reclaim his liberty, but as an expression of his profound disillusionment. He is angered, according to his testimony, by what he considers an act of betrayal on the part of his masters. His masters were reneging on an unwritten agreement by which years of faithful service would win him not only his freedom but also acceptance in the community. Despite all his efforts to assimilate, despite his conversion to Christianity, despite more than six years of loyal service, his masters were expelling him from their household and putting him up for resale.

Notes

1 Stephen P. Bensch, 'From Prizes of War to Domestic Merchandise: The Changing Face of Slavery in Catalonia and Aragon, 1000–1300,' *Viator* 25 (1994) 85.
2 'Il demeure que, du point de vue social, cet esclavage-là, celui des domestiques, constitue un procédé de christianisation et d'assimilation capable d'amener, de retenir puis de fondre dans ces villes méditerranéenes d'Occident des groupes humains fort divers, néanmoins presque toujours de race blanch.' Jacques Heers, *Esclaves et domestiques au moyen âge dans le monde méditerranéen* (Paris 1981), 287.
3 Referring to the sizable number of Muslim captives appearing on Valencian auction blocks subsequent to the fall of Málaga (1487) and Oran (1509), see M. A. Ladero Quesada, 'La esclavitud por guerra a fines del siglo XV: El caso de Málaga,' *Hispania* 27 (1967) 63–88; and Mark D. Meyerson, 'Slavery and Solidarity: Mudejars and Foreign Muslim Captives in the Kingdom of Valencia,' *Medieval Encounters* 2.3 (1996) 286–343.
4 Mudéjars constituted as much as 80 per cent of the kingdom's population at the time of conquest in the 13th century, and Jacqueline Guiral-Hadziiossif has estimated the number of Muslims living in the kingdom of Valencia during the 15th century at around 130,000 – or about 40 per cent out of a total population of 320,000. Jacqueline Guiral-Hadziiossif, *Valencia, puerto mediterráneo en el siglo xv (1410–1525)* (Valencia 1989), 435.
5 Based on my own research in the notarial records of the city of Valencia – records encountered both in the Archivo del Reino de Valencia (hereafter ARV) and the Archivo de Protocolos del Patriarca (APPV) – of 511 references to slaves or former slaves between 1460 and 1480, 276 were to males, 235 to females.
6 Of the aforementioned 511 references to slaves and former slaves in notarial records from the city of Valencia dating between 1460 and 1480, 204 were to blacks or mulattos. My findings generally seem to agree with those of D. Bénesse

Slaves as Violent Offenders in Fifteenth-Century Valencia 47

in an unpublished dissertation, 'Les Esclaves dans la société ibérique aux XIVe et XVe siècles' (University of Paris X, 1970). Based on statistics taken from the studies of Vicenta Cortes (for Valencia) and Charles Verlinden (for Barcelona), Bénesse notes that 21 per cent of the slaves imported into Barcelona in the 14th century were black, declining to 17 per cent between 1400 and 1450 and then increasing to 32 per cent in the latter half of the 15th century. In contrast, Bénesse shows how the number of black slaves being imported into the city of Valencia increased steadily during this period, constituting a significantly higher percentage of the slave population in the last decade of the 15th century. Seventy per cent of the slaves imported into the city of Valencia between 1489 and 1500 were black! Cited in Jacques Heers, *Family Clans in the Middle Ages: A Study of Political and Social Structures in Urban Areas* (Amsterdam 1977), 64.

7 ARV Justicia Criminal 44: Denunciacions: Manus 8: 13r–15v: 'Primo diu que en lo present dia de huy en hora quasi de mega tercie lo dit Miquel induhit desperit maligna la temor de deu et de la senyoria real apart posada pres un punyal et ab aquell se lexa correr contra la dita na Sibilia senyora sua la qual pastava et ab lo dit punyal dona diverses punyalades a la dita dona per les espatles en manera que sopte mori et passa de aquesta present vida. Et de aço es fama. Item diu ut supra que'l dit Miquel catiu no content de la mort que feit havia de la dona sua ab lo dit punyal dona dues punyalades al dit en Guillem Ros senyor seu lo qual sta en obte de mort. Et de aço es fama.'

8 ARV Justicia Criminal 44: Denunciacions: Manus 8: 13r–15v: 'Interrogat ... per que havia morta la dita na Sibilia senyora sua. Et dix que per tal com era fort irat et despagat com havia sabut de cert que lo dit en Guillem Ros volia vendre o havia venut a ell dit confesant a qui havia servit sis o set anys et que us tenia loch la dita na Sibilia.' Miquel was ultimately sentenced to being dragged through the streets of the city, having his hands and feet cut off and the limbs displayed, respectively, in the doorway of the municipal courthouse (left hand), the doorway of his master and mistress's household (right hand), the city marketplace (left foot), and the plaza in front of the cathedral (right foot). Miquel was then to be taken outside the city walls where he would be 'hung by the neck in a manner so that he dies.'

9 In the article that sparked my initial interest in this topic, Iris Origo describes the atmosphere in slave-holding households in 14th- and 15th-century Tuscany in the following terms. 'Many of the slave-owning households must have been divided into two camps, with sullen, resentful, half-savage slaves on the one side, and on the other, suspicious, and often extremely nervous masters. And indeed, their fears were natural enough.' Indeed, Origo's examination of criminal court records from Siena and Florence yielded cases in which one female slave was charged with sticking 'a small knife' into her mistress's thigh, resulting in 'some shedding of blood,' and another with hitting her mistress repeatedly with a stone. Iris

Origo, 'The Domestic Enemy: The Eastern Slaves in Tuscany in the Fourteenth and Fifteenth Centuries,' *Speculum* 30 (1955) 340–1.

10 In these petitions (*requestes*), masters and mistresses of conditionally freed slaves asked the civil justice to declare that, as a consequence of a slave's act of insurrection, their contract of manumission was null and void. Masters were seeking official confirmation of their right to retain these conditionally freed slaves in servitude, rather than the administration of any corporal penalty or punishment.

11 Sharply distinguishing between 'normal, everyday, or systemic' violence and 'abnormal or cataclysmic' violence, David Nirenberg has emphasized how violence and competition, hardly indicative of only the 'destructive breakdown of social relations,' can, in fact be viewed as manifestations of 'associative action.' He argues that 'violence was a central and systemic aspect of the coexistence of majority and minorities in medieval Spain, and even that coexistence was in part predicated on such violence.' David Nirenberg, *Communities of Violence: Persecution of Minorities in the Middle Ages* (Princeton 1996), 9–10.

12 Although the transcripts of the trials themselves are often incomplete (in most cases the criminal justice's ultimate ruling is missing), the *demandes* or *denunciacions* filed before the court upon the initiation of a trial are highly detailed. Rafael Narbona Vizcaíno describes the differences between these various types of lawsuits in his *Malhechores, violencia, y justicia ciudadana en la Valencia bajomedieval (1360–1399)* (Valencia 1987).

13 *Clams* normally consisted of two- to three-sentence statements in which the injured party seeking redress recounted the injury as well as fingered the accused.

14 Although technically the criminal justice could not prosecute an individual unless a plaintiff filed charges, in exercising his secondary function as the preserver of public order he also performed a role akin to that of the police, actively investigating crimes and pursuing criminals rather than just passively responding to victims' complaints. Upon learning of a suspicious death or a serious injury, lieutenants of the criminal justice would visit the crime scene, question witnesses, and ask the victim's family members if they wished to press charges. An affirmative response to this query seems to have carried about the same weight as registering a verbal complaint (a *clam*). In both cases, before the criminal justice could move forward, formal written charges had to be filed.

15 In only rare instances did the injured party disclose the reasons for subsequently withdrawing his/her charges. For one example, see ARV Justicia Criminal 102: M. 6: Clams: 7 November 1452.

16 In the context of an honour culture, the slave him/herself, by definition, was a person without honour. Although the honour and prestige of a master's household was magnified by a large and impressive retinue of slaves, a symbol of a master's wealth and power, the individual slaves themselves, as a consequence of their complete indebtedness and powerlessness, were persons without honour. As

Orlando Patterson states in *Slavery and Social Death: A Comparative Study* (Cambridge, MA 1982), 11, 'What was universal in the master-slave relationship was the strong sense of honor the experience of mastership generated, and conversely, the dishonoring of the slave condition.' See also Kenneth S. Greenberg, *Honor & Slavery: Lies, Duels, Noses, Masks, Dressing as a Woman, Gifts to Strangers, Death, Humanitarianism, Slave Rebellions, The Pro-Slavery Argument, Baseball, Hunting, and Gambling in the Old South* (Princeton 1996), esp. 33–9.

The condition of the slave as a person without honour was made patent by the legislation of the period. Hence, an injury done to a slave was deemed immaterial – not able to be the subject of prosecution – unless either the injury seriously disabled the slave (broken bone, loss of limb, etc.), rendering him/her incapable of providing service, or his/her master took offense, i.e., the injury to the slave was construed as aimed at dishonouring the master. In both cases, it was the slave's master, not the slave him/herself, who could claim offence. 'Si a servu chrestià, o serrahí de paraula, o de feyt serà alguna injúria feyta, aquell servu per rahó d'aquella injúria que li serà feyta no ha nenguna demanda. *Per ço car servu no ha persona de star en juhi ques pusca clamar de nengun hom:* emperò si a aquell servu serà feyta injúria axí com és que hom laura nafrat, o os trencat, o blavura feyta, o li haurà hom tolt algu de sos membres, o *en deshonour de son senyor lauran ferit, o batut:* la donchs és donada demanda a son senyor per rahó d'aquelles injúries que seran feytes al servu contra aquell qui les li haurà feytes. Mas si al servu seran dites algunes paraules quant que sien vils ne aontades nenguna demanda no és donada al senyor ne al servu per aquelles paraules injurioses les quals seran dites al servu.' *Furs de València* 9.5.3. Quoted from the edition by Germà Colón and Arcadi Garcia, 9 vols, Els nostres clàssics, col·lecció A, 101, 105, 113, 121, 130, 134, 136–8 (Barcelona 1970–2002), 7: 47.

17 Dennis Romano, in his study of master-servant relations in renaissance Venice, remarks that 'servants' identification with their masters was especially apparent when masters were under attack. Then servants closed ranks to defend masters and their family.' He further states that while 'masters may well have encouraged' this behaviour, these incidents show how servants themselves 'identify with and internalize the values of their masters.' Dennis Romano, *Housecraft and Statecraft: Domestic Service in Renaissance Venice, 1400–1600* (Baltimore 1996), 205–6. For a discussion of the problems and pitfalls in assuming that slaves internalized the ideology of their masters, see James C. Scott, *Domination and the Arts of Resistance: Hidden Transcripts* (New Haven 1990), 85–90.

18 While slaves could *not* be held personally liable in civil suits, this protection did not apply for criminal offences. 'Servu en juhii ne en pleit no pot ésser, ne condempnatió que sie feita en persona d'ell, no estie ni haje valor. En aquest fur adobà lo senyor rey que sie entès en pleit civil *e no en criminal.*' *Furs de València* 3.1.1; ed. Colón and Garcia, 3: 5 (emphasis mine).

19 ARV Justicia Civil 915: M. 16: 15r–19v; M. 16: 25r–32v.
20 When a pharmacist named Pere Martí died in 1460, for example, his widow Ursola felt it necessary to continue maintaining a household of at least ten dependents. Having lived (prior to her husband's death) 'very honourably, having in their household between thirteen and fourteen mouths to feed (*menjadors*),' Ursola struggled to continue living in the style to which she had become accustomed. In addition to the three male youths (*jovens*) who worked in the pharmacy, Ursola fed, sheltered, and clothed a young girl who was a distant relative of her husband's (*fadrina parenta del dit defunt*), a salaried female servant (*dona de soldada*), a young male servant (*fadri*), a female slave along with her ten-year-old son, as well as a young girl taken in from a local orphanage (*una borda del spital*). ARV Justicia Civil 923: M. 15: 30r–48r.
21 An analysis of contemporary documentation describing the individuals buying and selling slaves (as well as those purchasing captives recently presented before the court of the bailiff general) reveals that in addition to nobles and urban professionals (merchants, notaries, lawyers, and doctors), artisans such as tanners, cobblers, rope-makers, and (especially) bakers and carpenters were prominent among slave owners. The documents consulted include contracts of sales of captives recently ruled *de bona guerra* found in the records of the bailiff general of the kingdom of Valencia (ARV Bailia 219–21) and contracts of sale located among the voluminous notarial records of both the ARV and the APPV.
22 Social anthropologists such as Julian A. Pitt-Rivers and Julio Caro Baroja have all noted how the 'Mediterranean' notion of honour (particularly with regard to elites) is an 'honour of precedence,' derived from 'the domination of persons.' See Julian A. Pitt-Rivers, 'Honour and Social Status,' in *Honour and Shame: The Values of Mediterranean Society*, ed. J.G. Peristiany (London 1965), 19–78. See also, by Pitt-Rivers, *The Fate of Shechem* (Cambridge 1977), and 'Honor' in *International Encyclopedia of the Social Sciences*, ed. David L. Sills, 2nd ed. (New York 1968), 503–11. See further the articles by J.G. Peristiany and Julio Caro Baroja in *Honour and Shame*, as well as Frank Henderson Stewart's more recent *Honour* (Chicago 1994).
23 In connection with their historical studies investigating the significance of honour and violence in Valencian society, both Rafael Narbona Vizcaíno and Pablo Pérez García have discussed the intense feuding (*bandositat*) characteristic of Valencia in the 14th and 15th centuries. See Narbona Vizcaíno, *Malhechores, violencia, y justicia ciudadana*, esp. 83–123, and his *Pueblo, poder, y sexo: Valencia medieval (1306–1420)* (Valencia 1991), esp. 125–44; Pablo Pérez García, *La comparsa de los malhechores: Valencia 1479–1518* (Valencia 1990), esp. 267–306. See also Mark D. Meyerson, *The Muslims of Valencia in the Age of Fernando and Isabel: Between Coexistence and Crusade* (Berkeley 1991), esp. ch. 6.

For a discussion of how 'plebeians' (including slaves) in colonial Latin America – 'although they lacked the birth, race, and wealth necessary' – participated in the 'Iberian culture of honor,' see the essays by Richard Boyer, Lyman Johnson, Sonya-Lipsett-Rivera, and Sandra Lauderdale Graham in *The Faces of Honour: Sex, Shame, and Violence in Colonial Latin America*, ed. Lyman L. Johnson and Sonya Lipsett-Rivera (Albuquerque 1998).

24 Damiata Pardo claimed that her husband, said noble mossen Tristany Pardo ('de la casta cavaller'), 'acostuma anar pacificament per la present ciutat de Valencia axi a cavall com a peu sens portar armes algunes ab si sino tant com a vegades lo seu sclau li porta una spasa segons es costum entre los homes de be de la present ciutat.' ARV Justicia Criminal 52: M. 1: 28v; M. 4: 39r–45v.

25 ARV Justicia Criminal 36: Clams: 31 July 1464: 'Na Ursola, filla d'En Guillem Liniat quondam se clama al magnifich justicia de hun sclau negre de mossen Melchior de Vilanova appellat Anthoni e del dit mossen Melchior afermant que en lo dia de huy apres mig jorn lo dit negre *de manament del dit son amo* li ha pegat diversses bastonades de les quals la ha tota magnada en la persona. Requirent esser presos esser li feta justicia.'

26 To which he (Johan Nadal) responded, 'Shut up you drunk, you don't know anything!' ARV Justicia Criminal 99: Denunciacions (27 May 1441).

27 ARV Justicia Criminal 24: Cedules: M. 4: 14 September 1456: 'En Johan de Valencia mercader ciutada de Valencia e na Eyronis sa muller asseguren la persona homens coses e bens d'en Jacme Thopi payre [sic] e de Marta sclava d'aquell qui d'aquell se temen e han requests assegurament a pena de bars e traydors e CC florins aplicadors etc. presta sagrament e homenatge en poder del honourable justicia. Obligaren etc. Testes Bernat Bertran e Johan Sandoval saig. Et e comisero Testes proxime dicti. *Lo dit honourable justicia personalment mana a la dita Marta sclava que no diga paraules injurioses en presencia ne absencia als dits en Johan de Valencia ne a sa muller a pena de deu morabatins e si aquells pagar no pora correr la vila acots.*'

28 This, of course, would also have worked in the other direction. Assaults against slaves were viewed as assaults against their masters. Hence, slaves often found themselves caught in the crossfire, easy targets for someone wishing to offend or dishonour their masters. In the spring of 1452, for example, a Valencian butcher directed his (free) male servant to attack the female slave owned by his rival. This foray was only a prelude of sorts, perpetrated the day before the butcher himself attacked his rival's wife and mother-in-law. In the *clam* that the slave's master, Johan Pascual, a.k.a. Johan 'the Double-Chinned (*Gorgera*),' filed against the butcher Luis Martí, Pascual portrayed Martí's servant's attack against his female slave as the preliminary to Martí's own, more direct, assault against his kinfolk. After 'said Francesquet came to his household with a butcher's hammer or club

and deliberately, having been incited by and on the orders of said Luis Martí and his wife, gave Caterina, the slave of said Johan Pascual, two blows in her left arm,' Martí himself, the following Sunday, attacked Pascual's wife and mother-in-law. Ambushing them while they were on their way to attend vespers at their local parish church, Martí allegedly hit them repeatedly with a bat. ARV Justicia Criminal 102: Cedes: M. 2: 6 March 1452. On March 17th of the same year, Pascual and his wife dropped the charges.

29 ARV Justicia Criminal 36: Clams: 16 September 1464: 'En Francesch Miro se clama al magnifich justicia de lo qui sta en la casa de mossen Johan Vidal prevere affermant que en lo dia de hir ja vespre del dit dia stan ell clamant e hun quis diu Arigel tansat a la pena de ell clamant li lancaren de la terrat de la casa del dit mossen Vidal huna mongeta plena de fem e merda e per la differencia que es entre ell clamant e lo dit mossen Vidal. Requirent etc.'

30 ARV Justicia Criminal 36: Clams: 14 December 1464: 'En Anthoni Ferrer laurador de Benicalairet se clama al magnifich justicia d'En Anthoni Puig laurador del dit lloch e de Guillem Vilalba scuder del magnifich En Gizbert Valleriola e ... [blank] Manuel *e de Pere sclau negre del dit En Valleriolla* affermant que en la nit passada li son venguts e combatreli la casa am ballesta parada e altres armes sens causa alguna justa.' Cf. the assault against Na Caterina Gyronis, 'vaguera,' ARV Justicia Criminal 53: M. 3: 24r–26v: where the accused included Bernat Noguera 'fill d'En Noguert,' Perot 'cunyat de aquell dit Bernat Noguera,' Luis Maria, Bernat Bosch, Macia Polo, N'Alfonso Alvarez, En Johan Guimera, Anthoni Martí, En Jacme Martí 'fill de aquell... *e lo dit negre del dit Bernat Noguera.*' In the end, as I will emphasize below, the slave was held solely responsible for the attack.

31 ARV Justicia Criminal 99: Denunciacions (1441 March): 'Item dien ut supra que lo dit mestre Matheu e muller de aquell fahent volenca e ajuda als dessus dits qui combatren la dita casa isqueren a la lur finestra e participants e ajudants en lo dit combatiment tiraren e foren vists tirar diverses barres e fusts vers e contra lo dit en Johan Fababux e casa de aquell. En tant que'l crydaren matar a ell e a les altres quis meten per depertir. E axi es ver.'

32 For example, Franciscan moralist Francesc Eiximenis instructed '... for these ones, those who have submitted themselves to service, are obliged to defend their lords and present themselves whenever needed' (my translation). Francesc Eiximenis, *Dotzè llibre del Crestià*, cap. 338: '... aquests aitals servicials son tenguts de defendre llurs senyors e d'ensenyar-se per ells quan es hora.' Cited in *La societat catalana al segle XIV*, ed. Jill Webster (Barcelona 1980), 60–1.

33 The following portrayal of a black male slave's performance 'under fire' reflects how they were not viewed on an equal footing with free-born squires as loyal and valiant defenders of their master's honour. On the evening of 29 May 1452, a small company made up of a squire and a black male slave from the household of

'micer' Miquel Cabrugada and a squire from the household of nobleman Nicholau de Proxita were waylaid by a group of armed men on the royal highway leading from Valencia to Beniparrell. Rather than forming a united front against an equally matched group of three attackers, however, they immediately dispersed, each going off in a different direction. In the report of the incident filed before the criminal justice, their reactions to the ambush are differentiated and subtly ranked. When their attackers discharged their crossbows in their direction, only the squire of nobleman Nicholau de Proxita stood his ground: the squire and the black male slave of 'micer' Miquel Cabrugada both fled the scene. But, while the squire is said to have run off to get assistance, the black male slave is depicted as running away 'out of fear' and hiding in the bushes. Upon reaching the town of Beniparrell, Cabrugada's squire sounded the alarm, shouting 'Help! Help!' and urging the local authorities to come to their aid, for he had no doubt that their attackers were intent upon killing them. By the time the squire, the justice of Beniparrell, and 'nearly all the men of said place' arrived on the scene and found the savagely butchered body of Proxita's squire off to the side of the road, the attackers had escaped. The black male slave, however, was still hiding in the bushes. The officials of the justice noted how they had to make several appeals to get him to come out from his hiding place! ARV Justicia Criminal 102: Cedes: M. 3: 30 May 1452.

34 'De Jaumot Escrivà. En l'any de 1455, divenres, a 7 de noembre, Jaumot Escrivà venia del riu de Corbera de tirar a les fotges ab los arcs ... E ans que no fossen a la gola dels Tamarits, de la llastra ixqué Galceran Pardo, fill de mossén Joan, e lo fill d'en Bernat Fontanills, e Joan Estella, ab bons ginets, e un negre a peu ... *alancejaren lo dit Jaumot Escrivà e feren-lo degollar al negre*, e segons se diu, li llevaren la cadena d'or que porta al coll e cent timbres. Fon cas molt cruel sobre pau e treva e assegurament del senyor rey de Navarra.' Melchior Miralles, *Dietari del capella d'Alfons el Magnanim*, ed. Vicent-Josep Escarti (Valencia 1988), 181–2.

35 The 'lance' may only have been a scythe, since Miralles said that the slave seized it from the gardener after he returned from working in the fields.

36 'De la brega del paborde Sanç. Lo paborde Sanç, lo dijous, a 6 de noembre, estant en lo monestir de Sant Julià – lo seu esclau tent la mula – , venc a brega ab Bertomeu Bernat, hortolà de les monges del dit monestir, de què lo paborde fonc a la brega. L'esclau pres una llança e donà-li una llançada en les espatles, que fonc mort dissabte, a 25 de noembre. E a la muller de l'hortolà, en la llança li dona ba[s]collades; estava a dies de parir. La llança era del dit hortolà, que venia de llaurar, e dix: "Monsènyer, jo no vull haver brega ab vos." E lo pabordr[e] lo pres per lo cabells, e lo negre li donà la llançada. Tan poca menció se n'és feta com si fos mort un poll: paborde e negre van per València com si no haguessen fet res.' Miralles, *Dietari*, 396.

37 That this is a more than probable interpretation of these types of attacks is supported by the *denunciacion* filed against a pharmacist's apprentice/servant in

which the plaintiff, a physician's wife (Damiata, wife of 'honourable mestre Francesch Martí Gradano, mestre en medecina'), insisted that the apprentice (Johan Mestre, 'moco d'apothecari d'en Francesch Vilar,' accused of assaulting her husband) be sentenced to death since 'according to the disposition of the *Furs* of the most high King and according to ancient practice, when a vile and lowly individual harms or otherwise injures a man of honour (*hun hom de be*) he ought to be condemned to the death penalty.' 'Item diu ut supra que segons disposicio de fur del al Rey ... e segons pratica antiquada quant hun vila e menestra aminuara e dona de fet carech a hun hom de be deu esser condempnar a pena de mort. E axi es stat arbitrat et declarat lo fur del dit alt Rey en Jaume lo capitol qui comença aquell qui ferra en lo titol de crims per lo honourable o consell criminal de la ciutat de Valencie e etiam per lo spectable governador et etiam ... ha declarat e pronunciat la sacra audiencia real e en semblant cars per procurador de presencia es stat penjar home e contra altres es stat pronunciar per procurators de absencia a pena de mort et ... es notori en la present ciutat. E axi es ver e fama.' ARV Justicia Criminal 53: Denunciacions: M. 3: 6v–10v.

38 In his discussion of how slaves were regarded with 'un cierto aire de desprecio,' Vicente Graullera Sanz cites two sayings reflective of contemporary views of black Africans: 'Fes bé, encara que siga un moro de Guinea [Be good, for you too could end up like a Moor from Guinea!]' and 'Aná la negra al bany, y tingue que contar un any [A year will pass before a black woman returns to the bath house!].' Graullera Sanz, *La esclavitud en Valencia en los siglos XVI y XVII* (Valencia 1978), 142–3 [taken from Estanislau Alberola, *Refraner Valencià* (Valencia 1928), 19, 21].

39 ARV Justicia Criminal 25: Denunciacions: M. 2: 18r–22v: 'Item diu e posa ut suppra que dilluns que comptaven XX del mes de agost any present MCCCCLXXXVIII lo dit en Bernat Coll delat vench a la casa de la dita na Johanna Blasquo denunciador la dita na Johana demana al dit en Bernat Coll que li donas e pagas lo que li deuia donar per la concordia que entre ells era feta ... E lo dit en Bernat Coll no volent pagar ni fer raho de si mateix vench a moltes males rahons e paraules ab lo dit en March Blasquo *e que ell lo faria matar e castigar ab lo pus rohin negre de casa sua* o ab en Johan Coll fill de aquell delat e denunciat e que ell no'l tendria per fill si ell no feya. E axi es ver e fama publica.'

40 ARV Justicia Criminal 25: Denunciacions: M. 2: 18r–22v: 'Item diu e posa ut suppra que lo dit en Bernat Coll ... E venint lo sperit maligne o dins lo seu cors e en la pensa per mal husar de malvestats e maleses acostumades con deliberada pensa de matar o greument dapnificar los damunt dits compra hun negre appellat Mayniques al qual comprat *hague dix davant moltes e diverses persones que aquell negre havia comprat per matas an Sobrevero o alguna de ses jermanes* per husurparse los bens de la herencia de son pare per que nols haguessen aquells. *E vist que lo dit negre non volia fer* prengue'l fera'l e mete'l a la serra. E axi es ver.'

41 *Furs de València* 2.2.1; ed. Colón and Garcia, 2: 129.

42 See n. 18 above.
43 'Si ab volentat del pare lo fill, o ab volentat del senyor lo servu, usaran de menar nau, o usaran de tenir taverna, o usaran de tenir hostaleria, lo pare, o el senyor seran tenguts per lo tot de ço que serà feit per aquells.' *Furs de València* 2.16.4; ed. Colón and Garcia, 2: 245. See also Graullera Sanz, *Esclavitud en Valencia*, 156.
44 'Si catiu d'alcú donarà o farà mal o dan a alcuna persona, lo senyor, sabén o no sabén, e no·u podie vedar, aquel senyor no és tengut sinó que dó aquel catiu a aquel qui·l dan haurà suffert e pres, jasia ço que més sia el dan que no val lo catiu. Emperò si el catiu darà dan a alcú, e el senyor seu ó sabé e no·u volch vedar com ó pogués vedar, és tengut tot lo dan a restituir que aquel catiu haurà feit; ne és deliurat ne absolt si volrrà dar aquell catiu per lo mal ne el dan que haurà feit ne donat. E si aquel catiu qui haurà feit dan o mal, lo senyor sabén o no sabén, e no volch vedar com vedar ó pogués, vendrà en poder d'altre novell senyor per compra o per altra justa rahó, aquel novell senyor serà tengut tan solament a liurar aquel catiu per lo mal e per lo dan que haurà feit enans que vingués en son poder, car la malafeyta seguex aquel qui feita la haurà.' *Furs de València* 3.17.11; ed. Colón and Garcia, 3: 254–5.
45 A slave owner's success in doing so, however, clearly varied according to his/her relative power and socio-political influence. In a petition filed before the governor in 1479, for instance, reference is made to a sentence pronounced against a slave and his deceased master's son, by which they were both condemned to death (*pena de mort*) for having perpetrated 'certs furts ladronicis e roberies.' Both having been sentenced to the death penalty *in absentia*, however, it is unclear whether the penalty was ever actually applied to either master or slave. ARV Gobernación 2351: M. 16: 1r–2r.
46 ARV Justicia Criminal 53: Denunciacions: M. 3: 24r–26v.
47 ARV Justicia Criminal 53: 26r–v: 'Devant la presencia de nos molt honourable mossen Jacme d'Almenar cavaller justicia de la ciutat de Valencia en lo criminal compar la dona na Gyronis muller d'en Marti Vidal laurador et diu et expon que com ella ab denunciacio per ella proposada ... haia solempnialment denunciat en Perot Pont, en Bernat Noguera menor de dies, en Luis Marti alias Maria, e en Bernat Bosch et molt altres vehins de la partida de Campanar orta de la present ciutat dients los que serien stats complicies de certs e diverses crims e delictes en la dita denunciacio contenguts e expressats. E com a cascu per furs del present regne sia licit e permes de renunciat desistir relexar e abolir son propi clam acusacio et denunciacio e ella proposant regonexent sa consciencia *com sapia e sia certa que la naffra o naffres en sa persona fetes hauria e ha fetes Jordi sclau negre del pare del dit Bernat Noguera per son propi motiu e atreviment* e vulla a la dita denunciacio clam e acusacio renunciar desistir e abolir.' In this particular case, moreover, the master did not even have to sacrifice his slave. Caterina ultimately dropped her charges against the black male slave as well. Jordi was

subsequently remanded back into the custody of Noguera, who conceivably, as the slave's master, 'disciplined' him.

48 Indeed, Dennis Romano provides evidence to suggest that deflecting responsibility for crimes onto their slaves was a common tactic utilized by slave owners. Examining cases from the criminal court records of 16th-century Venice, in which individuals were banished by the *signori di notte al criminal* for having failed to respond to charges that they had murdered their servants, he notes how, 'tellingly,' none of those banished in contumacy between 1523 and 1559 involved members of the nobility, 'who proportionally employed the greatest number of servants in Venice.' While Romano remarks that 'it may well be that nobles had little to fear from the Venetian justice system, did not flee the city, and so were not included in these records,' he also notes that '*it is also possible that some noble masters made their servants take the blame for certain crimes*' (emphasis mine). In the footnote, Romano cites a case in which the *signori di notte* charged Niccolò Saraceno, the slave of nobleman Marino de Garzoni, with the death of a twelve-year-old boy named Giovanni, 'who, in all likelihood was another of Garzoni's servants.' He concludes by noting how the judges ultimately 'accepted the testimony of Garzoni's son Alvise [against the slave].' Romano, *Housecraft and Statecraft*, 296.

49 Romano, *Housecraft and Statecraft*, 205.

50 While the slave was armed with the aforementioned *lança de Xerez*, his master's son was armed with a *lança largua*.

51 ARV Justicia Criminal 99: Demandes (14 March 1441): 'Lo dit Gaspar Stheve s'en torna a la dita alqueria e torna tantost ab una lança largua e lo dit Marti sclau ab ell ab una lança de Xerez dient al dit Johan Galiot, que solament tenia hun punyal en la sinta e una lancura despuntada, "a mort a mort," tirant li de grans colps o lançades ... Item diu que lo dit Gaspar Stheve induhit del sperit maligne e aquell en aquell regnant no tement deu ni la senyoria reyal ni esser content de les lançades que havia tirades al dit pastor e dites moltes paraules injurioses afegint mal a mal *ab escalfament e ajuda del dit sclau* ab la dita lança larga que ab si portava se lexa anar vers e contra lo dit Johan Galiot tirant li molts e diverses colps lo que'l dit Johan hac a fogir com no tingues armes ab qu'es pogues defendre de les sobredits Gaspar e Marti sclau sino les armes damunt dites e fogint e reculant que feya caygue e caygut que fon lo dit Gaspar ab ajuda del dit sclau se abraça ab lo dit Johan Galiot e pres lo punyal que aquell portava en la correga e dona e fon vist donar e naffrar ab aquell dit punyal al dit Johan Galiot dos coltellades co es la una en lo cap e l'altre en lo front les quals naffres de continent vengueren a gran effussio de sanch e stampament e axi mateix no nafrare ab les lances en lo cors e li donaren moltes e diverses aristlades ... Item diu e posa ut suppra que los dits Gaspar Stheve e Marti sclau son homens molt moguts superbioses bregossos escandalosos movedors de bregues e fahedors de naffres e per tal son hauts tenguts e reputats entre los conexents aquells.'

3 The Murder of Pau de Sant Martí: Jews, *Conversos*, and the Feud in Fifteenth-Century Valencia

MARK D. MEYERSON

Just before sundown on 12 July 1430, the *converso* Pau de Sant Martí, then travelling on the royal road from Morvedre to his home in Valencia, approached the town of Puçol. Suddenly Mossé Maymó, a Jew from Morvedre, along with three Muslims and a Christian pimp, emerged from a roadside vineyard firing crossbows and brandishing lances and swords. A Muslim slave accompanying Pau heard Mossé growl, as he charged Pau with shield and lance, 'so you will die.' While the slave fell to his knees begging to be spared, the pimp unhorsed Pau. Mossé then pounced and dealt Pau the death blow, a sword cut extending from his left ear down to his mouth.[1]

Such acts of violence and aggression between Jews, or between Jews and Jewish converts, lend themselves to a variety of interpretations. Some scholars tend simply to categorize them with other kinds of 'crime,' regarding them as indicative of the moral decay of Spanish Jewry and as a result of the influence of Christian society. Love and good deeds, they assert, were nonetheless far more usual.[2] Others, keen to deny the existence of *converso* crypto-Judaism, might point to this particular homicide as a prime example of the hostility which Jews felt toward *conversos* because of the latter's assimilation into Catholic church and society.[3]

A close examination of the records of the trial of Mossé Maymó and his relatives reveals, however, more complex social realities and suggests different interpretations. As will become clear, in 1430 ties of kinship and friendship between Morvedre's Jews and Valencia's *conversos* remained strong and were fundamental to the formation of factions that cut across religious boundaries. Mossé's ambush of Pau had little to do with religious issues and much more to do with the dynamic of the blood feud, an extreme form of the aggressive status competition that had long characterized and structured social relations within Valencian Jewish communities. I want first to analyse Pau's murder as an act of normative violence guided by the dictates of a Jewish honour culture, and then, because this culture now included both *conversos* and Jews, to use the analysis as the basis for a discussion of social and cultural change among Jews and *conversos* in the fifteenth-century kingdom of Valencia.

In an honour culture like that of late medieval Valencia, aggression and violence were integral to the processes through which social status was contested and affirmed and economic resources allocated within the local community. These struggles for power were couched in an idiom of honour. Since honour was a social value, the possession of which depended on the community's evaluation of the conduct of an individual and his or her family, acts that entailed a challenge to or a defence of honour had a meaning recognized and understood by the entire community. Feuding violence, then, was a form of social discourse expressed by rival families and read by the community.[4]

What made the honour culture under consideration here 'Jewish' was, most importantly, the simple fact that its participants were all Jews or of Jewish origin. The aggressive social competition in which they engaged was group-specific and had meaning primarily for them. Valencian Christians and Muslims also participated in honour cultures, but it is by no means clear that Jewish cultural practices of this sort can be attributed to Christian or Muslim 'influence.' Because status contestation was group-specific, distinctive kinship and class structures, religious and textual traditions, and the nature of each religious community's relationship to royal authority were all bound to affect the manner in which the members of each community understood, perpetrated, and controlled violent behaviour.[5] I am not prepared at this point, however, to propose precise distinctions between the three honour cultures.[6] It may nonetheless be useful to consider violent contests among Jews for honour and prestige as part of Jewish popular culture in medieval Spain, a culture which in this respect differed significantly from that of its Ashkenazic counterpart. This violent honour culture was 'popular' not because it was exclusive to lower-class Jews – for the Jewish social elite certainly shared its values – but because it deviated from religious and legal norms.[7]

The connection of the Jews of Morvedre with the *conversos* of Valencia city, located less than twenty-five kilometres to the south, was continuous with links between the two Jewish communities which had been forged long before 1391 – a watershed year that saw the forced baptism or murder of Jews in many cities and towns in both Castile and the Crown of Aragon. The violence of 1391 nonetheless significantly altered the relationship, for while the Morvedre community emerged largely intact, most members of the huge *aljama* of Valencia were forcibly baptized. The royal ban of 1397 against the re-establishment of a Jewish community in Valencia forced unbaptized Jews there to settle elsewhere. Many moved to Morvedre, which had become the main Jewish centre in the kingdom. Valencia, which now housed the largest *converso* community, attracted *converso* immigrants from Morvedre, most of whom had converted after the preaching tours of the Dominican Vicent Ferrer and the Disputation of Tortosa (1413-14). Jews from Morvedre and elsewhere in the kingdom could, however, visit Valencia for ten days at a time, as long as they were not lodged in *converso* homes and parishes. Yet the latter provision was frequently honoured in the breach. There was, in other words, ample opportunity for contact of all sorts between Morvedre's Jews and Valencia's *conversos*.[8]

The murder of Pau de Sant Martí was neither the first nor the last act of violence in a feud that pitted Pau and his brother Luis, and their Jewish first-cousins from Morvedre, Abraham and Samuel Agí, against the brothers Jahudà and Mossé Maymó, their maternal uncle Salamó Tarfon, and their brother-in-law Gento del Castillo, the spouse of their sister Cinha (Simha), alias Alegra. Both sides had various Jewish and *converso* allies. Sometime before the spring of 1430 the two parties had sworn before royal officials not to attack one another.[9] Despite these assurances, Jahudà Maymó slashed the face of Abraham Agí during Holy Week.[10] Jahudà then headed for Valencia to explain his actions to the bailiff general, but en route he was assaulted by Samuel Agí, Pau de Sant Martí, and at least seven other Jewish and *converso* accomplices who wounded him with twelve or thirteen lacerations.[11] Meanwhile, the bailiff of Morvedre, who seems to have been favourable to the Agís, had begun the process of trying Jahudà *in absentia*; by July he had sentenced him to death by hanging.[12] The bailiff entrusted Pau, who just happened to be visiting Morvedre, with delivering the sentence against Jahudà to the bailiff general in Valencia, hoping that his superior would act on his recommendation.[13] When Jahudà's uncle Salamó Tarfon got wind of this, he sent a message to his other nephew Mossé, then at his workshop in the heavily Muslim-populated Vall d'Uixó, urging him to do something to help his brother.[14] Mossé and company immediately departed and murdered Pau.[15]

Officials from Puçol captured only Mossé and handed him over to the bailiff general. Mossé was hanged in Valencia on 17 July 1430.[16] Pau's brother Luis and his widowed mother then filed charges against Salamó Tarfon, Mossé's sister Cinha, and her husband Gento as accomplices in the murder of Pau.[17] As this trial dragged on – until July 1432 and without conviction – Jahudà Maymó prompted the authorities to initiate procedure against the Agís and their allies.[18] On 19 December 1432 the bailiff general sponsored a truce between the factions. Even so, before two months were out, Jahudà Maymó and Mossé Xamblell had wounded Abraham Agí on the face and shoulder.[19] Finally, after more judicial wrangling, in January 1436 Jahudà and Mossé paid compensation to Abraham through the office of the bailiff general. After this, tensions seem to have subsided.[20]

As is so often the case, it is nearly impossible to uncover the origins of the conflict.[21] With respect to the Maymó and Agí families of Morvedre, economic competition may well have caused animosity: the key players were all silversmiths, some of them living across the street from each other.[22] Violence among Muslim or Christian artisans practising the same craft and struggling for preeminence within the same occupational and social group was likewise frequent.[23] By besting their rivals on the neighbourhood stage, artisans were likely to increase their access to economic resources and to augment their social capital, in the coin of honour.

Indeed, when hostilities ensued in such cases, whether remaining at the level of verbal insult or escalating to the point of blood feud, the contenders and their audience talked not about economics but about honour.[24] Among families who were not distinguishable from each other by virtue of wealth or obvious signs of social rank it was the public's evaluation of which families had acted honourably and which shamefully that created a local pecking order. A crucial determinant of a family's honour in the eyes of its peers was the degree to which its members fulfilled responsibility to kin and friends in avenging the affronts which they had suffered.

The individuals involved in the Maymó-Agí feud could not have been unaware that their enactment of bloody deeds was a form of public theatre. News of each assault, including details about the nature of the wounds, spread rapidly within the Jewish quarter of Morvedre and the *converso* neighbourhood of Valencia.[25] The public recognized the gravity of Jahudà Maymó's cutting of the face of Abraham Agí, for it was a mark of humiliation Abraham could not hide.[26] The number of retaliatory wounds which Abraham's brother, cousin, and friends inflicted on the body of Jahudà in ritual fashion was also recorded on the public scorecard: the Agís were now ahead.[27] When Jahudà's sister Cinha, then in Valencia at the home of her *converso* brother-in-law, received word of this, she stood at the door of the house, beat her own face, and screamed, 'Oh wretch, ... by the hair that I have on my head, they [the Agís and Sant Martís] will pay for this soon!' As intended, many people on the *Carrer Nou*, the main street in the *converso* neighbourhood, heard her.[28] Pau's brother and mother later alleged that her words had brought about his murder.[29] Cinha's attorney countered that, after all, women, and Jewish women in particular, 'are accustomed to utter such words,' even more 'in the heat of anger.'[30] Indeed they were, precisely for the purpose of inciting male relatives to defend family honour. Cinha had publicly declared her family's intentions and had made it difficult for Mossé or other menfolk to back down.[31]

The testimonies of witnesses for the prosecution and the defence about the character of the various parties to the feud indicate that in such circumstances violent behaviour was normative and prescribed. Persons of allegedly bad character were labelled as liars, cheats, oath-breakers, gamblers, and so forth, but rarely as violent or bloodthirsty. Those of sterling character were described as trustworthy, honest, good Jews or, in the case of some *conversos*, good Christians. When witnesses felt obliged to comment on an individual's propensity for violence, they made a distinction between disreputable individuals who were 'quarrelsome' troublemakers and those who perpetrated violence out of a sense of loyalty to family and friends.[32] It was understood that sometimes good people had little choice but to exact vengeance.

Particularly revealing in this respect are the efforts of the royal prosecutor and the defence attorney, through their own arguments and through the supporting testimony of witnesses, to defend or besmirch the character of Jacme Català and Pere d'Artes, two *converso* witnesses for the prosecution. As for the quilt-maker Català, the defence attorney Berthomeu de Tolosa maintained that he was the first-cousin (*cosin germa*) of the Agís and the Sant Martís, with whom he had shared meals many times and whom he had accompanied on trips to Morvedre, and that he bore such 'great friendship' for the party inimical to the defendants that 'for love of it' he would say 'anything against the truth, even under oath.'[33] Tolosa then offered the statements of Johan Just, a *converso* shoemaker of Valencia, to corroborate his portrait of Català. Just testified that 'he had heard them [Català and the Agí brothers] call each other cousins all the time ... and had seen the said Agís, Jewish brothers, entering and leaving, and staying at the house of the said mossèn Jacme Català [and they were] hidden there ... in the time when the wounds were inflicted on the person of Jahudà [Maymó] ... and there they stayed eating and drinking.'[34] The implication, of course, was that Català had been an accomplice of the Agí brothers in their attack on Jahudà Maymó. The defendant and uncle of Jahudà, Salamó Tarfon, who was hardly an unbiased witness, testified that Català had acted truculently toward him and Jahudà. He had, moreover, welcomed 'their opponents [the Agís and Sant Martís] in his house and took up arms with them.'[35]

Tolosa attempted to undermine the testimony of the *converso* tailor Pere d'Artes by describing him as 'a breaker of oaths, a big gambler, a man of ill repute and evil life, and a very poor man ... and he is a bad Christian.'[36] The witness Johan Just added that Artes 'is a quarrelsome man ... [whom] he has seen start many fights with others.'[37] But the hosier Manuel Gorda, a witness produced by the prosecutor, painted a different portrait of Artes: he was a good

Christian who neither gambled nor assaulted people. Still, Gorda conceded that on one occasion, when Artes 'was afraid of enemies on account of disputes which they had had with his relative, he came upon these enemies, and believing that his said relative was present there [and in danger], the said Pere d'Artes wounded a man for reason of the dispute.'[38] In his own deposition Artes made no effort to conceal his readiness to shed blood to defend or avenge relatives or friends. A self-described 'great friend' of Pau de Sant Martí, he frankly testified that upon hearing of Pau's murder, he 'immediately grabbed a crossbow by the neck with some bolts and took the road to Morvedre.' He and an ally arrived in Puçol in time to taunt the jailed Mossé Maymó: 'Listen Maymó, you're not going to get away with this killing.'[39] Such behaviour, Artes assumed, the bailiff general would understand.

After Mossé's hanging, his uncle Salamó and brother-in-law Gento criticized his conduct – not the homicide per se but the manner in which he had committed it. Gento offered that if Mossé had wished to, he could have escaped hanging. Uncle Salamó agreed, pointing out that Mossé had acted as if 'desperate' and 'mad,' for a cool and prudent avenger would have killed Pau at night and not at the very gates of Puçol. Perhaps the two would have been happier if their kinsman had simply wounded Pau, severely enough to prevent him from delivering the letter to the bailiff general and to even the score with the Agís and Sant Martís, but not mortally. In any case, both expressed their chagrin at the damage Mossé's public execution had done to the family's honour.[40]

Mossé himself was a reluctant avenger and a rather tragic figure, one whose fate was sealed by the course of events, one who, despite his personal inclinations, could not escape the demands of responsibility to his family. When Pere d'Artes and his friend taunted him in the Puçol jail, he answered that he had not been accustomed to get involved in his brother's affairs since he knew that only bad would come of it.[41] Mossé's aversion for Jahudà's bloody games had earned him the disapproval of his family and left him feeling that he had something to prove. A fellow prisoner in Valencia heard Mossé mumbling in anguish just before his hanging: 'God pardon my uncle and some of my relatives who were always telling me I was worth nothing and who cursed me to my face. Well now I have done enough to be hanged, and enough evil for my uncle and other relatives who will remain in this world, which I will soon depart.'[42]

Given the social norms and assumptions that moved the players in this drama and framed the perception of those who observed their violent deeds, it should be reasonably clear that the murder of Pau de Sant Martí was not a bizarre occurrence, the act of a depraved Jew, but rather of one who thought himself to be acting responsibly, in accordance with the unwritten code of a

Jewish honour culture. Although many instances of violence among the Jews of the kingdom of Valencia between the 1230s and 1492 could be cited, the caveat that royal records do tend to focus inordinately on bloodshed and the like must be acknowledged.[43] In fact, a full-blown feud like that pitting the Maymós against the Agís was not so common. Yet if bloodshed and especially homicide were limited, it was not simply because good will and harmony normally prevailed, but because in an agonistic society such as this, in which aggressive competition was integral to the creation and maintenance of social order, the threat of retaliation and the fear that reciprocal affronts could spiral into a blood feud often served to inhibit the perpetration of violence.[44]

Royal courts and institutions provided other checks on violent behaviour and other avenues for pursuing and resolving conflict. Because the Jews had long been embedded in Christian power structures, and had at times been crown functionaries themselves, they were, rather like Christians, quite adept at manipulating public courts and officials to the detriment of rival coreligionists. Recall, for instance, Jahudà Maymó running off to the bailiff general to offer his account of his wounding of Abraham Agí. He hoped to get off with a fine – a small price to pay for dishonouring his enemy – and to avoid punishment at the hands of the local bailiff, who seems to have been in the Agís' pocket. Serious disputes among Jews over tax assessment, which perhaps most frequently brought Jews to blows precisely because their resolution could have a palpable effect on material wealth and social status, were often dealt with by Jewish communal and royal officials together after one of the disputants complained to the king.[45] In other words, the Jews' integration into the surrounding state and society made available to them a range of institutions and officials to which they could appeal or 'inform,' and which they could utilize for offensive and defensive purposes before resorting to violence. Despite its negative implications for communal autonomy, Jewish acculturation and familiarity with Christian courts and institutions may have had the benefit of attenuating intracommunal violence.[46] (Valencian Muslim society was, in contrast, more self-contained and less enmeshed in this institutional web. Among Muslims, feud was not only more frequent but approached being a self-regulating mechanism in and of itself, a social system per se.)[47]

The Jewish, Christian, and Muslim communities of Valencia each had honour cultures; within each one violence was a form of social discourse.[48] It is crucial to recall, moreover, that although the three groups in some respects shared an idiom of honour, aggressive social competition was group-specific and had meaning primarily for the members of a given religious group, the intended audience. Conflict and violence paradoxically enhanced group solidarity by channelling social energies inward.

Hence the case of the murder of Pau de Sant Martí is significant in that it shows *conversos*, a generation, more or less, after the period of conversions (1391–1416) forming factions with Jews to contest power and status with other Jews and *conversos*. The audience was a conglomerate of Jews from Morvedre and *conversos* from Valencia. What counted most to the *conversos* involved was how other *conversos* and Jews evaluated their conduct.

The transcripts of a murder trial, in which religion was not at issue, make it difficult to uncover the religious beliefs and practices of these *conversos*. Yet that ties of kinship and friendship were so strong as to have moved *conversos* to shed blood on behalf of Jews indicates the persistence of the sort of social intimacy that would have made *converso* Judaism more than possible.[49] Indeed, there was plenty of grumbling in ecclesiastical and royal circles about *converso* judaising in early fifteenth-century Valencia.[50] Some *converso* witnesses, however, were described, by way of vouching for their reliability, as good Christians who attended Mass and the like.[51] This of course says nothing about what they did at home or really believed, but it does raise the question of whether kinship ties were more powerful than religious ties, whether a truly Christian *converso* would fight for a Jewish relative.

Considered from the perspective of the Jews, the existence of this conglomerate Jewish-*converso* honour culture had some troubling and dangerous implications. For the Jewish performers in this theatre of *agon* the audience was no longer just Jewish, but Jewish and *converso*. Even if all the *conversos* involved were believing and practising Jews, the very presence of a large *converso* community made the Jews conscious of new possibilities and strategic options. Precisely because so many *conversos* were practising Jews and could still compete with Jews for honour before a Jewish audience, some Jews realized that under certain circumstances receiving baptism might be politic. One could convert, practise Judaism, and continue to appear honourable in the eyes of Jews and *conversos*.[52]

Such thoughts seem to have crossed the mind of Mossé Maymó on the eve of his execution. He decided to convert to Christianity and was given the baptismal name Pere de Cabanyelles. Mossé had not experienced a spiritual awakening, nor had the bailiff general induced him to convert with the offer of a pardon. Mossé sought baptism so that instead of being hanged upside down like a Jew, he could be hanged right side up like a Christian, so that he could die in a more honourable manner. Furthermore, because of his conversion, Mossé/Pere could be hanged in the city marketplace instead of on the *Rambla* by the Turia River, outside the city's walls. Hanging in the marketplace was no less public than hanging on the *Rambla*, but the *Rambla* intersected the royal road linking Valencia to Morvedre. Were Mossé/Pere executed there, the audience that really counted – the Jews and *conversos* passing back and forth between the two centres – would not fail to see his dangling body.[53] Before 1391 neither Mossé nor his fellow Jews would have deemed being executed like a Jew to be dishonourable; for, after all, only Jews would really have been watching. Only other Jews would have cared about the honour or disgrace of a particular Jewish family. But in 1430 New Christians were watching too; hence there were better ways to die. Perhaps Mossé thereby salvaged some of his family's honour.

Later Mossé's incorrigible brother Jahudà also converted. He took this dramatic step in February 1433, just when the bailiff of Morvedre was initiating legal procedures against him for having violated an official truce by attacking Abraham Agí again. Perhaps he hoped that his baptism would move the crown to reduce the heavy fine of 500 florins.[54] More likely he saw conversion as a ticket from Morvedre to Valencia, where he could lose himself and escape the Agís and the local bailiff, who was no friend of his. Things were now too hot in Morvedre.

A couple of generations later, by the time the Spanish Inquisition had set up shop in Valencia, there were still Jewish Agís in Morvedre, but no more Maymós. Jahudà, it seems, had been the last of the line. If by then the Maymó-Agí feud was but a fading memory, so too was the conglomerate Jewish-*converso* honour culture within which it had been enacted. As the generations passed, and as kinship ties between Jews and *conversos* inevitably weakened, such a conglomerate culture, which had been galvanized by competition between family and faction, could not sustain itself. The descendants of the individuals involved in the Maymó-Agí feud, and their Jewish and *converso* fellows, could not give such bonds of kinship the same significance; nor could they very well perpetuate them, for the simple reason that Jews and *conversos* could not intermarry. The family circles within which Jews and *conversos* situated themselves overlapped less and less, moving ever closer to mutual exclusivity.[55] After the Maymó-Agí feud, Jewish families in Morvedre did not recruit *converso* friends and relatives to combat their rivals. True, there persisted a great deal of contact and communication between the Jews of Morvedre and the *conversos* of Valencia who clung to Judaism, but this connection was mainly a religious one.[56]

The *conversos* of Valencia, whatever their religious inclinations, now performed in a different and wider arena of honour. The audience was *converso* and Old Christian. With the dissolution of the kinship ties that had involved Valencia's *conversos* in Jewish factions and feuds, the *conversos'* social centre of gravity had shifted toward Old Christian society. When *conversos* competed for social status in Valencia, their rivals and allies were other *conversos* and

Old Christians, not Jews. Jews and Judaism remained factors in the lives of some *conversos*, but only with regard to quiet household observances and matters of private conscience. Due to the *conversos'* greater integration into Old Christian society, which included more intermarriage with Old Christians, it had increasingly come to matter to *conversos* how Old Christians evaluated their social conduct; *conversos* wanted to appear honourable in their eyes. That the Jews had long shared an idiom of honour with Christians made the transition easier for *conversos*. They could play the game of honour by the Old Christians' rules.

There was, however, one new and important twist in the game: for Old and New Christians, public Catholic worship was increasingly a mark of honour. As the *conversos* assimilated more and more into Old Christian society and jockeyed for position and power there, uncertainty about their true religious allegiance persisted.[57] Since Old Christians would have deemed a *converso*'s adherence to Judaism dishonourable, if not heretical, *conversos* felt impelled to display publicly their fealty to the Catholic church, regardless of what they truly believed or practised at home. But Old Christians also, if they wished to best their *converso* rivals on the city stage, needed to ensure that everyone concerned knew that they too were devoted sons and daughters of the church. The new discourse of religion and race which the mass conversions of 1391–1416 had generated moved New and Old Christians to work ever more assiduously to construct façades proclaiming the Catholic orthodoxy of their families.

The association of overt displays of Catholic orthodoxy with family honour put considerable strain on those *conversos* still adhering to Judaism. The stress involved in playing the game of honour by the Old Christians' rules is reflected in the case of Joan Aldomar, a *converso* hosier burned in 1492 for relapsing into Judaism. Despite his Jewish leanings, he had attended Mass. During his trial Joan scoffed at the testimony of a witness who had claimed that he used to leave Mass in the middle. Joan said, 'for his honour itself he had to go [to Mass], and when he went, he had to hear it just like all the others who were there.'[58] Honour had to be upheld, for it defined the place of oneself and one's family in local society. But it was not everything: there was also the necessity of ensuring the salvation of one's soul, which, in the case of Joan, entailed following the 'law of Moses.' Those sincerely Catholic *conversos* whose honourable public behaviour was a natural extension of their inner faith were fortunate; their worldly and otherworldly concerns went hand-in-hand. For the others, like Joan Aldomar, the disjuncture must have been downright unbearable.

Notes

1 The file for this murder case can be found among the extant, fragmentary records of the tribunal of the bailiff general of the kingdom of Valencia: Arxiu del Regne de València (hereafter ARV): Bailia (hereafter B) Procesos, P. 2618 (1430). The case file, which begins on 30 June 1430, is incomplete and ends abruptly on 17 July 1432. It is 143 folios in length. Although it is unfoliated, I am indicating folio numbers here for the easier reference of interested readers. Details of the attack on Pau come from the accusations of his widowed mother Francesca and his brother Luis, which were presented to the court by the royal prosecutor Pere d'Anglesola (2v), and from the testimony of Mahomat, the Muslim slave of Johan Vives who accompanied Pau and heard Mossé utter 'açi morras' (9r–v). The three Muslims from the Vall d'Uixó who joined Mossé in the assault were Jafar Almasuet, Arramoni, and Mahomet Maçoda; the Christian pimp was one Domingo Colomer from Morella.

2 This is for the most part the approach of Yom Tov Assis, 'Crime and Violence in Jewish Society in Spain (13th–14th Centuries),' [Hebrew] *Zion* 50 (1985) 221–40, esp. 221–3, 233, 239–40, where he comments on Christian influence and 'moral deterioration.' See also his *Golden Age of Aragonese Jewry: Community and Society in the Crown of Aragon, 1213–1327* (London 1997), 279, 288–96. Assis does, however, lean a bit toward the interpretative stance I am taking here ('Crime and Violence,' 232). Elena Lourie does more in her 'Mafiosi and Malsines: Violence, Fear, and Faction in the Jewish Aljamas of Valencia in the Fourteenth Century,' in *Actas del III congreso internacional 'Encuentro de las tres culturas,'* ed. C. Carrete Parrondo (Toledo 1988; repr. in Elena Lourie, *Crusade and Colonisation: Muslims, Christians, and Jews in Medieval Aragon* [Aldershot 1990]), 79–80, though her emphasis is largely different. José Ramón Magdalena Nom de Déu, 'Delitos y "calònies" de los judíos valencianos en la segunda mitad del siglo XIV (1351–1384),' *Anuario de Filología* 2 (1976) 181–225, is mainly a catalogue of crimes committed and fines collected. For northern European Jews, see Zefira Entin Rokéah, 'Crime and Jews in Late-Thirteenth Century England: Some Cases and Comments,' *Hebrew Union College Annual* 55 (1984) 95–157, which offers little in the way of interpretation; and Avraham Grossman, 'Offenders and Violent Men in Jewish Society in Early Ashkenaz and their Influence upon Legal Procedure,' [Hebrew] *Annual of the Institute for Research in Jewish Law* 8 (1981) 135–52. Elliott Horowitz, 'The Rite to Be Reckless: On the Perpetration and Interpretation of Purim Violence,' *Poetics Today* 15 (1994) 9–54, considers ritual anti-Christian violence from the medieval period into the 20th century.

3 There is a vast and polemical historiography on the *converso* problem. The two poles of the debate are represented, on the one hand, by Yitzhak Baer and Haim

68 Mark D. Meyerson

Beinart, who argue for almost complete *converso* adherence to Judaism; and, on the other, by Benzion Netanyahu, who argues for almost full assimilation. See Yitzhak Baer, *A History of the Jews in Christian Spain*, trans. L. Schoffman, 2 vols (Philadelphia 1961), 2: 244–443; Haim Beinart, *Conversos on Trial: The Inquisition in Ciudad Real*, trans. Y. Guiladi (Jerusalem 1981); Benzion Netanyahu, *The Marranos of Spain from the Late XIVth to the Early XVIth Century, According to Contemporary Hebrew Sources*, 2nd ed. (New York 1973); idem, *The Origins of the Inquisition in Fifteenth Century Spain* (New York 1995). One proponent of the view held by Netanyahu is Norman Roth, *Conversos, Inquisition, and the Expulsion of the Jews from Spain* (Madison 1995), who pursues the kind of decontextualized analysis of Jewish-*converso* relations (74–82) that could easily lead to a misreading of the murder of Pau de Sant Martí. I would position myself in the grey area between the two camps and advocate more local studies as a means of understanding the complexities of the *converso* problem.

4 My reading of this case as feud and my understanding of honour culture in Valencia – Jewish, Christian, and Muslim – are informed by wide reading in the anthropological literature, including Jacob Black-Michaud, *Feuding Societies* (Oxford 1975); Pierre Bourdieu, *Outline of a Theory of Practice*, trans. R. Nice (Cambridge 1977); David D. Gilmore, *Aggression and Community: Paradoxes of Andalusian Culture* (New Haven and London 1987); idem, ed., *Honor and Shame and the Unity of the Mediterranean* (Washington 1987); Christopher Boehm, *Blood Revenge: The Anthropology of Feuding in Montenegro and Other Tribal Societies* (Lawrence 1984); Julian Pitt-Rivers, *The Fate of Shechem, or: The Politics of Sex. Essays in the Anthropology of the Mediterranean* (Cambridge 1977); idem, *The People of the Sierra* (Chicago 1961); J.G. Peristiany, ed., *Honour and Shame: The Values of Mediterranean Society* (London 1965); and Michael Herzfeld, *Anthropology Through the Looking Glass: Critical Ethnography in the Margins of Europe* (Cambridge 1987). Useful historical explorations of these themes are Edward Muir, *Mad Blood Stirring: Vendetta in Renaissance Italy* (Baltimore 1993); Robert Muchembled, *La Violence au village: Sociabilité et comportements populaires en Artois du XVe au XVIIe siècle* (Turnhout 1989); and William Ian Miller, *Humiliation, and Other Essays on Honor, Social Discomfort, and Violence* (Ithaca 1993). Natalie Zemon Davis, *Fiction in the Archives: Pardon Tales and Their Tellers in Sixteenth-Century France* (Stanford 1987) is quite helpful for the interpretation of judicial records.

5 The problems of disentangling specific Jewish cultural practices from those of the majority community, and of tracing the influence of one culture on another are emphasized by anthropologists studying North African Jewish communities. See Harvey E. Goldberg, 'Anthropology and the Study of Traditional Jewish Societies,' *Association for Jewish Studies Review* 15 (1990) 19–20; idem, *Jewish Life in*

Muslim Libya: Rivals & Relatives (Chicago 1990), 14 and 63–4; and Shlomo Deshen, *The Mellah Society: Jewish Community Life in Sherifian Morocco* (Chicago 1989), 6. In his 'Introduction' to *Judaism Viewed from Within and from Without: Anthropological Studies*, ed. H.E. Goldberg (Albany 1987), 13, Goldberg offers insightful comments as to the importance of texts for subtly shaping and giving meaning to social patterns. Elena Lourie, 'Cultic Dancing and Courtly Love: Jews and Popular Culture in Fourteenth Century Aragon and Valencia,' in *Cross Cultural Convergences in the Crusader Period: Essays Presented to Aryeh Grabois on His Sixty-Fifth Birthday*, ed. M. Goodich, S. Menache, and S. Schein (New York 1995), 151–82, presents a fascinating study of cases where Christian influence is more obvious but nonetheless difficult to trace. Ivan G. Marcus, *Rituals of Childhood: Jewish Acculturation in Medieval Europe* (New Haven and London 1996) offers a particularly interesting study of an aspect of Ashkenazic culture in this regard.

6 I have begun work on a large study, tentatively entitled 'Of Bloodshed and Baptism: Social Violence and Religious Conflict in Late Medieval Valencia,' which involves, on the one hand, a comparative anthropological history of conflict and violence within Christian, Muslim, and Jewish communities, and, on the other, an analysis of violence between these communities.

7 Aspects of Jewish popular culture have been treated by Lourie, 'Cultic Dancing and Courtly Love'; Horowitz, 'Rite to Be Reckless'; and idem, 'The Eve of Circumcision: A Chapter in the History of Jewish Nightlife,' *Journal of Social History* 23 (1989) 45–69, where he shows how in the early modern period Jewish communal authorities conducted a 'campaign against popular culture' (52) much like that promoted by the post-Tridentine church. As for regarding violence as an aspect of 'popular culture,' it is worth noting that Deshen, *Mellah Society*, 53–5, distinguishes between the realm of halakhic justice administered by the (rabbinic) 'sages' and that of lay, customary justice administered by the *nagid*, which included cases of personal violence and illicit sexuality. Moroccan Jews, many of them the descendants of Spanish exiles, were much concerned about family honour (82–4, 110, 117). The difference between Spanish Jewish and Ashkenazic culture has been emphasized by Daniel Boyarin, *Unheroic Conduct: The Rise of Heterosexuality and the Invention of the Jewish Man* (Berkeley and Los Angeles 1997), 1–185, who argues 'that the image of the ideal male as nonaggressive, not strong, not physically active is a positive product of the self-fashioning of rabbinic masculinity in a certain, very central, textual product of the culture, the Babylonian Talmud' (81). This ideal image shaped the outlook and behaviour of Ashkenazic males far more than it did those of their Spanish counterparts (though see Grossman, 'Offenders and Violent Men,' esp. 136–9), due in part to the markedly different 'sociopolitical conditions' of each community (164). Ephraim Kanarfogel, 'Rabbinic Attitudes toward Non-

Observance in the Medieval Period,' in *Jewish Tradition and the Nontraditional Jew*, ed. J.J. Schachter (Northvale, NJ 1992), 30, points out that 'Spanish [Jewish] society alone had a courtier class, whose life-style was especially conducive to religious malfeasance, and that the scholarly class of Spain was smaller and more detached from the rest of the population compared to its Ashkenazic counterpart.' This too may help to explain the Spanish Jews' valorizing of violence in defence of honour despite religious and legal proscriptions. The degree to which the rhetoric of honour, shame, and revenge infused the discourse of rival Spanish rabbis is striking, even if they did not (or usually did not) engage in acts of physical violence. See Bernard Septimus, 'Piety and Power in Thirteenth-Century Catalonia,' in *Studies in Medieval Jewish History and Literature*, ed. I. Twersky (Cambridge, MA 1979), 197–230. However, S.D. Goitein, *A Mediterranean Society: The Jewish Communities of the Arab World as Portrayed in the Documents of Cairo Geniza*, vol. 5: *The Individual: Portrait of a Mediterranean Personality of the High Middle Ages as Reflected in the Cairo Geniza* (Berkeley and Los Angeles 1988), 305–6, emphasizes a disjuncture between words and deeds, and sees 'aggressiveness and violence' as 'confined to the lower classes and, in general, petty circumstances.' Still, it must be kept in mind that to a 'modern' outside observer the punctilious concern about verbal and physical affronts inherent to an honour culture like that of late medieval Valencia might well appear 'petty.'

8   On the Morvedre community, see Mark D. Meyerson, *Jews in an Iberian Frontier Kingdom: Society, Economy, and Politics in Morvedre, 1248–1391* (Leiden 2004); and idem, *A Jewish Renaissance in Fifteenth-Century Spain* (Princeton 2004). For a brief overview of its 15th-century history, see idem, 'The Jewish Community in Murviedro [Morvedre] (1391–1492),' in *The Jews of Spain and the Expulsion of 1492*, ed. M. Lazar and S. Haliczer (Lancaster, CA 1997), 129–46. There is no adequate study of the Jewish community of Valencia, which prior to its destruction in 1391 numbered more than 2000, but see, for instance, José Hinojosa Montalvo, 'La comunidad hebrea en Valencia: Del esplendor a la nada (1377–1391),' *Saitabi* 31 (1981) 47–57; Jaume Riera i Sans, 'Jafudà Alatzar: Jueu de València (segle XIV),' *Revista d'Història Medieval* 4 (1993) 65–100; and Leopoldo Piles Ros, *La judería de Valencia: Estudio histórico*, ed. R. Magdalena (Barcelona 1991), which is largely a miscellany of data collected by the late Professor Piles. The violence and forced conversions in Valencia in 1391 have received more attention, however: Baer, *History*, 2: 99–102; Philippe Wolff, 'The 1391 Pogrom in Spain: Social Crisis or Not?' *Past and Present* 50 (1971) 4–18; Jaume Riera Sans, 'Los tumultos contra las juderías de la Corona de Aragón,' *Cuadernos de historia: Anejos de la revista Hispania* 8 (1977) 213–25; Eliseo Vidal Beltrán, *Valencia en la época de Juan I* (Valencia 1974), 53–70; and José Hinojosa Montalvo, *The Jews of the Kingdom of Valencia: From Persecution to Expulsion, 1391–1492* (Jerusalem

1993), 21–66. On the *conversos* of Valencia and the Spanish Inquisition, see Ricardo García Cárcel, *Orígenes de la Inquisición española: El tribunal de Valencia, 1478–1530* (Barcelona 1976), 37–108, 195–200; Stephen Haliczer, *Inquisition and Society in the Kingdom of Valencia, 1478–1834* (Berkeley and Los Angeles 1990), 209–43; and Angelina Garcia, *Els Vives: Una família de jueus valencians* (Valencia 1987). There is very little on the early period, but see Jaime Castillo Sainz, 'De solidaritats jueves a confraries de conversos: entre la fossilització i la integració d'una minoria religiosa,' *Revista d'Història Medieval* 4 (1993) 183–205; and José Luis Luz Compañ, 'Familias judías – familias conversas: Aproximación a los neófitos valencianos del siglo XIV,' *Espacio, tiempo, y forma: Historia medieval*, ser. 3, 6 (1993) 409–24. In *A Jewish Renaissance* I discuss contacts between Valencia's *conversos* and Morvedre's Jews between 1391 and 1492.

9 ARV: B Procesos, P. 2618. Both the plaintiffs, Francesca and Luis de Sant Martí (2r), and the defendant Cinha, sister of Mossé Maymó (18r), refer to prior 'assurances' (*asseguraments*) sworn to by the opposing factions. Naturally, both sides claimed that the other had violated them. On the function of the *assegurament*, or *pau*, in Valencia, see R. Ferrero Micó, 'Pau e Treua en Valencia,' in *Estudios dedicados a Juan Peset Aleixandre*, 3 vols (Valencia 1982), 2: 1–15. Esther Cohen, 'Violence-Control in Late Medieval France,' *The Legal History Review* 51 (1983) 111–22, treats the *assecuramentum* in France.

10 ARV: B Procesos, P. 2618: 1v, noting that the 'gran coltellada' was inflicted on Saturday, 'vespre de Rams' (the eve of Palm Sunday). ARV: B 1147: 219v (17 July 1430) [Hinojosa, *Jews*, no. 378] also mentions the attack on Agí. Black-Michaud, *Feuding Societies*, 86–118, emphasizes the perpetual nature of the feud; but see the qualifications of Boehm, *Blood Revenge*, 121–42, 220–1.

11 ARV: B Procesos, P. 2618: the testimonies of Cinha, Jahudà's sister (16r–v), and Bernat Torell, the royal *porter* who found the wounded Jew by the road (61v–62r). ARV: Cancilleria Real (hereafter C) 49: 1r–v (16 October 1430), regarding the 'causas seu questiones criminales' still pending between Jahudà and his assailants, with the exception, of course, of Pau de Sant Martí.

12 ARV: B 1147: 219v (17 July 1430), a letter of the bailiff of Morvedre, Bernat Çaydia, to the bailiff general, in which he notes his sentencing of Jahudà. In ARV: C 46: 24v (6 September 1430) King Alfonso orders the bailiff general to rule on the 'causam denunciationis' between Jahudà and Abraham Agí and prohibits the interference of the bailiff of Morvedre. This indicates that there were doubts about Çaydia's impartiality.

13 ARV: B Procesos, P. 2618: 2r.

14 ARV: B Procesos, P. 2618: 21r–22r, the confessions of Salamó Tarfon.

15 ARV: B Procesos, P. 2618. In response to the charges against him, Mossé initially

asserted, on 13 July, that he and his accomplices had killed Pau in self-defence (6r–v, 8v). The next day, however, he confessed under torture to having been the aggressor. When the judges took him to a separate room, where he could not see the instruments of torture, and asked him whether he wished to verify what he had just confessed, he replied in the affirmative (10r).

16 ARV: B Procesos, P. 2618: 3r for the capture, and 12v–13v for the hanging.
17 ARV: B Procesos, P. 2618: 14r–15r (19 July 1430). ARV: B 1150: n.f. (27 February 1431) is a letter of the bailiff general concerning the questioning of witnesses for the prosecution.
18 ARV: C 49: 1r–v (16 October 1430). On 17 March 1432 the bailiff general licensed Jahudà to bear arms for protection against the Agís, whom he feared 'per rahon del proces de denuncia que mena contra aquells' (ARV: B 1147: 375r [Hinojosa, *Jews*, no. 395]). While the case against Abraham Agí was pending, the bailiff general issued safe-conducts (*guiatge*) protecting him against any other judicial initiatives – ARV: B 1147: 387r (25 April 1432); and ARV: C 47: 114v (26 April).
19 ARV: B 1147: 469v–470r (5 February 1433) [Hinojosa, *Jews*, no. 402] treats the act of violence and mentions the prior truce.
20 ARV: B 1148: 172v (24 January 1436) [Hinojosa, *Jews*, no. 443]. It is worth noting here that Jahudà Maymó had converted to Christianity in 1433, taking the name Dionis Guiot, and was living in Valencia by 1436 (see n. 54 below, on his baptism). His removal to Valencia served to reduce tensions with the Agís in Morvedre.
21 There is some vague and unclear testimony regarding earlier attacks by the Maymós and their allies on the father (deceased by 1430) of Pau and Luis de Sant Martí (ARV: B Procesos, P. 2618: 18r, 59r, 60v, 67r), but it says nothing about the origin of the conflict between the factions.
22 A number of the documents already cited describe the Maymó brothers and the Agí brothers as silversmiths. ARV: B Procesos, P. 2618: 44v–45r (18 September 1430), an inventory of the property of the executed Mossé Maymó, lists his house (*alberch*) located in the Jewish quarter of Morvedre, which 'affronta ab cases de Samuel Agi e ab cases d'Astruch Saporta.'
23 Mark D. Meyerson, *The Muslims of Valencia in the Age of Fernando and Isabel: Between Coexistence and Crusade* (Berkeley and Los Angeles 1991), 244–5, treats feuding between Muslim artisans. For the Christians, see Rafael Narbona Vizcaíno, *Malhechores, violencia, y justicia ciudadana en la Valencia bajomedieval* (Valencia 1990), 108–20; and Pablo Pérez García, *La comparsa de los malhechores: Valencia, 1479–1518* (Valencia 1990), 253–306. Both authors, however, are primarily interested in the institutional history of the criminal justice of Valencia and less in explaining the violent behaviour of those arraigned before the justice's court. Pérez asserts that artisan violence resulted from the artisans' emulation of noble behaviour, an interpretation with which I disagree.

Cf. Pieter Spierenburg, 'Knife Fighting and Popular Codes of Honor in Early Modern Amsterdam,' in *Men and Violence: Gender, Honor, and Rituals in Modern Europe and America*, ed. Spierenburg (Columbus 1998), 103–27; and Thomas W. Gallant, 'Honor, Masculinity, and Ritual Knife Fighting in Nineteenth-Century Greece,' *American Historical Review* 105 (2000) 359–82, whose views accord more with my own.

24 The records of the criminal justice of Valencia, which I have been examining for the project mentioned in n. 6, demonstrate this quite clearly. Individuals frequently spoke of 'dishonouring' or being 'dishonoured' by foes.

25 E.g., ARV: B Procesos, P. 2618: 74r (17 August 1430), where the witness Mossé Levi, a Jew of Morvedre testifying about the events leading to the murder of Pau, comments 'e tal fama n'era per la vila de Murvedre.' Another Jewish witness from Morvedre, Samuel Corcos, recalled (75r–v [28 August]) how he had questioned Salamó Tarfon about his plans shortly after news circulated about the arrest of his nephew Jahudà for having assaulted Abraham Agí: 'e que demana ell dit testimoni al dit Salamo que que [*sic*] havia fet del fet de son nebot [Jahudà].'

26 ARV: B Procesos, P. 2618: 21r (19 July 1430): Salamó Tarfon testifies how the 'news' (*nova*) spread in the Jewish quarter of Morvedre after Jahudà wounded Abraham Agí. On 27 February 1431 Jacme Català, a *converso* of Valencia, testified (63r) that he had heard some *conversos* discussing the subsequent attack on Jahudà Maymó by Samuel Agí and company 'per ço com pledejaven [Jahudà and Samuel] abduys per una coltellada que lo dit juheu [Jahudà] havia donada al germa del dit Samuel *per la cara* en Murvedre' (emphasis mine).

27 ARV: B Procesos, P. 2618: 16r–v, 56v, 58v, 62r, 63r–v are all testimonies about the attack on Jahudà. I regard the violence as 'ritual' in nature because clearly the eight or more assailants could have killed Jahudà but chose not to, instead marking his body for all concerned – friends, enemies, and the Jewish-*converso* community – to see.

28 For example, the testimony of Vidal de Vilanova, a *converso* shoemaker, in ARV: B Procesos, P. 2618: 67r (28 February 1431): 'e la dita juhia dix "ho mesquina," donantse un colp en la cara ab les mans ... "per aquests vells que yo tinch en lo cap," metentse la ma al cap, "ells ho pagaran tost".' The *converso* witnesses Alvaro Roiz (58r–59r) and Rodrigo d'Abella (60r–v) offer similar accounts of Cinha's reaction, as does the royal *porter* Bernat Torell, who informed Cinha of her brother's misfortune.

29 ARV: B Procesos, P. 2618: 15r and 97v, where the prosecutor states that after Cinha cried out thus, 'se segui de contintent la mort en la persona del dit en Pau ... per que es presumida violentment que les paraules de aquella [Cinha] obraren lo malefici que apres se segui.'

30 On 3 July 1431 the defence attorney (or *procurador*), Berthomeu de Tolosa, presented arguments aimed at disqualifying various witnesses for the prosecution. Regarding the allegedly damning testimony about Cinha's words, he argued, 'cum quia fuissent prolata per mulierem et per juhia, les quales acostumen dir tals paraules. Tum car no consta que aquella fos tal que aco acostumas de duhir a essent les sues menaçes cum quia fuissent verba prolata calore iracundie' (ARV: B Procesos, P. 2618: 94v).

31 Among Valencian Christians and Muslims as well, women functioned as inciters of their menfolk in feuding situations. See Meyerson, *Muslims of Valencia*, 248; and (for Christian society) idem, 'Violence Against Women and the Power of Women in Late Medieval Valencia,' an unpublished paper presented at the American Historical Association meeting in December 1992. Women played this role elsewhere in Europe – see, e.g., William Ian Miller, *Bloodtaking and Peacemaking: Feud, Law, and Society in Saga Iceland* (Chicago 1990), 55, 170, 182, 212–14; Carol J. Clover, 'Hildigunnr's Lament,' in *Structure and Meaning in Old Norse Literature: New Approaches to Textual Analysis and Literary Criticism*, ed. J. Lindow, L. Lönnroth, and G. Weber (Odense 1986), 141–83; and Marjorie K. McIntosh, *Controlling Misbehaviour in England, 1370–1600* (Cambridge 1998), 58–65, 186–200.

32 E.g., ARV: B Procesos, P. 2618 includes various depositions about the character of Salamó Tarfon. Johan Ganer, a notary of Valencia who had once served as royal castellan in the Vall d'Uixó, where Salamó often worked as a silversmith, described him as 'home simple, benigne, *no bregos, no escandalos*, mas hom reposat e de bona fama' (73r, emphasis mine). The Jew Samuel Corcos stated that Salamó was a 'good man and a good Jew' and that he never heard of him being involved in a 'mal barat ne tracte mal' (76v). The rabbi Jacob Legem (79r) and the Christian innkeeper Na Pelegrina, the wife of Goçalbo de Vitoria (86r–v), offered similar statements.

33 ARV: B Procesos, P. 2618: 94v–95r: 'gran amistat ab la part adversa ... per amor de aquella tota cosa contra veritat, encara ab sagrament.' There was some uncertainty about Català's kinship ties with the Agís and Sant Martís. The prosecutor unsurprisingly argued that Català was not their *cosin germa* (98r). An elderly *converso* witness produced by Tolosa, the tailor Guillem de Reig, seems to have had the most precise knowledge of the matter (110v–111r). According to him, Català was indeed a relative of the Agí brothers: the Agís' mother was the first-cousin of the grandmother of Català. Reig knew this 'per ço com coneix per antiquitat los dessus dits e lur generacio e ell havia pus de LX anys e s'es criat entre lurs paretats.' Reig, who would have been in his twenties in 1391, must have been Jewish in his youth, when he had lived either with the Agís or with the Jewish ancestors of Jacme Català.

34 ARV: B Procesos: P. 2618: 108r–v: 'dix que per ço com los havia hoyts cridar cosins tostemps e ... havia vist entrar e exir als dits Aguis [sic], germans juheus, e estar e habitar en casa del dit en Jacme Catala amagats ... en lo temps que foren fetes les nafres en la persona de Jaffuda ... e alli stigueren menjaven e bevien.'

35 ARV: B Procesos, P. 2618: 102v: 'E dix ell dit responent que lo dit en Jacme Catala feu valença contra ell dit responent e per conseguent de Jaffuda Maymo, e tengut lurs contraris en sa casa e se arma ab aquells.'

36 ARV: B Procesos, P. 2618: 95r: 'trencador de sagraments, gran jugador, home de mala fama e mala vida, e home molt pobre ... e es mal cristia.'

37 ARV: B Procesos, P. 2618: 109r: 'que es home bregos ... per ço com ha vist moure moltes bregues ab altres.'

38 ARV: B Procesos, P. 2618: 117v–118r: 'Empero sab que lo dit Pere d'Artes anant sobre si recelantse de enemichs per noves que havien haudes ab un son parent, encontras ab los contraris d'aquell e creu que'y fos lo dit parent seu present e nafra lo dit Pere d'Artes un hom per la questio.'

39 ARV: B Procesos, P. 2618: 65r–v: 'per ço com lo dit Pau de Sent Marti era gran amich d'ell dit testimoni, de continent pres una ballesta al coll ab sos arreus e tira son cami de Murvedre anant.' The words to Maymó, recalled by Artes, were uttered by his companion, the tailor Bernat Sparça: 'Hoyda Maymo e aquesta mort no's podia scusar.'

40 On 24 April 1431 the woolworker Vicent Sala recounted overhearing the conversation between Gento and Salamó at the gates of the Muslim quarter. Gento said to Salamó, 'deus loy perdo a vostre nebot ... que si ell se volgues, ell no fora penjat e no aguerem nosaltres tant de mal com havem ens a mes a tots' (ARV: B Procesos, P. 2618: 57r–v). At the time Sala had been enjoying some leisurely activity, including a visit to the bordello, with his friend, the *converso* artisan Jacme Català. The latter's testimony (63v–64r) confirms that of his friend Sala. Prior to the court's reception of their depositions, Salamó Tarfon had already confessed the substance of his response to Gento's words, though he chose not to identify Gento in order to avoid incriminating him (48v–49r [30 January]): 'E dix ell dit confessant e responent que stava en veritat que apres mort del dit Mosse Maymo, alias appellat Pere [his post-baptismal name (see below at n. 53)], que rahonantse ell dit confessant e responent de la mort en seguida ... ab algunes persones – no li acorde a present qui eren ne en quin loch – dix tals o semblants paraules: "deus loy perdo a mon nebot, dientho del dit Mosse, que be feu com a desesperat e orat e be ha reebut com a orat e desesperat que ja tal malefici volia fer hagues so sperat a la sua salva e no'n hagues fet en tal loch com ho feu a les portes del loch de Puçol".'

41 ARV: B Procesos, P. 2618: 65v–66r: the testimony of Pere d'Artes (28 February 1431).

42 ARV: B Procesos, P. 2618: 68v (1 March 1431). The witness was Jacme de Vilabella who saw and heard Mossé 'congoxantse en si mateix, dient tals o semblants paraules: "o deu loy perdo a mon oncle" – nomenant nengu person nom – "e alguns de mos parents que'm deyen tots dies que no era pera res e'm lançaven en la cara blasfemies. Ara he fet prou pera mi a esser penjat e prou mal pera mon oncle e als altres parents que romanen en aquest mon que yo tost sere passat e la mia mort tost sera finida".'

43 This is the point of Assis, *Golden Age*, 279. For examples of violence among Valencian Jews in the 13th and 14th centuries, see Assis, 'Crime and Violence,' 230–3; Magdalena, 'Delitos y "calònies" '; and Lourie, 'Mafiosi and Malsines.' In 15th-century Morvedre the Agí-Maymó feud was by no means the only case of family rivalry or intracommunal politicking which led to bloodshed. For instance, Arxiu de la Corona d'Aragó (hereafter ACA): C 2205: 14v–15r (28 July 1407) treats the lethal wounding of Mossé Façan by Mossé Legem and Jahudà Arrami; or ARV: B 1151: 464v (9 February 1452) [Hinojosa, *Jews*, no. 526], which concerns the complaint of Jucef Gallego regarding the attempt of Isaac Bonet, the son of Jucef Bonet, to assault him inside his house. Meyerson, *Jewish Renaissance*, treats social conflict, including violence, in detail. ARV: B 1151: 769v (13 August 1453) [Hinojosa, *Jews*, no. 531], which concerns a brawl between a Jew and a Christian over gambling in Xàtiva, is worth noting because it shows that the Jew was, as a matter of course, armed with sword and buckler.

44 This is a point emphasized in almost all the anthropological literature on the feud.

45 Baer, *History*, 1: 212–31, 2: 35–94; and Assis, *Golden Age*, 76–87, 110–31, emphasize the role of fiscal issues in generating class conflict and institutional reform within the Jewish communities of the Crown of Aragon. This also emerges as an important problem in Meyerson, *Jews in an Iberian Frontier Kingdom*.

46 Most commentators – like Baer, *History*, and Assis, *Golden Age* – emphasize, and usually with good reason, the negative implications of informing. However, Lourie, 'Mafiosi and Malsines,' has shown that the accusation of *malshinut* was a double-edged sword, deployed not only by communal leaders endeavouring to protect their community from damaging external interference but also by unscrupulous 'mafiosi' who used it to dissuade well-intentioned Jews from complaining about their activities to royal officials. In any case, it is clear from archival records that many Jews turned to the crown to adjudicate their disputes with coreligionists over a wide range of matters, without ever being accused of 'informing.'

47 Meyerson, *Muslims of Valencia*, 232–54.

48 For the Christian case, see the works cited in n. 23, and for the nobility in particular, Rafael Narbona, 'Violencias feudales en la ciudad de Valencia,' *Revista d'Història Medieval* 1 (1990) 59–86.

49 Consider, for instance, the testimony of the *converso* Johan Just (n. 34) that the Jews Abraham and Samuel Agí lodged, ate, and drank in the home of their *converso* cousin, Jacme Català, when in Valencia. The willingness of the Agís to do so suggests that Català observed the laws of *kashrut* in his home. The same can probably be said of the *converso* mossèn Pujades, who welcomed his Jewish sister-in-law Cinha into his home (see p. 58 above).

50 For detailed treatments of the question, Mark D. Meyerson, 'Samuel of Granada and the Dominican Inquisitor: Jewish Magic and Jewish Heresy in Post-1391 Valencia,' in *The Friars and the Jews in the Middle Ages and Renaissance*, ed. S. McMichael and L. Simon (Leiden, forthcoming); and idem, *Jewish Renaissance*. See also Castillo, 'De solidaritats jueves a confraries de conversos,' 194–205, for relevant material.

51 Jaume Gençor (ARV: B Procesos, P. 2618: 118v–119r) and Miquel Sánxez (119v–120r) described Pere d'Artes in this fashion. The silversmith Francesc Stheve said the same of Jacme Català (122v–123r): 'que va volenterosament a missa e als divinals officis.' One wonders if Stheve knew that Català shared meals and lodging with his Jewish cousins.

52 The increasingly negative view of Iberian *conversos* expressed by North African rabbis in their *responsa* (Netanyahu, *Marranos*, 5–76) can be read in this light, i.e., less as an indication of the full assimilation and Christianization of the *conversos* (Netanyahu's interpretation) than as a rabbinic anxiety about and warning to unbaptized Jews who might be considering baptism in order to have the best of both worlds, to have their cake and eat it too. That a good number of Valencian *converso* families did just that over the course of several decades is clear enough from a careful reading of the trial records of the Spanish Inquisition, which began its work in Valencia in 1482. See the works cited above in n. 8.

53 ARV: B Procesos, P. 2618: 12v–13r: 'E en seguides les dites coses en aquell dia mateix lo dit Mosse Maymo, juheu e condempnat, qui dessus dix que volia esser cristia e per la dita raho fou batejat en lo archiu de la dita cort criminal per lo vicari de Sent Pere e meteren li nom Pere. E de feyt los dits honorables batle general e justicia en criminal comutaren la dita sentencia que axi com lo dit condempnat devia esser penjat en la Rambla que sia penjat en lo mercat. E axi com devia esser penjat cap avall que sia penjat cap amunt per raho del dit cristianisme.' Elena Lourie, 'Anatomy of Ambivalence: Muslims under the Crown of Aragon in the Late Thirteenth Century,' in her *Crusade and Colonisation*, 58–9, discusses the hanging of Jews by the feet; and Claudine Fabre-Vassas, *The Singular Beast: Jews, Christians, and the Pig*, trans. C. Volk (New York 1997), 125–6, points out that the upside-down hanging was reserved for pigs and Jews, which 'humanizes the former while animalizing the latter.' José Sanchis Sivera, *Vida íntima de los valencianos en la época foral* (Altea 1993 [repr. ed.]), 95,

treats sites of public hangings in Valencia. Those conducted on the *Rambla* were done under the bridge *dels Serrans* leading into one of the main city gateways.

54 ARV: B 1147: 469v–470r (5 February 1433) [Hinojosa, *Jews*, no. 402] for the violation of the truce and the procedure of the bailiff. B 1147: 468r (5 March 1433) shows that by then Jahudà had already received baptism, taking the name Dionis Guiot; while B 1148: 14v (23 February 1435) shows him still in debt to the crown for the fines he had incurred for attacking Agí.

55 It is significant in this regard that Guillem de Reig, the *converso* able to pinpoint the relationship between the *converso* Jacme Català and the Agí brothers, was already sixty years old in 1430 (see n. 33). In other words, by 1430 the *conversos* and Jews guarding the memories that sustained blood ties and lent them meaning were already dying out.

56 Meyerson, *Jewish Renaissance*, chs 5 and 6.

57 See, e.g., *Epistolari de la València medieval*, ed. Agustín Rubio Vela, 2 vols (Valencia 1985–98), 2: 338–9, no. 134, the letter of the *jurats* of Valencia to Berthomeu Abat, the city's ambassador at the royal court, instructing him to ask the king – Juan II – to prohibit *conversos* from holding office in municipal government because 'it is very true that the *conversos* practise the Jewish law so much ... that in all their way of life they are Jews and not Christians; for they wear the chrism like a safe conduct.' The *jurats* continue on to label the *conversos* as 'these rats of Pharaoh.' The *jurats*' request was motivated by a combination of ethno-religious animosity and socio-political rivalry. In the event, King Juan did not accede to their request. However, the new Spanish Inquisition, which set up shop in Valencia in 1482, would end the careers of many ambitious and influential *conversos*.

58 Archivo Histórico Nacional: Inquisición de Valencia: Legajo 536, caja 1, no. 1: 31r (30 September 1491): 'Empero per sa honra mateixa hi havia de hanar y quant hi hanava havia de hoyr aquella com feyen tots los altres que alli estaven.' Aldomar was responding to the testimony of Martí Garces, an Old Christian and also a hosier (4r–v).

4 Violence and the Sacred City: London, Gower, and the Rising of 1381[1]

EVE SALISBURY

As one of medieval England's most vocal urban poets, John Gower raises his voice to condemn the desecration of urban life by those in power and by those seeking power. Like Chaucer, who explores the destructive tensions of ancient Troy in *Troilus and Criseyde*, Gower's concerns, vocalized most stridently in book 1 of the *Vox clamantis*, focus on the questionable integrity of London's citizenry and the vulnerability of the city to outside attacks. Gower's response to the invasion of London by protesting rebels is provoked not only by the violence done inside the city, including the executions of Simon Sudbury, archbishop of Canterbury, and Robert Hales, the king's treasurer, and the burning of public buildings and official documents, but by what that violence could mean to the larger community outside the city walls. In what Derek Pearsall calls 'the most powerful and sustained account of the Peasants' Revolt,'[2] Gower allows us to see the symbolic meanings of violence in a way that the other chroniclers do not. When Wat Tyler, the rebel leader, is slain during his meeting with a youthful King Richard at Smithfield, his head substituted for Simon Sudbury's on the city gate, Gower casts the scene in terms of propitiation to the gods. When the murderous deed is attributed to William Walworth, the mayor of London, Gower renders him into something approaching a chivalrous urban saint. When the Flemings are murdered in the streets, however, the event is tantamount to the slaughter of the innocents.

René Girard's theories of sacrificial violence as articulated in *Violence and the Sacred* are particularly germane to a reading of Gower's response to the violent events of the Rising of 1381.[3] In Girard's theory, sacrificial violence functions to expunge any perceived contamination or threat from within the community:

The sacrifice serves to protect the entire community from *its own* violence; it prompts the entire community to choose victims outside itself. The elements of dissension scattered throughout the community are drawn to the person of the sacrificial victim and eliminated, at least temporarily, by its sacrifice ... [The] common denominator is internal violence – all the dissensions, rivalries, jealousies and quarrels within the community that the sacrifices are designed to suppress. The purpose of the sacrifice is to restore harmony in the community, to reinforce the social fabric.[4]

Integral to the motives for the kind of violence Girard describes between opponents is a process of mimetic rivalry and desire for an object imbued with value *because* it is desired by the opposing Other; the identities of opponents bent on acquiring the same objects intertwine and merge until violence separates them into autonomous entities. Moreover, Girard continues, 'once aroused, the urge to violence triggers certain physical changes that prepare men's bodies for battle ... when unappeased, violence seeks and always finds a surrogate victim. The creature that excited its fury is abruptly replaced by another, chosen only because it is vulnerable and close at hand.'[5]

The feast of Corpus Christi, the day on which the rebels invaded London, invited the mixing together of ancient sacred practices with social revolution. Suddenly, violent acts take on symbolic significance, Tower Hill becomes a sacrificial altar; the city gates, sites of triumph in battle; the city itself, a place where sacred blood is spilled and sanctified heads are hung in spectacular display. And because violence 'seeks and always finds a surrogate victim,' the wholesale slaughter of the Flemings, documented ever so briefly by Chaucer in the Nun's Priest's Tale, provides evidence that such operations take place.[6]

My reading of the memorable events in London over that three-day period as they are reconstructed by Gower examines the violence of groups and individuals – the rebels, members of the London oligarchy, the king – in relation to mimetic desire and identity formation. What Girard sees as both a prelude to and an effect of violence – mimetic rivalry and a simultaneous merging and consolidation of identity – I see as operating here among contesting factions both inside and outside London. Although I concur with scholars who see these struggles as motivated by a desire to claim control of official culture, its written and legal forms, and its ideological symbols, what I offer in this essay is a shift in focus both to the dynamics of mimesis and Gower's symbolic representation of the *forms* of violence.[7] Each of these groups and individuals competes for a place in the social order to gain public recognition, to purge the body politic of corruption, and to accrue public identities made puissant by the righteous cause they claim.[8] Moreover, the city, rendered sacred by the forms of violence carried out on its behalf, provides a convenient venue for battles of identity such as these. What becomes apparent in a study of book 1 of the *Vox clamantis* is that sacrificial violence inheres within the symbolic system itself, remaining dormant until a volatile mix of social, economic, religious, and political conditions triggers its reemergence.

Gower distinguishes himself from the other chroniclers of the London rebellion not only by the symbolic dimension he adds to his account of events, but by an unusual perspective on the city's social and political terrain. Living in close proximity to one of the rebels' gates of entry at Southwark familiarized the poet with the desperate conditions of the neighbourhood as well as the ongoing conflicts between city officials and residents over the area's notorious brothels. It is even quite possible that Gower was an eyewitness to some of the events of the rebellion. By way of contrast, six of the eight extant histories, other than Gower's, derive from ecclesiastical authors who neither lived in the city nor could have witnessed events directly: *Historia Anglicana* and *Chronicon Angliae*, by Thomas Walsingham, monk of St Albans; *Chronicon Henrici Knighton*, by Henry Knighton, Augustinian canon of St Mary of the Meadows, Leicester; *Anonimalle Chronicle*, by a Benedictine from St Mary's at York; *Chronicon Westmonasteriense*, by the chronicler of Westminster; the continuation of the *Eulogium historiarum sive temporis* (considered a separate text), by its unknown author; and the Evesham chronicle, or *Historia vitae et regni Ricardi secundi* as it is also known, by the monk of Evesham. These works, as well as the French chronicle of Sir Jean Froissart, were written from perspectives outside of London, removed from the politics and social conflicts of the city and its immediate environs.[9] Except for the author of the *Letter-Book H*, an account of events inside the city, all chroniclers were literally outsiders to a complicated and tense urban scene with moral and ethical agendas of their own to advance; chroniclers like Froissart, who was both priest and knight, promoted the efficacy as well as the shortcomings of chivalry. All eight chronicles are limited in their vision of events, biased in their views, and notoriously inconsistent as definitive and accurate historical documents.[10] Yet what is remarkably consistent among them, particularly considering the lack of their authors' close proximity to London, is the horror they express about the violence that took place there in those eventful three days.[11]

Gower expresses a similar horror, though in a notably different way, in book 1 of his *Vox clamantis*.[12] Written after the rest of the *Vox*, a lengthy Latin poem critiquing all levels of English society, including the king, book 1 describes the London rebellion from an eyewitness perspective similar to that claimed in the *Anonimalle Chronicle*.[13] Imbued with the anxiety and fear of apocalyptic doom, the poem, whose title evokes the prophetic agenda of John the Baptist, virtually screams out from the wilderness to be heard. Portions of the poem are written in *cento*, a poetic form that Gower derives from Proba, the early Christian poet and Roman matron, who became famous in the late Middle Ages for her *Cento Vergilianus de laudibus Christi*, in which she transforms themes of warfare in Virgil's *Aeneid* into a manifesto on Christian pacifism.[14] Fragments of the gods' debate on the war between Turnus and Aeneas in books 10 and 11, for instance, are converted into a plea for peace spoken by Christ to his disciples. The flight of Camilla's father with his infant daughter carried tenderly in his arms becomes Mary's flight from Herod with her infant son. Likewise, Virgil's depiction of Camilla's father feeding her on the 'milk of a wild mare' becomes the Virgin Mary who nurses her son in the Egyptian wilderness.[15] By making changes to certain masculine pronouns in Virgil's texts, Proba emphasizes the pacifying power of the maternal body.

Gower's attraction to Proba's work and his mimicry of her methods, undoubtedly fostered by a common interest in pacifist ethics as well as his own devotion to the Virgin Mother, contribute to his continuously evolving view of the role of compassion and mercy in the political arena of late fourteenth-century England. The poet's choice of *cento* style allows him to create a new work that literally embodies themes of fragmentation and disintegration, to inscribe the effects of violence in the very body of his poem. Not only is the form of the work suited to its subject matter, but so too is Gower's poetic technique. Inherently violent, *cento* requires the excision of parts of other works from poets of other times, such as Ovid's *Metamorphoses*, *Tristia*, and *Fasti*; Peter Riga's *Aurora*; Godfrey of Viterbo's *Pantheon*; Nigel de Longchamp's *Speculum stultorum*; and Alexander Neckam's *De vita monachorum*, which are sutured together again. *Cento* style allows the poet to speak overtly of present events while covertly representing violent events of the past; the result is a hybrid poetic, a Frankenstein's monster with the power to signify the divisive nature of violence itself.

Like Proba, who assumes the identity of *vatis* to signal her status as prophet and seer, Gower assumes the identities of John the Baptist and John the Evangelist as he clamours to warn his audience of impending apocalyptic doom. To underscore the urgency of his vision, the poet renders his narration into myth by likening the rebels to domestic beasts gone wild, as if some malicious Roman god had cast his spell upon them. For Gower, rebellion is a monstrous event brought about by the transformative nature of sin. When men become *like* the beasts instead of carrying out their duties as their masters as prescribed in Genesis, it is symptomatic of widespread corruption. Gower makes that clear when he castigates just about everyone in medieval English society. Having set the cycle of violence in motion in this way, Gower casts Wat Tyler's murder in terms of sacrifice to the gods: 'There was an outcry in the skies, there were tears and frequent groans, and the gods did not neglect to show mercy. But Neptune, who is god of the sea, demanded sacrificial offerings to calm the sea. ...'[16]

Gower mythologizes the sacrificial moment by portraying Tyler's death as the demand of a Roman deity, thereby marking a distinction between Christian and 'pagan' sacrifice. As both 'tyrant' and 'monster,' Tyler is a social and political heretic in Gower's view, an 'appropriate' sacrifice to the Roman god. He, like the other rebels, acquires the identity of a beast; he relinquishes his humanity through heinous physical acts as well as rhetorical violence. The rebel leader is made responsible not only for his part in the pillaging and plundering of the city but for inciting the mob to violence, committing speech acts provocative and threatening enough to warrant drastic retaliation. When Tyler is murdered by the mayor of London, William Walworth, as he is in the *Vox*, the mayor is commended for his contribution to the quelling of Neptune's sea; the hand that kills the rebel tyrant is the 'blessed hand, that so plentifully provided the sacrificial offering for which the sea's tempest grew quiet and subdued.'[17] Walworth is transformed into a chivalrous role model and bequeathed nearly divine authority as he becomes the new, official protector of the city.

Another of Gower's grievances against Wat Tyler is that the rebel presumes the king is a peer, his 'brother' rather than his sovereign 'father.' Tyler's action, as that of a subordinate member of the realm, is tantamount to a rebellious son's threat to his father's position in the family, an attempt to supplant paternal authority.[18] As Gower sees it, Tyler challenges the authority of the sovereign, the very office of the king. In so doing the rebel becomes a threat to the fundamental structure of medieval society, a structure based upon a metaphor of the body politic given currency in the twelfth century by John of Salisbury in the *Policraticus*.

In this influential treatise, the body politic is a metaphor for hierarchical corporate entities organized with the 'head' (the king or prince) at its apex, which governs the lower members construed either as classes of society or as particular groups, each with a prescribed duty to contribute to the welfare of the whole organism. Not only were the lowest members of society expected to contribute meaningfully to the community, but the king was also expected to perform his duties to the highest standard of kingship, a standard that demanded genuine concern for his subjects as well as exemplary personal conduct. As long as the king exhibited supreme virtue, his authority remained difficult to challenge. But when a king failed to uphold the precepts of his rule, when he was perceived to have succumbed to the weaknesses of the flesh, he could be subject to a charge of tyranny and its ultimate fulfilment at the hands of his subjects.[19] Since Edward II's ugly deposition was still within memory when Gower was writing the *Vox*, much of what the poet says by way of his frequent association of Wat Tyler with the tyrant king Antiochus serves as a warning to Richard and to anyone whose personal and public behaviour might exceed medieval norms of conduct and duty. Kings and archbishops could meet untimely death by the sword just as readily as members of the lower classes, at least in theory.

The sacrifice of Tyler to the gods in Gower's text takes on additional meaning when we remember that the day on which the rebellion began marked the feast of Corpus Christi, a symbolic event commemorating the crucified body, a day when all members of the mystical body of Christ were expected to remember the suffering of *the* sacrificial victim and consume *that* body symbolically in communion. That the occasion was plagued by conflict and confusion is attested to by many scholars. Sarah Beckwith, for instance, suggests that the body of Christ in late medieval England stood as a nexus of opposing forces: 'If Christ's body is the place where God materializes, if it is the meeting place of finite and infinite, of flesh and spirit, of the material and the immaterial, of the sacred and the profane in the destabilizing hybridity, the intoxicating boundary-blurring ambiguity of Christ's body, then either pole of that meeting can be stressed at the expense of the other.'[20]

The number of binary oppositions caught within a single signifier rendering it an 'intoxicating boundary-blurring ambiguity' suggests its potential both to destabilize as well as to unify the community. Indeed, Corpus Christi and its attending rituals sparked contests over who was and who was not to be included in the social order. Processions, intended to function as unifying social rituals when they were carried out throughout the streets of towns, villages, and cities, often became sites of contestation and dispute as participants jockeyed for the most prestigious positions closest to the Host. As Miri Rubin explains, 'processional ritual, possesses an inherent destabilising element ... By laying hierarchy bare [a procession] could incite the conflict of difference ever more powerfully sensed in a concentrated symbolic moment.'[21] Placing individuals in a linear formation ordered by social and political rank unveiled the truth of the hierarchical nature of society. Where would a mayor who is also a fishmonger belong in the procession? What might the factors determining his position in the procession be? his high rank? his lowly occupation? If this seems a rather obvious source of divisiveness and rivalry, then it is not surprising that the feast of Corpus Christi became even more politically charged during a time when the very meaning of the body of Christ was being contested by Wyclif and his followers. Needless to say, the symbols and rituals associated with this particular feast provoked emphatic and often violent responses; by the late fourteenth century it had acquired a long history of disorder.[22]

Despite the fact that the rebellion began long before the June celebration of the feast of Corpus Christi in outlying districts, the invasion of London nonetheless becomes associated with the feast day in Gower's recapitulation of events. In what Margaret Aston calls an 'ironic parallel with a Corpus Christi procession,'[23] though there is really nothing ironic about it, Gower introduces his dramatic explication of the moment of invasion: 'Behold it was Thursday, the Festival of Corpus Christi, when madness hemmed in every side of the city. Going ahead of the others, one peasant captain urged them all to follow him. Supported by his many men, he crushed the city, put the citizens to the sword, and burned down the houses. He did not sing out alone, but drew many thousands along with him, and involved them in his nefarious doings.'[24]

After situating the insurgency in time, Gower borrows and reconstructs a passage from Peter Riga's *Aurora*, the twelfth-century versified Bible.[25] The lines, taken from the Book of Maccabees and rearranged to address current events, refer to Antiochus's invasion of Jerusalem and the abomination of the Temple by idolatrous sacrifice. Gower uses the fragments to link the tyrannical Antiochus with Wat Tyler; at the same time he renders sacred the city of London by connecting it to the besieged Holy City. The *cento* fragments taken from the *Aurora* allow the poet to cast a sacred aura about the city of London without disturbing the metaphor of New Troy he uses later in book 1. The hidden *centonic* text silently recalls another time and place when a similar scenario of destruction took place; violence has emerged in history once again. Gower's reference to Tyler's 'singing,' toward the end of the passage, understood by some as another ironic allusion to the sacred ceremony of Corpus Christi is, like that identified by Margaret Aston earlier, not as ironic as it seems.[26]

The sacred celebration of the day was disrupted by rebels who attacked and ultimately executed Simon Sudbury, chancellor and archbishop. Along with two other official heads, the head of the archbishop, together with its crudely attached mitre, was impaled on a long pole and paraded in procession to the city gates where the three heads were arranged in mock trinity. As Steven Justice explains, 'the configuration of the heads, with Sudbury's "in the middle, and above the others," recalled the iconography of the Crucifixion, in which Christ hangs between the two thieves and is foregrounded, so that his cross stands higher than the others; on his head, often red with blood, is the crown of thorns – meant as a mockery but actually a proclamation of the true kingship displayed in his suffering. The rebel parody mocked the archbishop's pretensions to speak in Christ's name ...'[27]

Such a reconfiguration facilitated a transference of sacred theories into profane practices, literally literalizing the mysteries regarding the body and blood of Christ, making evident the contestation over ownership of religious symbols. When the rebels 'mocked the archbishop's pretensions to speak in Christ's name,' it is akin to the linguistic presumption that Gower imposes upon Wat Tyler. In the midst of mimetic rivalry, actions of one group are reproduced in the Other, as are the forms of violence accompanying the rivalry. Gower's lengthy description of the archbishop's death demonstrates how the forms of violence practiced by secular authorities were imitated by those against whom those forms of violence were most often carried out: 'After the altars of the deity had been profaned, the enemy held every side and sprang to the death of the presiding official. Feeling no pity, the murderers shouted, "This man shall be killed at our hands." ... Thus the pale, suffering victim, struck in the neck with an axe, spattered the ground with red blood.'[28]

Other chroniclers emphasize the ineptitude of the self-appointed executioners by describing the number of times it took to complete the task while the archbishop patiently waited for the job to be done. To enhance the pathos, however, Gower describes Sudbury as the 'pale, suffering victim,' an apparent allusion to Christ's passion on the cross. Yet what is peculiar about the lines that follow is the method of execution they describe – 'struck in the neck with an axe' – and the spilling of blood on the ground. What lies latent here is a *cento* passage from Ovid's *Tristia* in which the exiled poet describes an animal sacrifice carried out by the Romans to celebrate a military triumph.[29] Is Gower deliberately linking the death of the archbishop to his depiction of Tyler's sacrifice? If this is the case, then the form of violence used against Tyler is implied in the execution of the archbishop.[30]

Gower's description of Sudbury's execution is only one part of an elaborate analogy between Sudbury and Thomas Becket that plays upon similarities in order to make distinctions. Whereas the poet identifies the politically motivated death of St Thomas as 'caused by the wrath of a king' (*ira fuit regis*), he calls the murder of Sudbury, in contrast, an 'infamous patricide' (*obprobrium patricida*). The children of God have rebelled against their spiritual father: 'Simon fell by the sword in the midst of a crowd of his children' (*Natorum turba Simon in ense cadit*). The difference between the two high-profile homicides is significant; while the former underscores the contest of wills between king and archbishop, the latter represents a case of insubordination within the mystical body of Christ, whose legitimate authority in England resides in the office of the archbishop. The act of rebellion by the 'children' of this spiritual patriarch is tantamount to ecclesiastical treason and constitutes not only a sinful defiance of divine authority, but also an assault on the entire body politic.[31] Yet the setting in motion of the death of Thomas Becket by Henry II is also an assault on the mystical body. The children act in anger against their spiritual leader, in the way that the king acts. The power of the Crown to damage the ecclesiastical body is demonstrated implicitly in both acts, though they derive from differing sources and are surrounded by differing circumstances.

The analogy between Sudbury and Becket clarifies the operations of mimetic rivalry and the carrying out of secular authority that ultimately demonstrates the power of the Crown even when carried out by members of the lower classes. In order to expand on questions of who is to be condemned and executed and who has the legitimate authority to carry out the execution, Gower extends the analogy between Sudbury and Becket to include Helenus, the high priest of Troy, known among the *litterati* in the fourteenth century as having been a traitor to his city. Eric Stockton finds Gower's use of the analogy to Helenus curious, since his assumption is that Gower unequivocally supports Sudbury's bishopric.[32] Given the rumours of Sudbury's corruption,[33] however, it is likely that Gower's choice is not misguided, but deliberately made to draw attention to the disregard for the office of high priest demonstrated by the rebels, an action that implies the power of the Crown. When Gower says later that Priam was incapable of saving Helenus, the inference is that Richard has failed to protect the ecclesiastical body and done essentially what Henry II had done centuries earlier. Gower's three-way analogy – Sudbury to Becket to Helenus – begins a lengthy recapitulation of Troy's violent legacy to England.

Gower links his poem to a tradition of 'imaginative' histories that participate in maintaining the illusion of Trojan heritage, such as the *Chronicle of England* or the *Brut Chronicle*, as it is also known. Gower's lengthy allusion to these events begins in book 1, where he calls the native Britons 'wild' (*ritus*), with a naturally 'cruel fierceness' (*feritatis*), who 'overthrow right by force' (*sternunt sub viribus equm*) and defeat justice because of their violent warfare.[34] Yet the Britons would be the worthiest people under the sun if only they could learn to practise compassion and Christian charity.[35] Gower calls London 'New Troy' because he sees the past being enacted in the present as those fierce Britons fight among themselves again.[36] Just as his analogy of Sudbury to Helenus points to the shortcomings of ecclesiastical and secular authority, so too does his analogy of London to Troy point to the shortcomings of London's citizenry. Just as Troy falls at the hands of the invading Greeks, whose deadly gift is permitted to enter the city, London is invaded by outside forces admitted by her own citizens.[37] Like Troy, London falls as a direct result of the failure of her citizens to protect her interests and expose the treachery within her walls. Gower's allegiance to chivalry as the means by which to protect and defend the city is challenged when the gates are not adequately defended. He imagines London to be as 'powerless as a widow' (*vidue languida*), weak and in need of a knight to defend her. This is one reason Gower is so impressed by what he sees as chivalrous action taken by William Walworth against Wat Tyler that day at Smithfield.

In rather stark contrast to his obvious delight at Tyler's death, Gower takes no pleasure in reporting the 'slaughter' of the Flemings. Instead, like many of the chroniclers, he expresses outrage at the actions of the frenzied mob: 'The bodies dispatched in the slaughter were by no means carried off; instead they lay scattered everywhere in the open roads. And because there were no tombs for these men, the frenzied mob trod upon the dead bodies, torn limb from limb. They placed the corpses of the slain to hang from the walls, and like crude beasts they refused them even crude burials ... and the city which had been the greatest then fell, overwhelmed by the slaughter.'[38] He paints a graphic and shocking picture, a stunning spectacle of carnage to make those in his immediate audience, several of the most powerful ecclesiastics in England, pause and reflect upon the events of the moment.[39] Certainly *these* ecclesiastical readers would hear echoes of Herod's 'slaughter of the innocents' and consider how they might have averted mass murder. The detailed description, which some view as blatant hyperbole, may be prompted by Gower's concern not only that his audience heed the word, but that they remember it well beyond its present moment. As Jody Enders has amply demonstrated, medieval memory techniques were intensely violent; the more violent the image one could create in the mind, the better the chance of remembering the event.[40] Even if Gower's ecclesiastical readers were familiar with the other chronicles, the *Vox* would have signified the historical implications of such an event far more dramatically by keenly drawn, intensely violent biblical and classical allusions. Certainly *these* learned readers of biblical and classical texts would understand the implications of unburied corpses scattered about the city streets.

We must remember, however, that because differentiation and consolidation of identity occur simultaneously, the gap between subject and object, perpetrator and victim, cannot be too wide. Often it is the case that surrogate victims are not radically distinct from other members of the community, but rather a feature of it, assimilated, yet distinguished by differences not outwardly apparent, such as language. This is the case with the mix of participants in the rebellion. Originally called the Peasants' Revolt, groups once thought to be binary opposites – the peasantry and the aristocracy – are now understood to have been much more stratified and heterogeneous (hence the renaming of the event from 'Peasants' Revolt' to the 'Rising' or 'Uprising' of 1381). The rebels were not made up exclusively of 'rustics' or 'peasants' as the chronicles and Gower himself would have us believe. Rather, the group included members from a variety of guilds and occupations, many of whom lived and worked in London and had a say in its government.[41] These are the kinds of conditions that exacerbate competition and rivalry, which inevitably lead, according to Girard's theory, to violence.

Rodney Hilton, in *Bond Men Made Free,* points to just such competition and rivalry between native English weavers and the Flemings: 'The native weavers had certainly been jealous of the privileges the Flemings enjoyed. By 1378 there was a lot of anti-alien feeling in the city, though the Flemish weavers agreed in March 1380 to submit to some of the search regulations and financial obligations of the English craftsmen. It could also be that some of the attacks on the Flemings were mounted not by English weaving masters, but by English journeymen employed by Flemish masters, class antagonism being cloaked, consciously or unconsciously, by xenophobia.'[42]

Steven Justice agrees with Hilton's general assessment of the rivalry and competition between native Englishmen and the Flemings, arguing that linguistic difference added a significant dimension to the violence: 'Perhaps the attacks would be best described not as xenophobic, but as xenoglottophobic.'[43] This suggests that the Flemings were not the original target but became surrogate victims only when their ethnic identities were discovered in the language test they were given during the course of the rebellion, when their pronunciation of the words 'bread' and 'cheese' distinguished them immediately from native speakers.[44] Suddenly what many social historians have described as a long-standing anti-Flemish sentiment found a convenient venue for expression.[45]

The Flemings had acquired prominence in and around London despite intermittent breaks in relations between Flanders and England, during which time all Flemings were expelled, though they were invited back by Edward III with assurances that they would be protected.[46] Rivalry, according to the Girardian scheme of things, is exacerbated by jealousy, the object of which, in this case, could easily be construed as preferential treatment by the king himself. Nonetheless, aliens are marked as Other, though not so radically Other that their presence in society might be intolerable to the natives. Indeed, as long as there remains enough to go around, as long as there is no competition or rivalry for the same objects, and as long as there is a stable economic and social environment, aliens in a foreign land may be assured some measure of safety. This was not the case in late fourteenth-century England.

The pathos Gower expresses for the Flemings, a pathos he does *not* express for any other ethnic group, may derive from his close proximity and involvement with a substantial part of the Flemish community in Southwark, Gower's residence during the time he was writing the *Vox*. At the Priory of St Mary Overey, the poet lived a sequestered married life adjacent to religious men who practised charity by aiding the destitute and despairing in the neighbourhood. There is a possibility that Gower's wife, Agnes Groundolf, whom he married late in life, may have been Flemish, a young foreign woman whom Gower 'rescued' from a life of prostitution in the Southwark stews.[47] According to Rosamond S. Allen, 'it seems not impossible that a priest at St Olave's or the Master or a sister at the hospital might have recommended as a servant for the aged Gower an intelligent girl from a poor family whom they might have been anxious to protect from the life of the brothels.'[48]

If this is the case, Gower's compassion for the Flemings is a very personal part of his evolving views of prostitution and family life, both of which figure into his pacifist political philosophy.[49] His retelling of the story of King Apollonius in the *Confessio amantis* a few years later, when Gower sees London set on destroying itself from within, is about the king's innocent daughter, who is thrown into prostitution against her will but who is strong enough of character to rise above it. For this reason, and because her father happens to be a good king, the story stands as a moral *exemplum* for medieval society at large, a trope for the 'proper' relation of all subordinates to the authorities governing them.[50] Here, of course, Gower's view of family structure replicates his view of *all* medieval institutions. Social disruption derives from tyranny or rebellion in the family and extends outward into the larger community. Thus Antiochus, the tyrant whom Gower associates with Wat Tyler in the *Vox*, provides the negative example of paternal responsibility when he subjects his own daughter to incest. Such a model of kingship provides Gower with a legitimate reason to turn against Richard when he begins to see a promising young prince develop into a ruthless tyrant. Richard's attempts to take over the government of London and usurp the authority of the mayor, a man whose office was considered second only to the king's, demonstrate his inclination toward subsuming the identity of others while coming to grips with his own. Just as the invasion of London provided a pretext for the slaughter of the Flemings, it also provided an opportunity for the adolescent king to establish his authority over the city. In his confrontation with William Walworth and Wat Tyler, the king becomes a glorious leader while the rebel leader and all those associated with him suffer the ignominious consequences.

The sacrificial nature of violence that I am claiming for Gower's text acquires additional significance when the narrative is read against a visual representation of the meeting at Smithfield. It is to the illumination of this occasion that I now turn, since it depicts visually much of what Gower describes verbally in relation to Wat Tyler's murder.[51] It also depicts a stunning visualization of Girard's triangulation of desire and mimetic rivalry that is made evident in Gower's narrative. Read from left to right in diptych fashion there are two moments frozen in time; the first, on the left, shows the mayor's upraised sword aimed at a man, described as Wat Tyler, who is reaching for his own weapon. Tyler, the man about to be executed, is placed in a subordinate position in relation to his slayer, Mayor Walworth, who has laid on his other hand, perhaps to balance himself for the swipe he is about to make. The king, located to the right, has his hand extended toward the two men while his sheathed sword is held by a squire. The narration in Froissart's *Chronicles*, in which the illumination appears, asserts that King Richard proclaimed himself 'captain' of the rebels after Tyler's death became known to the rebel mob, essentially taking the place of the rebel leader. The visual dimension suppresses Froissart's narrative, however, and presents instead a surface glossing of events. What we do not see is the violence leading up to this scene. Instead, the illumination depicts the king gesturing first to the mayor on the left and then to the leaderless rebels on the right.

On the left side, the king's extended hand draws the viewer's eye to William Walworth's action, visually linking him with the mayor, suggesting official parity and the heroic status Gower describes. Yet the mayor does not hold the traditional broadsword of an English knight. Rather he brandishes a weapon much more akin to a falchion, a weapon associated with the Saracen enemies

1. The murder of Wat Tyler. London, British Library, MS. Royal 18.E.i, fol. 41v.
By kind permission of The British Library.

of Christianity. With this weapon Walworth will sacrifice the social heretic before him, the rebel Gower so frequently associates with Antiochus, the tyrannical invader of Jerusalem. Walworth holds the naked sword aloft as he prepares to expunge the polluted Other from sanctified ground just outside the sacred city walls. In so doing, the mayor – connected as he is with the gesturing Richard to the right – wields the sword that stands for the power of the Crown, its upright position frozen in perpetual readiness to quell any challenges to its tyranny. At the same time, Richard assumes the identity of London's chief peacemaker (he holds no sword) and visually usurps the authority of the mayor. Richard also acquires a public image that belies his cruel intention to rescind the amnesty he promises at Smithfield, an event told only in narrative accounts. This is one of the acts by which the young monarch attains a kingly identity at the expense of all those who died during the rebellion and its aftermath.

The right portion of the illumination depicts a later moment at Smithfield, and here too there is some disparity between the chronicle narratives and the illustration. Froissart says that Richard took the place of Wat Tyler when he proclaimed himself captain of the so-called rebel hoard surrounding him at Smithfield, a description that suggests he took command of a confused and disorderly mob. But the 'rebel hoard' appears to be regaled in full armour, as if it belongs to an organized regiment of chivalrous knights standing attentively in orderly formation. Certainly, depicting the rebellious throng in this way lends authority to Richard's already commanding presence. But there is also a striking similarity between the men brought by Walworth from the city in the left section and the rebel hoard in the right. They are all equipped militarily as if to fight in formalized battle, as if the opponents were equally matched for a tournament rather than a rebellion. At the same time the two groups are separated and made distinct from each another; their group identities are thus represented visually as having been consolidated within but differentiated from the opposition. Caught in the middle, visually identified with neither group, Wat Tyler stands as the destabilizing Other, a threat to corporate solidarity, frozen forever into a symbol of disorder.

The visual representation of this scene belies the realities of the violence that took place preceding the meeting at Smithfield. What remains is only the prelude to Tyler's death, the threat of a raised sword. To a modern audience, the exquisitely drawn event commemorates and glamourizes the rebellion, rendering chivalry a thing of beauty, knights and kings people to admire and emulate, medieval justice a successful deterrent to crime; in so doing it obfuscates the underlying motives for Tyler's death and erases the ugly realities of urban violence. Nowhere to be found in this beautiful illumination are the corpses of the murdered Flemings.

If we look beyond the attempts to erase the violence, however, it is possible to see how Wat Tyler and the Flemings function as scapegoats for everything that has gone wrong with English society in the late fourteenth century. Both Tyler and the Flemings are recognized as threatening to corporate solidarity and invested with all the evils that London society can muster. But as Girard reminds us, we cannot lose sight of the underlying impulses contributing to such violent events:

> The whole range of victim signs can be found in myths, a fact unnoticed because we focus on the victim's ethnic or religious minority. That particular sign cannot appear in the same form in mythology. We find neither persecuted Jews nor blacks. But their equivalent can be found in a theme that plays a central role in all parts of the world, that of the *foreigner* banished or assassinated by the community ... If a stranger behaves in a strange or insulting way in the eyes of his hosts, it is because he [or *she*] conforms to other customs.[52]

Tyler, who acts in a strange and insulting way to the king, by not doffing his hat or speaking courteously, is assassinated by the community because he does not conform to their customs. In a similar way, the Flemings, who are identified by their distinct speech, are intentionally expunged; covered up by the noises of rebellion, carried out under the pretext of defending the city, this group becomes the deliberate target of ethnic extermination done by members of the very community in which they lived and worked.[53]

However offensive we may find Gower's judgment of Wat Tyler, or his empathy for a corrupt archbishop, the fact remains that of the several contemporary chroniclers who commemorate the violent events in London in June of 1381, he alone points to the diachronic nature of sacrificial violence; he alone attempts to shape a social conscience where it is conspicuously absent in the institutions around him.[54] The decapitated heads on London's city gates and the dismembered bodies of innocent bystanders represent a warning to those who dare to cross boundaries made sacred; outsiders, however their status is construed, end up in the same broad category for whom violence is a historically recursive event.

Notes

1 I am grateful to the editors of this volume and to an anonymous outside reader for their helpful commentaries on earlier drafts.
2 Derek Pearsall, 'Interpretive Models for the Peasants' Revolt,' in *Hermeneutics and Medieval Culture*, ed. Patrick J. Gallagher and Helen Damico (Albany 1989), 63–70.
3 René Girard, *Violence and the Sacred*, trans. Patrick Gregory (Baltimore 1972).
4 Ibid., 8.
5 Ibid., 2.
6 The Nun's Priest's Tale, as quoted in *The Riverside Chaucer*, 3rd ed., ed. Larry D. Benson (New York 1987):
    So hydous was the noyse – a, benedicitee! –
    Certes, he Jakke Straw and his meynee
    Ne made nevere shoutes half so shrille
    Whan that they wolden any Flemyng kille,
    As thilke day was maad upon the fox. (lines 3393–7)
7 Scholars such as Susan Crane, 'The Writing Lesson of 1381,' in *Chaucer's England: Literature in Historical Context*, ed. Barbara A. Hanawalt (Minneapolis 1992), 201–21; Richard Firth Green, *A Crisis of Truth: Literature and Law in Ricardian England* (Philadelphia 1999); Nick Ronan, '1381: Writing in Revolt. Signs of Confederacy in the Chronicle Accounts of the English Rising,' *Forum for Modern*

Language Studies (1989) 304–14; Margaret Aston, 'Corpus Christi and Corpus Regni: Heresy and the Peasants' Revolt,' *Past and Present* 143 (1994) 3–47; and Steven Justice, *Writing and Rebellion: England in 1381* (Berkeley 1994), are among those who have addressed the means by which these struggles are symbolic.

8   Barbara A. Hanawalt, *'Of Good and Ill Repute': Gender and Social Control in Medieval England* (Oxford 1998), argues the importance of reputation to Englishmen.

9   Harriet Merete Hansen, 'The Peasants' Revolt of 1381 and the Chronicles,' *Journal of Medieval History* 6 (1980) 393–415, at 400: 'Froissart was at the court of the count of Blois.'

10 A strong sense of the inconsistency and unreliability of these documents emerges from Hansen's detailed comparative study (see n. 9 above).

11 Hansen's study maps out the interdependency of these documents. Other points on which the chronicles agree are: 1) the meeting was a confrontation between the king and Wat Tyler; 2) Tyler's actions were provocative (p. 408).

12 All English quotations are from Eric W. Stockton, *Major Works of John Gower* (Seattle 1962). Latin quotations derive from G.C. Macauley, *The Complete Works of John Gower: The Latin Works* (Oxford 1902).

13 John H. Fisher, *John Gower: Moral Philosopher and Friend of Chaucer* (New York 1964), 105.

14 Jane McIntosh Snyder, *The Woman and the Lyre: Women Writers in Classical Greece and Rome* (Carbondale 1989), esp. ch. 5.

15 Elizabeth Clark and Diane Hatch, trans. and eds, *The Golden Bough and the Oaken Cross: The Vergilian Cento of Faltonia Betitia Proba*, American Academy of Religion Texts and Translations 5 (Chico, CA 1981).

16 Stockton, *Major Works,* 90. The Latin reads:
    Clamor in excelsis, lacrime gemitusque frequentes,
    Non veniam cassi preteriere dei;
    Attamen ipse maris Neptunus qui deus extat,
    At mare pacificet, tunc holocausta petit. (1.1851–4)

17 Ibid. The Latin reads:
    O benedicta manus, tam sufficiens holocaustum
    Que dedit, unde maris victa procella silet. (1.1883–4)

18 For an interesting discussion of familial metaphors in the context of rebellion and social violence see Lynn Hunt, *The Family Romance of the French Revolution* (Berkeley 1992).

19 J.H. Burns, ed., *The Cambridge History of Medieval Political Thought, c. 350–c.1450* (Cambridge 1988), 496.

20 Sarah Beckwith, *Christ's Body: Identity, Culture, and Society in Late-Medieval Writings* (London 1994), 25.

21 Miri Rubin, *Corpus Christi: The Eucharist in Late Medieval Culture* (Cambridge 1991), 266.

22 Ibid.
23 Margaret Aston, 'Corpus Christi and Corpus Regni: Heresy and the Peasants' Revolt,' *Past and Present* 143 (1994) 3–47.
24 Stockton, *Major Works,* 70. The Latin reads:
    Ecce Iovis festiva dies de Corpore Cristi,
    Cum furor accinxit urbis utrumque latus,
    Precedens alios Capitaneus excitat unus
    Rusticus, ut cuncti consequerentur eum
    Ipse viris multis prefultus conterit urbem,
    Ense necat cives, concremat igne domos:
    Non solus cecinit, set secum milia traxit,
    Involuitque malo milia multa suo; (1.919–26)
25 Peter Beichner, 'Gower's Use of *Aurora* in *Vox clamantis*,' *Speculum* 30 (1955) 582–95. The *Aurora* passage reads as follows:
    Ipse viris multis prefultus conterit urbem
    Ense necat cives, concremat igne domos. (Beichner, 587)
26 Stockton, *Major Works*, 356.
27 Justice, *Writing and Rebellion*, 99.
28 Stockton, *Major Works*, 73.
29 Ovid, *Tristia* 4.2, esp. lines 1–10. Lines 5–6 read:
    Candidaque adducta collum percussa securi
        Victima purpureo sanguine tingat humum:
30 There seems to be historical verification for this. According to Hansen, 'Peasants' Revolt,' 411, the *Anonimalle Chronicle* and the *London Letter Book* report that the king, when he met with the rebels at Mile End, gave them permission to seize traitors: 'This causes the rebels to go directly to the Tower, to seize the archbishop and four others, and to execute them on Tower Hill.'
31 The Statute of Treason of 1352 is relevant here to indicate how seriously a threat even to the 'patriarch' of the household would be taken. The statute held that wives who murdered their husbands were guilty not merely of homicide, as husbands would be for the same act, but of petty treason, a crime against the peace of the king. If convicted, a woman could be burned at the stake. For an interesting discussion of 'treason in the household,' see the chapter by that title in Paul Strohm's *Hochon's Arrow: Social Imagination of Fourteenth-Century Texts* (Princeton 1994). See also Green, *Crisis of Truth*, for a comprehensive discussion of the transformation of treason from private betrayal to public crime.
32 Stockton, *Major Works*, 358.
33 According to Nigel Saul, *Richard II* (New Haven 1997), 58, Sudbury was 'perceived as the personification of the "Caesarean" clergy, the clerics who mingled the affairs of Church and realm.' He was particularly unpopular in the countryside.
34 The Latin reads:

>   Non metuunt leges, sternunt sub viribus equm
>   Victaque pugnaci iura sub ense cadunt. (1.1971–2)

35 The Latin reads:
>   Non magis esse probos ad finem solis ab ortu
>   Estimo, si populi mutuus esset amor. (1.1981–2)

36 Gower does not coin the term; the renaming of London to New Troy was actually proposed by Nicholas Brembre, who served as mayor of London before Walworth and immediately thereafter. Brembre's demise in the treachery that became known as the 'Merciless Parliament' demonstrates how precarious urban politics could be.

37 These suspicions were substantiated by the indictment of several aldermen after the revolt.

38 Stockton, *Major Works*, 75–6. The Latin reads:
>   Corpora missa neci nullo de more feruntur,
>   Immo iacent patulis undique spersa viis:
>   Et quod nulla viris, rabies, monumenta manerent,
>   Mortua membratim corpora scissa terit:
>   Corpora cesorum muris suspensa reponunt,
>   Brutaque brutorum more sepulta neganti ...
>   Urbs que summa fuit, cede repressa ruit. (1.1165–70, 1176)

39 According to Fisher, *John Gower*, 105, these powerful clerics would include William of Wykeham, bishop of Winchester, William Courtenay, bishop of London, Simon Sudbury, Thomas Brunton, bishop of Rochester, Ralph Erghum, bishop of Salisbury, and 'others of the "Caesarian" clergy.'

40 Jody Enders, *The Medieval Theater of Cruelty: Rhetoric, Memory, Violence* (Ithaca 1999). See also Mary Carruthers, *The Book of Memory: A Study of Memory in Medieval Culture* (Cambridge 1990).

41 Andrew Prescott, 'London in the Peasants' Revolt: A Portrait Gallery,' *London Journal* 7 (1981) 125–43.

42 Rodney Hilton, *Bond Men Made Free: Medieval Peasant Movements and the English Rising of 1381* (New York 1973, repr. 1977), p. 195.

43 Justice, *Writing and Rebellion*, 72–3.

44 Many historians mention this feature of the identification process. E.g., Caroline Barron, *Revolt in London: 11th to 15th June 1381* (London 1981), says (p. 6): 'Heaps of headless bodies could be seen lying in the streets. A London chronicler observed that the Flemings lost their heads because they could not say "Breede and chese, but case and brode". More likely they died because they were skilled weavers whose presence in London threatened the livelihood of the free weavers of the city who had petitioned against the Flemings as recently as 1378.'

45 Londoners, at least those who were native Englishmen, feared Flemish immigrants for three reasons: 1) their potential to assimilate quickly into a non-native cultural

environment, 2) their ability to dominate the weaving trade simply by their superior skill, and 3) the threat of a Flemish subculture in England via intermarriage with the English aristocracy (Edward III's queen was Philippa of Hainault). See, e.g., Martha Carlin, *Medieval Southwark* (London 1996).

46 Carlin, *Medieval Southwark*, 150.

47 Though Gower married Agnes after the *Vox* was written, the union validates his continuing concern for the Flemish community.

48 Rosamond S. Allen, 'John Gower and Southwark: The Paradox of the Social Self,' in *London and Europe in the Later Middle Ages*, ed. Julia Boffey and Pamela King (London 1995), 111–47. On the persistent rumour that William Walworth may have been involved in the operation she writes (p. 140): 'There seems to be no truth in the suggestion that William Walworth, Mayor of London in 1381, was one of the tenants. In the 1381 poll tax return there were seven "*stuynmongers*" or "*stuyvmongers*" (OED has a 14c form *stuyue*) in Southwark, and there are records from 1300 on of women there with the title "Frowe", showing that they were Flemish.'

49 Caution must be observed when using this term to describe a medieval philosophy, since modern connotations of resistance or opposition to war and violence do not hold true for the Middle Ages. Rather, what is built into the medieval philosophy of 'just' war is the 'right' use of violence as defined by those in positions of authority.

50 See Russell A. Peck, *Kingship and Common Profit in Gower's 'Confessio amantis'* (Carbondale 1978).

51 The illumination is found in London, BL, MS. Royal 18.E. i, fol. 41v.

52 Girard, *Violence*, 32. The bracketed, italicized feminine pronoun indicates the gender dimension that Girard does not address in his theories of violence and scapegoating. Feminist scholars such as Patricia Klindienst Joplin, 'The Voice of the Shuttle is Ours,' *Stanford Literature Review* 1 (1984) 25–53, and Carolyn Dinshaw, 'Rivalry, Rape, and Manhood: Gower and Chaucer,' in *Violence Against Women in Medieval Texts*, ed. Anna Roberts (Gainesville 1998), 137–60, have helped to fill in this gap.

53 According to Barron, *Revolt in London*, 6, the body count was around 140–160 people: This number may not warrant the use of the term 'ethnic extermination' for some statisticians, but the collective impulse to eliminate a particular group of people suggests that a purging operation was in effect.

54 A comprehensive discussion of the emergence of social conscience in late medieval England is by Russell A. Peck, 'Social Conscience and the Poets,' in *Social Unrest in the Late Middle Ages: Papers of the Fifteenth Annual Conference of the Centre for Medieval and Early Renaissance Studies*, ed. Francis Newman (Binghamton 1986), 113–48.

5 Bystanders and Hearsayers First: Reassessing the Role of the Audience in Duelling[1]

OREN FALK

> BENVOLIO: We talk here in the public haunt of men:
> Either withdraw unto some private place,
> And reason coldly of your grievances,
> Or else depart; here all eyes gaze on us.
> MERCUTIO: Men's eyes were made to look, and let them gaze;
> I will not budge for no man's pleasure, I.
> (William Shakespeare, *Romeo and Juliet* 3.1.50–5)

On a brisk midwinter morning early in the eleventh century, two men in eastern Iceland went up a hill to fight a duel. In some respects, this encounter between the *goði* [chieftain] Bjarni of Hof and his *bóndi* [free farmer] neighbour Þorsteinn of Sunnudalr, recounted in *Þorsteins þáttr stangarhǫggs*,[2] resembled most duels in medieval Iceland. The hillock on which they fought served as an impromptu duelling ring; they took turns taking swings at each other; shattered shields were discarded and replaced; and even a new, sharp blade could be substituted for a blunted one – all features that students of the Norse *hólmganga* (pl. *hólmgǫngur*) will recognize as standard practice in such incidents.[3] In two important ways, however, this particular combat differed radically from run-of-the-mill saga duels. One difference has often been remarked on and has led many scholars to consider this encounter a-historical – a pure, sermonizing fiction: that both parties survived and were even reconciled with each other.[4] Elsewhere in the sagas, even if both duellists live, they do not walk away arm in arm. The other difference, less frequently noted, is that this duel proceeded in almost complete privacy: each combatant stood alone, without allies or aides, and no audience witnessed their fight firsthand.[5]

This latter peculiarity is intimately linked to the former, I argue, and may serve as an entry point into my discussion of the role that 'third parties' play in violent events – even such strictly delimited, bipolar events as duels. I draw on the spotty evidence of Norse duels, supplementing it with comparative material on duelling in other cultures and on more plural forms of violence in medieval Scandinavia.[6] But the implications of my argument may reach beyond the cultural confines of Norse *hólmgǫngur* or even of the duel form in general, and may apply to most types of violence involving any element of formal structure and signification – i.e., most non-trivial violence of any sort. Such acts (of which the duel is only one specialized instance) form an idiom of social exchange, performed before an audience who are to a great extent the interpreters, enunciators, and indeed authors of unfolding events. Bystanders, in a very real sense, come first; only when this pivotal role has been manned can other, secondary participants in the violence – viz. the combatants themselves – assume their positions. We ought to be thinking not of witnesses to a fight, then, but of fighters to a witness.

Strictly speaking, of course, critics who say that the duel recounted in *Þorsteins þáttr stangarhǫggs* is fictional are right. Above, I used the indicative mood to refer to this event; I must now retract it and acknowledge that this specific fight probably never took place. But although the particulars that the saga author relates are surely elaborate artistic invention (as various students of this text have shown),[7] at a deeper level they vibrate with historicity. The Icelandic sagas, lively narrative fictions written mostly in the thirteenth century (or later) but referring mostly to the tenth and eleventh centuries, were long rejected by historians as containing too lean a diet of fact.[8] In the past twenty-five years or so, however, a new generation of historians, weaned on anthropology, have reinstated a reading of the sagas as a literature written under the sign of social realism: imaginary narratives have been shown convincingly to cohere perfectly with what we otherwise know of medieval Icelandic culture.[9] The sagas distil an essence of (real) social life from the accidence of individual (if fictional) lives.

In other words, had two actual men like the fictional Bjarni and Þorsteinn really existed, fighting a duel like the one imputed to their namesakes would have been sensible conduct for them.[10] For the purposes of this paper, therefore, I will treat the Icelandic family sagas (which provide the bulk of our knowledge about duelling in medieval Scandinavia)[11] as reliable historical sources on the notional mechanics of the duel. We must remain constantly alert to the strong possibility that particular fights described have been rigged to satisfy the demands of their literary context – allowing, for instance, an unpromising young protagonist to prove his worth by besting a hyperbolic rival.[12] But, aside from such high-handed authorial fabrication (which must be discounted locally on a case-by-case basis), saga duels do provide rich veins for historians to mine.

Of the wealth of information that the sagas provide about single combats, procedural and ceremonial details have attracted by far the most scholarly attention. The alleged religious underpinnings of duelling rituals, the regulations of a supposed Norse *code duello* and the apparent fit (or lack thereof) between fighting etiquette and social organization have all excited historians' imaginations.[13] Such avenues of research run the risk of overly reifying the *hólmganga*, however, drawing too systematic a distinction between proper duels and looser sorts of armed confrontation. Þorsteinn and Bjarni's clash is a case in point: although clearly patterned on the conventions of a formal duel, right down to the aural pun of convening the combatants on a hillock, it is never expressly styled '*hólmganga*.'[14] Should this combat therefore be excluded from consideration in an investigation of the Norse duel? Most authorities on the *hólmganga* think not, thus tacitly acknowledging the fluidity of the form even as they insist on its rigidity.[15]

Prudence dictates approaching the Norse duel with a working definition as broad as initially plausible. In the Norse political landscape of local, often petty disputes, typically centrifugal in their progression and seldom capable of final resolution – what is usually described as the 'feuding' society of the medieval Norse – duelling can fill a variety of functional niches, initiating, perpetuating or (rarely) ending ongoing conflicts.[16] I should clarify at once that by 'duel' I mean simply a combat in which only one man fights on each side, typically with deadly weapons; I disregard more specific niceties (such as the restriction of the tag to aristocratic engagements, insistence on a time-lag between challenge and execution, scrupulous observance of an equality of weapons, and so forth), which are, in any case, most often honoured in the breach.[17] Such a definition does not ensure complete, unambiguous neatness of categorization; for instance, backstabbings like Þorsteinn Kálfsson's abortive attack on Bjǫrn Hítdœlakappi are probably better classified as attempted murder than as duel.[18] The definition does allow, however, some tentative distinctions, as between one-on-one engagements and mass mêlées (or engagements between patently unequal numbers).[19] The typical resort to lethal weapons, meanwhile, helps distinguish between encounters in which mortal danger is actively courted and mere *pro forma* fights.[20]

Old Norse has several terms for 'duel.' The sagas primarily mention two forms, *hólmganga* and *einvígi*,[21] but do not distinguish between them with any consistency, nor can a definitive account of duelling procedure be gleaned from them. That there were indeed customary rules, likely varying locally or over time, is plausible, but saga accounts of these rules might be entirely fanciful.[22]

The words *hólmganga* and *einvígi*, like their equivalents in English and in other languages (μονομαχία, דו-קרב, *duellum*, *Zweikampf*, etc.), seem to emphasize the joining of battle by two combatants isolated – even insulated – from their surroundings. The more generic (but less frequent) *einvígi* can be translated fairly literally as 'single combat,' while *hólmganga*, lit. an 'isletgoing' or 'sojourn on a small island,' really means simply 'a fight in a ring': a patch of exposed ground just off-shore is supposed to have served as a site of choice for duels,[23] not only in archaic Scandinavia but throughout much of medieval Europe.[24] (As described in the sagas, *hólmgǫngur* actually take place for the most part in a ritually demarcated arena, on a cloak stretched out on the ground; the insistence on an island seems rather metaphoric.)[25] Circumstantial descriptions of duels, especially the detailed *locus classicus* in *Kormáks saga*, further stress this idea of the combatants' insulation from their surroundings: three concentric, foot-wide furrows mark the boundaries of the duelling arena, which is further roped off.[26] Despite this emphasis on the one-on-one quality of the engagement, however, we find in Scandinavia (as in other duelling cultures) evidence both of 'communal duels,' waged by up to a dozen combatants on either side,[27] and of single combats conducted in the presence of 'seconds.' I shall return to these latter shortly.

The very lexicon of duelling, then, reinforces an intuitive distinction between 'principals,' the two weapon-wielding duellists, and 'auxiliaries,' a more motley category that may include seconds, surgeons, spectators, and other assorted sideliners. Such a distinction is commonplace throughout the historical literature on duelling (as well as on other forms of violence, if perhaps less radically). Combatants are perceived as essential, defining constituents in violence; third parties, on the other hand, are viewed as optional and (if present) relatively inconsequential to the event as violence. Secondary participants may well play crucial roles – providing principals with moral or material support, negotiating an end to a fight or attending to casualties, giving testimony or seeking to enforce justice after the fact – but such activities are regarded as tangential to the specifically violent aspect of the event.

Thus Thomas Gallant, for example, writing of knife-fights in nineteenth-century Greek villages, notes that 'the rules compelled onlookers to refrain from interfering. They were to observe and evaluate performances, not become actors themselves.'[28] Gallant does profess the centrality of witnesses to the ritual of the duel, but insists that they are only active in 'the third and final act of the drama of the knife fight,' viz. the trial. During the first act – the combat proper – he sees their role as 'by and large a *passive* one.'[29] Higher up the social ladder and farther to the north, Victor Kiernan also sees 'two men [who] were left to face each other, but under scrutiny of representatives of their world. ... From one point of view we see a code of honour derived from the feudal past asserting itself; from another we see the bourgeois (and Protestant) rule of strict accountability of the *individual*.' Whereas in the early modern period seconds had been 'frequent participants,' by the 1800s they had 'reverted to their *proper* function as counsellors, observers, and directors.'[30] We have, then, a sharp dichotomy between 'violent' principals and 'non-violent' auxiliaries.

The violent clash of lethally equipped principals must often have led, in medieval Scandinavia no less than in other duelling societies, to a bloody outcome: one researcher notes that of two dozen *hólmgǫngur* surveyed, twelve 'result in the death of at least one combatant,' for a total of fifteen corpses. My own rough calculations, based on a more exhaustive sample, yield even steeper fatality rates.[31] In some of these cases, however, lives are claimed by bare fists or even bared teeth, not by edged weapons.[32] This detail alone should caution us against accepting the fatality rate of saga duels at face value: hyperbolic feats of physical daring-do seem more the stuff of literary sensibility than of historical record. Furthermore, as others have noted before, many such terminal duels form 'a plot device [designed] to enhance the hero's stature'; pitting the protagonist against a caricature villain, these 'are stereotyped comic scenes in which the hero's prowess is tested' and affirmed.[33]

We may suspect, therefore, that the paradigmatic Norse duel may only have gone as far as first blood. Certainly, this was the rule in a vast majority of single combats in most other duelling societies that historians have studied.[34] Cross-cultural analogy aside, we have several examples of such fights in the saga corpus, one of which is the single most detailed account of duelling to survive from medieval Scandinavia:

> It was Kormákr's turn to strike, so he struck at Bersi; he [Bersi] countered with Hvítingr. Skǫfnungr snapped the point off Hvítingr in front of the cutting edge, and the sword point ricocheted onto Kormákr's hand, and he got a scratch on his thumb; the knuckle was slit, and blood got on the cloak. After that people went in between them and would not let them fight any more.[35]

This incident, if indeed typical, reveals several important points (quite aside from the fact that Norsemen were on a first-name basis with their swords). First, we can clearly see how even the tiniest modicum of blood spilled can suffice for consummating the duel, creating conditions sufficient for deciding a victor.[36] As a form of violence, then, the goal of the duel is not mutual annihilation (although the conditions to make this outcome possible are insisted upon), but the infliction of some token damage. Second, we may already perceive one vital function an audience could fulfill in a duel: stepping in to physically separate the combatants and minimize bloodshed.

Well documented throughout the literature on duelling,[37] such conduct also recurs elsewhere in the sagas in connexion with more plural forms of violence (where two groups are engaged in a fight and the sideliners intervene to stop them – sometimes quite violently, as when a man goes between the combatants swinging a construction-beam so that both sides fall back before him).[38] It would seem, then, that in cases where the principals to the duel are hell-bent on fighting to the last drop, auxiliaries can act as brakes and shock-absorbers, transforming the encounter from violence to some milder idiom of interaction. There is no denying, however, that auxiliaries here play an active role in the violence *per se*, perhaps even introducing an added element of violence in order to quell the initial fight, even if their activity is temporally confined to the very last segment of the duelling sequence.

A glance at the ethnographic literature on contemporary and recent societies with an alleged propensity to everyday violence suggests that even this terminal role may not be quite so temporally bounded as it first seems. All across the Mediterranean (where such societies have been most comprehensively studied), anthropologists have found a recurring 'somebody hold me back' motif in the midst of what otherwise looks like heated fighting. In highland Greece, 'even when they seem to be in the grip of ungovernable rage[, villagers] do not draw a knife unless they see, or sense, that there are witnesses uncommitted by kinship obligation who will prevent them from using it.'[39] In Andalusia, young men have been observed to bluster and brawl but do no damage, 'since the combatants were on the whole more drunk than the public to whom it fell to hold back the assailants.'[40] And in Crete, 'the coffeehouses as well as the streets may become settings for violent quarrels, in which bystanders become advocates of restraint as well as the means whereby hatred can be safely displayed – because, as one [local] remarked, "if you hold someone back, he can afford to be brave."'[41] In other words, rather than a clash of wills between hot-blooded principals and cool-headed auxiliaries, a more complex picture of unspoken cooperation emerges.[42] The bloodthirstiness that we attribute to principals may need to be scaled back as we realize that they only indulge it when they can count on others to rein them in before anything too serious happens.

Such a pattern of institutionalized brinkmanship may be so manifest as to thrust itself on contemporary anthropologists, but in the historical record of past societies it is almost certain to remain invisible. On the one hand, disgruntled authorities, whose repressive vigilance provides historians of violence with most of our primary sources (judicial records, police blotters, coroners' reports, etc.), would have had no reason to intervene when no one got seriously hurt. Participants and their groupies, on the other hand, would have had trouble getting themselves worked up over the martial valour displayed in a confrontation that ended almost before it began. I suspect that a significant portion of the long-term 'Civilising Process' that Norbert Elias and his disciples claim to perceive, in which atrophied displays of posturing gradually supersede actual destructive violence, may be due to such skewing of contemporary vs past evidence.[43]

One saga passage does afford a rare glimpse into the psychology of premeditated curbed escalation. Two powerful brothers, Guðmundr and Einarr, are at loggerheads, though no open hostilities have erupted. Guðmundr is an overbearing man, but not a great fighter. He seems to have overreached himself when he provokes a client of Einarr's by the name of Þórir, to the point that the latter challenges him to single combat. 'That evening ... Guðmundr was cheerful,' the saga reports. 'But later at night [his client Vigfúss] woke up and said to [him]: "You sleep lightly tonight, Guðmundr. Aren't you looking forward to a duel with Þórir?"' Guðmundr puts on a brave face, but Vigfúss unmasks him, insinuating that he does not stand a chance in a fair fight. Then he adds:

> 'But I can give you good advice on this, by which your reputation may grow while you shan't be placed in any danger. ... I will challenge your brother Einarr to a duel, that he should fight with me this very day. ... It will not turn out any better for Einarr in a duel with me than for you against Þórir. Now let's first give him room to back-paddle if he doesn't dare take up the duel. But if he does fight me, I'll kill him. *Still, the chieftains will figure out some other solution than that you two brothers both be cut down here at the þing.*'[44]

As this episode reveals, bystander intervention to stop a duel (or even prevent it from taking place altogether) is not an accidental exception to the rule of an otherwise brutal, bloodthirsty society. Rather, it is a predictable-enough principle that Vigfúss can use it to lynchpin the entire strategy he devises. The plan, which Guðmundr readily adopts, works to a tee.[45]

Besides their role as terminators of raging conflict, auxiliaries often play a part as instigators who initially trigger the outburst of violence. In *Þorsteins þáttr stangarhǫggs*, neither Þorsteinn nor Bjarni had been eager to fight the other. But the night before their duel, Bjarni's wife had pointed out to him in no uncertain terms that his status as a local leader would be jeopardized if he did not move against his rival. '[P]eople can't imagine what Þorsteinn stangarhǫgg must do in order for you to see a need for vengeance,' she rebukes him. 'He has now killed three of your retainers ... and you just sit on your hands.' Bjarni at first responds icily, but then adds: 'still I shall listen to what you propose. But Þorsteinn has killed few without cause.'[46] This little interlude fits into a common saga topos, thought by many to have its basis in actual social praxis, of *hvǫt*, 'whetting' or egging on to battle, generally *of* men *by* women – though a symmetrical exchange takes place the next morning, when Bjarni shows up to issue his challenge, in which Þorsteinn is whetted by his grumpy old father.[47]

In the literature on duelling in other times and places, we likewise come across repeated mention of bystanders who actively incite the principals to fight. Even formal seconds in those carefully hedged-about encounters of the nineteenth century, men whose ostensible duty it was to try hard to arbitrate a peaceful outcome, sometimes '[took] an uncompromising tone and insist[ed] on action instead of accommodation, [allowing them to] feel more important and make a parade of vicarious courage.'[48] In other cases, when conscientious seconds proved too pacific for the trigger-happy principals, they could be replaced – with men of a more suitable disposition, presumably.[49]

We can see auxiliaries contributing to the violence of the duel at both ends, then: fanning the flames before or during the opening scene, throwing wet blankets over the fire during or after the closing vignette. Sometimes it is even the same supporting actor who plays the roles of both Mephistophelian goad and angelic voice of temperance. Bjarni's wife, after as good as putting the blade in his hand at bedtime, alters her tune in the morning when she discovers that he intends to challenge Þorsteinn to single combat rather than raise a posse and hunt him down. 'Don't do it,' she pleads with Bjarni, 'don't risk yourself on your own against the weapons of the fiend!'[50] She is evidently more effective at instigating violence than at deterring it.

And just as expected audience intervention to end the fight might exert influence over its beginning, motivating men to engage in it in the first place, so also provocative words need not be uttered ahead of time to have an impact: the retrospective judgement of bellicose bystanders (or at least fear of what such judgment might be) can be equally effective. The Georgia *Columbus Enquirer*, reporting on a victimless duel in January 1845, commented: 'We are tired of these bloodless fights and now give due notice that if somebody don't get killed pretty shortly we will quit noticing such contemptible freaks of martial honor. If men will fight we want them to do the thing a little less like they were taken with a shaking. Some uncharitable people have already surmised that of late there are no *bullets* used by these *braggers*. We venture no opinion on the subject ourselves.'[51] The sagas frequently do give notice to men who, when challenged by a martially superior rival, instantly opt for death over dishonour.[52] Even if no one on hand explicitly tells them so, these individuals realize what their peers' expectations of them are. Their rivals, too, are more interested in the rumours of war than in an anticipated victory in the one-on-one battle. When Egill Skalla-Grímsson, a seasoned fighter and a bit of a psychopath, proposes to stand in for his inexperienced friend Friðgeirr, the challenger, Ljótr, replies: 'Come here into the ring, you big fellow, and fight with me, if you're so eager to; we'll contend among us. It's much more equitable than if I fought with Friðgeirr, for I wouldn't be thought a bigger man, though I should lay him low.'[53] Although rightly confident that he could trounce Friðgeirr, Ljótr knows that mere practicalities like staying alive or killing his rival would miss the point of the engagement. What mattered to him was what the lads were going to say afterwards.

But if auxiliaries undoubtedly have roles to play before and after the main event, are they not at any rate secondary *during* the violent exchange itself? Where by-the-book duels are concerned, Gallant reiterates, '[i]t is empirically correct that the witnesses to the single combat between two men *were* largely passive: if they were not, then the fight would have been a brawl and not a duel.'[54] In Norse duels, seconds (*skjaldsveinar*, lit. 'squires,' 'shield-boys') were sometimes involved, acting, apparently, as shield-bearers.[55] In one instance, a second twists away a shield in which the opponent's blade has become lodged, thus allowing his man to land a decisive blow.[56] Olav Bø, a pre-eminent authority on the Norse duel, expresses puzzlement at this arrangement: 'This is rather strange, since the fight really ceases to be a duel in such cases. The result was dependent on all four participants.'[57]

These phrases – 'really ceases to be a duel'; 'a brawl and not a duel' – cut right to the heart of the matter, contrasting the roles appropriate to principals (thrusting and parrying) and those suitable for auxiliaries (everything else). But if spectators did not draw their own blades or knock away opponents', were they therefore necessarily 'passive,' as Gallant says? Only if one's sole measure of 'active' participation is the striking of blows. Even in a duel (and, all the more so, in more overtly plural violent scenarios), it need not be. A nineteenth-century anti-duelling polemicist 'exaggerated only slightly,' in one historian's estimation, 'when he claimed that "the principals in such affairs should be passive instruments, with no other function than to pull triggers at word of command."'[58] In the medieval Norse duel, with duellists' shield-play delegated to their seconds, the lives of the principals may quite literally have been in the hands of others.[59] Without getting too deeply into the question of apportioning passivity between principals and seconds in *hólmgǫngur*, however, I simply wish to draw attention again to two well-established facts: first, that no duel takes place in a social vacuum,[60] and second, that duels are seldom (if ever) really 'about' reciprocal murder. Their theme, rather, is honour: a negotiable form of social capital ('status, reputation, and esteem ... assessed, bestowed, or rescinded by the court of masculine public opinion'), a far scarcer commodity than life.[61]

In this contest for honour, bystanders perform a variety of active duties, even if they never set foot within the combat zone. Onlookers look on: their eyes evaluate; their mouths comment, cautioning or encouraging, assessing skill and bravery; and their arms may intervene at any moment, to pull combatants apart or to join them in melee. (Yes, such intervention, if it occurs, does turn the duel into a brawl. But brawl-*potential* management is as active a role as participation in one.)[62] Even indirect audiences – especially those culturally institutionalized audiences whose commentary can be foreseen, like newspaper reporters in nineteenth-century Georgia or the gossips and saga authors of medieval Iceland – directly determine the actions of duellists.[63] In this court of public opinion, spectators are judge, bailiff, and town crier; but even this metaphor is insufficient, since courts only react to infractions after the fact, while, where public opinion is concerned, its existence is what spurs men on to fight in the first place.[64]

The motivating logic of the duel, like the surface structure of any other narrative, is not causal but teleological.[65] According to Chekhov's famous dictum, the gun displayed onstage in Act 1 got there not because of some event in the characters' past but in preparation for events in their future, allowing it to go off on schedule in Act 4. Similarly, the violence of the duel is not intended to mend past wrongs but to create future rights: distribution rights over the participants' reputations. After all, '[w]hen the man of honor is told that he smells, he does not take a bath – he draws his pistol. In other words, a man of honor does not care if he stinks, but he does care that someone has accused him of stinking.'[66]

Combatants' knowledge of the non-combatant roles played by the supporting cast is decisive in initiating a fight, in determining its shape and outcome, and in formulating its impact for later consumption. Bystanders' intervention is not only effective but also structurally mandated. Witnesses may muzzle the violence of an antagonistic exchange before too much harm is done. But they also provide a setting for the exchange to occur at all, on the one hand by making up the audience before whom the rivals need to vie for honour, on the other by supplying the contest with a safety net.[67] Absent this audience, the antagonists may not feel a need to bare fangs; if they feel this need, they may not dare entertain it, fearing a bloody outcome with no one around to pry them from each other's throat at first blood; and if they dare, their actual encounter may go rather differently from the script enabled by having decidedly active (but non-brawling) witnesses all about.[68]

Before concluding, I wish to broaden the canvas briefly and contemplate the implications of such teleological, 'audience-response'-oriented analysis for understanding forms of violence other than the duel. Narratologists have long taken to heart Chekhov's dictum, shifting critical attention away from the past-looking realism of illusory narrative depth (*histoire*) and towards the anticipatory reality of surface-level textual manoeuvres (*récit*).[69] Similarly, historians of violence should do well to shed their preoccupation with some supposed chthonic aggression, fuelling the depths of warfare or murder, and focus instead on the surface context of signification within which violence unfolds. We often like to congratulate ourselves that, in the modern West at any rate, state vigilance is able to thwart most individual outbreaks of violence rather effectively, and that those irruptions of brutality which do mar our everyday lives and enliven our television shows – muggings, rapes, drive-bys, and school rampages – are the acts of poorly socialized deviants. Without, for the moment, taking issue with these claims, let me simply point out that even if they are accepted at face value, this still leaves action at the international level completely devoid of coercive restraints, subject only to the same feuding laws of honour and circumstance that operate in the Icelandic *hólmganga*. In this light, I think the Israeli columnist Ben Kaspit, writing shortly after the accession of Ariel Sharon in 2001, hit the nail right on the head:

> On Wednesday evening, Israel Defence Forces helicopters launched an assault on the Thursday morning newspaper headlines. Since it is impossible, under present circumstances, to curtail terrorism, and it is very difficult, in the prevailing situation, to reassure the [Israeli] public, all that was left to Ariel Sharon was to order that the front pages be stormed and held for as long as possible (until the next act of terrorism). 'We need pictures of smoke and fire from the other side, too,' said one of the Prime Minister's confidants over the weekend, 'if only for the sake of appearances.'[70]

Whatever the role of Yasser Arafat and other warmongers in this tragedy-ridden region – actors who have, of course, their own audiences before whom they must strive – their importance for making sense of Sharon's conduct is really only secondary. By focussing on the interplay between the Israeli prime minister and his domestic public, Kaspit provides the best possible key for decoding Sharon's military action.

The duel in *Þorsteins þáttr stangarhǫggs*, with which I began and with which I now conclude, is the exception that proves the rule. In this instance, with both principals painstakingly respectful of each other's honour and resolutely disinclined to hurt each another, it was only the incessant external pressure of their auxiliaries (personified in Bjarni's wife and Þorsteinn's father) that drove them to arms. Had any witnesses been present, one of the men would undoubtedly have had to leave the duelling ground feet first. By orchestrating their encounter in seclusion, Bjarni and Þorsteinn were able to enact the medieval Icelandic equivalent of those gallant French pistol duels where, as Mark Twain remarked, the safest place for the spectators was not on the sidelines but behind the two combatants.[71] To the audience that really mattered in the long run, the hearsayers and saga writers, Þorsteinn and Bjarni had comported themselves honourably, but, at the same time, they had managed to avoid the bloodthirsty spectatorship of their more immediate bystanders.

Reassessing the Role of the Audience in Duelling 109

Table 5.1: Provisional List of Family Saga Duels[72]

B = involves a *berserkr*.[73] F = fought on foreign soil.[74] S = involves seconds (in brackets if service refused). D = results in death of at least one principal (number of fatalities indicated in subscript).

Saga Reference (by chapter)	ÍF Reference	Principals	B?	F?	S?	D?
Egils saga 64	2: 203–6	Egill vs Ljótr	B	F		D_1
Egils saga 65	2: 208–10	Egill vs Atli	B	F		D_1
Gunnlaugs saga 7	3: 72–3	Gunnlaugr vs Þórormr	B	F		D_1
Gunnlaugs saga 11	3: 92–5	Gunnlaugr vs Hrafn			S	
Gunnlaugs saga 12	3: 101–3	Gunnlaugr vs Hrafn		F		D_{2-5}[75]
Bjarnar saga Hítdælakappa 4	3: 121	Bjǫrn vs Kaldimarr	B	F		D_1
Bjarnar saga Hítdælakappa 32	3: 200–3	Bjǫrn vs Dálkr				$[D_4]$[76]
Eyrbyggja saga 8	4: 13–14	Þórólfr vs Úlfarr	B			D_1
Gísla saga 1	6: 4	Ari Þorkelsson vs Bjǫrn inn blakki	B	F		D_1
Gísla saga 1	6: 5	Gísli Þorkelsson vs Bjǫrn inn blakki	B	F		D_1
Gísla saga 2	6: 10–11	Gísli Súrsson vs Skeggi		F		
Fóstbræðra saga 7	6: 149	Þorgeirr vs Þorgils				D_{1-7}
Fóstbræðra saga 24	6: 265	Þormóðr vs 14 men				D_{14}[77]
Grettis saga 4	7: 89	Vígbjóðr vs Ǫnundr tréfótr	B	F		$[D_1]$[78]
Grettis saga 25	7: 89	Þorgeirr vs Þorgils				D_{1-4}[79]
Grettis saga 40	7: 135–6	Grettir vs Snækollr	B	F		D_1
Kormáks saga 1	8: 204	Ǫgmundr vs Ásmundr	B	F		
Kormáks saga 9–10	8: 233–9	Kormákr vs Bersi			S	
Kormáks saga 12	8: 249–53	Bersi vs Steinarr			S	
Kormáks saga 12	8: 252	Steinarr vs 12 men				D_{12}[80]
Kormáks saga 14	8: 254–5	Bersi vs Þorkell			S	D_1
Kormáks saga 14	8: 255	Bersi vs 30 men				D_{30}[81]
Kormáks saga 22	8: 282–6	Kormákr vs Þorvarðr	B[82]			
Kormáks saga 23	8: 289–90	Kormákr vs Þorvarðr	B[83]			
Kormáks saga 27	8: 299–302	Kormákr vs monster	B[84]	F		D_2
Víga-Glúms saga 4	9: 12–13	Eyjólfr vs Ásgautr	B	F	[S]	
Víga-Glúms saga 6	9: 18–19	Víga-Glúmr vs Bjǫrn	B	F		D_1
Svarfdæla saga 9	9: 146–7	Þorsteinn vs Moldi	B	F	[S]	$[D_1]$[85]
Þorleifs þáttr jarlsskálds 7	9: 225–6	Þorleifr vs Þorgarðr	B			D_{1-2}[86]
Valla-Ljóts saga 4	9: 245–6	Valla-Ljótr vs Halli				D_1
Reykdæla saga 1	10: 155	Þorsteinn vs Eysteinn				
Reykdæla saga 19	10: 211–12	Þorkell vs Þorsteinn varastafr			S	D_1

110 Oren Falk

Saga Reference (by chapter)	ÍF Reference	Principals	B?	F?	S?	D?
Reykdæla saga 19	10: 212–13	Ófeigr vs Þorsteinn kvígr	B			D_1
Þorsteins þáttr stangarhǫggs	11: 74–6	Þorsteinn stangarhǫgg vs Bjarni				
Droplaugarsona saga 15	11: 178–9	Grímr vs Gauss	B	F		D_1
Brennu-Njáls saga 11	12: 35	Þjóstólfr vs Þorvaldr Ósvífrsson				D_1
Brennu-Njáls saga 17	12: 49–50	Þjóstólfr vs Glúmr Óleifsson				D_1
Brennu-Njáls saga 17	12: 51	Hrútr Herjólfsson vs Þjóstólfr				D_1
Brennu-Njáls saga 37	12: 97–8	Atli vs Víga-Kolr				D_1
Brennu-Njáls saga 38	12: 101	Brynjólfr rósta vs Atli				D_1
Brennu-Njáls saga 39	12: 104	Þórðr leysingjason vs Brynjólfr rósta				D_1
Brennu-Njáls saga 45	12: 115–17	Skarpheðinn vs Sigmundr Lambason				D_1
Brennu-Njáls saga 101	12: 258	Þangbrandr vs Þorkell				D_1
Þorskfirðinga saga 5	13: 190	Þórir et al. vs Háma, Hauknefr, et al.	B	F		D_{2-10}[87]
Þorskfirðinga saga 6	13: 191	Þórir et al. vs Gautr, Geirr, et al.	B			D_{2+}[88]
Flóamanna saga 16	13: 261	Þorgils vs Surtr járnhauss	B	F		D_1
Flóamanna saga 17	13: 263	Þorgils vs Gyrðr	B	F		
Flóamanna saga 17	13: 264–5	Þorgils vs Randviðr	B	F		D_1
Flóamanna saga 27	13: 311	Þorgils vs (another) Randviðr	B	F		D_1
Flóamanna saga 31	13: 317–18	Þorgils vs Bjálfi	B[89]			D_1
Flóamanna saga 34	13: 323	Þorgils vs Helgi				D_1
Kjalnesinga saga 9	14: 23	Búi vs Kolfiðr				
Kjalnesinga saga 18	14: 42–3	Jökull vs Búi				D_1
Víglundar saga 3	14: 65–6	Ketill vs 24 men		F		
Þórðar saga hreðu 13	14: 224	Þórðr vs Sörli				D_1
Brot af Þórðar sögu hreðu 2	14: 234–5	Þórðr Ketilsson vs Bárekr	B	F		D_1
Brot af Þórðar sögu hreðu 2	14: 236	Þórðr Þórðarson vs Bárekr	B	F		D_1
Totals: ca 132 duels[90]			29	48	5	96 $_{99-121+}$
Percentages: 100			22	36	4	73
Minimal Totals: ca 52 duels[91]			29	24	5	40 $_{43-65+}$
Minimal Percentages: 100			56	46	10	77

Table 5.2: Provisional List of Unconsummated Duels in the Family Sagas

B = involves a *berserkr*. F = fought on foreign soil.

Saga Reference (by chapter)	ÍF Reference	Principals	B?	F?
Egils saga 64	2: 201–3	Ljótr vs Friðgeirr	B	F
Gunnlaugs saga 12	3: 99–100	Norwegians mocking Gunnlaugr and Hrafn		F
Bjarnar saga Hítdœlakappa 4	3: 120–1	Kaldimarr vs Valdimarr	B	F
Heiðarvíga saga 15	3: 261	Narfi vs a Norwegian	B[92]	
Gísla saga 2	6: 9	Skeggi vs Kolbjǫrn		F
Grettis saga 19	7: 61	*berserkir* vs decent Norwegians	B	F
Grettis saga 40	7: 135	Snækollr vs Einarr	B	F
Vatnsdœla saga 33–4	8: 88–92	Finnbogi vs Þorsteinn, Bergr vs Jǫkull		
Vatnsdœla saga 47	8: 127	Þórarinn vs Hólmgǫngu-Starri[93]		
Hallfreðar saga 4	8: 149	Hallfreðr vs Gríss		
Hallfreðar saga 10	8: 190–3	Hallfreðr vs Gríss		
Kormáks saga 14	8: 255–6	Váli vs Bersi		
Kormáks saga 21	8: 279	Kormákr vs Þorvarðr		
Kormáks saga 21	8: 280–1	Kormákr vs Þorvarðr		
Víga-Glúms saga 14	9: 48	Víga-Glúmr vs Þjóðólfr		
Svarfdœla saga 7	9: 142	Moldi vs Herrøðr jarl	B	F
Ljósvetninga saga 6 [16–17]	10: 40–3	Þórir vs Guðmundr, Vigfúss vs Einarr		
Ljósvetninga saga 20 [30]	10: 102	Hrólfr et al. vs Eyjólfr et al.		
Vǫðu-Brands þáttr 4 [11]	10: 135	Þorkell vs Guðmundr		
Droplaugarsona saga 15	11: 178	Gauss vs Finngeirr	B	F
Brennu-Njáls saga 8	12: 27–8	Hrútr vs Mǫrðr		
Brennu-Njáls saga 24	12: 66–7	Gunnarr vs Hrútr		
Brennu-Njáls saga 42	12: 109	Þórðr leysingjason vs Sigmundr Lambason		
Brennu-Njáls saga 51	12: 131	Gunnarr vs Gizurr, Kolskeggr vs Geirr		
Brennu-Njáls saga 60	12: 152	Gunnarr vs Úlfr		
Brennu-Njáls saga 102	12: 265	Þórr vs Christ[95]	B	F
Flóamanna saga 15	13: 259	Óláfr jarl vs Surtr járnhauss	B	F
Flóamanna saga 17	13: 264	Randviðr vs Þrándr	B	F
Flóamanna saga 27	13: 310–11	(another) Randviðr vs Þorsteinn	B	F
Flóamanna saga 31	13: 317	Bjálfi vs Sámr	B	
Víglundar saga 6	14: 73	Þorgrímr vs Ketill		F
Finnboga saga 34[95]	14: 311	Jökull vs Finnbogi, Þorsteinn vs Bergr		

Totals: ca 31[96]   12   13
Percentages: 100   39   42

Notes

1 The ideas underlying this paper were first broached in a letter to the editor of the *American Historical Review* 105.5 (2000) 1868–9. Further-articulated versions were presented at the 36th International Congress on Medieval Studies at Kalamazoo (May 2001), and at seminars in the University of Illinois at Urbana-Champaign (January 2002) and Yeshiva University, New York (February 2002). I am grateful to Richard W. Burkhardt, S. Max Edelson, Will Lee, Kathryn J. Oberdeck, and other participants in these fora for illuminating comments and helpful criticisms. I am also indebted to Yad haNadiv in Jerusalem for the generous grant of a Fellowship in European and Western History. Special thanks go to Roberta Frank, Walter Goffart, Yael Levitte, and my fellow editors for their thoughtful suggestions. All translations are mine.

2 Editions: in *Austfirðinga sǫgur*, ed. Jón Jóhannesson, Íslenzk fornrit (henceforth ÍF) 11 (Reykjavik 1950), 69–79; also in *Austfirðinga sǫgur*, ed. Jakob Jakobsen, Samfund til udgivelse af gammel nordisk litteratur 29 (Copenhagen 1902–3), 73–92. Translations: Hermann Pálsson, 'Thorstein the Staff-Struck,' in his *Hrafnkel's Saga and Other Stories* (Harmondsworth 1971), 72–81; William Ian Miller, *Þorsteins þáttr stangarhǫggs*, in his *Bloodtaking and Peacemaking: Feud, Law, and Society in Saga Iceland* (Chicago and London 1990), 52–8; Anthony Maxwell, *The Tale of Thorstein Staff-Struck*, in *The Complete Sagas of Icelanders, including 49 Tales*, ed. Viðar Hreinsson et al., 5 vols (Reykjavik 1997), 4: 335–40, repr. in *Sagas of Icelanders: A Selection*, ed. Jane Smiley (New York 2000), 677–84.

3 On the features of the *hólmganga*, see, e.g., Gwyn Jones, 'Some Characteristics of the Icelandic "Hólmganga,"' *Journal of English and Germanic Philology* 32 (1933) 213–16; F. Wagner, 'L'Organisation du combat singulier au Moyen Âge dans les états scandinaves et dans l'ancienne république islandaise,' *Revue de Synthèse* 11 (1936) 49–54; Olav Bø, 'Holmgang,' in *Kulturhistorisk leksikon for nordisk middelalder, fra vikingetid til reformationstid* (henceforth *KLNM*), 22 vols (Copenhagen 1956–78), 6: cols 654–5; idem, '*Hólmganga* and *einvígi*,' *Mediaeval Scandinavia* 2 (1969) 133–4, 141, 143–4. The standardization of *hólmganga* practice can be easily overstated (as I argue below), but variations on all of the elements enumerated above do recur in many other Norse duels.

4 See, e.g., Jan de Vries, *Altnordische Literaturgeschichte*, 2nd ed., 2 vols, Grundriss der germanischen Philologie 15–16 (Berlin 1964–7), 2: 448–9; Paul Schach, 'Some Observations on the Generation-Gap in the Icelandic Saga,' in *The Epic in Medieval Society: Aesthetic and Moral Values*, ed. Harald Scholler (Tübingen 1977), 366–7, 380; Bjarne Fidjestøl, review of Theodore M. Andersson, *The Icelandic Family Saga: An Analytic Reading* (Cambridge, MA 1967), in *Maal og Minne* (1971) 81.

5 'Der Kampf unterscheidet sich in mehreren Punkten von allen anderen Zweikämpfen,' notes Gerd Sieg, enumerating first: 'niemand außer den beiden Gegner ist anwesend,' but he makes nothing of this point ('Die Zweikämpfe der Isländersagas,' *Zeitschrift für deutsches Altertum und deutsche Literatur* 95 [1966] 9).
6 The distinction between single and plural forms of fighting can be drawn too sharply (as I argue below); cf. V.G. Kiernan's (romantic) view: 'In older times, collective conflict tended to fall under the same kind of restraints as individual discord' (*The Duel in European History: Honour and the Reign of Aristocracy* [Oxford 1986], 22). Specifically in the Norse context, the sagas sometimes refer to 'duels' involving as many as two dozen combatants; see Wagner, 'L'Organisation,' 55, and n. 27 below.
7 See, e.g., Bertha S. Phillpotts, *Edda and Saga*, The Home University Library of Modern Knowledge (London 1931), 202; Heinrich M. Heinrichs, 'Die künstleriche Gestaltung des Þorsteins þáttr stangarhöggs,' in *Festschrift Walter Baetke*, ed. Kurt Rudolph, Rolf Heller, and Ernst Walter (Weimar 1966), 167–74; Sieg, 'Die Zweikämpfe,' 10, 24; Andersson, *The Icelandic Family Saga*, 3–6; Hermann Pálsson, 'Form and Meaning in Early Icelandic Fiction,' in *Les Vikings et leur civilisation: Problèmes actuels*, ed. Régis Boyer, Bibliothèque arctique et antarctique 5 (Paris 1976), 123–5; Edward G. Fichtner, 'The Calculus of Honor: Vengeance, Satisfaction and Reconciliation in the "Story of Thorstein Staff-Struck,"' in *Germanic Studies in Honor of Otto Springer*, ed. Stephen J. Kaplowitt (Pittsburgh 1978), 103–28; Peter Richardson, 'Tense, Structure, and Reception in Þorsteins þáttr stangarhǫggs,' *Arkiv för nordisk filologi* 110 (1995) 41–55.
8 Convenient discussions of the family sagas in their scholarly context include Carol J. Clover, 'Family Sagas, Icelandic,' in *Dictionary of the Middle Ages*, ed. Joseph R. Strayer et al., 13 vols (New York 1982–9), 4: 612–19; idem, 'Icelandic Family Sagas (Íslendingasögur),' in *Old Norse–Icelandic Literature: A Critical Guide*, ed. Clover and John Lindow, Islandica 45 (Ithaca 1985), 239–315; Vésteinn Ólason, 'Íslendingasögur,' in *Medieval Scandinavia: An Encyclopedia*, ed. Phillip Pulsiano et al. (New York and London 1993), 333–6.
9 Victor W. Turner's 'An Anthropological Approach to the Icelandic Saga,' in *The Translation of Culture: Essays to E. E. Evans-Pritchard*, ed. T.O. Beidelman (London 1971), 349–74, heralded the new sensibility in saga studies.
10 Cf. Miller's astute discussion of saga verisimilitude, *Bloodtaking and Peacemaking*, 46–8.
11 See Arthur Haase, 'Narrative Technique in Scenes of Combat in the Icelandic Family Sagas' (PhD diss. Yale University, 1970), 86–126; Jesse L. Byock, 'Hólmganga,' in *Medieval Scandinavia*, 289. Haase (following Sieg, 'Die Zweikämpfe') counts 24 saga duels; Jones, 'Some Characteristics,' ca 25. By my own rough tally, the family sagas mention or describe more than 80 (perhaps as

many as 160) duels; one to two of every five fights mentioned never actually take place (see tables 5.1 and 5.2). Several other narrative prose sources (kings' sagas, *Landnámabók*, Snorri's *Edda*, etc.) add a handful of references, as do skaldic stanzas and Saxo's Latin *Gesta Danorum*. The Icelandic law-codes do not contain any provisions for duelling, but the Norwegian *Ældre Gulathingslov* §216 (*Norges gamle Love indtil 1387* [henceforth *NGL*], ed. R. Keyser and P.A. Munch et al., 5 vols [Christiania 1846–95], 1: 74) and *Landslov* §5.19 (*NGL* 2: 90) supply information, as does the Swedish *Hednalagh* (relevant portion ed. Alvar Nelson in his 'Envig och ära: En studie över ett fornsvenskt lagfragment,' *Saga och Sed* [1944] 65–6). Occasional annal and diplomatic mentions round out this corpus. Unique, 9th-century evidence of Norse duelling practices is provided by the *Annales Bertiniani* s.a. 863, ed. G. Waitz, MGH Scriptores 5 (Hanover 1883), 66 (in English as *Annals of St. Bertin*, ed. and trans. Janet L. Nelson [Manchester and New York 1991], 110–11). Carolingian liberality in ascribing 'customary' behaviours to various Germanic peoples cautions, however, against accepting the reference to Norse tradition at face value, as does the animation of anti-duelling polemic in Frankish and papal circles of the mid-9th century (see Morton W. Bloomfield, 'Beowulf, Byrhtnoth, and the Judgement of God: Trial by Combat in Anglo-Saxon England,' *Speculum* 44 [1969] 552, 557).

12 See, e.g., Sieg, 'Die Zweikämpfe,' 13: 'Für gewöhnlich dienen die Zweikämpfe dazu, den Helden oder einen seiner Vorfahren als tüchtigen Krieger zu charakterisieren.' Cf. Kaaren Grimstad, 'A Comic Role of the Viking in the Family Sagas,' in *Studies for Einar Haugen: Presented by Friends and Colleagues*, ed. Evelyn Scherabon Firchow et al. (The Hague and Paris 1972), 249: 'the hero is always at a distinct disadvantage in his encounter with the villain. ... However, although the bully has the advantage in strength and invulnerability ... the hero possesses the intellectual advantage. ... [A]s in the folktale, the theme of brains over brawn is emphasized in the saga episodes. We find the same pattern in the familiar cat and mouse cartoons of our modern culture. ... The audience, aware of the trick about to be played on the cat and firmly on the side of the mouse, derives pleasure from seeing the anticipated defeat of the bully.'

13 On magic and paganism in the *hólmganga*, see, e.g., Magnus Olsen, '*Tjǫsnur* og *tjǫsnublót*,' *Arkiv för nordisk filologi* 26 (1910) 342–6; Gwyn Jones, 'The Religious Elements of the Icelandic "Hólmganga,"' *Modern Language Review* 27 (1932) 307–13; Wagner, 'L'Organisation,' 51–3, 57; Oskar Lundberg, 'Holmgång och Holmgångsblot,' *Arv* 2 (1946) 125–38; Bø, 'Holmgang,' col. 654; Marlene Ciklamini, 'The Old Icelandic Duel,' *Scandinavian Studies* 35.3 (1963) 181–90; and Byock, 'Hólmganga,' 289–90. On procedure, see works cited in n. 3 above. On the social matrix to which the *hólmganga* belongs, see, e.g., Jones, 'Some Characteristics,' 218–24; Wagner, 'L'Organisation,' 44–6, 59–60; Ciklamini, 'Old

Icelandic Duel,' 176–7, 190–1; idem, 'The Literary Mold of the *Hólm-gǫngumaðr,' Scandinavian Studies* 37.2 (1965) 117–18, 122–3; Bloomfield, 'Beowulf,' 549 ('apparently [the *hólmganga*] was frequently used as a kind of legal robbery'); R.S. Radford, 'Going to the Island: A Legal and Economic Analysis of the Medieval Icelandic Duel,' *Southern California Law Review* 62.2 (1989) 615–44; and Jón Viðar Sigurðsson, *Chieftains and Power in the Icelandic Commonwealth*, trans. Jean Lundskær-Nielsen, The Viking Collection 12 (Odense 1999), 170–9.

14 Bjarni announces before the fight: 'Þú skalt til einvígis *ganga* við mik í dag, Þorsteinn, *á hól* þenna, er hér er í túni' [You will meet me in single combat today, Þorsteinn, on this knoll that is here in the infield] (ÍF 11: 74, emphasis mine; cf. the idiom *ganga á hólm*).

15 Sieg, e.g., excludes from consideration 'die Fälle, in denen sich zwei Gegner mehr zufällig in einem an keine festen Regeln gebundenen Kampf gegenüberstehen' ('Die Zweikämpfe,' 1 n. 1). Nevertheless, he admits the *Þorsteins þáttr stangar-hǫggs* duel as a single exception to his otherwise narrow definition of *hólmgǫngur*.

16 For comprehensive overviews of Norse feuding practices, see esp. Jesse L. Byock, *Medieval Iceland: Society, Sagas, and Power* (Berkeley and Los Angeles 1988), and Miller, *Bloodtaking and Peacemaking*. If the essential characteristic of feud is privatized enforcement of the social contract, then the duel can be seen as the distilled acme of feuding logic: 'Wager-of-battle, like blood-vengeance, was a feud proceeding, and it relied upon personal effort for the realization of the participators' aims. ... Dahn has aptly called it "eine – allerdings geregelte und auf zwei Personen beschränkte – vom Gesetz selbst sanctionirte Fehde"' (Jones, 'Some Characteristics,' 205, citing Felix Dahn, *Studien zur Geschichte der germanischen Gottesurteile* [orig. Munich 1857; repr. in idem, *Bausteine*, 6 vols (Berlin 1879–84), 2: 57]).

17 Similarly, several historians have recently argued for broadening the definition of the duel form in other historical contexts where it allegedly represents a strictly delimited category; see, e.g., Elliott J. Gorn, ' "Gouge and Bite, Pull Hair and Scratch": The Social Significance of Fighting in the Southern Backcountry,' *American Historical Review* 90.1 (1985) 22–3, 41; Bertram Wyatt-Brown, *Southern Honor: Ethics and Behavior in the Old South* (New York and Oxford 1982), 353–4 ('Just as lesser folk spoke ungrammatically, so too they fought ungrammatically, but their actions were expressions of the same desire for prestige,' 353); Kenneth S. Greenberg, 'The Nose, the Lie, and the Duel in the Antebellum South,' *American Historical Review* 95.1 (1990) 58; Pieter Spierenburg, 'Knife Fighting and Popular Codes of Honor in Early Modern Amsterdam,' in *Men and Violence: Gender, Honor, and Rituals in Modern Europe and America*, ed. Spierenburg, History of Crime and Criminal Justice Series (Columbus 1998),

103–27; and Thomas W. Gallant, 'Honor, Masculinity, and Ritual Knife Fighting in Nineteenth-Century Greece,' *American Historical Review* 105.2 (2000) 360–2, 372–5. James R. Farr, *Hands of Honor: Artisans and Their World in Dijon, 1550–1650* (Ithaca and London 1988), 180, speaks of violent confrontations among artisans as 'an apparent parallel to the noble contests of honor.' For an opposite view see, e.g., Robert A. Nye, *Masculinity and Male Codes of Honor in Modern France*, Studies in the History of Sexuality (New York and Oxford 1993), 136.

18 *Bjarnar saga Hítdœlakappa* 19 [all saga citations refer to chapter numbers] (ÍF 3: 166). The saga concurs with this judgment, noting that '[Bjǫrn] grunaði, at [Þorsteinn] myndi vera flugumaðr' [(Bjǫrn) suspected that (Þorsteinn) might be an assassin]. Later in the saga, Bjǫrn is again attacked in an unchivalrous manner: while he is engaged in a horsefight, his arch-foe Þórðr Kolbeinsson stabs him from the sidelines; Bjǫrn requites the injury with a staff blow before the two are separated (*Bjarnar saga Hítdœlakappa* 23, ÍF 3: 175). A more successful back-stabbing occurs in *Vatnsdœla saga* 40 (ÍF 8: 106); though mortally injured, Guðbrandr Þorsteinsson does cut down his treacherous killer, Svartr. Another Svartr fails to murder Þorgils Þórðarson under similar circumstances in *Flóamanna saga* 19 (ÍF 13: 273), paying with his own life. In *Þorleifs þáttr jarlsskálds* 7 (ÍF 9: 226), the automaton Þorgarðr takes Þorleifr by surprise and strikes him a killing blow, melting into the ground when Þorleifr swipes back at him. Of all these examples, I consider only the last one a species of duel, since it involves face-to-face confrontation. The fact that Bjǫrn, Guðbrandr, and Þorgils all manage to strike back at their assailants does suggest combat (if not necessarily equitable), however, rather than simply treasonous attacks on helpless, unwary victims.

19 The distinctions can never be more than tentative, of course. For instance, group melee is frequently described in terms of serial single combats (see, e.g., *Hávarðar saga* 21, ÍF 6: 350–2). In *Víga-Glúms saga* 19, Vigfúss's two companions at first declare that they will not participate in an attack on Bárðr ('Þá mæltu austmenn, at þeir myndi heima hafa setit, ef þeir vissi ørendit, en létusk þó ekki lið veita mega, ef menn kœmi eigi til fulltings við Bárð, er fǫrunautr hans hleypði í brott' [Then the Norwegians declared that they would have stayed at home if they had known (Vigfúss's) intent; all the same, they made it known that they might offer no help if no one came to aid Bárðr, whose companion had run away]), but later, when they see that Vigfúss is being bested in single combat, they jump into the affray and finish Bárðr off (ÍF 9: 65).

20 Unarmed or stylised combat is not always sportsmanlike and danger-free, either; when treacherously set upon by an axe-wielding assassin, for instance, an unarmed Bjǫrn Hítdœlakappi tackles and strangles him to death (*Bjarnar saga Hítdœlakappa* 19, ÍF 3: 166). In like fashion, the unheroic-seeming Víga-Glúmr uses a piece of firewood to beat to death an infamous, heavily armoured viking (*Víga-Glúms saga* 6, ÍF 9: 19).

21 Other, less common terms include *kerganga*, lit. a 'tub-going' or 'sojourn in a confined space,' a (possibly jocular) hapax legomenon (*Flóamanna saga* 17, ÍF 13: 264–5; see Richard Perkins, '*Kerganga*,' in *Sjötíu Ritgerðir helgaðar Jakobi Benediktssyni 20. júlí 1977*, ed. Einar Pétursson and Jónas Kristjánsson, 2 vols [Reykjavik 1977], 2: 640–53); *kamp*[*r*?], lit. 'fight,' a late, non-saga term (possibly a Norwegianism; see, e.g., *Diplomatarium Islandicum*, 16 vols [Copenhagen and Reykjavik 1857–1952], 9: 727, §604 [27 April 1535]); and *hólmstefna*, lit. an 'islet summons' or 'islet meeting' (see, e.g., *Egils saga* 64, ÍF 2: 202). Also related are *hólmsǫk*, lit. an 'islet lawsuit,' i.e., 'cause for a duel' (*Bjarnar saga Hítdœlakappa* 32, ÍF 3: 201), and the adj. *hólmfœrr*, lit. 'islet-fit,' i.e., 'fit for combat, able-bodied' (*Landslov* §5.19, var. lect., *NGL* 2: 90 n.). References to a fight *á eyri*, 'on a sandy bank,' seem to be circumlocutions for *hólmganga* (see, e.g., *Helgaqviða Hjǫrvarðzsonar* st. 33, line 5, in *Edda: Die Lieder des Codex Regius nebst verwandten Denkmälern*, ed. Gustav Neckel, rev. Hans Kuhn, 4th ed., 2 vols [Heidelberg 1962–8], 1: 147; *Hallfreðar saga* 10 [v. 27], ÍF 8: 190; *Gunnlaugs saga* 11 [v. 17], ÍF 3: 93).

22 See details in Jones, 'Some Characteristics,' 212; Olav Bø, 'Einvígi,' *KLNM* 3 (1958), col. 534, and 'Holmgang,' col. 653; Byock, 'Hólmganga,' 289.

23 Thus Richard Cleasby and Gudbrand Vigfusson, *An Icelandic-English Dictionary*, 2nd ed., rev. William Craigie (Oxford 1957), s.v.; Jones, 'Some Characteristics,' 213–14; Bø, 'Holmgang,' col. 655. Kirsten Hastrup, *Culture and History in Medieval Iceland: An Anthropological Analysis of Structure and Change* (Oxford 1985), 214, notes the presence of islets at all known Icelandic *þing* [judicial assembly] sites. Peter Foote and David Wilson, *The Viking Achievement* (London 1970), 380, remark that 'islets must have been favoured as sites for such fighting: they had ready-made barriers which made interference and escape difficult, and possibly it was felt that they were neutral ground where blood might be shed without danger.' Cf. Bø, 'Einvígi,' col. 533, who remarks that *einvígi* is a fairly common place-name element in Iceland, denoting 'steder, der af naturen egne sig for enkeltmands forsvar' [places that naturally lend themselves to defence by a solitary man].

24 See Gertrude Schoepperle, *Tristan and Isolt: A Study of the Sources of the Romance*, 2 vols, New York University, Ottendorfer Memorial Series of Germanic Monographs 3–4 (Frankfurt a.M. and London 1913), 2: 338–67; Bloomfield, 'Beowulf,' 549–50 n. 11; Matthew Strickland, 'Provoking or Avoiding Battle? Challenge, Duel and Single Combat in Warfare of the High Middle Ages,' in *Armies, Chivalry and Warfare in Medieval Britain and France: Proceedings of the 1995 Harlaxton Symposium*, ed. Strickland, Harlaxton Medieval Studies 7 (Stamford 1998), 328–9.

25 Bø, 'Holmgang,' col. 655, and '*Hólmganga* and *einvígi*,' 133–4, summarize the evidence. See, primarily, *Kormáks saga* 10 (ÍF 8: 237–9); also *Egils saga* 64 (ÍF

2: 202, 204); *Svarfdæla saga* 9 (ÍF 9: 146–7); *Kjalnesinga saga* 9 (ÍF 14: 22–3). Cf. François Billacois, *Le Duel dans la société française des XVIe–XVIIe siècles: Essai du psychosociologie historique*, Civilisations et sociétés 73 (Paris 1986), 24–5 (in English as *The Duel: Its Rise and Fall in Early Modern France*, ed. and trans. Trista Selous [New Haven and London 1990], 10), on the significance of a designated duelling field in 16th- and 17th-century France.

26 'Þrír reitar skulu umhverfis feldinn, fets breiðir; út frá reitum skulu vera strengir fjórir, ok heita þat hǫslur; þat er vǫllr haslaðr, er svá er gǫrt' [Three grooves, a foot in breadth, are to be outlined around the cloak; outside the grooves shall be four cords, and those are called hazels; that which is so prepared is (called) a hazeled field] (*Kormáks saga* 10, ÍF 8: 237).

27 For a detailed description of a multiple *hólmganga*, see Snorri Sturluson's *Óláfs saga Tryggvasonar* 32 (in *Heimskringla*, ÍF 26: 268–9): 'Býðr Alvini Óláfi Tryggvasyni til hólmgǫngu um þetta mál. Þeir leggja með sér stefnulag til bardaga, ok skulu vera tólf hvárir. En er þeir finnask, mælir Óláfr svá við sína menn, at þeir geri svá sem hann gerir. Hann hafði mikla øxi. En er Alvini vildi hǫggva sverði til hans, þá laust hann sverðit ór hǫndum honum ok annat hǫgg sjálfan hann, svá at Alvini fell. Síðan batt Óláfr hann fast. Fóru svá allir menn Alvina, at þeir váru barðir ok bundnir' [Alvini offers Óláfr Tryggvason a duel over this matter. They agree on a time for the fight, and were to have twelve men each. But when they meet, Óláfr instructs his men to do as he does. He had a big axe. Just when Alvini was going to strike him with the sword, he knocked first the sword out of his hands, then him with another blow, so that Alvini fell. Then Óláfr bound him fast. So it went for all of Alvini's men, that they were beaten and bound]. From Óláfr's words to his men to observe his actions and emulate him, it would seem that the sg. noun refers to a dozen discrete *hólmgǫngur* fought simultaneously. See also *Ljósvetninga saga* 20 [30] (ÍF 10: 102), where a quadruple *hólmganga* is contemplated. For multiple duels in other historical contexts, see, e.g., Christopher Boehm, *Blood Revenge: The Anthropology of Feuding in Montenegro and Other Tribal Societies* (Lawrence, KS 1984), 118; Billacois, *Le Duel*, 107 (*The Duel*, 65); Ute Frevert, *Ehrenmänner: Das Duell in der bürgerlichen Gesellschaft* (Munich 1991), 23–5 (in English as *Men of Honour: A Social and Cultural History of the Duel*, trans. Anthony Williams [Cambridge 1995], 11–12); Nye, *Masculinity*, 25.

28 Gallant, 'Honor,' 363. Similarly, James Kelly, *'That Damn'd Thing Called Honour': Duelling in Ireland 1570–1860* (Cork 1995), 177: '[H]owever much blame or praise is directed at individual seconds, it was the principals alone who made the final decision [to fight] and there were invariably some so incandescent with rage that no amount of intercession could persuade them to conclude a rencontre without bloodshed' (see also 265–6); Spierenburg, 'Knife Fighting,' 111: 'Everybody might be involved in the preliminaries, but when two men had

actually started to fight, others normally stepped aside.' And cf. Frevert, *Ehrenmänner*, 195 (*Men of Honour*, 149): 'Das männliche Individuum begab sich einsam, bar jedes familialen Anhangs, auf das Feld der Ehre, wo es nur die Gesellschaft von Männern zuließ, die es in seinem Vorhaben unterstützten und ihm das Gefühl vermittelten, in einer Gemeinschaft Gleichgesinnter aufgehoben zu sein. Beim eigentliche Waffengang trat dann auch diese Gemeinschaft zurück, und beide Duellanten standen sich, umrahmt zwar von Sekundanten, Zeugen und Ärzten, als einzelne gegenüber, Auge in Auge mit dem Tod.'

29 Gallant, 'Honor,' 370–1, emphasis mine.

30 Kiernan, *The Duel*, 137, emphases mine. Similarly, Frevert complains that '[s]elbst die Einführung von Sekundanten vermochte den Zweikampf der Frühen Neuzeit nicht grundlegend zu "zivilisieren." Anstatt, wie später überlich, auf Regelkonformität und kämpferische Fairness zu achten, verstanden sich die Sekundanten des 16. und 17. Jahrhunderts als Helfer und Beschützer ihrer Klienten und griffen *aktiv* in das Gefecht ein' (*Ehrenmänner*, 25, emphasis mine; *Men of Honour*, 12). Kelly, noting that seconds' 'main function [by the mid-1700s] was to ensure fair play ... serv[ing] to mitigate the undisciplined character of so much [earlier] Irish duelling,' is outspoken in his characterization of earlier duels as 'generally bloody and, not infrequently, vicious encounters in which ill-temper usually triumphed over etiquette.' In the 17th century, 'it was quite normal for seconds [when present] to support their principals by fighting by their side,' with the consequence 'that seconds were as likely to get killed or injured as the principals' (*Damn'd Thing*, 74, 49, 32).

31 See Haase, 'Narrative Technique,' 86–9. My analysis suggests that as many as 3 duels out of every 4 result in at least one death. The overall body count may be as high as sixty-some dead in 40 engagements, if not twice these numbers and more. See table 5.1.

32 Fists: see *Kormáks saga* 27 (ÍF 8: 299); fangs: see *Egils saga* 65 (ÍF 2: 210). Cf. also a fatal wrestling match in *Kjalnesinga saga* 18 (ÍF 14: 42–3).

33 Jana Kate Schulman, 'Women Between the Texts: Legal License and Literary Discourse in Medieval Iceland' (PhD diss. University of Minnesota, 1995), 190. Many duel deaths seem to stem from narrative necessity rather than verisimilitude. The stock character of the *berserkr* is involved in over half of all circumstantially described duels (29 of 52, ca 56 per cent; see n. 91 below for duels omitted from this count); a similar proportion (24, ca 46 per cent) of all duels take place outside Iceland, i.e., in locales where saga authors' commitment to realism appears generally more lax. (Indeed, 22 duels, ca 42 per cent of the total, both take place on foreign soil and involve *berserkir*.) Fatality rates in such cases are staggering: lives are lost in ca 83 per cent of duels involving *berserkir* (24 of 29), ca 83 per cent of foreign duels (20 of 24), and ca 86 per cent of duels with both features (19 of 22), as opposed to ca 71 per cent (15 of 21) of duels distinguished by neither

feature. Of 40 identifiably lethal duels, 20 (ca 50 per cent) are set outside Iceland, 24 (ca 60 per cent) involve *berserkir*, 19 (ca 48 per cent) share both features, and only 15 (ca 38 per cent) are marked by neither.

34 See, e.g., Dickson D. Bruce, Jr, *Violence and Culture in the Antebellum South* (Austin and London 1979), 36–8; Billacois, *Le Duel*, 39, 74, 332 (*The Duel*, 19, 42, 197); Kiernan, *The Duel*, 20–1; Nye, *Masculinity*, 141–2.

35 'Þá átti Kormákr at hǫggva; síðan hjó hann til Bersa; hann brá við Hvítingi; tók Skǫfnungr af oddinn af Hvítingi fyrir framan véttrimina, ok hraut sverðsoddrinn á hǫnd Kormáki, ok skeindisk hann á þumalfingri, ok klofnaði kǫggullinn, ok kom blóð á feldinn. Eptir þat gengu menn á milli þeira ok vildu eigi, at þeir berðisk lengr' (*Kormáks saga* 10, ÍF 8: 238). Cf. *Gunnlaugs saga* 11 (ÍF 3: 94–5): 'Hrafn átti fyrr at hǫggva, er á hann var skorat, ok hjó hann í skjǫld Gunnlaugs ofanverðan, ok brast sverðit þegar sundr undir hjǫltunum, er til var hǫggvit af miklu afli. Blóðrefillinn hraut upp af skildinum ok kom á kinn Gunnlaugi, ok skeindisk hann heldr en eigi. Þá hljópu feðr þeira þegar á millim ok margir aðrir menn' [Hrafn was to strike first, for he had been challenged, and he swung at the top of Gunnlaugr's shield; the sword snapped at once beneath the hilt, for it had been swung too forcefully. The sword-point bounced off the shield and hit Gunnlaugr on the cheek, and he got rather more scratched than not. Then their fathers ran between them at once and (so did) many other men]; *Kjalnesinga saga* 9 (ÍF 14: 23): 'Búi hjó þá til Kolfinns ok gerði ónýtan fyrir honum skjöldin ok særði hann miklu sari á höndina; var Kolfiðr þegar óvígr. Menn hlupu þá í millum þeira, ok váru þeir skildir' [Then Búi struck at Kolfiðr and rendered his shield useless, wounding his arm severely; Kolfiðr was immediately *hors de combat*. People then ran in between them and they were separated]. Cf. also *Kormáks saga* 12 (ÍF 8: 250), where it seems that only the furious speed with which insults and injuries are traded prevents the auxiliaries from separating the principals before both have been wounded.

36 Cf. Billacois, *Le Duel*, 332: 'Une simple égratignure, une seule goutte de sang peut permettre de conclure honorablement un duel' (*The Duel*, 197); Kormákr accepts his defeat on the technicality, though not very graciously. The analogous scene in *Gunnlaugs saga* 11 (ÍF 3: 95, quoted above, n. 35) demonstrates how contestable the outcome might remain: Hrafn claims victory because a shard from his shattered sword drew first blood, but Gunnlaugr refuses to concede it, pointing out that his rival is now effectively disarmed and hence incapacitated.

37 See, e.g., Kelly, *Damn'd Thing*, on the theory: 113, 170; and numerous examples: 105, 120 (Table 3.8), 140, 141, 144, 145–6 (unsuccessful), 151, 156, 173, 175, 185 n. 99, 194–5 (unsuccessful), 201, 207, 208, 209, 214 (Table 5.6), 227, 228, 269.

38 See *Vápnfirðinga saga* 18 (ÍF 11: 61–2): 'Eyvindr svarar: "Fǫrum vér sem skjótast ok hǫfum klæði með oss ok kǫstum á vápnin." Eyvindr tók upp stokk ok reiðir um ǫxl sér ok hljóp þar út af garðinum. ... Þá kom at Eyvindr ok gekk svá hart

fram með setstokkin milli manna, at þeir hruku hvárutveggju vegna. Konur váru með honum ok kǫstuðu klæðum á vápnin, ok stǫðvaðisk bardaginn' [Eyvindr answers, 'Let's go as quickly as possible and take clothes with us and throw them over the weapons.' Eyvindr picked up a beam and hikes it over his shoulder and then ran out of the yard. ... Then Eyvindr arrived and went in with his crossbeam so vigorously among the men that they shrank back on both sides. The women were with him and they threw clothes over the weapons, and the fighting subsided]. For similar scenes, in which bystanders physically interpose themselves between warring groups (sometimes with tragic results), see, e.g., *Eyrbyggja saga* 9 and 18 (ÍF 4: 16, 36); *Grœnlendinga þáttr* 5 (ÍF 4: 287); *Laxdœla saga* 14 (ÍF 5: 29); *Grettis saga* 15 (ÍF 7: 43–4); *Vatnsdœla saga* 32 (ÍF 8: 86–7); *Ljósvetninga saga* 14 [24] and 17 [27] (ÍF 10: 80–1, 89–90); *Þórðar saga hreðu* 3 and 11–12 (ÍF 14: 178, 218, 220, 222). In a well-known passage in *Brennu-Njáls saga* 139 (ÍF 12: 371–3), the Machiavellian Snorri *goði* eggs on two other chieftains to attack a third, promising that his own men will step in once all those for whom compensation can be paid have been killed – from a group perspective, a (rather sinister) equivalent of individual fighting *au premier sang*.

39 J.K. Campbell, *Honour, Family and Patronage: A Study of Institutions and Moral Values in a Greek Mountain Community* (Oxford 1964), 97. (In contrast, Boehm finds that it is precisely those most implicated by kinship obligations who intervene to restrain Montenegrin fighters: *Blood Revenge*, 95–9; photos on 95–8 and 104–5.) Cf. Gallant, 'Honor,' 376.

40 Julian Pitt-Rivers, *The Fate of Shechem; or, The Politics of Sex: Essays in the Anthropology of the Mediterranean*, Cambridge Studies in Social Anthropology 19 (Cambridge 1977), 32; cf. Gallant, 'Honor,' 376. Cf. also Miguel Vale de Almeida, *The Hegemonic Male: Masculinity in a Portuguese Town*, New Directions in Anthropology 4 (Providence and Oxford 1996), 101–2: 'The brawl that followed was very ritualistic, as they almost always are: they take place in public and there is always someone there to restrain the contenders just in time.'

41 Michael Herzfeld, *The Poetics of Manhood* (Princeton 1985), 51. Boehm, *Blood Revenge*, 16–17, is only slightly less explicit: 'my cultural intuitions [in retorting to an insult] were sound. Public opinion was with me. ... [My adversary] was quite angry, visibly very disturbed over losing out in public to a victim who usually behaved rather meekly. ... Afterwards I was congratulated in private by several people [who] also suggested, with knowing looks, that it was just as well that there had been a large group of people present' (cf. also 91–2, 145).

42 Cf. Miller, *Bloodtaking and Peacemaking*, 260: 'Peacemaking [by physically intervening in a fight] required strength and courage more than negotiating skills. One suspects, however, that these frontline peacemakers were assisted in their efforts by the expectation on the part of the combatants that they would be separated by bystanders.'

43 See, e.g., Gallant, 'Honor,' 376: 'Even among contemporary groups known for their sensitivity to honor in Greece and elsewhere, then, violence in defense of reputation has been largely *reduced* to ritualized symbolic forms. *This was definitely not the case in the past*' (emphases mine); similarly, Boehm, *Blood Revenge*, 146 (but cf. 94 on other types of events likely to go unrecorded). Contrast Farr, who (though he finds the artisans of Dijon ca 1600 'an exceedingly rough and tumble lot, easily angered, and often at each other's throats') also notes that 'the public nature of most quarrels and the rapidity with which peace-keeping neighbors arrived at a scene of conflict may ... reflect a general wish to prevent blows. Brandish a knife or a sword, shriek insults and threats, and one could expect that neighbors would quickly arrive to stop the action' (*Hands of Honor*, 186).

44 '[Þ]at kveld ... var Guðmundr allkátr. En eptir um nóttina ... vaknaði Vigfúss Víga-Glúmsson ok mælti til Guðmundar: "Lítt sefr þú í nótt, Guðmundr. Hyggr þú eigi gótt til hólmgǫngunnar við Þóri?"... "En ek kann þér gott ráð hér til, þat er virðing þín megi af vaxa, en þú verðr þó í engri mannhættu. ... [M]un ek skora til hólmgǫngu Einar bróður þinn, at hann berisk nú við mik í dag. ... Horfir Einari engum mun betr hólmgangan við mik en þér við Þóri. Nú látum hann first hafa hvikunarrúmit, ef svá er, at hann Þórir eigi á hólm at ganga. En ef hann bersk við mik, þá mun ek drepa hann. *En hǫfðingjar munu leita annars ráðs en þit brœðr séð hǫggnir hér niðr á þinginu báðir*"' (*Ljósvetninga saga* 6 [17], ÍF 10: 40–1, emphasis mine). A somewhat similar dynamic unfolds in a less formal confrontation in *Eyrbyggja saga* 57 (ÍF 4: 158–60): Óspakr Kjallaksson and his ruffians intend to rob a group of whale-flensers of their catch. Þórir Gull-Harðarson, who tries to oppose them, is quickly knocked unconscious. When he comes to, Þórir berates his comrades for standing idly by while they are despoiled – but takes care to leap vigorously to his feet only when Óspakr's gang are safely away.

45 As Theodore Andersson and William Ian Miller comment, '[one] important reason people went to law [was that p]rocessing a lawsuit forced the parties to meet, but to meet in the presence of a large number of neutral parties. These neutrals were generally a force for peace. And ... the litigants did not always leave the matter of a strong third-party presence to chance; rather, they ensured their presence as an indirect consequence of the support-mustering process. Litigants could expect that if things threatened to get too far out of hand, the onlookers would mobilize to keep things within bounds' (*Law and Literature in Medieval Iceland* [Stanford 1989], 31).

46 ' "[M]enn þykkjask eigi vita, hvat Þorsteinn stangarhǫgg mun þess gera, at þér muni þurfa þykkja at hefna. Hefir hann nú vegit húskarla þína þrjá ... ok eru þér mjǫk mislagðar hendr í kné."... Bjarni svarar: ... "[E]n hlýða mun ek þér, hvat er þú mælir. Hefir Þorsteinn ok fá saklausa drepit"' (*Þorsteins þáttr stangarhǫggs*, ÍF 11: 74).

47 *Þorsteins þáttr stangarhǫggs* (ÍF 11: 75). On *hvǫt*, see Rolf Heller, *Die literarische Darstellung der Frau in den Isländersagas*, Saga: Untersuchungen zur nordischen Literatur- und Sprachgeschichte 2 (Halle [Saale] 1958), 98–122; Carol J. Clover, 'Hildigunnr's Lament,' in *Structure and Meaning in Old Norse Literature*, ed. John Lindow, Lars Lönnroth, and Gerd Wolfgang Weber (Odense 1986), 141–83; Miller, *Bloodtaking and Peacemaking*, 212–14; Judith Jesch, *Women in the Viking Age* (Woodbridge 1991), 188–91; Jenny Jochens, *Old Norse Images of Women* (Philadelphia 1996), 162–203; cf. Preben Meulengracht Sørensen, *The Unmanly Man: Concepts of Sexual Defamation in Early Northern Society*, trans. Joan Turville-Petre (Odense 1983), esp. 21, 179. Heller, Jesch (p. 190), and Jochens (174–203) view *hvǫt* as pure literary convention; Clover (180), Miller (212), and Sørensen (179) argue in favour of its social plausibility. Cf. Cecilia Morgan, ' "In Search of a Phantom Misnamed Honour": Duelling in Upper Canada,' *Canadian Historical Review* 76.4 (1995) 543, on 'women [in 19th-century English Canada, who] could help shape the events that might lead up to a duel, possibly even instigating them.'

48 Kiernan, *The Duel*, 140. 'Young hotheads were always objectionable picks [to serve as seconds] because a phlegmatic temperament was indispensable to the negotiation of a mutually amicable arrangement,' notes Kevin McAleer. Thus Irishmen, for instance, in a fine display of prejudicial profiling, 'were expressly precluded from consideration in eighteenth-century England' (*Dueling: The Cult of Honor in Fin-de-Siècle Germany* [Princeton 1994], 49); cf. Kelly, *Damn'd Thing*, 74, 176, 263–4. See also Bruce, *Violence and Culture*, 36: 'Daniel Dugger proposed [merely to fire without hurting his opponent], but was dissuaded by his second's refusal to serve in such an instance.'

49 See, e.g., Nye, *Masculinity*, 140.

50 ' "Gerðu eigi þat," segir hon, "at hætta þér einn undir vápn heljarmannsins" ' (*Þorsteins þáttr stangarhǫggs*, ÍF 11: 75).

51 Editorial of 29 January 1845; quoted by Bruce, *Violence and Culture*, 36.

52 See, e.g., *Gísla saga* 1 (ÍF 6: 4–5): 'Bjǫrn gerir Ara tvá kosti, hvárt hann vill heldr berjask við hann í hólmi ... eða vill hann selja honum í hendr konu sína. Hann kaus skjótt, at hann vill heldr berjask en hvárttveggja yrði at skǫmm, hann ok kona hans. ... Þá berjask þeir, ok lýkr svá, at Ari fellr ok lætr líf sitt. Þykkisk Bjǫrn hafa vegit til landa ok konu. Gísli segir, at hann vill heldr láta líf sitt en þetta gangi fram, vill hann ganga á hólm við Bjǫrn' [Bjǫrn gives Ari two options, whether he would rather fight a duel with him ... or he would give over his wife to him. He chose quickly, that he would rather fight than bring calumny upon them both, himself and his wife. ... Then they fight, and it ends thus: that Ari falls and loses his life. It seems to Bjǫrn that he has won the land and the woman. Gísli says that he would rather lose his life than let this come about, (that) he wishes to fight a duel with Bjǫrn].

53 'Ljótr ... mælti: "Gakk þú hingat, inn mikli maðr, á hólminn ok bersk við mik, ef þú ert allfúss til, ok reynum með okkr; er þat miklu jafnligra en ek berjumk við Friðgeir, því at ek þykkjumk eigi at meiri maðr, þó at ek leggja hann at jǫrðu"' (*Egils saga* 64, ÍF 2: 203).

54 Gallant, 'Reply to a Letter to the Editor,' *American Historical Review* 105.5 (2000) 1869, emphasis his. Cf. the normative tone of indignation adopted by Kiernan, Frevert, and Kelly when describing early modern duels in which seconds pitched into the fighting (cited above, n. 30).

55 See Haase, 'Narrative Technique,' 90: 'The main combatants are usually assisted by seconds, who hold their shields for them'; cf. Jones, 'Some Characteristics,' 214–15; Bø, 'Holmganga,' col. 655. I have located only seven cases where shield-bearing seconds are mentioned (see table 5.1). In numerous other instances, however, combatants are accompanied by partisans whose precise role is unstated; see, e.g., *Kormáks saga* 12 (ÍF 8: 250): 'Óláfr pái fær Bersa lið til holms; var Þórðr Arndísarson vanr at halda skildi fyrir Bersa, en nú varð þat ekki; gengr Bersi þó til holms, ok er eigi nefndr skjaldsveinn hans' [Óláfr Peacock supports Bersi in the duel. Þórðr Arndísarson usually held the shield for Bersi, but now that did not happen. Still, Bersi went into the ring and his shield-bearer is not named].

56 'Kormákr skal halda skildi fyrir Steinari. ... Bersi hjó til Steinars, en Hvíting festi í járnrendingunni á skildi Steinars. Kormákr brá upp skildinum; í því hjó Steinarr til Bersa, ok kom á skjaldarrǫndina ok hljóp af skildinum ok á þjón-hnappa Bersa' [Kormákr is to hold the shield in front of Steinarr. ... Bersi struck at Steinarr, but Hvítingr stuck in the iron rim of Steinarr's shield. Kormákr wrenched the shield up; at that (moment) Steinarr struck at Bersi, and (the blow) landed on the shield's rim and bounced off the shield and to Bersi's buttocks] (*Kormáks saga* 12, ÍF 8: 250).

57 Bø, '*Hólmganga* and *Einvígi*,' 144. Cf. Jones's understated allusion to this incident: 'A good second was a great help to his principal' ('Some Characteristics,' 215).

58 Bruce, *Violence and Culture*, 35, quoting from an (anonymous?) article on 'Duelling in America,' *Living Age* 15 (1847) 468. Cf. McAleer, *Dueling*, 49.

59 Seconds' actions could as easily jeopardize combatants as enhance their chances; not surprisingly, perhaps, a duellist in one classic saga passage spurns the help of a second and lauds the merit of trusting only one's own prowess: 'sjálfs hǫnd er hollust' [one's own hand is most reliable] (*Víga-Glúms saga* 4, ÍF 9: 12; for the idiom, cf. *Færeyinga saga* 48, ed. Ólafur Halldórsson, Stofnun Árna Magnússonar á Íslandi 29 [Reykjavik 1987], 121). In modern pistol duels, the ability of seconds to influence the outcome of the engagement directly was also no metaphor: the mechanics of the smoothbore pistol meant that imperfect loading 'not only greatly reduced the shot's muzzle velocity but rendered its exterior ballistics extremely fickle' (McAleer, *Dueling*, 66; cf. Kelly, *Damn'd Thing*, 176–7).

Seconds' agency is further exemplified by an incident from Spain in the 1830s, in which the principals, who could not be dissuaded from fighting, were set 'on the beach at San Sebastian, on sand too loose to enable either of them to shoot straight' (Kiernan, *The Duel*, 140).

60 'Often men of various positions in the local hierarchy ac[t] as a Greek chorus in a Sophoclean drama,' notes Wyatt-Brown; they manipulate the duelling principals in a '[t]yranny of the community' (*Southern Honor*, 356–7). 'The prolific [19th-century] duelist and journalist Henri Rochefort observed that the duel could be abolished straightaway in France "if there weren't always four gentlem[e]n available to draw up a duel-report, and fifty newspapers to print it. In ninety-one out of ninety-two cases, one duels for the gallery. Suppress the gallery and you exterminate the duel"' (McAleer, *Dueling*, 192). On duelling as a frank mechanism for promoting personal and political reputation, see Nye, *Masculinity*, 187–200. Cf. also Frevert, *Ehrenmänner*, 212–14 (*Men of Honour*, 170–1).

61 Gallant, 'Honor,' 375. '[T]he central, unifying tenet of [the duelling code] was the right and responsibility of certain men to defend their reputations with a public display of physical courage,' notes Morgan ('Phantom,' 531; see also 551). See also Bruce, *Violence and Culture*, 37–41; Wyatt-Brown, *Southern Honor*, 350–61; Billacois, *Le Duel*, 136, 345–52 (*The Duel*, 81–2, 205–8); McAleer, *Dueling*, 81. (Radford only concludes that Norse duelling 'was not primarily an expression of a code of honor' due to excessive legal formalism; 'Going to the Island,' 616. Contrast his discussion of audience participation in lawsuits, 636.)

62 An incident in *Laxdœla saga* 87 (ÍF 5: 246), though it involves a battle of two groups rather than two individuals, clearly demonstrates the utility of menacing combatants with a widening of the conflict: 'Nú er at segja frá Óttari; hann ríðr upp á Vǫllu til Ljóts, ok þegar þeir finnask, mælti Óttarr: "Eigi er nú setuefni, Ljótr," sagði hann, "ok fylg þú nú virðing þinni er þér liggr laus fyrir." "Hvat er nú helzt í því, Óttarr?" "Ek hygg, at þeir berisk hér niðri við ána Þorsteinn af Hálsi ok Bolli, ok er þat in mesta hamingja, at skirra vandræðum þeira." ... Ljótr brá við skjótt ok við nǫkkura menn, ok þeir Óttarr báðir. Ok er þeir koma til árinnar, berjask þeir Bolli sem óðast; váru þá fallnir þrír menn af Þorsteini. Þeir Ljótr ganga fram í meðal þeira snarliga, svá at þeir máttu nær ekki at hafask. Þá mælti Ljótr: "Þér skuluð skilja þegar í stað," segir hann, "ok er þó nú œrit at orðit. Vil ek einn gera milli yðvar um þessi mál, en ef því níta aðirhvárir, þá skulu vér veita þeim atgǫngu"' [To tell now of Óttarr; he rides up to Ljótr at Vǫllr, and as soon as they meet, Óttarr declared: 'The business at hand isn't to be sitting, Ljótr,' he said; 'now do what your honour (demands) and that's plain to see.' 'What's mostly involved in that, Óttarr?' 'I believe that they're fighting here below at the river, Þorsteinn of Háls and Bolli, and it would be a most fortunate thing to curb their hostilities.' Ljótr jumped up quickly and he and several men (accompanied)

Óttarr. And when they reach the river, Bolli and his men are fighting furiously: three men of Þorsteinn's had already fallen. Ljótr and his men quickly go forth between them, so that they were unable to go at each other at all. Then Ljótr spoke: 'You are to separate at once,' he says; 'quite enough has been done now. I alone will rule between you in this case, and if either of you refuses, we will attack him']. Cf. *Eyrbyggja saga* 44 (ÍF 4: 123).

63 Numerous first-person testimonies from duellists of later ages bear witness to their having undertaken this violent course of action in a conscious effort to conform to society's expectations of them. 'All defenses of the Practice [of dueling] are derived from sophistry,' opined a 19th-century Virginian, 'whilst most of the arguments against it are pure reason and common sense. Yet so strong is the force of imperious *opinion*, that I may again be *compelled* to fight' (Francis Gildart Ruffin's diary, 13 June 1838 [Richmond: Virginia Historical Society], as quoted by Bruce, *Violence and Culture*, 28). 'Various gossip mongers, as [Andrew] Jackson himself recognized, had more to do with staging the event than either of the duelists,' writes Wyatt-Brown of Jackson's famous shoot-out with Charles Dickinson in 1806 (*Southern Honor*, 356); cf. Frevert, *Ehrenmänner*, 218 (*Men of Honour*, 175–6); McAleer, *Dueling*, 69–70. See also Gorn, 'Gouge and Bite,' 27–33, on the interpenetration of actual fighting and fighting folklore. In the age of mass media, men of honour also became adept at manipulating their opponents by publicizing partisan accounts of conflicts; see, e.g., Wyatt-Brown, *Southern Honor*, 558 n. 46; Kiernan, *The Duel*, 138–9; Greenberg, 'The Nose,' 62; Edward Muir, *Mad Blood Stirring: Vendetta & Factions in Friuli during the Renaissance* (Baltimore and London 1993), 265–72; McAleer, *Dueling*, 192; Kelly, *Damn'd Thing*, 109; Morgan, 'Phantom,' 553 ('Ironically, attempts to keep duels out of the public eye seemed to result in their landing in the pages of the press; it is hard to imagine a more "public" spot than behind the colonial seat of government,' a favoured duelling locale in Toronto around the turn of the 19th century).

64 Several men mentioned in the family sagas and elsewhere are nicknamed 'Hólmgǫngu-' [the Dueller]; next to nothing is known about their careers or how they earned their sobriquets. Contrasting the reputation of Hólmgǫngu-Bersi (the only renowned duellist of whom any details are known) with that of a minor villain, Þórarinn, a saga character comments: 'Mun nǫkkut alllíkt garpskapr Bersa eða stulðir Þórarins?' [Is there any similarity between Bersi's bravery and Þórarinn's thievery?] (*Kormáks saga* 15, ÍF 8: 257); as Ciklamini notes, '[i]n this scene, [Bersi's career] of duels has found its appropriate end. Bersi's stature has been established even without revealing how [he] had acquired his epithet "the Duelist," in duels preceding the events narrated by the saga. What we know of Bersi's self proclaimed record of thirty one slayings is that he has killed two

[*recte*: one] opponents in duels. We need not know more' ('Literary Mold,' 126). Cf. Kelly, *Damn'd Thing*, 104, on the effect that a (false) rumour about a duel he allegedly participated in had on Sir George Macartney's reputation in 1769 Dublin.

65 See Shlomith Rimmon-Kenan, *Narrative Fiction: Contemporary Poetics*, New Accents (London and New York 1983), 17–18, 48. Contrast Bloomfield, 'Beowulf,' 552: 'The oracle, usually though not always, attempted to determine the truth of the future; the ordeal [of which the duel is a sub-category] that of the past.'

66 Greenberg, 'The Nose,' 67. It is crucial to note that duelling aims to avert loss of face with respect to society at large, not merely vis-à-vis an individual: '[Eighteenth-century Irishmen] felt compelled to [duel] because displays of the "white feather" would expose them "to insufferable insults, not only f[ro]m the challenger, but from every other impertinent coxcomb, who would fain establish his own reputation of courage on the known timidity of a man branded with the infamous name of coward"' (Kelly, *Damn'd Thing*, 280, citing M. Corr, 'Reminiscences of duelling in Ireland,' *Macmillan's Magazine* 29 [1873–4] 306, 312–13).

67 Cf. Herzfeld, *Poetics of Manhood*, 80–1: '[In coffeehouse confrontations between feuding kin groups, o]utsiders both provoke and restrain violence. They provoke it implicitly, since they provide the audience in front of which the patrigroup's reputation is at stake. They also restrain that same violence, usually through physical intervention – whether by expelling the "offending" visitors, or by holding back their furious covillagers. ... On the mountainside, by contrast, with no critical eyes watching them, some members of the dead man's patrigroup regularly share food and drink with [the opposing kin group's] shepherds – an amiable reciprocity that leaves the fighting to those most immediately involved.'

68 Campbell notes that, while knives are readily drawn in public brawls, 'in boundary disputes, where two shepherds may sometimes find themselves alone, quarrels are more often decided with iron-hooked shepherds' crooks, capable of ugly but generally not mortal wounds' (*Honour, Family, and Patronage*, 97). Kelly's account of an 1807 duel, conducted 'in the absence of seconds or other witnesses,' is complementary; when one combatant was shot dead, the survivor was hanged as a murderer (*Damn'd Thing*, 233).

69 Gérard Genette, *Figures III*, Collection poétique (Paris 1972), 71–6; in English as *Narrative Discourse: An Essay in Method*, trans. Jane E. Lewin (Ithaca 1980), 25–32. Lewin renders *histoire* as 'story' and *récit* as 'narrative.' Different authors use different terms for this conceptual pair, or closely analogous ones; Rimmon-Kenan, for instance, speaks of 'story' and 'text,' respectively (*Narrative Fiction*, 3), while the traditions of Russian formalism have disseminated the terms *sjužet* and *fabula*. I prefer Genette's (untranslated) terminology mainly for reasons of convenience: for one thing, it has acquired a degree of currency; for another, it allows me to retain the relevant English vocabulary for less technical uses.

128 Oren Falk

70 Ben Kaspit, 'Ariel Sharon Now Learns in Person the Lesson that Finished Baraq,' *Ma'ariv* Musaf leShabbat (Friday, 30 March 2001): 4–5 and 25, at 4 [original in Hebrew].
71 Mark Twain, *A Tramp Abroad* (New York 1879), 59, as quoted by McAleer, *Dueling*, 190.
72 Adapted and expanded from Haase, 'Narrative Technique,' 89–90. This list and the next cannot claim to be exhaustive. Aside from duels I may have missed, problems in delimiting the family saga genre and in defining a duel prevent me from establishing an entirely closed database. The lists have been compiled mostly in the old-fashioned manner, by reading through the sagas; supplementary keyword searches were conducted using the online corpus at <http://www.snerpa.is/net/fornrit.htm> (normalized as Modern Icelandic).
73 As suggested above, duel narratives involving *berserkir* are usually highly conventional and unlikely to be realistic; cf. Sieg, 'Die Zweikämpfe,' 6: 'Durch ihre übernatürlichen Kräfte bieten sich die Berserker als ungewöhnlich gefährliche Gegner an; sie zu besiegen, zeichnet einen Mann besonders aus. Und sie werden, trotz ihrer Stärke, trotz ihrer übernatürlichen Kräfte, stets besieget'; see also 24. I include not only cases in which one of the combatants is expressly labelled a *berserkr* or *víkingr* (for the interchangeability of these terms, see Sieg, 'Die Zweikämpfe,' 2–3; Grimstad, 'Comic Role,' 245, 250–2), but also those in which he displays prominent *berserkr* qualities (such as Atli's invulnerability to iron, *Egils saga* 65).
74 As suggested above, duel narratives set outside Iceland are likely to be unrealistic.
75 Besides the two principals, three of their supporters are killed in the preliminaries and are hence direct (anticipatory) casualties of Gunnlaugr and Hrafn's duelling. Only one of the three, however, is dispatched in one-on-one combat.
76 The saga says of Dálkr, one of Bjǫrn's (many) attackers at his last stand, that 'þóttist hann varla án holmsǫk við Bjǫrn' [he considered himself hardly without a cause for duelling with Bjǫrn] (*Bjarnar saga Hítdœlakappa* 32, ÍF 3: 201). Dálkr is disabled before he can do Bjǫrn any harm, but the latter eventually succumbs to the group assault. (For other duels encapsulated within group melees, see, e.g., *Þorskfirðinga saga* 5–6.) Four men, in all, die in this engagement, though only in a very broad sense may they all be considered duelling casualties.
77 In reply to King Óláfr's question, Þormóðr reports having single-handedly ('í einvígi,' *Fóstbrœðra saga* 24, ÍF 6: 265) killed fourteen (unnamed) men throughout his career.
78 The saga relates that Vígbjóðr, severely wounded in the fight, is at death's door shortly afterwards; I take this to mean that he did not survive, though the saga does not mention explicitly that he expired.
79 This is the same engagement reported in *Fóstbrœðra saga* 7, above. Both sagas report that, besides Þorgils, three of his men (according to *Grettis saga*) or three

men on each side (according to *Fóstbrœðra saga*) were slain in fighting immediately subsequent to the duel.

80 Steinarr, who predicts that his encounter with Bersi will have been his last duel, states in a convoluted verse (*Kormáks saga* 12 [v. 42], ÍF 8: 252) that he has previously fought, and probably killed, twelve men ('létk ... fyr Skrýmis eggju ... verða,' lit. 'I've let [them] come before the Skrýmir's [= sword's?] edge'; cf. Finnur Jónsson's translation in his edition of *Den norsk-islandske skjaldedigtning*, 4 vols [Copenhagen and Christiania 1910–15], vol. B1 [Rettet Tekst]: 89 n.: 'Jeg har ladet 12 krigere blive genstand for [hug af] den blanke Skrymirs æg' [I have made 12 warriors become objects for (cut down by) the gleaming Skrymir's edge]). There is no clear indication that Steinarr's victims were slain in duels, but the context makes this somewhat likely.

81 After killing Þorkell, Bersi boasts in a verse (*Kormáks saga* 14 [v. 44], ÍF 8: 255) that this has been his thirty-first kill. It is not clear whether all of Bersi's victims were slain in duels, but his nickname 'Hólmgǫngu-Bersi' [Duelling-Bersi] suggests that this is somewhat likely. (Later in the saga, however, Bersi kills five more men, none in a duel.)

82 Þorvarðr is said to employ the protection of a witch, who blunts Kormákr's sword (*Kormáks saga* 22, ÍF 8: 284–5); I thus consider him under the same supernatural rubric as *berserkir*.

83 Þorvarðr is again said to employ the protection of a witch, who blunts Kormákr's sword (*Kormáks saga* 23, ÍF 8: 289).

84 The saga describes Kormákr's opponent as a 'blótrisi Skota' [Scottish sacrificial giant (?)] (ÍF 8: 299). Although not, technically, a *berserkr*, I consider this supernatural foe under the same rubric.

85 The account of this duel is truncated because the chief MS is missing half a folio at this point (ÍF 9: 147 n. 2), but it is clear that Moldi does not survive the encounter.

86 Þorleifr's opponent is an enchanted wooden golem (*trémaðr*); having struck Þorleifr a lethal blow, he disintegrates as Þorleifr strikes back at him. Whether this is because of the counter-blow or because the spell wears off once his mission is completed is unclear. Although not, technically, a *berserkr*, I consider Þorgarðr (like the giant in *Kormáks saga* 27, above) under the same rubric of supernatural foes.

87 An initial double duel, in which two *berserkir* are slain, develops into a fight in which eight more die.

88 An initial double duel, in which two *berserkir* die, develops into a fight in which an unspecified additional number perish.

89 Although he is not explicitly called *berserkr*, Bjálfi's behaviour is typical of one: he demands Sámr's wife and is described as an 'œirðarmaðr' [ruffian] (*Flóamanna saga* 31, ÍF 13: 317).

90 I arrive at this tally by counting the encounter between Þorgeirr and Þorgils (*Fóstbrœðra saga* 7 and *Grettis saga* 25) only once, but considering all fourteen duel killings Þormóðr reports (*Fóstbrœðra saga* 24), all forty-two kills Steinarr and Bersi boast of (*Kormáks saga* 12, 14 [vv. 42, 44]), and all twenty-four duel victories imputed to Ketill (*Víglundar saga* 3) as separate incidents. The tally of deadly duels is calculated in the same way.

91 The overall statistics on saga duels are significantly skewed by the duels attributed to Þormóðr (*Fóstbrœðra saga* 24), Steinarr and Bersi (*Kormáks saga* 12, 14 [vv. 42, 44]), and Ketill (*Víglundar saga* 3), which together comprise 61 per cent of the total number and concerning which next to no details are known. I therefore calculate minimal totals and percentages, disregarding these 80 putative duels.

92 Narfi's claim that he has been challenged by a foreigner because of a dispute over the hand of a woman – a fabrication – is nevertheless strongly reminiscent of an encounter with a *berserkr* ('Narfi ... segir, at einn Austmaðr norðr í Øxnadal hafi skorat á sik til einvígis út af konu einni, er báðir vildu hafa' [Narfi says that a Norwegian had called him out to single combat, north in Øxnadalr, on account of a woman whom they both wanted], *Heiðarvíga saga* 15, ÍF 3: 261).

93 This planned duel only receives mention in passing. It is unclear whether it is supposed to have taken place.

94 Even if not technically a *berserkr* abroad, Þórr's duelling exploits should certainly be viewed as no less legendary than those of other foreign wildmen.

95 This is the same engagement that fails to come to pass in *Vatnsdœla saga* 33, above.

96 Cases like Narfi's alleged plan to duel with an unnamed Norwegian (*Heiðarvíga saga* 15), presented within the saga as an outright lie, Þórr's supposed challenge of Christ, reported by a pagan priestess (*Brennu-Njáls saga* 102), or challenges left unanswered by their original addressee but superseded by a fight between the challenger and a stand-in champion (such as Ljótr's challenge of Friðgeirr, *Egils saga* 64), complicate the question of just how many abortive duels the family sagas mention.

6 Scottish National Heroes and the Limits of Violence

ANNE McKIM

>> Thus thai slayand ware sa fast
>> All the day, qwhill at the last
>> This Kyng Edward saw in that tyde
>> A woman slayne, and off hyr syde
>> A barne he saw fall owt, sprewland
>> Besyd that woman slayne lyand.
>> '*Lasses, lasses,*' than cryid he;
>> 'Leve off, leve off,' that word suld be.
>
> (Andrew of Wyntoun, *Orygynale Cronykil of Scotland* 8.11.1831–8)[1]

[Thus all day they were killing so quickly, until at last this King Edward saw at that time a woman slain, and from her side he saw a child had fallen out, and lay sprawling beside that slain woman. 'Laissez! Laissez!' then he cried. 'Leave off! Leave off!' that is to say.]

So, according to the early fifteenth-century Scottish chronicler, Andrew of Wyntoun, is Edward I of England prompted to call a halt to the wholesale slaughter of the inhabitants of the town of Berwick on Good Friday 1296. The sight of the mutilated corpse of a pregnant woman provides the appalling climax to Wyntoun's account of the indiscriminate killing of Scots by Edward's English army, regardless not only of sex but also of religious or lay status, social rank, or age:

>> Bath awld and yhowng, men and wywys,
>> And sowkand barnys thar tynt thare lywys:
>> Yhwmen and gentilmen alsa,
>> The lywys all thai tuk [thaim] fra. (*Cronykil* 8.11.1823–6)[2]

[Both old and young, men and women, and suckling babes lost their lives there.
Yeomen and noblemen as well, they took the lives of all of them.]

Altogether this is a severe indictment of the king's breach of conduct. Edward's order to stop the killing itself constitutes an acknowledgment that the violence has reached an unacceptable level, but rather than credit the English king with a healthy sense of disgust, Wyntoun chooses to underscore the atrocity by telling his readers that the final body count was 7500 and that the streets of the town ran with 'rede blude' (line 1844) for two days. Wyntoun, prior of St Serf's in Lochleven, Fife, proceeds to condemn Edward for carrying out this attack on a Good Friday, a transgression against the law of arms that prohibited fighting on religious feastdays, except in self-defence.[3] Moreover, the spiritual consequences of his sinful conduct are driven home to the reader through grim and ironic wordplay: Edward observes the holy day by his 'devotyown' (1847) to the 'Passyown' (1848) of the many 'innocentis' (1854) who died during the 'serwys' (1857) he leads. Through his 'offyce ... that Gud Fryday' (1853) thousands of 'pure' (1850) souls are transported:

> quhare his sawle nevyrmare
> Wes lyk to come, that is the blys,
> Quhare alkyn joy ay lestand is. (*Cronykil* 8.11.1860–2)

[where his soul was never likely to come, that is, the bliss of heaven, where all joy is everlasting.]

Wyntoun's moralization on Edward's lack of 'pete' (line 1858) – clearly piety as well as pity – serves to highlight the literariness and conventionality of his representation. Attributing atrocities against non-combatants to the nation's enemies, a familiar *topos* in medieval historical narratives, is, as Ruth Morse has noted, the clerical historian's 'mark of the wickedness of those who perpetrated such deeds – a dramatisation of their *ethos*.'[4] Equally conventional is the characterization of Edward as a tyrant, for although Wyntoun's explicit denunciation of him as 'noucht kyng, bot a fell tyrand' (1846) goes further than earlier Scottish chroniclers had been prepared to go, it nevertheless derives from his predecessors' work.[5]

Medieval Scottish historiography, the 'matter of Scotland,' both produced and was shaped by what Eugene Vance has called a 'commemorative culture': one in which 'events of violence are given great prominence.'[6] Well into the sixteenth century, Scottish historians were producing images of Scotland as 'first and foremost a nation-in-arms' whose history provided many examples of acts of aggression against its sovereign status and the successful defence of the nation's freedom by warrior heroes.[7] These later writers also appropriated 'the chivalrous lineage culture' created by the acknowledged 'fathers' of Scottish history and literature, John Fordun and John Barbour, both of whom were clerics at Aberdeen cathedral in the second half of the fourteenth century.[8] This culture is best articulated by Barbour at the beginning of his memorializing narrative about the Scottish national heroes, Robert Bruce and James Douglas:

> For auld storys y*at* men redys
> Representis to yaim the dedys
> Of stalwart folk y*at* lywyt ar
> Ric*ht* as yai yan in p*r*esence war
> And cert*is* yai suld weill hawe prys
> Yat in y*ar* tyme war wyc*ht* and wys,
> And led y*ar* lyff in gret t*r*awaill,
> And oft in hard stour of bataill
> Wan gret p*r*ice of chewalry. (*Bruce* 1.17–25)

[For old histories that men read, present again to them the deeds of brave people who lived formerly as though they were present now; and indeed they should be esteemed who in their time were bold and wise, who led their lives in great struggle, and often in the hard press of battle won a great reputation for chivalry.]

Theirs is a chivalrous struggle to right wrongs and avenge atrocities attributed to the English occupying forces in Scotland.

All of the early Scottish accounts of the wars of independence criticize to some degree the conduct of Edward's troops at Berwick – as well as during the occupation of Scotland that followed – and all protest about the killing of women, children, and priests.[9] Contemporary English accounts confirm that there was a bloodbath when the town was sacked in 1296, some putting the death toll even higher than Wyntoun did, reflecting the numbers of ordinary townspeople killed, but they claim that the women and children were allowed to leave.[10] Wyntoun's description is by far the most lurid and, as his is the only one of all the surviving accounts to assign the event to Good Friday, this embellishment may well have been introduced to heighten the 'unthinkable' nature of Edward's offence.[11] Recently historian Michael Prestwich, in what almost appears to be an unconscious rebuttal of Wyntoun, has written that 'Edward himself waited, with due piety, until the Easter celebrations were over before crossing the Tweed' to unleash his anger against the inhabitants who had dared to offer resistance to his occupying army.[12]

There can be little doubt that the massacre at Berwick in 1296 came to

134 Anne McKim

acquire iconic significance in medieval Scottish historiography. The savage capture of the town and subsequent installation of English government officers marked the beginning of Edward's invasion and occupation of Scotland. The behaviour of his occupying forces was invariably attributed to his aggressiveness. One particularly influential account links Edward's covetous attitude towards Scotland with the licensed covetousness of his officers that leads to the rape of Scottish women:[13]

> To Scotland went he yan in hy,
> And all ye land gan occupy
> Sa hale y*at* bath castell & toune
> War in-till his possessioune
> [Fra Weik anent Orknay]
> To Mullyr snwk in Gallaway,
> And stuffyt all w*ith* Inglis-men.
> Schyrreffys and bail3heys maid he ye*n*,
> And alkyn oyer office*ris*
> Y*at* for to gowern land affe*ris*
> He maid off Inglis nation,
> Yat worthyt yan sa rych fellone
> And sa wykkyt and cowatous
> And swa hawtane and dispitous
> Yat Scott*is*-men my*cht* do na thing
> Y*at* euer my*cht* pleys to y*ar* liking.
> Yar wyff*is* wald yai oft forly
> And y*ar* dochtrys dispitusly
> And gyff ony of yaim y*ar*-at war wrath
> Yai watyt hym wele w*ith* gret scaith. (*Bruce* 1.183–202)

[To Scotland he then went in haste and occupied the whole land, so completely that he gained possession of both castles and towns from Wick next to Orkney to the Mull of Galloway and filled them all with Englishmen. He then appointed sheriffs and baillies and all kinds of other officers required to govern the country, all Englishmen, who then became so extremely cruel and so wicked and greedy, so haughty and arrogant, that Scots men could never do anything that might please them. Their (the Scots') wives and daughters they would often rape and if anyone was enraged about that they punished him severely.]

For Hary, author of the first Life of William Wallace (ca 1477), the ensuing brutality was nothing more nor less than 'wyrkand [performing] the will of Eduuard, that fals king.'[14] He goes on to provide examples of the atrocities committed by the occupying army, reserving the worst for last:

> Mony gret wrang thai wro*ch*t in this Regioune;
> Distroyed our lordys and brak thar byggynys doun;
> Both wiffis, wedowis, thai tuk all at th*ar* will,
> Nonnys, madyns, quham thai likit to spill.
> King Herodis part thai playit in-to Scotland
> Off ʒong child*y*r that thai befor thai*m* fand. (*Wallace* 1.161–6)

[Many great wrongs they carried out in this country, destroyed our lords and demolished their buildings. They took both wives and widows entirely at their will, and nuns and maidens whom they liked to dishonour. They played the part of King Herod towards young children in Scotland wherever they found them.]

The analogy drawn with the slaughter of the innocents tends to alert readers to the literary quality of Hary's portrayal of events, to a rhetorical representation of violent events that derives from a Scottish historiographical tradition at least a hundred and seventy years old when he wrote.

* * *

Condemnations of Edward's behaviour at Berwick, including Wyntoun's, make an implicit appeal to the laws of arms, which codified limits on violence. Honoré Bonet, author of the influential *L'Arbre des batailles*, for example, is absolutely firm on the immunity of non-combatants.[15] Sir Gilbert Haye, who translated Bonet's treatise on warfare into Scots in 1456, deplores the mistreatment of women, children, the elderly, and priests: even taking them prisoner is regarded as a form of oppression, 'for thare is na vailliaunce na worschip tharin' [for there is neither honour nor glory therein].[16] Since it is the duty of 'noble men of armys' to protect such 'innocentis,' to do 'the contraire' 'suld be erar [rather] callit cruell and pillarde [pillaging].'[17] In another work, *The Buke of Knychthede*, he takes to task those who fail to show pity, without which 'na knycht mycht sustene the grete charge of knychthede.'[18]

It has been said often enough before that the theories and the practice of warfare in the Middle Ages were very different things.[19] Perhaps embodying this tension and conflict, again and again in medieval chivalric chronicles and biographies violent conduct that is condemned in the enemy may be condoned in national heroes. Robert Bruce and his companion-in-arms James Douglas owed much of their success in the Scottish wars of independence to the brutal and destructive form of warfare they adopted, yet the chivalry of these heroes is celebrated by Bruce's first biographer, John Barbour.[20] His poem, *The Bruce,* depicts numerous episodes in which Bruce excels in individual feats of prowess as well as in military manoeuvres. There is no disputing, however, that Robert Bruce secured his accession to the throne of Scotland by murdering his rival, John Comyn, in front of the high altar of a Dumfries church.[21] Barbour goes as far as he can to justify the killing, adopting what had become – well before he completed his biography in 1376 – the 'party line' of accusing the murdered man of treachery (disclosing the pact and conniving with Edward I to kill Bruce), but he can't overlook the sacrilege which gave 'na girth' to the altar [failed to respect sanctuary], so he concedes that the hero-king 'mysdyd thar gretly' (2.43). Because Bruce is constructed in Barbour's text as a model king, with a righteous cause, he is able to expiate his sin through suffering many setbacks before winning the war (or what proved to be the first phase of the struggle for independence).[22]

But even Archdeacon Barbour can remain conspicuously non-judgmental when the man he depicts as the perfect knight, Sir James Douglas, attacks and kills an English garrison as they attend church on Palm Sunday, and, taking a few prisoners to gain entry to Douglas Castle, proceeds to decapitate them, mixing their blood with meal, flour, malt, and wine in the cellars to make a concoction that came to be called 'the Douglas Larder.' Barbour ventures the understatement, 'Yat was wnsemly for to se' (*Bruce* 5.407).

If, as Lee Patterson has argued, 'violence legitimised the knight's social identity' then it can also be said that chivalry legitimized violence in medieval historical narratives.[23] Just as knights are almost invariably 'trew' or 'fals' (depending on whether they have the writer's sympathy and approval), so in chivalric historiography violent acts ('violent' not itself a neutral description)[24] are usually designated 'gret' and 'rychtwis' or 'felloun' and 'wrang,' and a 'felloun' deed justifies violent retribution. It is in this light that we are to understand Hary's celebration of William Wallace as a man distressed at the general oppression of his fellow-countrymen by the English occupying forces, and finally provoked beyond endurance by the murder of his new wife by the English sheriff installed by Edward I at Lanark:

> Sichand he said, 'Sall neuir man me se
> Rest in-till eys quhill this deid wrokyn be,
> The saklace slauchtyr off hir blith and brycht.
> That I awow to the makar off mycht,
> That off that nacioune I sall neuir forber
> 3hong nor ald that abill is to wer. (*Wallace* 6.213–18)

[Sighing, he said, "No men shall ever see me rest easy until I have avenged this deed, this slaughter of a blithe, fair, and innocent creature. I vow to the Almighty Maker that I shall never spare any of that nation, neither young nor old, if they are able to fight.]

From the start of his armed resistance, Wallace's mind is set on 'wer and werray rychtwisnes' [war and very righteousness] (2.6), just as Barbour's Bruce and Douglas take up arms against Edward to avenge

> ye harme and ye contrer
> At y*a*t fele folk and pautener
> Dyd till sympill folk and worthy (*Bruce* 1.461–3)

[the harm and wrong that many cruel folk did to few worthy people.]

If, in other words, it is wicked (*felloun, fals*) to violate and oppress the innocent (*saklace, sympill*), then, according to the operating binary, it is just (*rychtwis, lele*) to defend them through resistance. This is a classic instance of what Foucault termed a 'relationship of violence,' a struggle marked by domination and subordination.[25]

Like Barbour, Hary opens his life of Wallace by highlighting his commemorative purpose, and by attacking the 'sleuthfulnes' that has meant that William Wallace has not been given the recognition he deserves.[26] A little later in his poem Hary avers that Wallace challenges comparison with the great Bruce, and indeed surpasses the king in respect of his military audacity:

> He was als gud, quhat deid was to assaill,
> As off his handis, and bauldar in battaill. (*Wallace* 2.354–5)[27]

[He was as good with his hands, and bolder in battle, whatever feat of arms he attempted.]

But whereas Bruce inherited the kingdom by a right retrospectively established by royal propagandists, Wallace was merely the son of a knight, a member of the lesser aristocracy, and therefore a man who never commanded the full support of Scottish magnates.[28] This perhaps explains why almost all the other medieval Scottish chroniclers, as well as Hary, denote Wallace's nobility chiefly in terms of his prowess and his courage: his 'gud deidis and his manheid' is a common collocation.[29] The most obvious measure of Wallace's manliness is his physical strength, which is frequently demonstrated in violent actions. (The adjectives *stalwart, stark,* and *wicht,* for example – which are repeatedly applied to his actions – mean, according to the *Dictionary of the Older Scottish Tongue*, 'violent' as well as 'strong.') Wallace's reputation for violence is well attested in contemporary English sources, and the kind of atrocities (and worse) attributed to Edward I by Wyntoun, for example, are alleged against him.[30] Even in celebratory accounts, Wallace is presented as a violent man who thirsts for English blood. Wyntoun wryly suggests the economy of his violence and the national benefit that accrues from it:

> To sla he sparyd noucht Inglis men.
> Till Scottis he dyd gret profyt then. (*Cronykil* 8.13.2127–8)

[In slaying he did not spare English men. He therefore greatly profited the Scots.]

Again and again Hary tells of attacks on English-held castles and towns that are characterized by 'full gret slauchter' (*Wallace* 9.644), as Wallace carries out his vow never to spare the lives of Englishmen. Almost always, however, we are told that even in his revenge-driven fury, Wallace invariably exempts non-combatants:

> He sparyt nane that abill was to wer,
> Bot wemen and preystis he gart thaim ay forber. (*Wallace* 3.217–18)

[He spared none who were able to fight, but he always saved women and priests.]

For instance, after various raids in northeast Scotland in which English soldiers who sought sanctuary in Dunottar church are burned 'in powd*ir* cauld' [to a cold powder] (*Wallace* 7.1058) and the enemy fleet in Aberdeen harbour is put to the torch, with anyone who gained land 'bertynyt bayne and lyr' (1074), burned flesh and bone, the reader is told 'yeid nane away bot preistis, wyffis and barnys' (1075). On another occasion when his army is in full 'burning and slaying' mode, Wallace orders the last minute evacuation of the 'waik folk' (identified as mainly women and children) from the blazing town of Ayr (*Wallace* 5.1128). To give only one more instance, because peace is 'wncorduall' to his nature (5.558), during a sojourn in France Wallace cannot resist mounting an attack on a town held by the English. When all the able-bodied men are killed:

> Wemen and barnys, the gud thai tuk thaim fra,
> Syn gaiff thaim leyff in-to the realm to ga,
> And preystis als th*at* war nocht in the feild,
> Off agyt men quhilk my*ch*t na wapy*n*nis weild.
> Thai slew nayn sic, so Wallace chargis was,
> Bot maid thaim fre at thar largis to pas. (*Wallace* 9.647–52)

[They took possessions from the women and children, then gave them leave to go into the realm, along with priests who were not on the battlefield and old men who were not capable of wielding weapons. They slew none of these, but made them free to go at their liberty, as Wallace commanded.]

So, while extensive killing and destruction of property that cannot be pillaged are presented again and again as the norm for Wallace and his followers, so too is the sparing of noncombatants, specifically identified here as priests who had not fought on the battlefield and men too aged to bear arms, as well as women and children. Highlighted are Wallace's noble leadership in this respect, and his magnanimity. Observing – as well as commanding his men to observe – limits to the violence that is otherwise depicted as acceptable, is consistently ascribed to Wallace by medieval Scottish writers: it is an integral part of his 'manheid.' As he tells the queen of England on one of only two occasions in Hary's poem when a woman is given an individual identity and the power of speech, no honour can be gained from warring on women (*Wallace* 8.1440).

Nevertheless, in Hary's book the rules are there to be broken, and although he never acually depicts his hero transgressing these particular limits, the possibility is admitted by Wallace himself, when he says:

> Preystis no wemen I think nocht for to sla
> In my defaut, bot thai me causing ma. (*Wallace* 6.219–20)

[I do not intend to kill priests and women wrongfully, unless they give me cause.]

This 'personal' code of conduct is later endorsed by Hary when he describes the party of ladies, widows, nuns, and elderly priests who make up the queen of England's peace-seeking embassy to Wallace, and comments:

> Wallace to sic did neu*ir* gret owtrage
> Bot gyff till him thai maid a gret offens. (*Wallace* 8.1222–3)

[Wallace never committed an outrage on such people unless they offered him great provocation.]

Interestingly, in each of these statements, the same adversative conjunction, *bot*, introduces the same kind of qualification.[31] Noncombatants are spared *unless* they give cause or provocation for dealing with them less mercifully. Quite simply, their immunity exists only as long as these 'waik folk' remain just that, passive and unresisting; the alternative is chillingly, if briefly, conveyed:

> ƺeid nane away bot preistis, wyffis and barnys:
> Maid thai debait thai chapyt nocht but harmys. (*Wallace* 7.1075–6)

[None went away except priests, women, and children: if they resisted they did not escape without harm.]

Active resistance is seen as grounds for dispatching the enemy, regardless of status, sex, or age, a view expressed not only by Wallace and his biographer, but also by those English chroniclers who justified Edward I's brutal sack of Berwick because of the inhabitants' resistance.

140 Anne McKim

This, of course, brings me full circle. If the man constructed as a national hero is just as capable of committing a 'gret owtrage' against women, children, and priests as the man constructed as a cruel 'tyrand,' then respecting or transgressing the limits of violence is no longer the absolute, distinguishing criterion it at first appears to be. One writer's hero can be another's villain, and vice-versa.[32] Transgressing the boundaries is what the enemy does, and the 'war of historiography' – which on the one hand paralleled the physical struggle for independence that Edward I's claim to suzerainty in Scotland prompted, and on the other hand intersected it, engaged, participated in, and shaped that struggle – highlights in an appreciable sense that historical writing in medieval Scotland was a symbolic practice, 'a form of violence in its own right.'[33]

Notes

1 Andrew of Wyntoun, *The Orygynale Cronykil of Scotland*, ed. David Laing, 3 vols, Historians of Scotland 2, 3, 9 (Edinburgh 1872–9). The influence and popularity of this rhyming vernacular chronicle have been stressed recently by R. James Goldstein, '*For he walde vsurpe na fame*: Andrew of Wyntoun's Use of the Modesty Topos and Literary Culture in Early Fifteenth-Century Scotland,' *Scottish Literary Journal* 14.1 (1987) 5–18, at 5.
2 The lines immediately preceding these stress the wholesale nature of the massacre through repetition of 'all' and 'allkyn,' and reiteration of the claim that no one was spared:
> The Inglis [men] thare slwe downe
> All hale the Scottis natyowne,
> That wyth in that towne thai fand,
> Off all condytyowne nane sparand;
> Leryd and lawde, nwne and frere,
> All wes slayne wyth that powere:
> Off allkyn state, off allkyn age,
> [Thai] sparyd nothir carl na page. (*Cronykil* 8.11.1816–24)

[There the Englishmen completely slaughtered the native Scots they found within that town, sparing no one, whatever their status. Learned and ignorant, nuns and friars, were all slain by that army. Whatever the rank, whatever the age, they spared no one, neither peasant nor page.]
3 Honoré Bonet, *The Tree of Battles*, trans. G. Coopland (Liverpool 1949), 155.
4 Ruth Morse, *Truth and Convention in the Middle Ages: Rhetoric, Representation, and Reality* (Cambridge 1991), 117. The tendency of clerical historians to dramatize and exaggerate accounts of military conflicts has been noted by J.F. Verbruggen,

The Art of Warfare in Western Europe during the Middle Ages (Amsterdam etc. 1977), 12–13; and by H. J. Hewitt, *The Organisation of War under Edward III* (Manchester 1966), 123.

5 E.g., John of Fordun (ca 1363) attributes the massacre at Berwick to the tyrannous rage (*in sua tirannide*) of the king. *Johannis de Fordun chronica gentis Scotorum*, ed. William Skene, 2 vols, Historians of Scotland 1, 4 (Edinburgh 1871–2), annal 90. The second volume is a translation. On another occasion in his chronicle Wyntoun accuses Edward of being a 'tyrand' immediately after a long quotation from Barbour's *Bruce* (written in 1376) in which the brutality of Edward's occupying forces towards the Scots is described (*Cronykil* 8.18.2733–62).

6 Eugene Vance, *Marvelous Signals: Poetics and Sign Theory in the Middle Ages* (Lincoln 1986), 54. In his recent book, *The Matter of Scotland: Historical Narratives in Medieval Scotland* (Lincoln and London 1993), R. James Goldstein considers the formation of the Scottish national ideology.

7 Roger Mason, 'Chivalry and Citizenship: Aspects of National Identity in Renaissance Scotland,' in *People and Power in Scotland*, ed. Roger Mason and Norman Macdougall (Edinburgh 1992), 62.

8 Almost nothing is known of Fordun, except that his authorship of his *Chronica* and *Gesta annalia* is attested by MSS as well as by his 15th-century continuator, Walter Bower. One MS says that he was a priest at Aberdeen Cathedral when he worked on his history, during the period Barbour was archdeacon (1357–95). Barbour's major surviving work is *The Bruce*, a romantic biography of Robert the Bruce, written in 1376 during the reign of Robert II, for whom he also composed a genealogy of the Stewarts, now lost. *Barbour's Bruce*, ed. Matthew P. McDiarmid and James A.C. Stevenson. 3 vols, Scottish Text Society 4th ser. 12, 13, 15 (Edinburgh 1980–5).

9 The earliest surviving criticism is found in the so-called Instructions of 1301, written by Scottish canon lawyers to counter claims contained in Edward I's letter to Pope Boniface VIII written in May of the same year. Versions of the text are preserved in the *Scotichronicon*, the generic name given until fairly recently to a Scottish chronicle tradition begun in the second half of the 14th century by John of Fordun (see n. 8 above) and subsequently revised, expanded, and continued by others, most notably in the 1440s by Walter Bower, abbot of Inchcolm. Fordun's description of the sack of Berwick is contained in a brief annal entry, number 90. Walter Bower essentially adopted Fordun's version but changed the date of the attack from 30 March (a date supported by various English chroniclers too) to 29 March. See *Scotichronicon* 11.20, ed. D.E.R. Watt, 9 vols (Aberdeen 1987–98), 6: 57–61.

10 *Willelmi Rishanger ... chronica et annales*, ed. H.T. Riley, Rolls Series 28.2 (London 1865), 373–4; *Chronicon de Lanercost* ed. Joseph Stevenson, Bannatyne Club

Publications 65 (Edinburgh 1839), 173; *The Chronicle of Walter of Guisborough*, ed. Harry Rothwell, Royal Historical Society, Camden 3rd ser. 89 (London 1957), 274–5. Michael Prestwich cites a number of these, as well as the London Hagnaby chronicle, in his *Edward I* (London 1988), 471.

11   I borrow the term from Morse, *Truth and Convention*, 117 (who may be making an oblique allusion to Foucault). Walter Bower assigns the sack of Berwick to 29 March, which in 1296 was the Thursday after Easter, although a scribe's marginal note mistakenly identifies the date as Good Friday.

12   Prestwich, *Edward I*, 470. G.W.S. Barrow assigns sole responsibility for the slaughter of Berwick's inhabitants (mainly the burgesses, since knights were able to negotiate surrender terms) to the king. *Robert Bruce & the Community of the Realm of Scotland*, 3rd ed. (Edinburgh 1988), 71.

13   Wyntoun, e.g., was so impressed with these lines (and those following) that he quoted them more or less in their entirety (*Cronykil* 8.18.2732–60).

14   *Hary's Wallace* 1.160, ed. M.P. McDiarmid, 2 vols, Scottish Text Society 4th ser. 4–5 (Edinburgh and London 1968–9), 1: 6. Hary – whether this is his first or last name is unknown – drew heavily, in various ways, on Barbour's *Bruce*. His editor also detects the influence of Wyntoun's description of the sack of Berwick in this and the following lines.

15   See *Tree of Battles* pt 4, chs 70 and 93–5.

16   *Gilbert of the Haye's Prose Manuscript*, vol 1: *The Buke of the Law of Armys or Buke of Bataillis*, ed. J.H. Stevenson, Scottish Text Society 44 (Edinburgh and London 1901), 233. In his preface Haye describes himself as a knight, a Master of Arts and Bachelor in Decrees, and former chamberlain to the king of France. He seems to have spent much of his life in service in France before translating several French texts into Scots for the earl of Orkney and Caithness in 1456.

17   Ibid. 233.

18   *Gilbert of the Haye's Prose Manuscript*, vol. 2: *The Buke of Knychthede and The Buke of the Governaunce of Princis*, ed. J.H. Stevenson, Scottish Text Society 62 (Edinburgh and London 1914), ch. 7, p. 54.

19   For recent discussions see Michael Prestwich, *Armies and Warfare in the Middle Ages: The English Experience* (New Haven 1996), esp. on 'Chivalry,' 219–43; and Richard Kaueper, *Chivalry and Violence in Medieval Europe* (Oxford 1999).

20   Barrow, *Robert Bruce*, 312.

21   Barbour admits, though, that at the time he was writing – seventy years after the event – there was still debate about some of the details (particularly the motives behind the fatal encounter). *Bruce* 2.39–42.

22   *Bruce* 2.45–8.

23   *Chaucer and the Subject of History* (London 1991), 191.

24   Philippa Maddern, *Violence and Social Disorder in East Anglia* (Oxford 1992), 9:

'The description of an act as violent is not a neutral one: it involves the ascription of meaning and purpose, ethical and otherwise, to the act.'
25 Michel Foucault, 'Afterword: The Subject and Power,' in *Michel Foucault*, ed. and trans. H. Dreyfus and P. Raisinow (Chicago 1982), 220.
26 He begins:
> Our antecessowris that we suld of reide
> And hald in mynd thar nobille worthi deid
> We lat ourslide throw weray sleuthfulnes. (*Wallace* 1.1–3)
> [Our ancestors, that we should read about and keep in mind their noble worthy deeds, we neglect through very sloth.]
and later writes:
> Gret harm I thocht his gud deid suld be smord. (*Wallace* 9.1434)
> [I thought it a great pity that his good deeds should be forgotten.]
27 Hary fabricated many of his hero's deeds and had the 'audacity' himself to plunder Barbour's text for episodes and heroic feats he then attributed to his hero. See G. Neilson, 'On Blind Harry's *Wallace*,' *Essays and Studies* 1 (1910) 93–8.
28 Barrow, *Robert Bruce*, 138; Goldstein, *Matter of Scotland*, 233.
29 Fordun, *Chronica*, annal 98; Wyntoun, *Cronykil* 8.13.2125, 8.15.2299, 8.16.2462; Hary, *Wallace* 8.1477.
30 See Walter of Guisborough's account of his raids in Northumbria in October and November 1297: *Chronicle of Walter of Guisborough*, 303–7. Also *Chronicon de Lanercost*, 190–1.
31 For an interesting examination of the use of the same adversative conjunction by other writers see Judith Grossman, 'The Correction of a Descriptive Schema: Some "Buts" in Barbour and Chaucer,' *Studies in the Age of Chaucer* 1 (1977) 41–54.
32 This is nowhere more apparent than in Scottish and English accounts of William Wallace. See Goldstein, *Matter of Scotland*, 215–16.
33 Nancy Armstrong and Leonard Tennenhouse, *The Violence of Representation* (London and New York 1989), 2. The 'war of historiography' is a term coined by Goldstein, *Matter of Scotland*.

PART II

VIOLENCE AND THE TESTAMENT OF THE BODY

7 Seeing the Gendering of Violence: Female and Male Martyrs in the *South English Legendary*

BETH CRACHIOLO

The tortured body in medieval Christian hagiography is, for the hagiographer and his Christian audience, a testimony to the power of God and the church, and the tale of a martyred saint is an important way to illustrate that power – often by providing details of horrific torture, the failure of which functions as proof that steadfast spiritual faith can overcome physical suffering. Particularly graphic in its torture descriptions is the *South English Legendary*.[1] The *SEL* narratives of martyrs' Lives are structured around a pattern of represented violence that constructs vivid pictures of torn limbs, rent bellies, and blood that runs 'Bi stremes ... so water doþ of welle' [By streams ... as water does from a well].[2] Both women and men suffer torture at the hands of authorities in the *SEL*, but the narrative function of the representation of violence differs according to gender. An examination of the rhetorical details of the narratives shows that representations of the torture of women encourage the narrative's audience to concentrate its attention on the sight of a suffering female body, while representations of the torture of men focus attention away from the suffering male body. The audience of the *SEL* narratives is encouraged to gaze on the female body both by the differences in the ways male and female saints respond to torture and by narrative reminders in women's Lives of issues of sight and visualization.

Originating in the southwest of England in the thirteenth century, the *SEL* is a collection both large and popular. Made up of *sanctorale* and *temporale* material, its purpose seems to have been, as Klaus P. Jankofsky describes it, 'instruction of the laity in matters of the faith, mainly through straightforward stories that could be understood at first hearing ...' and its popularity is implied by the number of manuscripts that survive.[3] The collection's scope is extensive; though the bulk of its narratives are martyrs' Lives, much other material is included as well. The Life of Theophilus, for example, is dominated by tales of miracles wrought by the Virgin Mary; the Life of saints Simon and Jude includes a physical description of Jesus. Michael's Life is divided into three parts, one of which is concerned with ways by which humans can recognize the devil and his works, another of which is essentially a geography/astronomy lesson giving precise locations for heaven, hell, the stars, and the planets. The *SEL* also includes histories of two figures who are not saints, Judas and Pilate.

Though it appears to be a didactic text, the *SEL* is noticeably lacking in doctrinal teachings, especially in the Lives of the martyrs, where violence is rhetorically privileged over models of doctrine. One of the two prologues to the collection (called the 'Banna sanctorum' in some manuscripts) promises a series of narratives that will appeal to a popular audience in the same ways that romance and epic do:

> Men wilneþ muche to hure telle · of bataille of kynge
> And of kniʒtes þat hardy were · þat muchedel is lesynge
> Wo so wilneþ muche to hure · tales of suche þinge
> Hardi batailles he may hure · here þat nis no lesinge
> Of apostles & martirs · þat hardy kniʒtes were
> Þat studeuast were in bataille · & ne fleide noʒt for fere
> Þat soffrede þat luþer men · al quik hare lymes totere (lines 59–65, *SEL* 1: 3)

[Men wish much to hear tales of the battles of kings and of knights who were strong, of which the most part is false. Whoever wishes much to hear tales of such things may hear about strong battles here, which is not false, of apostles and martyrs who were strong knights, who were steadfast in battle and did not flee for fear, who suffered while evil men tore apart their limbs (while they were) alive.]

The prologue thus promises nothing new, nor does it suggest a need for didactic material. Rather, it introduces this collection as a replacement for the already familiar, with the added bonus that there will be 'no lesinge' as there is in other forms of popular entertainment. It further advertises a gory form of entertainment through an extended metaphor in lines 1–22 of the 'sed' of Christianity, planted by God, watered first by Christ's blood and then by the blood of martyrs:

> Verst þe martir seinte Steuene · & þe appostles þat were ded
> Þat hare blod and hare lyf ʒaf · to norisschi þat swete sed
> And þis oþer martirs ek · þat oure Louerdes knyʒtes were
> Þat schadde hare blod for Cristendom · þat it yperissid nere (17–20, *SEL* 1: 1)

[First the martyr saint Stephen, and the apostles who died, who gave their blood and their life to nourish that sweet seed, and the other martyrs who were our Lord's knights, who shed their blood for Christianity so that it did not perish.]

The suggestion of gore combines with the promise to replace other popular material to imply that stories of violence and torture were at least assumed to appeal to a popular audience and, indeed, the stories in the *SEL* are overwhelmingly accounts of martyrdom; of the ninety-one narratives in Charlotte d'Evelyn's and Anna J. Mill's edition, forty-four are martyrs' Lives, most of which are formulaic, describing the same torments in nearly the same language as they are perpetrated on saints whose personalities are remarkably similar. The formula follows a specific pattern: the set up; the interrogation; the first beating; prison; the second beating; fire (which is sometimes accompanied by molten metals and/or torture involving a griddle or oven); and, finally, death by decapitation or as the result of the saint's request to God. The narratives all end with a short prayer of one or two lines. There is little room in the pattern for theological instruction; most of the narratives are less than three hundred lines, and Jankofsky has estimated that most of them can be read aloud in under thirty minutes.[4] The repetitive nature of the narratives and their depictions of violence, along with the absence of doctrine, make each Life seem much like the others, so that the modern reader's experience of reading the collection from start to finish can be, as Jankofsky comments, 'deadening, depressing, and utterly boring.'[5] Hearing them read over the course of the church's calendar year, however, would surely have been a different experience in the thirteenth century. Jankofsky is undoubtedly right in asserting that 'interest in this kind of story surely existed, for the tales of adventure of the then popular romance heroes have much in common with the lives of the Christian protagonists of the saints' lives. And tales of exotic lands and peoples, vicarious experiences in the world of the marvelous and the miraculous seem to have delighted equally the "lewed and the learned."'[6]

Assuming that manuscript survival is indeed an indication of popularity, the *SEL* must truly have delighted medieval audiences. The repetitive, formulaic nature of the texts indicates a tried-and-true method of capturing audience attention and further implies shared assumptions among the compilers and copiers about audience expectations. The Banna sanctorum makes it clear that the popular appeal of the *SEL* lies, at least in part, in its depictions of violence and gore following the expected pattern. Stephen Wilson has argued that 'saints' Lives could fulfil functions similar to those fulfilled later by serial stories or *romans-feuilletons*, and ... by horror films,'[7] and the Lives in the *SEL* certainly do so. That they follow a distinct pattern and are presented over the course of the church's calendar year allies them with the *roman-feuilleton*; the overarching story in the serial, of course, is the church's growth and survival. The martyrs' Lives are violent episodes of that larger narrative.

Karen A. Winstead observes: 'One of the distinguishing features of the *South English Legendary* is its graphic description of violence, which by far exceeds what we find in both the *Legenda aurea* and in most contemporary vernacular legends.'[8] A gruesome moment from Juliana's Life illustrates how graphic violence in the *SEL* is:

> A weol of ire swuþe strang · byuore hure hy caste
> Al were þe uelien aboute · wiþ rasours ystiked uaste
> Þat weol hi turnde al aboute · þe maide þerbi hi sette
> Dupe wode in hure naked fleiss · þe rasors kene iwette
> Þat þo hure uless was al to torne · so deope wode & gnowe
> Þat þe bones hy to slitte · and þe marrou out drowe
> Þat marrou sprang out alaboute · so ouercome he[o] was
> Þat he[o] almest ȝaf þe gost · & no wonder it nas   (141–8, *SEL* 1: 67)

[They cast before her a very strong wheel of iron; on the rims all around it razors were stuck fast. They turned the wheel all around; they set the virgin on it. The keen, sharpened razors penetrated deeply into her naked flesh so that then her flesh was all torn, so deeply penetrated and gnawed that they slit the bones and drew out the marrow. The marrow sprang out all around; she was so overcome that she almost gave up the ghost, and it was no wonder.]

Such a close, detailed description of this scene is not found in other contemporary versions of Juliana's Life; the same incident in Jacobus de Voragine's *Golden Legend*, for example, is described as: ' ... [the prefect] had Juliana stretched on a wheel until all her bones were broken and the marrow spurted out, but an angel of the Lord shattered the wheel and healed her instantly.'[9] In the *SEL*, even the angel's intervention emphasizes violence rather than, say, the miraculous healing of Juliana. Jankofsky reads this episode as an illustration of 'the mood of compassion and warm human participation in the description of the lives of saints, disciples, apostles, confessors, virgins, and martyrs which permeates the entire collection.'[10] These characteristics of the *SEL*, Jankofsky argues, are 'the result of a more "realistic" and purposely heightened depiction of the sufferings and joys of the protagonists and of the direct appeal to the emotions and empathy of the audience.'[11]

Complicating such a reading, however, is the observation of Winstead that 'descriptions of grisly tortures are almost invariably accompanied by assurances that the saint feels nothing.'[12] Though Juliana is not described here as feeling nothing before the angel heals her, Winstead's point is well taken, since it is not only true that other saints are so described, but Juliana herself compares her ordeal to Christ's, and Christ wins the suffering contest. Winstead further argues that such representations of violence may have actually distanced the audience from the saint: 'Ultimately, the saints' extraordinary imperviousness to pain may have *discouraged* many people from identifying with them. In fact, given the highly subversive actions of virgin martyrs in these legends, it seems likely that one reason that Middle English hagiographers emphasized the saints' resilience was to distance readers from their heroines and in so doing to make it less likely that they would imitate their unruliness.'[13]

Since works such as the *Golden Legend* achieve the same distancing effect with much less gore, it is reasonable to assume that representations of violence in the *SEL* have the additional function of entertainment described by Jankofsky. If the audience is indeed distanced from the saint, as Winstead argues, that very distance can be part of what allows the audience to be entertained, imagining the spectacle of torture through the *SEL*'s careful descriptions.

The martyrological narratives of the *SEL* thus function more as audience entertainment than as didactic models of the Christian life. The repetition of the same tortures perpetrated on the saints suggests that violence is a major component of the Lives' entertainment function. But precisely *how* violence is coded as entertainment in the martyrs' Lives of the *SEL* is gendered. Though the Lives of female saints comprise the smallest group in the *SEL* (fourteen narratives; there are sixteen *temporale* pieces, and sixty-one Lives of male saints), the torture of women is noticeably more spectacular than the torture of men.[14] The distinct gendered difference in the representations of violence in the *SEL* is illustrated by the degree to which the narratives focus on the body itself. There are, for example, two concerns in the Life of a male saint: how he deals with torture, and who he is, especially in ecclesiastical terms. Neither concern specifically focusses on the body. The two concerns in the Life of a female martyr, however, are both bodily concerns: her virginity, and how she looks while being tortured.

Similar episodes in the Lives of female and male martyrs point out the difference. In Margaret's Life, for example, witnesses to Margaret's torture, including the justice who orders it, find it too shameful to watch:

> And þe Iustice for ssunnesse · nolde loky þerto
> Ac bihuld abac and hudde is eiȝen · & moni oþere also (127–8, *SEL* 1: 296)
> [And the justice for shame would not look toward there, but looked back and hid his eyes and many others (did) also.]

So pitiful is the scene, in fact, that spectators in the narrative beg Margaret to

> Haue reuþe of þi faire bodi · þat me let þus torende (132, *SEL* 1: 296)
> [Have pity on your fair body that men order thus tormented.]

Her response is to denounce them:

> And sede ȝe wikkede conseillers · goþ fram me anon
> Anoþer conseil ich habbe itake · ich forsake ȝou echon (135–6, *SEL* 1: 296)
> [And she said, 'You wicked counsellors, get away from me immediately. I have taken another counsel; I forsake each one of you.']

When, however, Vincent is faced with a similar request from the justice responsible for his torture to

> Ne let namore þin hendi bodi · wiþ tormens defouly (50, *SEL* 1: 26)
> [Let no more of your gracious body (be) defiled with torments]

his response is to pity the justice's foolishness and call for more torture:

> Hit me greueþ þat þou feinest þe · more þanne al þe pine
> And al þe tormens þat þou me dest · þou & alle þine
> Ne bilef noȝt ȝut ne be[o] þou noȝt · so sone bineþe ibroȝt
> Þou most ȝute more ioie bringe · & gladnesse in my þoȝt (55–8, *SEL* 1: 27)
>
> [It grieves me more that you dissemble than all the pain and all the torments that you do to me, you and all your (followers). Don't give up yet; you are not so soon brought down. You must yet bring more joy and gladness to my mind.]

In this way, Vincent keeps some amount of control over what happens to him, and the responsibility for more torture rests partly on him, not on 'anoþer conseil.' The only witnesses to Vincent's tortures are the men following the justice's orders, and nothing is said about their reactions; they are described only as acting and speaking, never as witnessing or lamenting. The justice is not even present at several of Vincent's torments; his men repeatedly have to go to him to report failure. Witnessing, then, is not a part of Vincent's Life. It is replaced five times with reports of Vincent's speaking, praying, or singing. With the exception of the (unquoted) prayer at his death, Vincent's speech is a dangerous response to the situations in which he finds himself; his reward is more severe punishment. Torture in the Life of a male martyr is thus an event in which he is involved, while torture in the Life of a female martyr is a spectacle that she must endure.

Modern theorists of pain argue that torture, by its very nature, is a spectacle defined primarily by its judicial use and the body of the prisoner. Edward Peters finds a single common element in the definitions of torture given by lawyers and historians: 'it is torment inflicted by a public authority for ostensibly public purposes.'[15] Michel Foucault argues that: 'The tortured body is first inscribed in the legal ceremonial that must produce, open for all to see, the truth of the crime.'[16] The judicial process of torture, then, produces the 'truth of the crime' via the tortured body; the suffering body, therefore, is crucial to the definition of torture as spectacle. To this definition Elaine Scarry adds the necessity of bodily pain. Pain, in fact, is central to the three elements that Scarry argues make up the structure of torture: 'the infliction of pain,' 'the objectification of the subjective attributes of pain,' and 'the translation of the objectified attributes of pain into the insignia of power.'[17] For Scarry, the translation of pain into power makes 'torture ... a grotesque piece of compensatory drama.'[18] The body alone is not enough; torture needs visible pain as well. Foucault argues: 'Torture rests on a whole quantitative art of pain' and, in fact, 'public torture and execution must be spectacular, it must be seen by all almost as its triumph.'[19] The spectacle of bodily pain makes torture simultaneously an exercise of power and a warning against transgression; the tortured body-in-pain is a text to be read by the torturer as affirmation and by others as confirmation. Those who read must also interpret, assessing what has been done, and why.

Though such theorists provide an opening for ways of thinking about the roles of violence, pain, and suffering in medieval saints' Lives, their theories fail to map entirely onto medieval hagiographic practices in two key ways. First, the lack of felt pain in Christian martyrs' Lives contradicts what Scarry says the function of pain in torture is: 'in serious pain the claims of the body utterly nullify the claims of the world.'[20] In accounts of torture such as those found in the *SEL* the opposite occurs: the *lack* of felt pain – the torturer's inability to cause pain in torture – nullifies 'the claims of the world,' defined in a collection like the *SEL* as the claims of the pagan world, which contradict the spiritual claims of the Christian world. The result is that the nature of the spectacle is changed. Rather than the sight of a body-in-pain, the sight is now of a body that resists pain, a change that leads to fuller concentration on issues other than torture in men's Lives and to a conflation of violence and sexuality in women's Lives. The latter results in the second key point of departure between modern theory and medieval hagiography: the spectacle of torture is present when the victim is female, but absent when the victim is male.

Because it should not be forgotten that there is a vast difference between *torture* and *representations* of torture, it is necessary to note that Scarry, Peters, and Foucault are writing about real world torture; hagiographic texts are not. Medieval hagiographers' accounts of early Christian martyrs are drawn from a long tradition that began with lists of the names of martyrs, to which details were added later. Thus, torture in the *SEL* is of an imaginary and rhetorical nature, which may in part explain why it bears little resemblance to real world torture as described by Scarry, Peters, and Foucault. Nevertheless, the lack of felt pain on the part of the martyrs and the repetitive nature of torture in the *SEL* point to an important function of the *SEL*'s textual representations of violence: the normalization of torture as an event with little or no real world consequence. Descriptions of torture, therefore, are connected not to actual suffering but to the 'vicarious experiences in the world of the marvelous and the miraculous' that Jankofsky mentions.[21] As such, they are not warnings against transgression but safe, entertaining episodes of the larger narrative of church history.

Because women's participation in the *SEL*'s narrative of church history is largely limited to their steadfast insistence on virginity, the forms of entertainment in their Lives are also limited; there are no other issues to distract from the violence of any given torture scene. Men's more varied roles in church history, however, open possibilities for other types of entertainment, such as humour that serves to distract from bodily violence. Gregory M. Sadlek points out the humour in the Lives of saints Alphege and Vincent, arguing that the apparently inappropriate humour in those Lives 'might ... indicate that an author is striking out beyond traditional generic boundaries, that the text in question ... occupies a generic middle ground' between romance and hagiography.[22] Whether it so indicates or not, the incidents Sadlek cites are indeed funny. Poor, hapless Alphege, mucking around in the swampy ground to which the devil has led him, finally realizes that he has been tricked and calls on God for help. God sends an angel, whose greeting to Alphege is comically stern:

> Þou fol he sede wy wenstou [·] mid him þat doþ þe ssame
> Þat haþ iheued to þe envie · suþþe þou were ibore (138–9, *SEL* 1: 152)

['You fool,' he said, 'why did you go with him who does you shame, who has had envy for you since you were born?']

As Sadlek suggests, one might expect derisive laughter to be directed at the devil, but instead the narrative paints a comic picture of the mud-spattered Alphege meekly returning to the prison from which he will be martyred the following day. In the Life of Vincent, the comic elements highlight the torturer Dacian's pitiful attempts to use torture to illustrate his power. That power is nullified, however, as Vincent shows himself eager for his torment, referring to it as a 'game' (line 27) and comically rushing to the gibbet from which he is to be hanged (61–2). Dacian cannot, it turns out, even kill Vincent with torture: Vincent dies when Dacian gives up and orders him placed in a soft bed.

Humour in male martyrs' Lives is sometimes juxtaposed with a graphic description of a torture performed on the saint. In Lawrence's Life, for example, the narrator provides specifics about the destruction of Lawrence's face:

> His cheken & is mouþ aboute · hi lete bete wiþ stones
> And dasste out is teþ of his heued · & debrusede þe oþer bones
> (149–50, *SEL* 2: 363)

[His cheeks and his mouth he ordered beaten with stones, and dashed his teeth out of his head and destroyed the other bones.]

The narrator immediately follows the description with a joke:

> He was an vuel dobbe dent · þer uore i ne rede ʒou noʒt
> Hure him to deore to hele ʒoure teþ · i not ware ʒe habbe iþoʒt (151–2, *SEL* 2: 363)

[He was an evil dentist; therefore I do not advise you to hire him at a high price to fix your teeth.]

Attention is thus diverted from the horror of Lawrence's destroyed face, and the pain that such a beating would cause gets no mention. Lawrence himself later participates in the grim humour when he is being roasted on iron pikes:

> þou wrecche he sede þou hast irosted · þulke side inou
> Turn is upward & et is nou · for ȝare he[o] is þerto
> Wend þe oþer side & roste is ek · forte he[o] be[o] inou also (174–6, *SEL* 2: 364)

['You wretch,' he said, 'you have roasted this side enough. Turn it upward and eat it now, for it is ready. Turn the other side and roast it, too, until it is done also.']

Making a joke of the torture of male martyrs means that neither the audience nor the men upon whom torture is perpetrated need take it seriously, nor does the audience need to focus on the horrific sight of a tortured body. Vincent's game, Alphege's helplessness, and Lawrence's joke stand not only as examples of the saints' steadfastness but of their lack of concern for what is happening to them as well. Pity for the suffering of the tortured male body is replaced by laughter at the jokes, giggling at the saint's all-too-human confusion, and admiration of his wit.

In only one female martyr's Life is the joking humour pointed out directly: Juliana's. Her battle with the devil is full of comic moments, as when she tosses him into a full chamberpot (lines 129–33). Unlike Lawrence, however, Juliana is not described as laughing at her own joke; it is the narrator who points out the comedy:

> Day þat him wolde ricchore bed · biseche oþer bidde
> For it was god inou to him · wiþinne & eke aboue
> Wat segge ȝe segge ich soþ · ne lieþ noȝt for is loue (134–6, *SEL* 1: 67)

[They that would (wish) a richer bed for him, ask another prayer, for it was good enough for him.]

The joke is not about Juliana or the torture of her body, but about the suitability of a chamberpot as a devil's bed. The same devil later becomes a maniacally comic figure when he appears at the scene of Juliana's execution to warn her executioners to beware of her and to ask them to protect him from her (lines 191–200). Juliana herself displays little humour in the narrative; she laughs once while being beaten (44), tosses the devil into a chamberpot when 'reuþe of him heo [h]adde' [she had pity on him] (130), and rolls her eyes at his antics at the site of her execution (193). She is not ever the object of the joke, as Alphege is. Furthermore, the joke is not connected to her body or to her suffering – as in the cases of Alphege, Vincent, and Lawrence – and thus it does not rewrite that suffering and distract from it. Because the humour does not distract from or make light of Juliana's torture, there is still room to focus on her body and to pity what happens to it.

This is not to say that there are no humorous possibilities in female martyrs' Lives. The chaos of Christina's encounters with various justices, for example, probably struck medieval audiences as funny. Women martyrs in the *SEL*, however, do not participate in humour by making jokes, nor are they directly associated with slapstick moments. They are, instead, distanced from narrative humour, and are thus focal points of serious, steadfast piety in the face of opposition and torture.

The narratives of the *SEL* do not rely on humorous distraction as the only rhetorical device for shifting focus away from tortured male bodies. Men have other roles besides being martyrs: Lawrence is an archdeacon, Vincent a deacon. Alphege holds a series of offices: abbot, bishop of Winchester, archbishop of Canterbury. These roles give the male martyr an additional identity not directly connected with the body. They also provide reasons other than bodily suffering for the man's sanctity, as well as further justifications – from the pagan point of view – for his initial arrest. The male martyr's ecclesiastical activities, not the state of his body, are what irritate the authorities. Though refusal of marriage is the most common reason for a female martyr's arrest, this issue is entirely absent in the Lives of male martyrs. Vincent, for example, is arrested along with Valerian, his bishop; Valerian's inability to evangelize effectively gets him released, but Vincent is held and subsequently tortured because he is 'renable inou · to prechi uer & ner' [eloquent enough to preach far and near] (line 8). Lawrence is arrested because he has been entrusted with 'Al þe tresor of Holy Churche' [All the treasure of holy Church] (11), which turns out to be poor people. Alphege is taken prisoner by the Vikings because he offers his life in exchange for those of the 'selymen' [simple men] (86) of Canterbury. Moreover, once in prison, some male martyrs continue their ecclesiastical activities; Lawrence, for example, heals and converts people while he is in prison. The male martyr's activities and ecclesiastical identity remain, therefore, his major identifying characteristics, and they both define his role in church history and join his wit and steadfastness as the narrative's main focus.

But in women's Lives, the mutilation of a female body is of sufficient interest that it constitutes the major concern of the narrative. The female martyr's most important identity is that of virgin, an identity entirely dependent upon the state of the body. In prison, therefore, a virgin martyr primarily waits; any prison activities are the result of visits from outsiders. A visit from her mother, for example, leads to Christina's disowning of her family. Two more extended examples are Juliana's and Margaret's battles with the devils who visit them in prison. Both episodes involve physical prowess on the part of the saint and, significantly, both function to keep the saint's biological sex and cultural gender foregrounded. The battles initially appear to shift the focus away from the saint's tortured body, even if only for that episode. But the details of the fight scenes emphasize the gendered nature of violence, highlighting as they do the unusual occurrence of a 'maid' being physically able to beat up the devil. The devil who visits Juliana is frightened by the gender reversal:

> Maidens ichelle euere eft drede · inabbe aȝen hom no miȝte (120, *SEL* 1: 66)
>
> [Virgins I shall ever after dread; I have no power against them.]

Despite this professed fear of virgins, his plea to her for release is based on her gender and sexual status, which, as he puts it, are at odds with her aggression:

> Þench þat maidens ssolde milde be[o] · & bring me of þis bende
> War is þe kunde of þi maidenot · þat ssolde be[o] milde & stille
> & þou ert aȝen me so sterne · hou miȝtou habbe þe wille (126–8, *SEL* 1: 66)
>
> [Remember that virgins should be mild and release me from this bond. Where is the nature of your virginity, which should be mild and quiet, and you are so fierce against me? How can you have the will?]

The devil who is seized by Margaret makes a similar plea:

> Haue ruþe of me ich bidde þe · & bring me of þis wrechede
> And þench þat maidens ssolde be[o] · fol of milce and ore (228–9, *SEL* 1: 299)
>
> [Have pity on me, I beg you, and release me from this wretchedness, and remember that virgins should be full of mercy and grace].

When Margaret rises up 'wel baldeliche' [very boldly] (174) to seize the devil and throw him to the ground, his lament at his predicament is based on her sex:

> Alas þat ich here com · mi miȝte me is bynome
> Alas þat a tendre maide · me ssel þus ouercome
> Ȝif it were a man of eni strengþe · me þingþ me nere noȝt
> Ac issend ich am þat a maide · me haþ to grondre ibroȝt (185–8, *SEL* 1: 298)
>
> [Alas that I came here! My power is taken from me. Alas that such a tender virgin shall thus overcome me! If it were a man of any strength, it seems to me it would be nothing, but I am ashamed that a virgin has brought me to the ground.]

Thus, rhetorically, the unusual nature of the reversal – a female in the position of torturer – is emphasized.[23] Margaret's battle with the devil actually follows the most horrifying of her torture sessions, in which the narrator focuses the audience's attention on pity, crying 'Alas' three times in four lines:

> Alas hure swete tendre body · so villiche todrawe so
> Alas hou miȝte enyman · such dede for ruþe do
> Wiþ oules hi todrowe hure wombe · þe gottes isene were
> Alas also þe ssendfol dede · hure deorne limes hi totere (123–6, *SEL* 1: 296)

[Alas, her sweet tender body so vilely rent! Alas, how might any man do such a deed for pity! With hooks they tore her belly so that the guts were seen. Alas, too, the shameful deed: they ripped her private parts.]

Though Christian steadfastness is at least part of what allows Margaret to endure, it is only part of the point. Encouraging the text's audience to visualize what the spectators within the narrative are witnessing – the mutilation of Margaret's female body – the narrator connects female Christian steadfastness with female bodily suffering: it is through such suffering that Margaret is proven a steadfast and devout Christian.

The bodies of female martyrs are put on imaginative rhetorical display with the obligatory removal of their clothing by the pagan torturers. Women martyrs are routinely deprived of their clothes just before they are tortured, and the resulting nakedness has a dual function. Because there is no resistance on the part of the martyr, nakedness is first a symbol of rejection of the secular world and of the strength of the martyr's faith; as Margaret R. Miles observes: 'Nakedness in martyrdom, in asceticism, and in medieval practices of evangelical poverty was voluntary and active, the result of an adamantly confessed faith.'[24] But, Miles points out, nakedness also connects with issues of power and shame: 'The mark of powerlessness and passivity, nakedness was associated with captives, slaves, prostitutes, the insane, and the dead. Also, as we have seen in martyrdom accounts, the prerogative of imposing nakedness on others to humiliate, torture, or punish was an important social power.'[25]

Nakedness represents shame and display most clearly in the Life of Agnes. The narrator highlights the social shame of nakedness by attributing to the pagans who strip Agnes the motive of humiliating her:

> Me let somny al þan toun · þe maide ham stod byuore
> Þe constable hure let strupe · so naked so he[o] was ibore
> Þat echman ssolde hure de[o]rne lymes · ise[o] hure to ssende (41–3, *SEL* 1: 20)

[Men ordered all the town summoned; the virgin stood before them. The officer ordered her stripped as naked as she was born, so that everyone should see her private parts to shame her.]

Agnes is protected from shame only because she is hidden from pagan eyes; the narrative assumes that her naked body is shameful. Nakedness in martyrdom itself is not gender specific – male martyrs are sometimes also deprived of their clothing before torture – but rhetorical emphasis on it and its association with shame are.[26]

Even more striking than nakedness in these narratives is the way in which saints and tormenters *see* versions of truth. In Christina's Life, for instance, Christian and non-Christian visual abilities are juxtaposed. The three justices Christina faces can *see* her defiance but not the power of God. Early in the narrative, Christina's father is 'So gelous ... of hure fairhede · þat noman hure ne seie' [So jealous ... of her beauty that no one saw her] (line 16). He knows trouble is afoot when he spies on her (56) and later when he 'bihuld & miste is false god' [looked and missed his false gods] (102). By contrast, Christina's nightly viewing of the stars leads to her realization that, as a pagan, she is living 'in luþer þoȝt' [in an evil state] (37), and her conversion is confirmed when an angel appears to her to tell her that she will suffer torture under three justices but will 'ouercome alle þre[o]' [overcome all three] (76). Later, Christ himself baptizes her in the ocean. Christina never sees another Christian or even a church, but she does see that

> He is God of alle god · þat al þis made of noȝt (38, *SEL* 1: 316)
>
> [He is God of all gods who made all this from nothing.]

Christina's ability to see the narrative's truth of Christianity and pagan error, as well as her own future identity as a Christian martyr, is juxtaposed with pagan literal and spiritual blindness, and all of these issues have Christina's body as their locus. The power of her Christian body to blind pagans is first suggested when she nearly blinds her father:

> Þis maide gripte pece and oþer · & fram hure body rende
> And caste hure uader aȝen þe teþ · & almest him ablende
> Nim þere he [*sic*] sede þ[ou] luþer best · þou vnwreste uode
> And fret al rau þi nowe fleiss · and þin owe blode
> For þou nere neuere uol · monnes fleiss to drawe
> Þer þou miȝt of þin owene inou · bo[þ]e frete & gnawe (157–62, *SEL* 1: 320–1)
>
> [The virgin gripped a piece, and another, and tore (them) from her body and threw (them) at her father against his teeth and almost blinded him. Take there, she said, you evil beast, you wicked creature, and chew all raw your own flesh and your own blood.]

Christina's father responds not to what she has said but to what he has seen: 'Þe fader þo he þis isei · he nuste hou on take' [When the father saw this he did not know how to proceed] (163). Unable to respond in any rational way because he cannot see Christina's spiritual truth, he has her cast into a fire while men pour pitch and oil over her head. The spectacle that ensues – the fire 'bigan to sprede abrod' [began to spread about] (174) and 'forbarnd al to noȝt · þat misbiluued were' [burned all to nothing those who were unbelieving] (176) – leads to the father having his daughter dragged to prison to be out of sight 'Forte he hadde bet biseie · to bringe hure of lif dawe' [Until he had better seen how to bring her from life's days] (180). That the father's response is to what he sees and not to what he hears is a subtle encouragement to the narrative's listeners to picture what they hear.

A similar encouragement is in the next episode of Christina's Life; the shortest torture sequence, Christina's encounter with the second justice contains the clearest indication to the narrative's audience that picturing what happens to Christina is important. Female onlookers in the narrative chastise the second justice for treating a woman so shamefully:

> Wymmen þat þere stode aboute · & yseie hure defouled more
> And euere naked so uilliche · hom ofssamede sore
> Iustice hi seide þou art · an vnwreste man
> Þat þou so ssenfolliche · defoulest a womman
> In ssennesse of alle oþere · boþe nou and er
> Alas þat eny womman · so luþer mon ber (241–6, *SEL* 1: 323)

[Women who stood about there and saw her defiled more and ever so vilely naked felt very ashamed. Justice, they said, you are a wicked man that you (would) so shamefully defile a woman, to the shame of all others both now and before. Alas that any woman bore so evil a man.]

The reaction of the women emphasizes the spectacle with terms like 'defouled' and 'euere naked so uilliche'; it also invites the narrative's listeners to join the female onlookers in seeing and understanding the shame of the justice's behaviour. Seeing the consequences of his actions, in fact, kills this second justice:

> Þe Iustice isei þat þis folk · toward þis maide drou
> For wraþþe he uel upriȝt ded · and deide in sorwe inou (263–4, *SEL* 1: 324)

[The justice saw that the people drew toward the virgin; for anger he fell dead and died in great sorrow.]

The third justice in Christina's story is, of course, the one who is blinded in an incident that shows the audience the spectacle of the gender-specific mutilation of cutting off Christina's breasts (lines 321–3). Instead of blood, the wounds produce milk, to which Christina responds by praising God: 'For nou ichot clene ich am' [For now I know that I am pure] (328). The sight is meaningless to the pagan justice, however, and his anger is 'mest for hure speche' [most for her speech] (329); he orders her tongue cut off to silence her. When this fails and Christina continues to speak, the Justice responds by seizing her 'holi tonge' [holy tongue] (329), and angrily flinging it at her. Though the causes of the justice's anger – 'hure speche' [her speech] (329) and 'ȝute spak þis holy maide' [yet the holy virgin spoke] (332) – suggest that narrative focus has shifted to speech, no direct speech is actually attributed to any of the characters. What Christina 'ȝute spak' about is not given. When the justice throws Christina's tongue at her, the narrative returns explicitly to sight, as the tongue blinds the tormenter, and turns *him* into a spectacle: 'Me miȝte segge wo him iseie · þere sit þe blinde wrecche' [Men who saw him might say, there sits the blind wretch] (337). Christina's death follows shortly thereafter, out of the sight of her pagan enemies and with one more reminder of her torture: 'To ȝer in such torment he[o] liuede · and in such ssame' [She lived two years in such torment and in such shame] (360). Violence, the witnessing of torture both in the narrative and outside of it, and the spectacle of the suffering female body are thus brought together at the close of Christina's Life.

While men in the *SEL* are models of Christian steadfastness and action, and are thus subjects who have at least some control over their fate, women are models of steadfastness and *reaction*, and are therefore objects to be acted upon. Male and female martyrs share the active decision to be Christian, but women's roles in church history end with their acceptance of Christianity. Men's Lives generally begin with the martyr acting in some way on behalf of the church. Women's Lives begin with the martyr *reacting* to the pursuit of a potential lover/husband or the disapproval of a cruel father. With their joking, eagerness, prison activities, and preaching, male martyrs retain their active status, goading their tormenters to respond to their steadfast faith with further punishment. Women, on the other hand, continue to react, enduring the spectacle of torture.

The narrative of the *SEL* collection as a whole is the story of church history, struggle, and growth. Men's Lives – those of both martyrs and non-martyrs – each represent a moment in church history when a saint helped further the interests of the church in some important way, and their identities span a broad range of church history, from biblical figures to Thomas Becket; the most recent Life in the *SEL* is Edmund of Canterbury (d. 1242). By contrast, all but one of the female martyrs in the *SEL* were martyred by Roman authorities in a past already distant in the thirteenth century.[27] They make no direct contributions to the church itself, either through ecclesiastical office or evangelical activities; instead, they are bodies to be gazed at by audiences both within and outside of the narrative. The focus in women's Lives on the female body and what is done to it combines with the *SEL*'s project of capturing the attention of the laity to suggest an assumption that the female body itself is an object of entertainment. While torture in all the *SEL* martyrs' Lives functions as a way to nullify the claims of the material world and emphasize the claims of Christian spirituality, its particular rhetorical emphases in women's Lives on the visual appearance of the body are central to those Lives' entertainment elements. The narratives' relentless training of the audience's gaze on the naked female body having violence enacted upon it leads to the disturbing suggestion that violence against women itself is somehow entertaining. By turning female bodies into objects to be enacted and gazed upon, the *SEL* narratives ultimately turn the torture of those bodies into a prurient sport designed to help lure audiences away from the 'lesynge' of other forms of popular entertainment. They are not, then, narratives about women as subjects, but narratives about women's bodies as objects.

Notes

1 *The South English Legendary*, ed. Charlotte d'Evelyn and Anna J. Mill, 3 vols, EETS 235, 236, 244 (London 1956–9). All citations of the *SEL* in this article are taken from this edition of the 'Banna Sanctorum' (*SEL* 1: 1–3), 'De sancta Agneta' (1: 19– 23), 'De sancto Vincencio' (1: 25–31), 'De sancta Iuliana virgine' (1: 62–70), 'De sancta Margareta' (1: 291–302), 'De sancta Cristina' (1: 315–27), 'De sancto Alphego' (1: 148–55), and 'De sancto Laurencio martire' (2: 358–64).
2 'De sancta Margareta' line 120, *SEL* 1: 295.
3 Klaus P. Jankofsky, 'National Characteristics in the Portrayal of English Saints in the *South English Legendary*,' in *Images of Sainthood in Medieval Europe*, ed. Renate Blumenfeld-Kosinski and Timea Szell (Ithaca 1991), 83. In his study of the *SEL*'s textual tradition, Manfred Görlach, *The Textual Tradition of the South English Legendary*, Leeds Texts and Monographs n.s. 6 (Leeds 1974), x, lists 62 MSS, which he categorizes as follows: 25 MSS containing the bulk of the collection, 19 fragments, and 18 miscellanies with one *SEL* item; he also lists 4 MSS 'now apparently lost.' Jankofsky asserts elsewhere ('Foreword,' in *The South English Legendary: A Critical Assessment*, ed. Janofsky [Tübingen 1992], ix) that the number of surviving *SEL* MSS 'rank it with Chaucer, Langland, and *The Pricke of Conscience* as one of the most widely read, copied and distributed texts of the Middle English period.'
4 Jankofsky, 'National Characteristics,' 84.
5 Klaus P. Jankofsky, 'Personalized Didacticism: The Interplay of Narrative and Subject Matter in the *South English Legendary*,' *TAIUS: Journal of Texas A&I University* 10 (1977) 70.
6 Ibid.
7 Stephen Wilson, 'Introduction,' in *Saints and Their Cults: Studies in Religious Sociology, Folklore, and History*, ed. Wilson (Cambridge 1983), 16.

8 Karen A. Winstead, *Virgin Martyrs: Legends of Sainthood in Late Medieval England* (Ithaca and London 1997), 73.
9 Jacobus de Voragine, *The Golden Legend: Readings on the Saints*, trans. William Granger Ryan, 2 vols (Princeton 1993), 1: 161.
10 Klaus P. Jankofsky, 'Entertainment, Edification, and Popular Education in the *South English Legendary*,' *Journal of Popular Culture* 11.3 (1977) 710–11.
11 Ibid., 711.
12 Winstead, *Virgin Martyrs*, 73.
13 Ibid., 74.
14 Of the 14 Lives of women saints in d'Evelyn and Mill's edition, 9 are martyrs' legends. Of the 61 Lives of men saints, 35 are martyrs' legends.
15 Edward Peters, *Torture*, expanded ed. (Philadelphia 1996), 3.
16 Michel Foucault, *Discipline and Punish: The Birth of the Prison*, trans. Alan Sheridan (New York 1995), 35.
17 Elaine Scarry, *The Body in Pain: The Making and Unmaking of the World* (New York 1985), 51.
18 Ibid., 28.
19 Foucault, *Discipline and Punish*, 34.
20 Scarry, *Body in Pain*, 33.
21 Jankofsky, 'Personalized Didacticism,' 70.
22 Gregory M. Sadlek, 'Laughter, Game, and Ambiguous Comedy in the *South English Legendary*,' *Studia neophilologica* 64 (1991) 46.
23 For an excellent discussion of the anxieties and challenges posed by similar gendered reversals in early modern Europe, see Natalie Zemon Davis, 'Women on Top,' in her *Society and Culture in Early Modern France* (Stanford 1975), 124–51.
24 Margaret R. Miles, *Carnal Knowing: Female Nakedness and Religious Meaning in the Christian West* (Boston 1989), 81.
25 Ibid.
26 Of the nine female martyrs in the d'Evelyn and Mill edition of the *SEL*, only two – Ursula and Agatha – are not specifically described as being stripped naked. In the case of Ursula, the omission is not surprising; her Life is not concerned with Ursula as an individual martyr but with the story of the Eleven Thousand Virgins, and it is the only Life of a female martyr that diverges from the general pattern of martyrs' Lives. In Agatha's Life, the stripping of her clothing is replaced by the gender-specific torture of tearing off her breasts, an act that obviously could not be accomplished if Agatha were clothed.
27 The exception is the story of Ursula and the Eleven Thousand Virgins. But, again, this Life is set in the distant past: 'Ac þen nas ȝute in Engelond · no Cirstendom ibroȝt' [But no Christianity was yet brought to England] ('De vndecim milia virginum' 12, *SEL* 1: 443–8, at 443).

8 Violence or Cruelty?
An Intercultural Perspective

DANIEL BARAZ

Violence and cruelty are close but not identical concepts. Both involve primarily, though not exclusively, the application of physical force. By modern standards burning heretics at the stake would undoubtedly be a violent act. Yet is it also a cruel act? A modern answer would most likely be again 'yes.' But in other periods and in other cultures the answer would be different. Violence and cruelty are both cultural constructs, but that does not entail that they are objective or subjective to the same extent. What I would like to argue in this paper is that cruelty, much more than violence, is related to specific cultural conventions and traditions, and hence is less 'objective.'

The modern concept of physical violence is, to a considerable extent, objective and quantifiable. Violence can be defined as the application of physical force against an individual or a group of people. It can be organized according to standard – mostly legal – categories, such as murder, rape, assault, robbery. Categorization serves primarily as a basis for comparison. Thus, for instance, one can compare the levels of violence in Los Angeles and Seattle, or observe patterns of rise and decline of violence in New York. Classification also permits comparison of violence across different cultures and historical periods.

Records of violence can provide a rough idea of the levels of violence within a specific society or community. However, categorization is problematic, since it is inevitably affected by the cultural, organizational, and personal biases of the compilers of the statistics. Yet the problems of dealing with modern violence dwarf in comparison to those that have to be tackled when dealing with violence in previous periods.

The issue of violence is an essential background for understanding medieval perceptions of cruelty. The various attitudes to cruelty stand out only by comparing the different modes in which similar acts of violence are represented.

In this respect *violence* will be used here in the modern sense of the concept, as a quantifiable and comparable category and, to the extent possible, morally neutral.[1] Yet, to avoid unnecessary anachronism, I have chosen to examine the medieval representations of actions that were invariably deemed violent in the Middle Ages as well: killing that is extraordinary either in the number of victims or in the extent of suffering inflicted (or both), and demolition of property and of shrines (churches, monasteries, or mosques).

The Implications of Terminology

What renders a violent action cruel is primarily its definition as such. Some acts of violence are defined as cruelty, and some are not. Moreover, the specific manner of description is a conscious choice. Cruelty is a label that involves moral judgment. One can speak about 'justified violence,' but much less so – if at all – about 'justified cruelty.'[2] Thus, cruelty is a more subjective and culturally dependent concept than violence. The choice of labelling actions as cruel is moderated by cultural, social, and political factors.

The implications of this choice for key aspects of medieval society and culture render the distinction between the two concepts important. Marking the border between violence and cruelty had practical implications in medieval Western societies. The distinction between violence and cruelty had a crucial political significance. Violence was, to a certain degree, the prerogative of the legitimate ruler. Cruelty, on the other hand, was the sign of an illegitimate tyrant. Consequently, in the medieval period there were numerous mechanisms, religious and political, whose function was to manipulate this border.

The Threshold

The ability to distinguish between violence and cruelty bears directly upon the historian's understanding of medieval societies; reconstructing the way in which people perceive violence aimed against them is one of the more complex tasks in reconstructing medieval 'world views.' The problem in the attempt to distinguish between violence and cruelty is the overlap between the concepts. Moreover, the preoccupation with this issue was not always explicit. In the early Middle Ages, for instance, violence was presented as cruelty only implicitly. Although the presence of explicit references to cruelty is significant in itself, their absence does not necessarily indicate that the action was not perceived as morally wrong or cruel.

Thus, passage from violence to cruelty hinges on the concept of the threshold, which separates two distinct entities. Violence can be presented as part of an open-ended continuum, from lesser to greater violence. The introduction of the concept of cruelty closes the upper end of the continuum: when the level of violence crosses this threshold it turns into something else. In the medieval West, when violence was considered excessive – for various reasons – it was defined as cruelty.

Cruelty and Tyranny

Justified and unjustified violence were, to a considerable measure, legal issues. Violence was justified, with qualifications, as self-defence.[3] Violence was also necessary in the enforcement of the law. The extent of this violence, however, was limited; excessive violence – even in self-defence or in the application of the law – ceased to be legitimate.[4]

The concept of *cruelty* is of Latin classical origin. It is related to the issue of tyranny, more accurately to the abhorrence of tyranny in Latin culture, which is evident in episodes such as the killing of Sextus Tarquinius following the rape of Lucretia, or in the murder of Julius Caesar. Hence cruelty appears as an object of theoretical speculation in the writings of Seneca, who lived under the emperors Caligula, Claudius, and Nero. These rulers became emblems of cruelty and tyrannical rule as early as the first century AD.[5]

This conceptual structure is reflected in the key theoretical text on cruelty in the Middle Ages, a question in Thomas Aquinas's *Summa theologiae*. Thomas refers to cruelty as *superexcessus poenarum* [excess in punishing].[6] Legal treatises dealing with torture, which was not reprehensible *per se*, warned against its excesses, claiming that the judge responsible for these excesses is to be considered as having broken the law.[7]

Yet the threshold that indicates when an action ceases to be 'merely' violent and becomes cruel shifts considerably when examined from late antiquity to the early modern period, or across cultures. More significantly, even the existence of the threshold is not constant, since cruelty as a concept is sometimes represented implicitly and sometimes is absent altogether. Thus, cruelty is the main characteristic consistently attributed to the Mongols in Western accounts of the thirteenth century. Examined cross-culturally, such references to cruelty are completely missing from non-Western sources dealing with the Mongols, although the peoples of the East were subjected to the same, if not higher, degree of violence. Thus, acts which were defined as cruelty in one culture were not defined so in a different medieval culture.

The scope of this essay is not wide enough to encompass all the issues related to the border between violence and cruelty. I shall deal with three essential ones. Firstly, I shall examine the implicit modes of representing cruelty, what mechanisms they employ to indicate that they are dealing with cruelty (and not with the more neutral concept of violence), and how these implicit representations are related to the more explicit ones. Secondly, I shall examine non-Western representations of violence that do not use distinct conceptual categories for violence and cruelty, and try to outline the main factors that shape the divergent attitudes to this issue in Western and Eastern sources. Finally, I shall examine the implications of the choice between the various modes of addressing violence.

1. The Implied Threshold: Accounts of the Vikings

The border between violence and cruelty can be observed with the greatest clarity in descriptions of violence attributed to external 'others' who threatened the medieval West. The violence of external invaders, mostly non-Christian, was their primary claim to 'otherness.' Thus it was a priori excessive, and provides an ideal context for examining the manner in which it was represented: i.e., as 'mere' violence or as cruelty.

In the West one can see a succession of such external invaders from late Antiquity to the late Middle Ages: Vandals, Muslims, Magyars, Vikings, Mongols, and Turks. In the early medieval period the Vikings seem to present such violence in its purest form. Their raids, like those of the Muslims, spanned a long period of time. They seem, however, to have inspired more fear than those of the Muslims since it was difficult to foresee where they would strike, they usually had the advantage of surprise, and they were not confined to a specific geographic frontier.

The *Annales Bertiniani*, one of the most important sources on the Viking incursions upon Francia, report their raids with surprising aloofness:

> (836) At that same time, the Northmen again devastated Dorestad and Frisia.
> (844) The Northmen sailed up the Garonne as far as Toulouse, wreaking destruction everywhere, without meeting any opposition.
> (848) The Northmen laid waste the township of Melle and set it on fire.[8]

These entries are brief: they do not specify exactly what happened in these targets of Viking raids and, more importantly, they do not offer any appraisal or authorial comment on the events. The Vikings were evidently perceived as violent, but were they in fact seen in terms of a separate category, or merely as somewhat more violent than the 'norm' of internal violence? Was a threshold crossed in the chroniclers' perception of the Vikings, from either the quantitative or the qualitative point of view?

The answer to these questions is not self-evident. The apparent detachment of the chronicles has been taken by some scholars as evidence that the Vikings were seen as merely another nexus of violence in a society that suffered primarily from a high level of internal violence. According to this view, the

Viking raids were not perceived as exceptional when compared to the ravages of local armed men.[9]

A broader perspective is needed for interpreting the representations of violence in these accounts. For this purpose it is necessary to address several problems. First – using the more detailed entries relating to the Vikings – one needs to reconstruct what types of violence were attributed to them. Then, how are the Vikings and their actions characterized in the chronicles, if at all? And finally, how do these accounts fit into previous, contemporary, and subsequent representations of violence?

Components of Viking Violence
What did the Vikings do during their raids? A few of the entries in the chronicles are less laconic than most. The attack on Quentovic is described thus in the *Annales Bertiniani*:

> (842) At that time, a fleet of Normans made a surprise attack at dawn on the *emporium* called Quentovic, plundered it and laid it waste, capturing or massacring the inhabitants of both sexes. They left nothing in it except for those buildings which they were paid to spare.

In the following year, the chronicle tells, the Vikings attacked Nantes, killing the bishop, other clergy, and lay people 'of both sexes.'[10] One entry in the somewhat later *Annales Vedastini* explicitly defines the massacres and the demolition of churches as cruelty.[11]

The types of violence repeatedly emphasized in relation to the Vikings are indiscriminate massacres (i.e., without sparing women and children), violence against religious officeholders and holy places, and plunder. The entries that do refer to cruelty explicitly, like the one referred to from the *Annales Vedastini*, mention precisely these same actions.

Characterization of Viking Violence
This aloofness in depicting violence against the ingroup is related in part to the writers' understanding of the historical function of the invaders. They perceived them as a punishment sent by God on account of the sins of Christendom.[12] Thus – as a reincarnation of the Old Testament Assyrians and Babylonians – they were an instrument of God's justice and their cruelty was, to a certain extent, deserved. This, however, is only one factor that made the issue of cruelty less relevant for the early medieval writers. As we shall see later, the perceptions of the 'other' as a godsent punishment and as cruel are not mutually exclusive.

Nevertheless, identifying the characteristic actions associated with Viking violence does not solve the hermeneutic problem of understanding whether this violence was perceived as crossing the threshold between 'mere' violence and cruelty. Since there is a tradition in Western culture associating the 'other' with cruelty, part of the solution would be to examine whether, or how, the accounts of the Vikings fit into existing traditions of describing the violence of the 'other.'

Traditional 'Others'

Other early medieval chronicles shed little light on this problem. Chronicles referring to the Muslim conquests report their violence in terms similar to those used for the Vikings.[13] In late Antiquity, however, representations of violence are more elaborate and their meaning is clearer. Christian writers of the fourth and fifth centuries wrote at length about the incursions and conquests of the various barbarians within the empire. Following the pagan classical tradition, such writers, like Lactantius and Victor of Vita, saw cruelty as a natural quality of the Barbarians.[14]

In the fifth century Victor of Vita wrote an account of the Vandal conquest and subsequent rule of North Africa. His references to the violence of the Vandals are lengthy, and more affective than early medieval references to the Vikings. Moreover, he presented cruelty as one of the Vandals' main characteristics. Setting the tone in the opening sentence of the first chapter Victor wrote: 'this is now the sixtieth year since the cruel and savage [*crudelis ac saevus*] people of the Vandal race set foot on the territory of wretched Africa ...'[15]

The types of action by which Victor characterizes the cruelty of the Vandals are very similar to those attributed by early medieval chroniclers to the Vikings. Victor writes about the killing of women and children, focusing on images of infants snatched from their mothers' breasts and dashed to the ground or cut in two by the Vandals.[16] In other places he emphasizes the Vandals' violence against religious officeholders, and against Christianity.[17] Pagan writers, such as Ammianus Marcellinus, also referred explicitly to the cruelty of the barbarians, with some differences of emphasis consisting mainly of more explicit references to sexual cruelty.

The observed similarities between the representations of the violence of the 'other' in late Antiquity and of the references to the Vikings in the early medieval period would have suggested that, like the barbarians, the Vikings were also perceived as cruel. However, because of the conceptual difference between violence and cruelty, this is *not* a necessary conclusion. It has been claimed that early medieval people were desensitized by the endemic violence of their society, and hence did not consider the Vikings as exceptional in this sense. Since cruelty involves the crossing of a threshold from 'mere' violence, it is possible that the threshold was higher in the early Middle Ages than in later periods, and it was not crossed in the case of the Vikings.

The Second Tradition of Representing Viking Violence

A new perspective on this issue is gained by examining early medieval hagiographic sources. While most of them describe Viking violence in the same manner as the chronicles, a minority continues the tradition of late antiquity. In a collection of miracles attributed to St Germain at the time of the Viking incursions, cruelty becomes one of the chief characteristics of the invaders:

> The aforesaid Normans ... issued from their ships, and scattered far and wide ... without anyone resisting [them], they started to take as captives or kill the people of both sexes, to devastate monasteries, to lay waste or burn churches or villages on which they could lay hands, to plunder sheep; and they began to revel with every cruelty [*cum omni crudelitate ... debachari*] against the one-time people of God, and exercise their desires against [the people of God] on account of the enormity of their sins.[18]

The actions described are similar to those of the chronicles, but the mode of representation is different, since cruelty *is* an issue. Likewise, elsewhere in this collection, the author tells of a public execution of eleven captives by the Normans, the purpose of which was to humiliate Charles the Bald. The enemy is characterized there as 'the most impious and most cruel [*impiissimi ac crudelissimi*] Normans, blasphemers of God.'[19] The chronicles also characterize the Vikings as pagans, but only here is this characteristic linked to cruelty.

The explicitness of the hagiographic mode of representing cruelty is even more evident in the *Passio* of St Edmund, written by Abbo of Fleury (d. ca 1004). The chronicles reporting Edmund's execution are laconic as always. Asser reports Edmund's death following a battle against the Vikings in less than a sentence: 'he, together with a large part of his [men], was slain.'[20] In contrast, the *passio* refers extensively to the cruelty of the Vikings. Moreover, Abbo exposes the specific cultural tradition upon which he draws. His description of the Viking goes back to the classical tradition of describing the 'other,' originating in Herodotus's accounts of the Scythians.[21]

Thus, non-reference to cruelty was not a matter of necessity, due to the lack of vocabulary or relevant cultural traditions: it was a positive choice of representational mode. The continuity of classical tradition, even if only as a thin thread, indicates that the implicit mode of representing violence was not a result of desensitization, due to the continuous exposure of early medieval people to violence. The representation of violence as cruelty in the medieval West in this period was a matter of cultural choice, and related to the specific literary genre selected by the author. Hence the co-existence, side by side, of the implicit and explicit modes of representation is significant. It shows that the crossing of the threshold could be represented implicitly, and – at the same time – that the absence of explicit references did not imply the absence of the threshold. The interpretation of implicit representations of cruelty as distinct from representations of 'mere' *violence* depended upon the identification of the specific contexts and literary traditions identifying them as cruelty.

Western representations of violence referred to cruelty in an increasingly explicit manner from the central Middle Ages onwards. This tendency is reflected in the accounts of the Vikings written in the twelfth and thirteenth centuries. It is particularly manifest in the later transmission of the early medieval texts we have examined. Thus, Henry of Huntington and Matthew Paris add explicit references to cruelty when they cite earlier sources such as Asser's *De rebus gestis Alfredi* or the *Historia regum*. This, it must be pointed out, is not a necessary part of the 'encyclopedic' tendency of thirteenth-century writers to elaborate and expand on what they borrowed from their predecessors. Sometimes the later entry is less detailed than its sources, but nevertheless adds an explicit reference to cruelty.[22]

The increasingly explicit mode of reference to cruelty is evident when writers of the twelfth and thirteenth centuries narrate contemporary events. Thus, for instance, in his account of child martyrdom, William of Norwich repeatedly refers to the cruelty of the Jews who are accused of the murder. Some of the authors writing about the *passio* of Thomas Becket elaborate on the cruelty of the murderers, comparing them to the pre-Constantinian persecutors. The references to cruelty in these texts are embedded in an affective, even sentimental, narrative.[23]

This tendency culminates in the accounts relating to the Mongol incursions upon central Europe in the middle of the thirteenth century. Cruelty becomes an anthropological category of primary importance in the descriptions of the Mongols, and is represented as one of the main characteristics of the 'Mongol way of life.' Thus, in the accounts relating to them one can find chapter headings such as 'De victu eorum' and 'De crudelitate ipsorum et fallacia,' or 'De natura Tartarorum' and 'De sevicia Tartarorum.'[24]

The literature on the Mongols reflects the extent of the change that took place in the span of one century – from the middle of the twelfth to the middle of the thirteenth. During this period there is a remarkable rise in the cultural preoccupation with cruelty in the West. The Mongol invasions, however, affected vast areas beyond western Europe. In fact, most of their conquests were in the far and near East. All sources, Western and Eastern alike, attest to the unprecedented violence that accompanied the Mongol conquests. Thus, they can serve as a focus for cross-cultural comparison of modes of representing violence and cruelty. Such a comparison brings into relief some of the unique traits of the developments in the West.

2. Violence as an Unbroken Continuum: Eastern Sources

The cultural factors that shape the positioning of the threshold between violence and cruelty are brought into relief when Western sources are compared with non-Western ones dealing with similar subject matter. Thus, non-Western authors treat the Mongol incursions of the thirteenth century in different terms than Western ones do.

The extreme violence that was almost invariably practised by the Mongols can lead to the expectation that their actions would be characterized as cruelty. Yet Islamic sources report the Mongol massacres matter-of-factly, and present a striking contrast to the affective tone of Western narratives. Thus Ibn al-Athīr (1160–1233) writes that 'these [Tartars] did not spare anyone, but killed the women, the men, and the children; and split the bellies of the pregnant [women], and killed the fetuses.'[25] Al-Jūzjānī (1193–after 1260), writing in Persian in the middle of the thirteenth century, refers in a similar manner to the Mongol conquest of Merv: 'In the year 617 H., Tūlī [Tuloi] turned his face from the [great camp at the] Pushtah-i-Nuʿmān towards the city of Marw [Merv] and took that city and martyred its inhabitants.'[26] This tone is representative of the manner in which Islamic sources describe the Mongol massacres. The accounts they give vary in length and detail, but their tone of narration is only seldom affective, and they do not refer explicitly to the issue of cruelty. Eastern Christian sources dealing with the Mongols present, with few exceptions, a similar attitude to the representation of violence. The Christian Bar Hebraeus (1225/6–1286) describes the massacre that followed the Mongol conquest of Harim in a similar vein: 'And the King of Kings commanded, and they were all killed, men and women, and sons, and daughters, [and] also nursing children.'[27]

The crucial role of cultural traditions in the choice of the mode of representation is best reflected in the issue of Mongol cannibalism. Western sources consistently attribute cannibalism to the Mongols. Non-Western sources ignore this issue altogether. The reason for this discrepancy is the persistence of the classical image of the Scythians, the prototypes of the cannibal 'other.' Since Western authors viewed the Mongols simply as Scythians or as a reincarnation of this people, they projected upon them all the attributes of the Scythians, including cannibalism, regardless of the actual facts.[28]

We have observed that in the West the reference to cruelty, or lack thereof, is genre-dependent: i.e., there are periods in which most sources represent violence without referring to cruelty, with the exception of some hagiographic sources. It is, in many respects, understandable that hagiography is the exception: the ordeals of the martyrs generally involve a significant amount of violence, and the authors' critical attitude towards it is axiomatic. The morally unambiguous character of violence in hagiographic texts renders it an interesting focus for an intercultural comparison between Western and non-Western texts. I shall examine the way in which violence is represented in three types of Eastern Christian martyrdom accounts, stretching over a period of six centuries: in Coptic martyrdoms of Byzantine Egypt, in accounts relating to martyrs executed in Palestine in the ninth century, and in the Coptic Synaxary, which was probably compiled towards the end of the thirteenth century.

Coptic Martyrdoms of Byzantine Egypt
Post-Constantinian hagiography is preoccupied to a considerable extent with reprocessing and retelling the accounts of the early Christian martyrs. These are second-generation accounts, in the sense that they are based on earlier *acta* rather than on eyewitness accounts. They were produced in both the eastern and the western parts of the empire mainly in the fourth and fifth centuries. The comparison with the early *passiones* points to the different emphases chosen by the authors of the second-generation accounts.

In his seminal study of martyrdom accounts Hippolyte Delehaye classified a subgroup within this genre as 'epic' due to its exaggerated characteristics.[29] The tendency to overstate relates mainly to the representation of violence, emphasizing the cruelty of the persecutor and the suffering of the martyrs. In the West such accounts not only exaggerate the violence inflicted on the martyrs: they specifically add, or intensify, explicit references to the cruelty of the persecutors.[30] How is violence represented in Eastern second-generation accounts? A preliminary examination of several texts written in Byzantine Egypt indicates a strong tendency (as in their Western counterparts) to assign demonic characteristics to the persecutor's violence.[31] Similarly, the martyrs undergo a long list of tortures, which at times reaches grotesque proportions. Yet they do not always suffer from these tortures. The martyrs Paese and Thecla benefited from a personal bodyguard, the archangel Raphael who accompanied them in all their ordeals. The author indicates specifically, in more than one instance, that they did not feel pain.[32] In the case of another martyr, Shenoufe, the archangel Michael fulfilled the same function.[33] Using Esther Cohen's distinction between *impassivity*, the ability to tolerate pain without any noticeable reaction, and *impassability*, the actual absence of the feeling of pain, it is important to point out that these saints are presented as being *impassable* to pain.[34]

Yet while Delehaye makes this insensitivity to pain a general characteristic of the 'epic' martyrdoms, this is true only to a limited extent.[35] In many cases the relief comes only halfway through the martyrdom, and in other instances it never arrives. The martyrdom of Sts Apaioule and Pteleme, for instance, emphasizes the martyrs' suffering by vivid descriptions that make the reading of the account unsettling. It brings forth the real presence of violence, not merely as a stylized ornamental background to martyrdom:

> [The Count] was furiously angry, and he ordered Apaioule to be brought forward; he was seated upon an iron bed, and ⟨the count ordered⟩[36] that a red-hot instrument be brought and thrust into his right eye; and he had it stirred up until its pupil sprang out on the ground. And he was distressed, and he looked up to the heaven, and cried out, saying, 'My Lord Jesus Christ, look, and see my light which I have lost for Thy Holy Name's sake. And I believe in Thee, that Thou has the power to [do] anything.'[37]

Second-generation *passiones* in the West resemble the Coptic accounts mentioned here in the gradual demonization of the persecutor and in the more detailed descriptions of the torture of the martyrs. Moreover, the types of torture that are added in subsequent versions are similar. Thus, the second Coptic version of the martyrdom of Coluthus adds to the earlier narrative the amputation of the saint's tongue, a type of torture relished also by Western accounts.[38] Yet in the West, the process of *showing* more severe physical violence is complemented by more detailed *telling* – i.e., more explicit references to cruelty. In the Eastern accounts only the first half of the process occurs: the scenes of physical violence and torture are shown in detail, but they are not accompanied by any explicit commentary on their cruelty. The Eastern Christian accounts that emphasize the suffering of the martyrs only make this absence more prominent.

Palestinian Neo-Martyrs of the Eighth and Ninth Centuries
The Coptic martyrdom accounts discussed above were written under Christian rule. Christian domination, however, was relatively short-lived in Egypt as in much of the Near East; it came to an abrupt end with the Islamic conquests of the seventh and eighth centuries. For the Christian subjects Muslim rule was significantly different from pagan rule. Islam acknowledged the right of the ancient 'people of the book,' Jews and Christians, to practise their religion and did not require their conversion to Islam. Thus, Christians may have been humiliated and persecuted but, unlike in the pagan persecutions, there was no systematic persecution of Christianity as a religion. The execution of Christians was formally allowed only if they publicly reviled Islam or Muhammad, or if they were apostatized Muslims.[39]

Nevertheless, Christians *were* executed sporadically by the Muslim authorities, and these instances provide a new setting for examining the treatment of violence inflicted on Christians by external enemies of the faith. I will refer to several such texts commemorating the execution of a number of Christians in Palestine in the eighth and ninth centuries.

As could be expected, these texts present the Christians as martyrs executed by the Muslim authorities on account of their faith.[40] Yet most of these martyrs fall into the categories punishable by execution according to the rules of Islam. This in itself indicates the sporadic and non-systematic nature of these martyrdoms, and also points to some analogies with what is known as the Cordovan martyr movement, i.e., the execution of more than fifty Christians by the Muslim authorities between 850 and 859.[41] Most of these martyrdoms were self-inflicted, i.e., the Christians were apostates from Islam or they publicly reviled Islam, and knew their offences were punishable by death. In contrast to the situation in Cordova, most of the Palestinian martyrdoms were not self-inflicted. The initial contact between the martyr and the Muslim authorities was not the result of a willful act committed by the martyr in order to obtain martyrdom, even though later he may have consciously behaved in a way that would lead to his execution.

The story of St Michael of the Mar Sabas monastery is representative of the almost random chain of events leading to martyrdom. The Muslim authorities did not initially intend to execute Christians or engage in any anti-Christian activity, and the martyr himself did not set out to achieve martyrdom. This is true of most of the Palestinian martyrs. Michael was brought before the authorities following a false accusation by the emir's wife to the effect that he had insulted her.[42] The emir realized that the charges were false and released him. But immediately afterwards the emir engaged in a learned religious polemic with the monk, summoning a Jew to participate as well. In the course of this discussion Michael insulted Islam and the Prophet, and was given the choice of conversion or execution.

Michael's martyrdom is described in a factual and detached manner.[43] The execution of another martyr, St Anthony Rawḥ, is even more sparing in its report of the physical details of his martyrdom. Anthony was beaten before he was imprisoned, and was then decapitated. Only after he was dead was his body crucified. The actual martyrdom is described in one sentence: 'And when [Hārūn] al-Rashīd heard his words he cut his throat for the belief in our Lord Jesus the saviour.'[44] The account of the martyrdom of 'Abd al-Masīḥ al-Najrānī al-Ghassanī, executed in the middle of the ninth century, is likewise laconic: 'And [the governor] gave the command to behead him. They carried it out in fact.'[45]

Other accounts contain more elaborate torture descriptions. Romanos, who was martyred towards the end of the eighth century, suffered more than the martyrs mentioned above. He underwent one session of severe torture, in which fifteen men were assigned to whip him with dry tendons of oxen, in a manner meant to ensure that the effect would be painful. Yet, the author does not comment on this episode, and mentions that he was not tortured again until his swift beheading. What seems to grieve the author more than Romanos's suffering is the scattering of his remains over the Euphrates.[46]

The accounts of the Palestinian neo-martyrs contain no explicit references to cruelty. As in the case of the Cordovan martyrs, this is due primarily to the actual circumstances. The majority of these martyrs seem to have been executed in a swift and straightforward manner, and since the Christian community was aware of this, the martyrdoms could not be described in too gruelling terms. However, even in those cases in which they *were* tortured and these tortures were recorded by the authors of the accounts, there are no explicit references to the cruelty of the persecutors. The closest these accounts come to this issue is the reference to the persecutors as tyrants. The metonymic use of tyranny as an indicator of cruelty is common to both the Greek and the Latin settings in late antiquity. In the Latin context, however, there are usually additional explicit references to cruelty. Mostly the accounts adopt a matter-of-fact, unaffective, attitude to the issue of physical suffering in general. Thus, pain is also not an important issue. In the case of Michael of Mar Sabas it is stated several times that he did not suffer from the punishments inflicted on him.[47]

In sum, in spite of the significantly varied historical circumstances under which these accounts were composed, there seem to be only minor differences between the martyrdom accounts of Byzantine Egypt and those of the Islamic period regarding cruelty. All of them avoid referring to cruelty explicitly. Their mode of representing cruelty bears a marked resemblance to that of ninth-century authors in the West.

The Coptic Synaxary

The martyrdom accounts from Byzantine Egypt and those of the Palestinian martyrs present one basic attitude: they report violence in a matter-of-fact way, without passing explicit judgment, and without defining it as cruelty. The Coptic Synaxary, compiled three centuries and more after the accounts of the Palestinian martyrs, points to the perseverance of this static attitude. Thus it stands in opposition to the significant changes that occur in the West during this period: the contrast between the factual and minimalist early medieval chronicles relating to the Vikings and the detailed and affective thirteenth-century reports on the Mongols bears witness to the dynamic development in Western representations of violence.

The Synaxary is a hagiographic calendar arranged according to the Coptic year. But its importance extends beyond that of a mere liturgical text, since it is the semi-official compilation of the Coptic hagiographic heritage in Arabic. Like the Western martyrologies, it mentions, in varying detail, the saints whose feasts are celebrated on each day. Most of the entries in the Synaxary refer to the pagan persecutions of the first centuries AD. The Synaxary was most probably compiled in the thirteenth century, but most of the material is much older and originally written in Coptic.[48]

The entries in the Synaxary, even the longer ones, are naturally briefer than full-fledged *vitae* or *passiones*. Most of the saints commemorated are either martyrs or ascetic monks; the latter's feats of physical endurance are sometimes even more impressive than those of the martyrs. The more detailed accounts concentrate on the torments undergone by the saint. Thomas of *Shandalat* was an eleven-year-old swineherd when the archangel Michael ordered him to go forth and confess his faith. He found his opportunity when he was ordered to worship the idols, and instead of complying he assaulted the governor of Alexandria. He was arrested, and after some additional confrontations and tortures, his head was covered with boiling oil and pitch. Then he was cooked in a cauldron, castrated, hung with a heavy stone on his neck, and finally decapitated.[49] This account and similar ones are dry and factual, without any explicit reference to pain and suffering.[50] In some instances the tortures are described in detail, but from a certain stage onwards it is related that divine intervention came to the saint's relief, and he did not feel the pain.[51]

References to the persecutor are scant in the accounts of martyrdom in the Synaxary. His motivations are not relevant. He has a role to fulfill, and in this sense he is merely a tool. Given the self-inflicted character of many of these martyrdoms, the distance between the martyrs and the ascetics diminishes and the persecutor seems yet another instrument of self-chastisement. The lack of reference to cruelty may be partly a result of the fact that self-inflicted torments fit less easily into the category of cruelty. This has implications for the way in which the problem of theodicy is handled: a view that shifts the responsibility for martyrdom to the martyr also, as it were, 'absolves' God of his responsibility for the martyr's suffering.

But the Synaxary's handling of the problem of suffering and theodicy provides another important insight into its treatment of cruelty and the Eastern mode of reference to the issue when compared to the Western one. The problem of 'why God makes the just suffer' has several solutions. As mentioned above, one solution is to claim that they did not suffer. Another is to imply that the suffering was self-inflicted. Yet another solution, inconceivable from a Western perspective, but nevertheless present in the Synaxary, is to imply that the martyrs were not just.

In Western sources of the early medieval period the affliction of God's people by various 'others' is commonly explained as a punishment for their sins. Such an explanation is employed in the West only at the group level. On the personal level the martyr is intrinsically virtuous: his afflictions cannot be perceived or presented as a punishment. Yet in the Coptic Synaxary this causal relationship *is* suggested at times, in the case of martyrs who were notorious sinners before their conversion. Thus, the Synaxary tells of Abu Musa al-aswad [Moses the Black], a licentious sinner who repented and became an ascetic. But his conversion did not obliterate his sins. Near the end of his life, after years of ascetic practices and after having been consecrated as a priest, he went to visit St Macarius in the company of other ascetics. Macarius observed that one of them was about to become a martyr, and Musa came forth and declared: 'It is I, for it is written that he who has killed with the sword, with the sword he shall be killed' [Mt 26:52]. Later, when the Berbers arrived, they let the people escape without harm. Musa, however, remained, declaring that he awaited the fulfillment of the verse from Matthew, and was slain by the Berbers.[52]

This attitude to the martyrdom of saints who converted many years previously and led a saintly life originates in a very severe view of sin and redemption, which is characteristic of the Synaxary in other contexts besides martyrdom. It is not unique to the Coptic Synaxary, but appears in other Eastern sources as well: in the story of St Anthony Rawḥ it is implied that he sees martyrdom as the expiation of his sins. Yet in the Coptic Synaxary this attitude is revealed in multiple examples, not just in isolated cases. The perception of martyrdom as a punishment renders the issue of cruelty less relevant. Such a view of martyrdom sets it in a legitimate legal context. If death serves as a punishment, it is not by itself a crossing of the threshold separating 'mere' violence from cruelty. This attitude does not have a parallel in Western accounts and is probably unique to the Eastern ones.

In the West hagiography turned out to be the most explicit genre in relation to cruelty. This is most evident in the early medieval period, in which other genres, such as chronicles, do not distinguish explicitly between violence and cruelty. The types of non-Western chronicles examined here do not seem to position a threshold separating violence from cruelty during the Middle Ages. They do not attribute cruelty even to perpetrators of extreme acts of violence. The contrast between Eastern and Western sources stands out in such periods as the central Middle Ages, during which cruelty becomes a major issue in Western sources of all types.

The association between hagiography and cruelty is intuitive: martyrdom is a context in which violence is inflicted by the wicked on the just. I have therefore examined here whether in Eastern Christian hagiography one can locate such a threshold – implicit or explicit – separating violence from cruelty. None of the Eastern hagiographic sources I examined here – ranging from the early Middle Ages to the thirteenth century – pointed to the existence of such a threshold. The texts seem dominated by the perception of violence as a godsent punishment for sins, even to the extent of questioning the basic moral premises of martyrdom. This attitude exists, if only at the group level, in the

West as well. It is dominant, but not exclusive, in non-hagiographic texts of the early Middle Ages. But, in contrast to the Eastern Christian sources, it becomes more and more marginal in later periods.

3. Categorizing Cruelty

The preceding analysis brings out clearly one general conclusion, that the distinction between violence and cruelty is culturally dependent. There are periods and cultures in which this distinction is made explicitly, others in which it is indicated implicitly, and others in which it does not exist at all. When there is no distinction between violence and cruelty, violence is perceived as an unbroken continuum from lesser to more severe, which can be perceived as more, or less, justified. A conscious move to distinguish between violence and cruelty seems to have existed in the medieval West, but not in most Eastern Christian societies.

What are the factors affecting the presence or absence of this distinction, and what are its implications? On the most basic level this variability in the representation of violence indicates that there is no 'natural' way of representing violence. Hence the modes of representing it in the medieval West are the result of conscious choices on the part of authors dealing with violence. These observations are borne out by the early medieval accounts of the Vikings. They were generally perceived as cruel, but in some instances their cruelty was indicated implicitly and in others explicitly. The coexistence of these two modes of representation shows that the two options were accessible, and that early medieval authors usually opted to use the implicit mode. The shift, in the central Middle Ages, to increasingly explicit references to cruelty is yet another indication that the representation of cruelty depends upon cultural variables, more than on actual historical circumstances.

Non-Western authors represented violence in a more uniform manner. They generally refrained from distinguishing between the general concept of violence and a category of cruelty. They did not refer to cruelty explicitly. Yet, to a limited extent one can still argue that, at least for Arabic-speaking Christians and Jews, this mode of representation is also the result of a conscious choice. It is evident that Jews and Christians writing in Arabic were aware of the existence of the concept of cruelty in cultures other than their own. When translating from Latin or Hebrew sources they consistently translated the Latin *crudelitas* and the Hebrew *akhzariyut* into the Arabic term *qaswa*,[53] using this term almost exclusively for the purpose of translation. Non-Muslim writers in Arabic did not use this term in their own texts in contexts similar to those in which *crudelitas* was used in the West (such as accounts of martyrdom or of attacks by external invaders).

Why did some authors choose to represent violence as cruelty while others did not? The choice of mode for representation of violence was influenced by a complex web of cultural factors. As suggested above, the reluctance to characterize as cruel the Vikings or the persecutors of the ancient martyrs had as its background a view of God as actively engaged in the world. Consequently, suffering was a punishment for sin, and the perpetrators of violence were the agents of God. Attributing cruelty to them was in a sense meaningless, since they were merely tools carrying out divine justice. Moreover, defining these agents of violence as cruel could imply that this characterization extended to God. This instrumental attitude is adopted in some early medieval Western chronicles and by Islamic sources dealing with external invaders. Eastern Christian sources display a similar attitude even when they deal with martyrdom.

In the West there was a shift away from this attitude in the twelfth century. It is apparent in the larger sphere of perceptions of sin and culpability. Procedures such as the ordeal, which were based on the immanence of divine judgment and on its manifest nature, were discredited and replaced by a system that locates culpability in intentions, not in outward actions.[54] Sinfulness was made manifest, or explicit, through a system of guided introspection – i.e., confession to the priest. These changes brought about a new attitude to violence that enabled distinction between the more ambiguous concept of violence and an a priori reprehensible category of cruelty.

This distinction served several purposes. The role of intentions in the moral appraisal of violence could serve to justify instances of commendable violence, such as the Crusades. At the same time it was employed for assigning cruelty to archetypal external invaders, the 'others' of the past and present. Both processes can be clearly observed in the writings of Bernard of Clairvaux. In *In Praise of the New Knighthood* he celebrates the transformation of 'bad' violence into something praiseworthy. Likewise, the Vikings could still be perceived as a godsent punishment for the sins of the Christians. But at the same time they could be presented as cruel, with increasing explicitness in twelfth- and thirteenth-century chronicles. The violent action could be perceived as a legitimate punishment, but its perpetrator could be characterized as cruel according to his intentions.

It is primarily this perceptual change that brings the category of cruelty into prominence, namely, the ability to judge the perpetrator of violence while ignoring the justification for his actions, be the justification cosmic or the perpetrator's subjective point of view. While in describing the action there is much overlap between cruelty and violence, the new attitude enabled judging themas separate concepts. Violence in this sense is a negotiable concept, in that it is quantitative; it can be placed on a continuum going from lesser to greater.

Cruelty, on the other hand, seems to have been envisioned as a *discrete* entity, above the upper hand of the continuum. Consequently, the violence of persecutors of Christianity or that of external invaders could be set aside from ordinary violence. Whereas in earlier periods greater violence could be presented as the result of the greater sinfulness of the victim, the new paradigm of violence points to a category set apart, which is non-negotiable or debatable and hence non-justifiable.

The creation of a separate category of cruelty had far-reaching implications. The appearance, or reappearance, of cruelty in the central Middle Ages did not represent only a cultural or religious change. This development was interwoven with contemporary eleventh- and twelfth-century politics, in particular with the fierce struggle between church and state.[55] The movement toward an introspective view of sin which was subject to the scrutiny of the church was part of the efforts of eleventh- and twelfth-century reformers to consolidate the church's control over most aspects of life. The conceptual category of cruelty was aggressively employed in the struggles between the church and lay rulers of the central Middle Ages. The issue of cruelty was manipulated and used as a delegitimizing label, initially by the church and subsequently in power struggles between lay parties as well. A ruler labelled as cruel was thus illegitimate, since his violence was perceived as having crossed the threshold of justified violence. This process was linked to revival of interest in the Latin classics, and it brought once more into the fore the association of cruelty and tyranny.[56]

In the twelfth century Roger of Sicily was the object of such delegitimation. Tyranny was used interchangeably with cruelty (as one of its manifestations) in sources written by Roger's many opponents, who had both secular and religious motives for their rivalry. The concept of cruelty as excessive punishment – with reference to what is prescribed by law – points to Roger's status as a tyrant. Allegations that he was a usurper further underlined the illegality of his actions.[57] Moreover, in Roger's case one can see the prominence of classical culture in the formation of the cultural construct of cruelty. If Abbo of Fleury presented the Vikings as a reincarnation of the Scythians, Roger was seen as an heir to the long tradition of Sicilian tyrants, foremost among whom was Phalaris.[58]

Another ruler who suffered from the emergence of the category of cruelty was King John of England. John had his ample share of conflicts with Innocent III, arguably the most powerful medieval pope. In John's case the link between lack of legitimacy, cruelty, and conflict with the church is even clearer: he was presented simultaneously as an unbeliever and a cruel tyrant. Guillaume le Breton, for instance, describes him in the following manner: 'He despoiled churches, pillaged the goods of the clergy, confiscated all the ancestral goods of country dwellers and of [town] citizens ... he relaxed the reins of [his] gluttony, and stained the body with lust,' and goes on to describe how John inflicted slow and painful deaths upon those whose goods he wanted to confiscate. Guillaume claims that in England the clerics have ceased to praise God, nor does anyone celebrate the offices of the church, and concludes by saying that for seven years England turned back to paganism.[59] Another French source of the early thirteenth century states that John was 'cruel to all men; too covetous of beautiful women.'[60] The truthfulness or otherwise of this image of John or the hidden agendas of those responsible for its creation are not relevant here. Regardless, these examples show once more that the classical (and early Christian) imagery of the cruel tyrant was the primary tool for delegitimizing a ruler.[61]

Cruelty as a primary delegitimizing label was first employed by the church in its struggles with lay rulers, but soon spread into other areas, such as the struggle against heresy. Thus, Peter of Vaux-de-Cernay, the chronicler of the crusade against the Albigensians, labels certain actions of the Albigensians as cruelty even in instances where no real violence takes place. This indicates that, while in the previous century heresy or unbelief were in themselves the primary delegitimizing labels, they were now superseded, or at least equalled, by cruelty. In the fourteenth century one can see this issue raised in the context of pure power struggles between lay rulers. The civil war in Castile between Henry of Trastámara and Pedro I of Castile is perhaps the most obvious example of the manipulative use of cruelty. Pedro, the legitimate heir to the throne (Henry was the bastard son of the former king), was defeated and entered posterity as 'Pedro the Cruel,' the epithet given to him by Henry.

Cruelty, as a conceptual category, played such an important role in Western medieval culture and politics because its sphere of reference was human. Cruelty was excessive violence employed by secular powers. It was judged as excessive in relation to human (in contrast to divine) law. Thus, some types of violence could be relegated to a category that was qualitatively different from others, and this classification depended upon human interpretation since it was related to law, in its earthly technical meaning.

The establishment of a separate category of cruelty, and shifting the distinction between it and violence into the realm of human hermeneutics was a decisive factor in the bringing of accountability into Western political systems. According to the political scheme implied in the 'great chain of being,' the king is set by God to rule over the people. He is accountable for his deeds only to God, not to any human agency. His violence is described quantitatively, and only God can pass the final judgment whether it was justified or not.[62] The introduction of the category of cruelty breaks this hierarchy. It introduces an element that is not part of the hierarchy, but parallel to it in the sense that the ruler's actions can be judged by humans and not by God alone.

In conclusion, in this article I have suggested that cruelty is a cultural construct in which violence is a priori severe, unjustified, and morally reprehensible. As such its existence and the modes in which it is used are culturally dependent. In the medieval period cruelty as a distinct category was peculiar to Western culture. Non-Western sources, both Islamic and Eastern Christian, do not reflect the presence of such a category. In the medieval West there were changes over time: cruelty is of only minor importance in the early medieval period, while in the central Middle Ages it emerges as a distinct concept and not as part of a continuum of varying degrees of violence. This process is part of more wide-ranging changes in the conceptualization and appraisal of sin and culpability, and it was influenced also by the revival of interest in the Latin classics. These developments were not only cultural: they were closely related to the political struggles of the eleventh and twelfth centuries between the church and lay rulers. The most far-reaching implications of the introduction of the category of cruelty seem to have been in the political sphere, where cruelty functioned, and was manipulated, as a delegitimizing label against lay rulers.

Notes

1 One can speak of justified or unjustified violence, the underlying assumption being that the same violent actions can acquire different meanings in different moral and cultural contexts. This was not the case for medieval writers. For them *violentia* was not an objective category; it was morally wrong. For a debate on the meaning of

violence and the possibility of quantifying and comparing it, see: Thomas N. Bisson, 'The "Feudal Revolution,"' *Past and Present* 142 (1994) 6–42, esp. 15–21; Stephen D. White, 'Debate: The "Feudal Revolution,"' *Past and Present* 152 (1996) 205ff., 209ff. My position is closer to Bisson's end of the spectrum revealed in this debate. The opposite view, that violence is purely contextual and subjective, is problematic. The claim that violence, or certain types of it, are not really violent since they were primarily a tool of conflict resolution does not eliminate the need for a prototypical construct of violence. Such a construct is necessarily implied when one later disproves that the actions perpetrated were 'merely' violence. The implicit existence of such a construct is reflected in the common denominator of the specific actions that were part of such a process of conflict resolution: they all 'look like' violence (see Bisson, ' "Feudal Revolution,"' and comments by: Dominique Barthélemy and Stephen D. White, *Past and Present* 152 [1996] 196–223; Timothy Reuter, Chris Wickham, and Thomas N. Bisson, *Past and Present* 155 [1997] 177–225).

2 See William I. Miller, *Humiliation* (Ithaca 1995 [1993]), 70–1: 'Violence can bear positive moral significations in certain settings; cruelty seldom can.' In this article I refer to violence and cruelty in their basic physical meaning, ignoring the extension into other spheres embodied in such concepts as psychological and verbal violence, or mental cruelty. I also ignore Miller's 'cruelty by omission,' i.e., inaction that is cruel (like choosing not to save a person in danger). 'Justified cruelty' *is* used rarely, but only to attract attention by means of this paradoxical and provocative formulation.

3 See Augustine, *De libero arbitrio* 1.5, ed. W.M. Green, CCSL 29 (Turnhout 1970) 217–19. See also Thomas A. Cavanaugh, 'Aquinas's Account of Double Effect,' *The Thomist* 61.1 (1997) 107–21, which discusses Aquinas's views on violent self-defence as expressed in *Summa theologiae* 2.2.64–7.

4 See Daniel Baraz, *Medieval Cruelty* (Ithaca 2003), 14–28 passim.

5 See Andrew Lintott, 'Cruelty in the Political Life of the Ancient World,' in *Crudelitas: The Politics of Cruelty in the Ancient and Medieval World*, ed. Toivo Viljamaa, Asko Timonen, and Christian Krötzl, Medium Aevum quotidianum (Krems 1992), 9–27. On the Roman emperors of the 1st century see Suetonius, *Caligula* 11, 27–32, 36; *Claudius* 34; *Nero* 27–38.

6 *Summa theologiae* 2.2.159; in English as *Summa theologica*, trans. Fathers of the English Dominican Province (Westminster, MD 1981 [1920]), 4: 1838–9.

7 See the 13th-century treatise attributed to Guido de Suzzara, *Tractatus de tormentis*, published, along with other works influenced by it, in *Tractatus de indiciis homicidii* (Venice 1549). The relevant passages are: Guido de Suzzara, 68r, 83r–v; Baldo de' Perigli of Perugia (13th-century), 99r; Francesco Bruni (15th-century), 37v–41r; Marc'Antonio Bianchi (1498–1548), 7r.

8 *Annales de Saint-Bertin*, ed. Felix Grat, Jeanne Vieilliard, and Suzanne Clemencet (Paris 1964), 19, 49, 55; in English as *The Annals of St Bertin*, trans. Janet L. Nelson (Manchester 1991), 35, 60, 66.

9 One of the main exponents of the view that underplays the argument for Viking violence is Peter H. Sawyer, *The Age of the Vikings* (London 1962), ch. 6 ('The Raids'), 117–44; this position is repeated in his *Kings and Vikings: Scandinavia and Europe AD 700–1100* (London 1982), 95. See also Thomas Lindkvist, 'The Politics of Violence and the Transition from Viking Age to Medieval Scandinavia,' in *Crudelitas*, 141; Luigi de Anna, 'Elogio della crudeltá: Aspetti della violenza nel mondo antico e medievale,' in *Crudelitas*, 102. Also relevant in this respect is Bisson's ' "Feudal Revolution" ' and the ensuing discussion (see n. 1 above).
10 *Annales de Saint-Bertin*, 42, 44; *Annals of St Bertin*, 53, 55–6.
11 Using the phrase *saevire coeperunt* (*Les Annales de Saint-Bertin et de Saint-Vaast*, ed. Chrétien C. A. Dehaisnes [Paris 1871], 322).
12 See, e.g., *Annales Bertiniani* s.a. 845 (after a report of a Norman incursion): 'Sed licet peccatis nostris diuinae bonitatis aequitas nimium offensa taliter christianorum terras et regna attriuerit'; s.a. 881 (after the Franks are defeated in a battle): '... diuino manifestante iudicio quia quod a Nortmannis fuerat actum non humana sed diuina uirtute patratum extiterit' (*Annales de Saint-Bertin*, 50, 244). On the origin of the concept of defeat as punishment of sin, see E. Siberry, *Criticism of Crusading 1095–1274* (Oxford 1985), 70–2. On the specific application of this conception to the Norsemen (and references to more sources expressing this position) see Simon Coupland, 'The Rod of God's Wrath or the People of God's Wrath? The Carolingian Theology of the Viking Invasions,' *Journal of Ecclesiastical History* 42.4 (1991) 535–54.
13 Thus, e.g., Paul the Deacon describes the conquest of Spain and the incursions into southern France: 'Eo tempore gens sarracenorum in loco qui Septem dicitur ex Africa transfretantes, universam Spaniam invaserunt. Deinde post decem annos cum uxoribus et parvulis venientes, Aquitaniam Galliae provinciam quasi habitaturi ingressi sunt.' (*Historia Langobardorum* 6.46, ed. G. Waitz, MGH Scriptores rerum Langobardicarum et Italicarum [Hanover 1878], 180).
14 'Inerat huic bestiae naturalis barbaries, efferitas a Romano sanguine aliena: non mirum, cum mater eius Transdanuuiana infestantibus Carpis in Daciam nouam transiecto amne confugerat' (Lactantius, *De mortibus persecutorum* 9.2, ed. Joseph Moreau, 2 vols, Sources chrétiennes 39 (Paris 1954), 1: 87. 'Numquid alio proprio nomine vocitari poterant nisi ut barbari dicerentur, ferocitatis utique, crudelitatis et terroris vocabulum possidentes?' (Victor Vitensis, *Historia persecvtionis Africanae provinciae temporibus Geiserici et Hvnirici regvm Wandalorum* 3.62, ed. C. Halm, MGH AA 3 [Berlin 1879], 56; in English as *Victor of Vita: History of the Vandal Persecution*, trans. John Moorhead [Liverpool 1992], 89).
15 Victor Vitensis, *Historia* 1.1.2; Moorhead, 3.
16 Ibid., 1.6–7.3; Moorhead, 4–5.
17 The Vandals were Arians, and therefore not recognized as Christians by Victor.
18 *Ex miraculis Sancti Germani in Normannorum adventu factis* 4, ed. G. Waitz, MGH

Scriptores 15.1 (Hanover 1887), 11, my translation. There is no explicit reference here to sexual cruelty, unless the phrase *exercere libidinem* is interpreted as pointing in this direction. Towards the end of *De infantia Sancti Eadmundi*, written around the middle of the 12th century by Galfridus de Fontibus, we find the following reference to the Norsemen: 'Isti [Hingwar, Ubba, and Wern] in aquilonali sinu Dacorum propter Gothos commanentes, ex antiqua consuetudine piraticam rabiem exercentes, latrociniis et depraedationibus ex toto se mancipaverant, et plurimas provincias crudeli exterminio dederant' (*Memorials of St Edmund's Abbey*, ed. Thomas Arnold, 3 vols, Rolls Series 96 [London 1890], 1: 102).

19 *Ex miraculis Sancti Germani* 12.12.
20 'ipso cum magna suorum parte ibidem occiso' (*Asser's Life of King Alfred* 33, ed. W.H. Stevenson [Oxford 1904], 26), my translation.
21 See François Hartog, *The Mirror of Herodotus: The Representation of the Other in the Writing of History*, trans. Janet Lloyd (Berkeley 1988 [1980]), 187.
22 See Baraz, *Medieval Cruelty*, 66–7. Stephen of Bourbon's writings are a good example of this 'encyclopedic' tendency.
23 See Dawn Hayes's article in this volume (chapter 9).
24 Simon de Saint-Quentin, *Histoire des Tartares [Historia Tartarorum]* 30.77–8, ed. J. Richard (Paris 1965), 38–41; Thomas of Salona, *Ex Thomae historiae pontificum Salonitanorum et Spalatinorum,* ed. L. de Heinemann, MGH Scriptores 29 (Hanover 1887), 590, 593.
25 Ibn al-Athīr, *Al-kāmil fī al-ta'rīkh*, ed. Carl J. Tornberg, corrected ed. (Beirut 1966 [1851–76]), 12: 359.
26 Al-Jūzjānī, *Tabakāt-I-Nāsirī*, trans. H.G. Raverty, 2 vols (London 1881), 2: 1026–7. For Ibn al-Athīr's account see: *Al-kāmil fī al-ta'rīkh* 12: 392–3.
27 Bar Hebraeus, *Chronography*, trans. E.A. Wallis Budge, 2 vols (Amsterdam 1976 [1932]), 1: 436. For other examples see Ibn al-Athīr, *Al-kāmil fī al-ta'rīkh* 12: 366–8, 373, 381, 383, on various cities conquered by the Mongols; Juvaini, *The History of the World-Conqueror*, trans. J.A. Boyle, 2 vols (Manchester 1958), 1: 127–8. For a detailed comparison of the different representations of the Mongols see Baraz, *Medieval Cruelty*, 89–122.
28 See Baraz, *Medieval Cruelty*, 120–2.
29 Hippolyte Delehaye, *Les Passions des martyres et les genres littéraires*, 2nd ed. rev. and corrected (Brussels 1966), 225–6.
30 There are accounts in Coptic which seem rather accurate translations of the original *acta*, unlike the more elaborate texts I am analyzing here. See, e.g., the martyrdom of Coluthus (Eve A.E. Reymond and John W.B. Barns, 'Introduction,' in *Four Martyrdoms from the Pierpont Morgan Coptic Codices*, ed. Reymond and Barns [Oxford 1973], 9–19). On Western second-generation accounts see Baraz, *Medieval Cruelty*, 39–46.
31 My remarks here are based primarily on three accounts, the *passiones* of Saints

Paese and Thecla, Shenoufe, and Apaioule and Pteleme. All three survive in MSS of the mid 9th century (and are edited in Reymond and Barns, *Four Martyrdoms*). For the demonization of the persecutor see ibid., 173, 202, 223, 225.

32 A youth named Victor was tortured before Paese, but 'he did not feel [the tortures] at all' (ibid., 156; see also 161).

33 'The governor was angry, and he ordered the holy Apa Shenoufe to be seated upon an iron couch, him and his brethren, and fire be kindled under them ... Straightaway the Archangel Michael stretched his hand over the fire, and it became like dew' (ibid., 194).

34 See Esther Cohen, 'Toward a History of European Physical Sensibility: Pain in the Later Middle Ages,' *Science in Context* 8.1 (1995) 47–74, 51–3. On medieval attitudes to pain see idem, 'The Animated Pain of the Body,' *American Historical Review* 105.1 (2000) 36–68 (pp 38 and 62–3 on pain in the context of martyrdom).

35 Delehaye, *Les Passions des martyres*, 207–13.

36 My emendation; the problematic nature of the text here is noted by Reymond and Barns, *Four Martyrdoms*, 227, n. 31.

37 Ibid., 226–7.

38 See Reymond and Barns, 'Introduction,' in *Four Martyrdoms*, 9–19.

39 Peter Brown compares the situation of pagans and Jews in the late Roman Empire under the Christian emperors to that of the Christians in the Islamic Empire. Pagans and Jews could keep their beliefs as long as they did not in any way detract from the dominance of Christianity (see Peter Brown, 'Christianization and Religious Conflict,' in *Cambridge Ancient History*, vol. 13 [Cambridge 1998], 640–1).

40 My discussion is based on Sidney H. Griffith's seminal study of these texts: 'Christians, Muslims, and Neo-Martyrs: Saints' Lives and Holy Land History,' in *Sharing the Sacred: Religious Contacts and Conflicts in the Holy Land*, ed. Aryeh Kofsky and Guy G. Stroumsa (Jerusalem 1998), 163–207.

41 See Ann Christys, *Christians in al-Andalus 711–c. 1000* (Richmond 2002); Kenneth B. Wolf, *Christian Martyrs in Muslim Spain* (Cambridge 1988); Clayton J. Drees, 'Sainthood and Suicide: The Motives of the Martyrs of Córdoba, AD 850–859,' *Journal of Medieval and Renaissance Studies* 20.1 (1990) 59–89; Jessica A. Coope, 'Religious and Cultural Conversion to Islam in Ninth-Century Umayyad Córdoba,' in *Journal of World History* 4 (1993) 47–68; idem, *The Martyrs of Córdoba: Community and Family Conflict in an Age of Mass Conversion* (Lincoln, NE 1995). There may have even been some direct influence by the Palestinian neo-martyrs on the Cordovan martyrs: a monk named George, of the Mar Sabas monastery (to which some of the Palestinian martyrs were attached), was present in Cordova during the decade in which the martyrdoms took place (see Griffith, 'Christians, Muslims, and Neo-Martyrs,' 203).

42 The text presents the accusation as the result of a failed effort on her part to seduce Michael, patterned upon the story of Joseph and the wife of Potiphar.

188 Daniel Baraz

43 This text was originally written in Arabic, but is extant only in a Georgian version: M. Blanchard, 'The Georgian Version of the Martyrdom of Saint Michael, Monk of Mar Sabas Monastery,' *ARAM* 6 (1994) 149–63.
44 Ignace Dick, 'La Passion arabe de S. Antoine Ruwah, néomartyr de Damas († 25 déc. 799),' *Le Muséon* 74 (1961) 109–33. The Ethiopian version of the passion is similar in this respect (Paul Peeters, 'S. Antoine le néo-martyr,' *Analecta Bollandiana* 31 [1912] 410–50).
45 For the text, translation, and commentary see Sidney H. Griffith, 'The Arabic Account of 'Abd al-Masih al-Najrani al-Gassani,' *Le Muséon* 98 (1985) 331–74; for the quoted passage see pp 369 and 373.
46 The emir is termed tyrant several times in this account; yet it is impossible to provide more accurate comments on this martyrdom, since it exists only in a Georgian version that is not easily accessible. I have been able to consult only the Latin translation of Paul Peeters, 'S. Romain le néomartyr († 1 mai 780) d'après un document géorgien,' *Analecta Bollandiana* 30 [1911] 393–427).
47 Most elaborate in this respect is the description of Peter of Capitolias's martyrdom, which takes place in public in the presence of his children. First Peter's tongue is cut off; on the next day a hand and a foot are amputated; on the next Sunday the other hand and foot are amputated; then he is crucified and left on the cross for five days. Unfortunately, I was able to examine only the summary of the story made by Paul Peeters, and could not therefore analyse the treatment of violence in this text (Peeters, 'La Passion de S. Pierre de Capitolias († 13 janvier 715),' *Analecta Bollandiana* 57 [1939] 299–333; the passion of the martyr is summarized in 311–16). The full text exists only in an untranslated Georgian version.
48 The formation of the Coptic Synaxary is a complex issue; despite the efforts to create a canonical text there are many variants of the version published by Basset in the Patrologia orientalis (hereafter PO): *Le Synaxaire arabe jacobite*, ed. René Basset, 6 vols, PO 1.3, 3.3, 11.5, 16.2, 17.3, 20.5 (Paris 1907–29). For a recent summary of the state of the research see Gerard Colin, 'Le Synaxaire éthiopien: Etat actuel de la question,' *Analecta Bollandiana* 106 (1988) 273–317.
49 PO 17.3: 602–3.
50 See PO 17.3: 607 for a reference to 'great tortures.'
51 The motif of the saint cured or relieved by divine intervention is common in the Synaxary. See PO 17.3: 609 (Anba Hur), PO 11.5: 698 (St Abadius), and PO 11.5: 707 (St Bajush).
52 PO 17.3: 591–4.
53 The primary meaning of this term is 'hardness of heart.' It is important to stress that this is not an exact equivalent of *crudelitas*; further, *qaswa* does not generally appear in Islamic sources as characterizing actions that are associated with *crudelitas* in the Latin West.

54 See Robert Blomme, *La Doctrine du péché dans les écoles théologiques de la première moitié du XIIe siècle* (Louvain 1958); see also Baraz, *Medieval Cruelty*, 15, 22–5 passim.
55 Dawn Hayes, in her article in this volume, refers in passing to the struggle between church and state in the case of Becket's martyrdom.
56 On the link between the two concepts in ancient Rome see p. 166 above.
57 See Helene Wieruszowski, 'Roger II of Sicily, Rex-Tyrannus, in Twelfth-Century Political Thought,' *Speculum* 38 (1963) 46–78, at 56–7.
58 Otto of Freising, e.g., writes on the conquest of Bari: 'Tradunt eum in prima irruptione ac Barrensis urbis expugnatione crudele et inhumanum piaculum perpetrasse ... Haec et alia crudelitatis opera ad antiquotum Siculorum formam tyrannorum, quae indesinenter de ipso audiuntur, quia pene cunctis nota omittimus' (Otto of Freising, *Chronica* 7.23, ed. Adolf Hofmeister, MGH Scriptores 45 [Hannover 1912], 347–8; see also Otto of St Blaise, *Chronica* 37, ed. Adolf Hofmeister, MGH Scriptores 47 [Hannover 1912], 56; both sources mentioned in Wieruszowski, 'Roger II of Sicily,' 66). On the motif of Phalaris see Gideon Bohar, 'Classica et Rabbinica I: The Bull of Phalaris and the Tophet,' *Journal for the Study of Judaism* 31 (2000) 203–16.
59 '... cleri tacet omnis ubique / Vox a laude Dei, nec sacramenta nec ullum / Ecclesia officium celebrat, septemque per annos / Se paganismi fedat tota Anglia ritu' (Guillaume le Breton, *Philippidos* 8.887–913, in *Oeuvres de Rigord et de Guillaume le Breton,* ed. Henri F. Delaborde, 2 vols [Paris 1882–5], 2: 244).
60 'Crueus estoit sor tot homes; de bieles femes estoit trop couvoiteus' (*Histoire des ducs de Normandie et des rois d'Angleterre*, ed. Francisque Michel [Paris 1840], 105). His aid to the Albigensian heretics is mentioned in the same source in another place, not necessarily related (ibid., 121–2). For similar imagery, see Queen Urraca's description of her husband, Alfonso I of Aragon: *Historia Compostellana* 1.64, ed. Emma Falque, CCCM 70 (Turnhout 1988), 102–3.
61 The Magna Carta can be seen as an extension of these principles, in its sanctions against arbitrary behaviour by the king and its emphasis on the superiority of the law.
62 See Ralph V. Turner, 'King John's Concept of Royal Authority,' *History of Political Thought* 17.2 (1996), 159ff. On the implications of the king's ruling by the grace of God see Walter Ullmann, 'The Medieval Papal Court as an International Tribunal,' *Virginia Journal of International Law* 11 (1971) 356–71, at 362–5 (repr. in Ullmann's *Papacy and Political Ideas in the Middle Ages* [London 1976]). On the decline of this ideology in the late medieval period and the rise of the concept that sees the people as the source of the king's legitimacy see ibid., 364–9.

9 Body as Champion of Church Authority and Sacred Place: The Murder of Thomas Becket

DAWN MARIE HAYES

In the late afternoon of Tuesday, 29 December 1170, four barons of the English king, Henry II, perpetrated what quickly became one of the most notorious violent acts of the Middle Ages when they murdered Thomas Becket, archbishop of Canterbury, in his cathedral.[1] Thomas's murder is one of the best-documented events of the Middle Ages; the sources, particularly the accounts of the five eyewitnesses to the murder, are well known for the information they provide regarding the political conflict between Thomas and Henry over the rights of *sacerdotium* and *regnum*. These documents, however, are more than testimonies to the political discord that existed between the king and the primate of England; they are rich sources of medieval cultural history. Specifically, they reveal information about medieval attitudes toward bodies, in particular the consecrated body of Thomas, and how it negotiated church authority and the sacred place of Canterbury Cathedral in twelfth-century England.

The accounts of the murder of Thomas Becket offer an unparalleled opportunity to observe the dynamic relationship between church and body, the two facades of Christian sacred place, and how they could simultaneously exist in one person. The narratives of the murder reveal that all parts of Thomas's body were not equal. Although medieval people believed that a person's head was a particularly important part of the body because it contained the soul, Thomas's head was that much more special since it was the locus of an archiepiscopal consecration.[2] In his *Rationale divinorum officiorum* William Durandus, a thirteenth-century bishop of Mende, writes that the sacred unction of a bishop is applied to his head, since in his pontifical office he represents the head of the church, Christ.[3] Durandus notes that, although bishops and kings are both anointed, only bishops are anointed on the head. The consecration of this part of the body signifies the dominant power bishops have over the Christian body.[4]

1. Thomas Becket arguing with Henry II. London, BL, MS. Royal 20 A. ii, fol. 7v.
By kind permission of The British Library.

Durandus maintains that since the time of Christ kings have been anointed on the arm or shoulder, parts of the rulers' bodies that represented their powers.[5] So when Edward Grim, one of the eyewitnesses to the murder who was seriously wounded during the attack, describes the prelude to the first blow, he writes that the infuriated knight 'brandished his sword against the sacred head' (*contra sacrum verticem*).[6] Grim's belief in the specialness of the archbishop's head is made more explicit in his description of the attack itself: Reginald fitz-Urse 'suddenly sprang up against [Thomas] and, shaving off the summit of the crown which the unction of the sacred chrism dedicated to God, he wounded the lamb that had to be sacrificed to God in the head …'[7]

Grim's account continues that Thomas 'presented his body to the attackers so that he might preserve his head – i.e., his soul and the church …'[8] Since he had just recounted the first blow to Thomas's head, this is a curious statement,

2. Assassination of Thomas Becket. London, BL, MS. Harley 5102, fol. 32r.
By kind permission of The British Library.

unless Grim saw Thomas as having two parts to his head. One was part of his natural body, the part that Grim witnessed being severed. The other part contained his spirit or *anima*, a dichotomy shared by all people. But Thomas's role as priest enriched the metaphor, so that his spiritual head contained more than his soul. As the archbishop of Canterbury he was also a church (*ecclesia*), and the focus of this manifestation was in his consecrated head. Thomas's sacrifice for his church, therefore, is a confirmation of René Girard's theory that all victims of sacrifice bear a resemblance to the objects for which they give their lives.[9] William fitzStephen, the archbishop's hagiographer, relates a dream Matilda, Thomas's mother, had when she was pregnant: 'The Lord knew and predestined the blessed Thomas [to His service] before he ever issued from the womb, and revealed to his mother what manner of man he would be. For during pregnancy she saw in a dream that she carried in her womb the whole church of Canterbury.'[10] This message is repeated in a marginal illustration in an early fourteenth-century psalter, depicting the baptism of Thomas's mother. One of the four men accompanying Matilda holds a small church in his hand: a symbol of the child she is to bear. The following folio contains a symmetrical marginal illustration of Thomas's consecration. In this image Thomas is also flanked by four men. Yet the church is noticeably absent, because through his archiepiscopal consecration Thomas has become Canterbury Cathedral. Grim seems to be suggesting, therefore, that Thomas sacrificed his natural body (including his head) in order to protect his spirit and the church that resided in him.

Thomas's sacrifice invited parallels between the archbishop and Christ. To suggest that Thomas was a church was to invoke the biblical verses that affirm Christ as head and saviour of the church body.[11] Like Christ, Thomas became the pillar and head of his church. Guernes (or Garnier) of Pont-Sainte-Maxence, a twelfth-century French clerk, sees the pillar near which Thomas was killed as a symbol of Christ, who supports the church, and of Thomas, who supports the cathedral: 'Then the sons of the devil took hold of him and began to tug and pull at him, and tried to heave him up onto William's shoulders, for they wanted to get him out of there, and kill or bind him; but they could not get him away from the pillar. For Saint Thomas was set firm against that Pillar who died on the cross to establish his church, and from this Pillar no one could ever detach him. But now the people's salvation demanded that one man be given over to death, beside the pillar of the church.'[12] It was fitting, then, that the barons could not remove the human Pillar (Thomas), who was joined to Christ the spiritual Pillar, from a stone pillar in the north transept. Guernes writes that 'those who ought more than any others to have protected holy church, were trying to destroy her and her members, to bring that Pillar and the Head which it supported crashing to the ground.'[13]

3. Baptism of Thomas Becket's mother. London, BL, MS. Royal 2 B. vii, fol. 289r. By kind permission of The British Library.

4. Consecration of Thomas Becket. London, BL, MS. Royal 2 B. vii, fol. 290r. By kind permission of The British Library.

Herbert of Bosham, one of Thomas's closest companions, conflates the cities of Jerusalem and Canterbury: 'Had you seen it, you would certainly have said that the Lord was a second time approaching His Passion, and that, amidst the rejoicing of children and the poor, He, who died once at Jerusalem for the salvation of the whole world, was now again ready to die a second time at Canterbury for the English Church.'[14] As Jean-Pierre Perrot notes, God had chosen both men to participate in salvific plans.[15] Beyond linking Canterbury to Jerusalem, Herbert argues that the archbishop suffered for the English church. Thomas was the new Christ; however, the focus of the salvation he offered was not universal but geographically limited to England. As Jerusalem was the navel of the medieval universe, Canterbury was the spiritual centre of the English realm.[16]

David Knowles wonders if Thomas had the rhythm of Christ's Good Friday reproaches in mind when he said, according to William of Canterbury, 'Reginald, Reginald, I've done you many favours. You dare to engage me armed?'[17] John of Salisbury also notes a similarity between the words Thomas and Christ spoke during their passions. 'Didn't his words appear to imitate Christ's when during the passion he said, "If you seek me, allow them to leave?"'[18] William fitzStephen reports that Thomas shared Christ's last words, 'Into thy hands, O Lord, I commend my spirit,' though we are left to wonder if it was Thomas or William or both who had the biblical precedent in mind.[19] Although the archbishop certainly could have seen himself as a second Christ, these passages might have been added by the narrators, who were, whether consciously or unconsciously, echoing deeply internalized texts in pursuit of political agendas.

The similarities between Christ's crucifixion and Thomas's murder multiply in the hands of the narrators. In the Gospels nature signals the death of Christ, while at Thomas's death 'the sun averted its eyes, hid its rays, concealed the day, so that it might not see this wicked deed, and a terrible storm encroached on the sky, rain poured suddenly, and it thundered from the heavens. Afterwards a copper red colour appeared in the sky, a sign of the shed blood ...'[20] As the sky darkened and Thomas lay dead in his cathedral, the king's knights plundered the archbishop's palace. The knights who killed the archbishop 'divided [his things] between them, made imitators of them who divided up between themselves the clothes of Christ, for it was permitted to them to exceed in wickedness those [men].'[21] Finally, the story of the terrible crime ends at the crypt tomb in which Becket's body will rest, a tomb hewn from rock that has never contained a body.[22]

Beyond being the new Christ and, to some degree, a manifestation of his own church (pillar and head), Thomas, like all priests, was the spouse of the female church. In other words, he was not only the church and part of the church but, at one and the same time, he was married to her female nature.

FitzStephen remarks that 'The sons slew their father in the womb of their mother.'[23] It is this mother who mourns her slain spouse. The anthropomorphized church weeps and 'cries constantly for a long time.'[24] She is also silent; her bells do not ring.[25] Her general appearance reveals intense grief 'with the ornaments removed from the altar, and with the walls bare everywhere the appearance of the [church] represented sorrow …'[26] 'The house of our sanctification has been abandoned; the lady of the people waits in sorrow; all her friends scorn her, and none from all her beloved people console her.'[27]

Thomas's bride is physically changed at the time of his death. Although she suffers, she also gains strength, because when he is attacked, the sacred energy from Thomas's head is released to the church building. Edward Grim offers an eerie image when he writes: 'the blood turns white with the brain and the brain turns no less red from the blood, enpurpling [*purpuraret*] the face of the church with the colours of the lily and the rose, of the Virgin and Mother, and with the life and death of the martyr and confessor.'[28] Although technically Thomas was not a martyr, his supporters saw him as one.[29] As the defender of Christian hierarchy, administration, and political power, Thomas was a martyr of the institutional church. His *causa* represents the struggle of the structural (as opposed to the communal) church in medieval society.[30] Thomas's energies were not solely focused on living a life based on the New Testament (as were those of St Francis of Assisi). This is not to say that the archbishop was not a spiritual man, but his concerns often reflected the worldliness of his earlier life. It is fitting, therefore, that the most significant change that Thomas's persistence reaped for the church was the expansion of papal jurisdiction.[31]

Medieval people expressed a variety of opinions about blood, including blood spilled in holy places. The *Decretum* clearly states that an effusion of blood in a church required that the church be consecrated anew.[32] Yet Durandus's thirteenth-century *Rationale* maintains that the intentional shedding of blood warrants only reconciliation: 'A church is reconciled from homicide whether accompanied by an effusion of blood or not … If, however, [blood] flows without violence either from an old injury to the nose or the mouth, or by bloodletting … or by menstruation, or in any other natural way in the church – either by accident in a game or in any other accidental manner – or if any animal is killed there, or if anyone should suddenly die there by his own hand, or is killed by falling stone or wood or lightning, on behalf of these and similar things it is not reconciled. Nor indeed if anyone wounded flees to the church and there in a great effusion of blood dies, since then the homicide was not perpetrated in the church.'[33] Thomas's blood, however, was different. John of Salisbury exposes the contradiction between the barons' wicked deed and Thomas's sacred blood when he notes that sacraments were suspended at Canterbury because the church had been violated, 'or rather consecrated,' by bloodshed.[34] The need to reconcile Canterbury, which wasn't done until almost a year later, was not an issue of ritual purity.[35] Thomas's blood itself did not profane the church. Instead it was the knights' crime, what Benedict of Peterborough calls the shameful parricide (*parricidali flagitio*), that had polluted the cathedral.[36] In fact, Benedict maintains that the Canterbury monks did not have to anoint Thomas's body with perfumes, since God had arranged for Thomas to be anointed with his own blood.[37] Indeed, Guernes believes that Thomas's blood purified the church. His circular argument is that Thomas, as the head's (church's) head, had to be sacrificed in order to purify the church of the sin of murder.[38] Ralph of Diss states that the cathedral's honour was restored through repeated miracles mediated by Thomas's relics.[39] Ralph does maintain, however, that the church's reconciliation which occurred almost a year later was necessary to restore it to purity.[40]

Thomas's murder during the Octave of Christmas was particularly shocking because, as well as profaning a person and place, it compounded the sin by violating a sacred trinity of time, space, and body. That Thomas was killed within the eight days following the Nativity, a time reserved for the celebration of the birth of Christ, did not escape those who wrote about the murder: Guernes suggests that the murderers were aware of the season, for it was on Christmas Eve that Henry's knights swore the season would not protect their intended victim.[41] William fitzStephen writes that some of the archbishop's companions believed the barons would do no harm, because they were assured the king's peace at Christmastide.[42] John of Salisbury mentions that the murder was not committed during a profane time but on a day reserved for the celebration of Christmas.[43]

The location of the murder also deeply offended the writers. William fitzStephen suggests that Thomas's murderers were parricides, since the church building, a female body, was a wife and mother who was forced to witness her sons murder their father.[44] In order for William to express his feelings about the slaughter of his friend and master, he has to access vocabularies of intimacy – words that evoke images of family and body. In so doing William demonstrates the particular horror of the murder. The men who killed Thomas were guilty not only of taking the natural life of their spiritual father but also of violating the consecrated space of the cathedral, the womb of spiritual life.

William, however, is not the only biographer to comment on the location of the murder. Drawing a distinction between Christ's crucifixion, which occurred outside Jerusalem proper, and Thomas's murder, John of Salisbury emphasizes the heinousness of the crime and remarks that not only was Thomas killed inside the city but inside the church itself.[45] Edward Grim reports that the knights had intended to drag Thomas outside the walls of the church, there to kill or imprison him; the assassins apparently realized that their crime would be compounded if they killed the archbishop in a consecrated place.[46] William of Canterbury adds that the knights' fear of Thomas's rescue by the townspeople persuaded them not to force Becket out of the cathedral.[47] Of all the narrators it is Guernes who seems to be most sensitive to the location of the murder; his narrative is sprinkled with references to the sacrilege committed in Holy Church ['And so holy church was profaned and desecrated'].[48]

Although the time and place of Thomas's murder were shocking, it was the attack on his body that truly seared the narrators' sensibilities. This was still the case by the thirteenth century when the Italian Dominican Thomas Aquinas wrote that there were two categories of sacrilegious acts: the more serious, which warranted major excommunication, included the violation of a sacred person; any other sacrilegious deeds (with the exception of burning or wrecking a church) called for minor excommunication.[49] Thus, according to Aquinas, the offence against Thomas's body would have been seen as much worse than the violation of season and sacred place. Though they didn't have access to the great theologian's reasoning, Thomas's biographers certainly agreed.

Although numerous churches were powerfully touched by the murdered prelate, it was at Canterbury that Becket's body would have the strongest presence. Even at the time of Thomas's death, the townspeople and the clergy of Canterbury expected that his body and blood would become mediators of local miracles. Anonymous I records that 'with the crowd of people sent away from the church, the monks closed the doors and gathered the blood and the brain of the new martyr that had spilled on the pavement and stored [them] in vessels ... And they put vessels under [the body] to catch the blood that flowed; they were not ignorant that this was the most precious blood of a martyr which had been spilled for the love of God and the liberty of the Church.'[50] Although spiritual benefits were transferred to objects associated with the saint's figurative relics, the saint's power would be focused in Canterbury Cathedral. The three areas that had the most intimate and extended contact with his corpse, the north transept where he was killed, the high altar where his body rested for a night, and the final place of burial, were membranes of the spiritual world, places where the barrier between saint and believer was thin. They were places where God via Thomas's intercession revealed his power in the temporal world. According to John of Salisbury: 'in the place of his passion, in the place before the high altar where he spent the night before he was buried, and in the place where at last he was buried, the paralysed are cured, the blind see, the deaf hear, the mute speak, the lame walk, lepers are cleansed, the feverish come to, those seized by an evil spirit are liberated, the sick are cured of various diseases, the blasphemous who are seized by an evil spirit are made whole, and – not since the days of our forefathers has this been heard of – the dead rise up ...'[51]

The places touched by Thomas's body retained their high spiritual energies. Ronald Finucane notes that after the archbishop's bones were translated in 1220 to a new shrine located on the cathedral's main level, pilgrims continued to visit

Becket's empty tomb in the crypt, which itself had become a relic.[52] The residual sanctity of Thomas's body was considered so powerful that when Benedict was transferred against his will to Peterborough Abbey in 1177, he brought with him the pavement stones on which Thomas had fallen. He later used the stones for two altars he had made there.[53] The stones that had borne the slain martyr's body would now be part of the altars on which Christ's body was sacrificed and made anew. Despite the extraordinary holiness of physical spaces sanctified by Becket's death, reliquaries of Thomas's blood worked to decentralize the cult, with the famous phials of the martyr's blood serving as perambulatory shrines.[54]

The political conflict that ultimately claimed Becket's life is reflected in the descriptions of his body. Thomas sacrificed his natural body and offered his blood so that the church might be free from the power of the English monarchy. John of Salisbury writes that at the moment of his death Thomas said, 'I embrace death freely, provided that the Church will obtain peace and liberty with the effusion of my blood.'[55] Recall Grim's comment about Thomas's blood 'purpling' (*purpuraret*) the church.[56] The man who was Christlike and a spiritual king charged the church building with his royal life-blood. The colour says something very powerful about Thomas and his church. Purple is a royal as well as an episcopal colour. It is also the colour of liturgical penitence and mourning. Becket's blood reifies his connection to Christ while emphasizing the sacramental quality of his life-giving death. Grim argues for Thomas's prestige at the expense of Henry's authority while conveying Becket's sacrifice and Canterbury's grief.

The superiority of archiepiscopal power over royal authority is also stressed in the discussion of another royal symbol: the crown or *corona*. Grim plays on the word a number of times. The large and sacred crown of Thomas's head was the locus of his consecration as well as the part of his natural body that he sacrificed for the crown of immortality (and presumably martyrdom).[57] Grim says that: 'the invincible martyr, seeing that the hour which would bring the end to his miserable mortal life was at hand, and the crown of immortality already prepared for him and promised by God to be next, with his neck bent as if he were in prayer and with his joined hands elevated above, commended himself and the cause of the church to God, St Mary, and the blessed martyr St Denis. He had barely finished speaking when the impious knight ... set upon him suddenly, and shaving off the summit of his crown, which the unction of sacred chrism had consecrated to God, wounded the lamb sacrificed to God in the head ...'[58] Benedict of Peterborough even speaks of Thomas as having a diadem of blood that may have foreshadowed his sanctity.[59] Clearly Henry's royal crown of gold and jewels paled in comparison to Thomas's bloody head.

The attack on Thomas's body was also an assault on the church and the tradition it represented, and the accounts of Thomas's body during the martyrdom are laced with affirmation of ecclesiastical triumph. Benedict interprets the shattering of the sword that severed Thomas's crown as evidence of ecclesiastical victory: 'How indeed does the breaking of the sword of the adversaries appear except to signal the true ejection of hostile power and the victory of triumph through the blood of the Church's martyr?'[60] The same sword sent a similar message to William of Canterbury: 'with the broken point the Lord showed that the Church would triumph in the blood of the martyrs, that malice would be overcome.'[61] William read Becket's body, which was unblemished, as having overcome the assassins. The archbishop's 'limbs were not trembling, there was no rigour in the body, nor was fluid flowing from the mouth or nose ... the flexibility of his fingers, the arrangement of his limbs, the cheerfulness and integrity of his appearance announced the glorious man ...'[62] Edward Grim differs, writing that Thomas's corpse was spattered with blood and brain. Becket's posture, however, emphasized his piety as his head (*caput*) was gathered into Abraham's spiritual bosom.[63] To Grim the archbishop sacrificed his body 'so that the affairs of the Church might be managed according to the paternal traditions and ordinances of the Church.'[64] John of Salisbury also considered Thomas's body to be an offering, one that brought peace to his enemies' land.[65] John's perception of Thomas's sacrifice, therefore, conforms to Girard's theory that the purpose of sacrifice is to restore harmony to the community.[66] The hostility and violence that might have continued to target those who had fallen out of Henry's good graces was instead deflected onto Thomas, whose murder restored some degree of peace between England and the Roman church.

The most intriguing expression of ecclesiastical triumph, however, was written by Benedict of Peterborough, who recounts that an iron hammer as well as a double-edged axe was found underneath Becket's body. To Benedict this was a symbolic statement of Thomas's victory.[67] Benedict's choice of *malleolus* for hammer, a word that can also mean a recently planted vineyard, suggests that Thomas's purple blood was the newly planted fruit, which would grow into the cathedral.[68] If *malleolus* was meant to be a double entendre, it is fitting that this sign of life be coupled with a *bisacuta*, a double-sided axe. The former is a symbol of life and spirituality. The latter is a weapon of death, wielded by secular officers. Did Becket's corpse not plant the seeds of spiritual life while overcoming bodily death?

Thomas was rapidly transformed from a living archbishop into an idealized martyr, changing his role in medieval society. He became an intercessor, a mediator of miracles. His body and the material with which it was vested bridged the journey from man to martyr. Before they prepared the body for burial some monks had doubted Thomas's sanctity.[69] But in removing the bloody clothes from the body the monks came upon a monastic cowl and shirt as well as a hair shirt and breeches riddled with lice and worms. The revelation of Becket's penitential garb and monastic clothing under his splendid archiepiscopal trappings powerfully affected the doubters. 'Had his furs been of gris and vair and his underclothes of samite and silk there might easily have been no martyr. And it was probably because of the changed atmosphere that some monks, led by Arnold the Goldsmith, went to collect in a basin what remained of the archbishop's blood ...'[70] During and just after Becket's murder his body revealed the superiority of his power, the just nature of his cause, and his relation to Christ himself. As the days wore on it became clear that his body and blood would serve as bridges between heaven and earth. Although King Henry and his supporters could not be reconciled with Thomas in life, the archbishop's transformation in death made this possible. Twelfth-century attitudes about holy bodies provided society with the elasticity necessary for the inevitable give-and-take between the competing jurisdictions of *sacerdotium* and *regnum*.

The sociologist Hans Mol argues that a relevant religion will 'reflect, reconcile, and sublimate' the strains of its society.[71] The Becket affair suggests that Mol is right. Thomas and Henry's struggle reflected the competition between church and secular authority that was a constant theme in medieval culture. The reconciliation was both fascinating and complex. After Thomas paid the ultimate price for resisting the king, within two years Henry submitted to the church for his penance. The king's penances were intended to extend church authority, the very power against which he had agitated. For example, in 1171 Henry acted on the papal bull *Laudabiliter*, given to him by Pope Adrian IV in 1154, which sanctioned the Angevin conquest of Ireland. In a letter of approval Adrian writes: '[We] are well pleased to agree that, for the extension of the boundaries of the Church, for the restraint of vice, for the correction of morals and for the implanting of virtues, and for the increase of the Christian religion, you may enter that island and perform therein the things that have regard to the honour of God and the salvation of that land ...'[72] Both Adrian and his successor, Alexander III, had hoped that the king, while attending to political changes developing in his realm, would help them extend episcopal control in Ireland, a land that was heavily influenced by monasticism.[73] Henry disappointed Rome's hopes and the Irish church retained its independence after his visit. Yet it is significant that at least on a superficial level Henry felt that it was politically correct to act on the bull. The king, who was not noted for being particularly religious, even called a synod across the Irish Sea.[74] One year after Thomas's murder Pope Alexander wrote a letter in response to Henry's intervention in Ireland in which he called him a 'devoted son of the Church' and a 'catholic and most Christian king.'[75] This may have seemed odd to those who were familiar with the Becket affair. But to the power brokers of twelfth-century Europe it was simply political expedience.

The English king made other gestures to appease the papacy. He contributed some 60,000 gold pieces to the defence of Jerusalem, and after the mid-1170s significantly increased his donations to churches.[76] Thomas would have been quite pleased to know that, according to the Concordat of Avranches, the peace treaty established in 1172 between Pope Alexander and King Henry, ecclesiastical cases could be appealed to Rome, bishops were no longer obliged to observe the customs of the realm, and clerical criminals were immune from secular jurisdiction.[77] These were the privileges that Becket struggled for most fiercely. Avranches marks a change in Henry's political nature, which had become less obstinate and insistent on royal privilege.[78] The king became a compromiser who made concessions while maintaining his own authority. England's church was free once again to fit into Rome's orbit as Alexander and his cardinals scrutinized the ancient customs of the realm.

Yet it seems that it was not until Henry experienced what was probably the toughest challenge of his life that he made the pilgrimage to Thomas's tomb. In April of 1173 a rebellion against his rule began in which his wife, Eleanor, their elder sons, the kings of France and Scotland, and disgruntled barons from various parts of the Angevin empire participated. Henry believed that the revolt was God's vengeance for Thomas's murder. In the summer of 1174, when it looked as if Henry was about to lose his kingdom, he made his way to Canterbury in order to atone for his role in Thomas's murder, hoping, as Perrot remarks, to break the cycle of expiatory violence. In engaging in ritual behaviour Henry not only makes reparation through suffering flagellation by members of the church on which he has previously inflicted violence, but also, by taking responsibility for a crime for which he was not directly responsible, he himself becomes a sacrifice.[79] In other words, during his penance at Canterbury Henry accepted the collective blame of all who had participated in the murder. The violence committed against Thomas was now deflected onto Henry, who received the punishment. The purpose of this act was to restore harmony between Henry and God and, by extension, between Henry and those who were rebelling against him. In so doing Henry hoped to break the cycle of vengeance that had begun with the martyrdom. Through God's good will or sheer coincidence, the penance worked. Within two months all of the king's enemies had been defeated or were ready to surrender.[80]

Henry certainly was not the only person to do penance for the murder. The four barons were coopted into acknowledging ecclesiastical authority. The church required that the murderers crusade in the Holy Land as penance for their crime, and Barlow notes that although many believed that all four died 'soon, in, or on the way to, the Holy Land,' this may not have been the case.[81] Though the fates of the barons remain uncertain, there is evidence that at least two of their descendants paid tribute to the Canterbury martyr. The grandson of Reginald fitzUrse, who was also a relative of William de Tracy, founded the Augustinian priory of Woodspring in Thomas's honour.[82] One of the de Broc family, perhaps even Ranulf himself, founded a chapel in Thomas's honour in the castle of Vernay at Airvault in Poitou.[83] But perhaps most significantly a number of the many miracles attributed to Thomas actually benefited his enemies. Ward points out that 'what impressed [Thomas's] chroniclers about St Thomas was ... that he worked miracles for his enemies: for Henry II, in the victory over Scotland at the time of his penance; in a cure of both a servant of Gilbert Foliot and of Foliot himself; and in the cure of a member of the De Broc family, one of whom had assisted in his death.'[84] Thomas's role as a thaumaturgical saint sublimated the attack against his body as the mutilated martyr helped make damaged bodies whole.

The threat against church authority was further sublimated when Canterbury Cathedral, which had been violated by the evil deed, became more powerful as it absorbed its violated human self. The church helped heal Thomas by sheltering him and providing a focus for his veneration. Thomas helped heal Canterbury by restoring honour to and enhancing the authority of his violated bride when his body and blood soon became the focus of one of the most successful cults of medieval Europe.[85] Canterbury blossomed into a national shrine. Before 1170 'England lacked a really popular national shrine, like St Denis in France. St Edmund was only of limited interest, the cult of St Edward at Westminister always precarious.'[86] Henry's posthumous reconciliation with Thomas was, no doubt, partially motivated by his intention to prevent the French from turning Thomas into a national saint.[87] Through its association with Thomas's body the sacred place of Canterbury Cathedral became a site of political and religious reconciliation and, as a national shrine, an architectural expression of twelfth-century conflict resolution.

Notes

1   Once close friends, Thomas and Henry II later became bitter enemies as they fought over the competing jurisdictions of ecclesiastical and royal power. Over time their quarrel became so heated that Thomas fled to France, where for the next six years he waged a campaign for the rights of the English church. The two men were ultimately reconciled in July of 1170 at Fréteval, near the Franco-Norman border, and Thomas prepared to return to England later in the year. In late November he sailed for England. The weeks following his landing bristled with conflicts between the archbishop and Henry's supporters. The situation became so tense that many believed there would be no peace in England while Thomas lived. This sentiment might have needled Henry into uttering at the Angevin court at Bur-le-Roi – possibly on

Christmas Day – the ambiguous plaint that precipitated the assassination ('What miserable drones and traitors have I nourished and promoted in my household, who let their lord be treated with such shameful contempt by a low-born clerk.') Four of Henry's barons (Hugh de Moreville, Reginald fitzUrse, Richard le Bret, and William de Tracy) interpreted these words as a challenge and plotted Thomas's death. By December 29 they had crossed the English Channel and reached Canterbury. The barons met Thomas in his palace and their exchange soon blossomed into a shouting match of insults and threats. As the barons sealed off the archbishop's palace from the town and began to let in the rest of the royal soldiers, Thomas reluctantly sought sanctuary in the church. The archbishop entered the cathedral through the north transept, and the barons pursued, entering through the same door. A scuffle ensued as they tried to arrest him. The verbal and physical efforts to force Thomas out of the church escalated; in the mounting violence Thomas, realizing he was about to be killed, commended himself to God, the Virgin, St Denis, and the patron saints of the church. One of the barons, probably Reginald fizUrse, raised his sword and struck the archbishop on the head. The second blow, probably inflicted by William de Tracy, drove Becket to the ground. While he lay on the floor another knight, perhaps Richard le Bret, finished the job by completely severing the crown from Becket's head. Before the barons fled the carnage, Hugh of Horsea (also known as Mauclerc) stuck his sword into the gaping opening of Thomas's head and with its point smeared the archbishop's blood and brains across the church floor. By 4:30 that afternoon Thomas, archbishop of Canterbury, lay dead on the paving stones of his own cathedral. For a general survey of the historical background to the murder see Frank Barlow, *Thomas Becket* (Berkeley and Los Angeles 1986).

2 Jacques Le Goff, 'Head or Heart? The Political Use of Body Metaphors in the Middle Ages,' in *Fragments for a History of the Human Body*, pt 3, ed. Michel Feher, Ramona Naddaff, and Nadia Tazi (New York 1989), 13: 'The head (*caput*), seat of the brain, was for the Romans – and for most peoples – the organ that contained the soul (that is, a person's vital force) and that exerts the directing function within the body.' Later he writes: 'The symbolic value of the head became unusually strong in the Christian system. It was enriched by the increased value given to that which was *high* within the fundamental subsystem *high/low*, an expression of the Christian principle of the *hierarchy*, and by the fact that not only is Christ the Head of the Church, that is of society, but also that God is Christ's head ... It seems that the metaphorical use of bodily parts took shape during the early Middle Ages, in the writings of Gregory the Great, in Bede's *Commentary on the Song of Songs*, and in Beatus' *Commentary on the Apocalypse*. In successive phases, these metaphors became politicized during the Carolingian period, then during the Gregorian reform, and finally during the twelfth century, which was particularly enamored of this comparison' (14–16).

3 *Guillelmi Duranti Rationale divinorum officiorum I–IV*, ed. Anselmus Davril and Timothy M. Thibodeau (Turnhout 1995), 106: 'In capite uero pontificis sacramentalis est delibutio obseruata quia personam capitis, scilicet Christi qui est caput Ecclesie, in pontificali officio representat.' Durandus (also known as William Duranti or Durantis, Durandus of Mende, and Durandus the Elder) was born in Provence around 1230. Although he had held a titular canonry of Chartres in the 1260s and became a dean of its chapter in 1279, he spent little if any time there. Instead Durandus lived a good number of his years in Italy while he served as part of the papal curia. In 1285 he was elected bishop of Mende, in Narbonne, and died in Rome in 1296. Durandus's *Rationale* is an exceptionally important source of information for 13th-century symbolism and ritual.

4 Ibid., 105: 'Secundo, caput ungitur propter auctoritatem et dignitatem quia non solum episcopus sed etiam rex constituitur.'

5 Ibid., 106: 'ut princeps, a tempore Christi, non ungatur in capite sed in brachio siue in humero uel in armo in quibus principatus congrue designatur ...' Durandus notes that in the Old Testament kings were anointed on the head. This practice changed, however, when Christ was anointed with the Holy Ghost and the locus of a king's consecration shifted from head to arm or shoulder.

6 'Ensemque vibrans contra sacrum verticem.' *Materials for the History of Thomas Becket, Chancellor of England and Archbishop of Canterbury*, ed. J.C. Robertson and J.B. Sheppard, 7 vols, Rolls Series 67 (New York 1965 [London 1875–85]), 2: 436.

7 'Insiliit in eum subito, et summitate coronae, quam sancti chrismatis unctio dicaverat Deo, abrasa, agnum Deo immolandum vulneravit in capite ...,' *Materials*, 2: 437 (Edward Grim). John of Salisbury qualifies Thomas's crown with the same words (*Materials*, 2: 320): 'quam sacri chrismatis unctio Deo dicaverat ...' See also his *Policraticus* where he writes that 'within that state, the prince occupies the place of the head; he is subject to the unique God and to those who are his lieutenants on earth, for in the human body the head is also governed by the soul.' Quoted from Le Goff, 'Head or Heart?,' 17. See *Joannis Saresberiensis episcopi Carnotensis Policraticus, sive: De nugis curialium et vestigiis philosophorum*, ed. C.C.J. Webb, 2 vols (Oxford 1929 [1909]), 2: 282.

8 *Materials*, 2: 437 (Edward Grim): 'qui corpus percutientibus opposuit, ut caput suum, animam scilicet vel ecclesiam, conservaret ...'

9 René Girard, *Violence and the Sacred*, trans. Patrick Gregory (London and Baltimore 1977), 11: 'We have remarked that all victims, even the animal ones, bear a certain *resemblance* to the object they replace; otherwise the violent impulse would remain unsatisfied.'

10 *The Life and Death of Thomas Becket, Chancellor of England and Archbishop of Canterbury*, ed. and trans. George Greenaway (London 1961), 35. *Materials*, 3:

13 (William fitzStephen): 'Beatum Thomam, antequam exiret de ventre, novit Dominus et Praedestinavit; et qualis quantusque futurus esset, matri per revelationem declaravit. Siquidem illa praegnans adhuc vidit per somnium quod archiepiscopalem ecclesiam Cantuariensem totam in utero haberet …'

11 See, e.g., Eph 5:23.

12 Garnier of Pont-Sainte-Maxence, *Garnier's Becket: Translated from the Twelfth-Century 'Vie de Saint Thomas le martyr de Cantorbire' of Garnier of Pont-Sainte-Maxence*, trans. Janet Shirley (London 1975), 147. *La Vie de Saint Thomas Becket*, ed. Emmanuel Walberg (Paris 1971 [1936]), 171:

> Dunc l'unt saisi as puinz li fil a l'aversier,
> Sil comencent forment a traire e a sachier,
> E sur le col Willaume le voldrent enchargier;
> Car la hors le voleient u oscire u l'ïer.
> Mais del pilier nel porent oster ne esluignier.
> Car sainz Thomas s'esteit apuiez al piler
> Qui suffri mort en cruiz pur s'iglise estorer;
> Ne l'en poeit nuls huem esluignier ne oster.
> Mais ore en coveneit un sul a mort livrer,
> Al piler del mustier, pur le pueple salver. (lines 5546–55)

13 Shirley, *Garnier's Becket*, 147; *Vie*, ed. Walberg, 171:

> Car cil qui mielz deüssent saint' iglise tenser,
> La voldrent, e ses menbres, del tut agraventer,
> Le piler e le chief qu'il sustint, aterrer. (5556–8)

Garnier [Guernes] dramatizes the comparison by likening Henry's men to Jews (*Vie*, ed. Walberg, 173):

> E si cum en Calvaire unt Deu crucifié
> Gïeu, qui si fil erent, e pur l'umain pechié … (5616–17)

14 Greenaway, *Life and Death*, 143. *Materials*, 3: 478 (Herbert of Bosham): 'si videres, Dominum secundo ad passionem appropinquare, et imminente passione in pueris et lactantibus et pauperibus secundum Domino praeparatum occursum, et venire iterum moriturum pro Anglicana ecclesia Cantuariae qui Hierosolymis pro totius mundi salute semel mortuus est.'

15 Jean-Pierre Perrot, 'Violence et sacré: Du meurtre au sacrifice dans la *Vie de Saint Thomas Becket*, de Guernes de Pont-Sainte-Maxence,' in *La violence dans le monde médiéval*, Sénéfiance 36 (Aix-en-Provence 1994), 405–6: 'Bien plus, lorsque Guernes cherche systématiquement à établir d'étroites analogies entre les circonstances du martyre de Thomas et celles de la Passion du Christ, il s'agit, bien au-delà de la loi du genre hagiographique et des règles de la rhétorique, de forcer la conviction que Dieu, comme pour le Christ, a non seulement agréé la mise à mort, mais que celle-ci faisait partie des desseins divins.'

Whereas Perrot and I both draw on Girard's theory to make sense of our evidence, he applies the theory mainly to Guernes of Pont-Sainte-Maxence's Old French biography of Thomas, the *Vie de Saint Thomas Becket*. I have chosen to focus on a broader document base, concentrating primarily on the five eyewitness accounts of the murder, but also incorporating evidence from other narrators. In addition, whereas Perrot and I interpret Thomas's murder and Henry's penance within their sociological context, arguing that both events were part of a complex process of medieval conflict resolution, we have different emphases. Perrot is interested in establishing violence – both Thomas's cathartic murder and Henry's expiatory sacrifice – as the vehicle through which resolution is achieved and the cycle of injury is broken. While acknowledging this resolution, my interest is also cultural: establishing the central role that Thomas's consecrated body, complexly constructed by his biographers, plays in this process. In addition to violence, whose role, as Perrot notes, could be ambiguous, holy bodies and the miraculous powers people believed they contained provided medieval society with the flexibility needed to resolve some of its most divisive conflicts.

16 William fitzStephen writes (*Materials*, 3: 142): 'Et quidem, sicut quondam Christo patiente in proprio corpore, ita et eodem nunc patiente in milite suo Thomas …' He also believed that Christ was again suffering in Becket's person.

17 *Materials*, 1: 133 (William of Canterbury): 'Reginalde, Reginalde, multa tibi contuli beneficia. Ingrederis armatus ad me?' See David Knowles, *Thomas Becket* (Stanford 1971), 147 n. 1. See also Grim's account in *Materials*, 2: 436.

18 *Materials*, 2: 319–20 (John of Salisbury): 'Verba ejus nonne Christum exprimere videntur in passione dicentem, 'Si me quaeritis, sinite hos abire?''

19 *Materials*, 3: 141(William fitzStephen): 'In manus tuas, Domine, commendo spiritum meum.'

20 Ibid., 143: '[A]vertit sol oculos, abscondit radios, obtenebravit diem, ne videret scelus hoc, et horrida tempestas caelum contraxit, subiti ruerunt imbres, intonuit de caelo. Postea rubor aeris magnus emicuit, in effusi sanguinis signum …' See Mt 27:45–51, Mk 15:33, and Lk 23:44–5.

21 *Materials*, 2: 321 (John of Salisbury): 'Ut libuit, inter se diviserunt, imitatores eorum facti qui inter se Christi vestimenta partiti sunt, licet eos quodammodo praecedebant in scelere.'

22 *Materials*, 3: 522 (Herbert of Bosham): 'Erat autem in crypta ecclesiae monumentum novum, excisum de petra a multis diebus, quasi ad hoc a Deo praeparatum, in quo nondum quisquam positus fuerat. Et propter metum in ecclesiae crypta illud quasi abscondentes posuerunt corpus Thomae in hoc monumento novo, quod erat excisum de petra …'

23 *Materials*, 3: 143 (William fitzStephen): 'Occiderunt filii patrem in utero matris suae.'

24 'Cantuariensis ecclesia post necem gloriosissimi martyris continuis diu perstitit in lamentis.' Ralph of Diss (Diceto), *Radulfi de Diceto decani Lundoniensis opera historica*, ed. William Stubbs, 2 vols, Rolls Series 68 (Wiesbaden 1965 [London 1876]), 1: 349.

25 Ibid.: 'Et quia communis laetitia cleri et populi crebris versa est in gemitibus, sonitum campanarum qui ad psallendum horis invitabat statutis oportuit intermitti.'

26 Ibid.: 'Et quoniam percusso pastore dispersae sunt oves, detractis ab altaribus ornamentis, nudatis parietibus, circumquaque tota loci facies induerat solitudinem ...'

27 *Materials*, 2: 22 (Benedict of Peterborough): 'Desolata est domus sanctificationis nostrae; sedit in tristitia domina gentium; omnes amici ejus spreverunt eam, nec erat qui consolaretur eam ex omnibus caris ejus.'

28 *Materials*, 2: 437–8 (Edward Grim): 'Sanguis albens ex cerebro, cerebrum nihilominus rubens ex sanguine, lilii et rosae coloribus virginis et matris ecclesiae faciem confessoris et martyris vita et morte purpuraret.'

29 Knowles, *Thomas Becket*, 170. Barlow, *Thomas Becket*, 267, notes: 'The murder in his cathedral of an archbishop who was fighting for a cause could not fail to be regarded by some people as a martyrdom ...'

30 Drawing on Victor Turner's organizing principles of society, *communitas*, and structure, Gábor Klaniczay offers interesting suggestions about the polarity inherent in Christianity. *Communitas* is a social force that emphasizes the equality within a group of people while structure stresses the differences that are manifested in categories such as gender, age, and wealth. In a Christian context these two principles have a fascinatingly complex relationship. As Turner points out, although structure is present in Christianity (which had a *highly* developed hierarchy by the 12th and 13th centuries), nevertheless *communitas* has been a vitally important principle that was infused into the religion by Jesus himself and later expanded on by St Paul (Mt 20:26–8; Gal 3:28). See Gábor Klaniczay, 'Religious Movements and Christian Culture: A Pattern of Centripetal and Centrifugal Orientations' in his *Uses of Supernatural Power: The Transformation of Popular Religion in Medieval and Early-Modern Europe*, ed. Karen Margolis, trans. Susan Singerman (Princeton 1990), 28–50. For Turner's discussion of the principles of *communitas* and structure, see Victor Turner and Edith Turner, *Image and Pilgrimage in Christian Culture: Anthropological Perspectives* (New York 1995 [1978]); also see Victor Turner, *Dramas, Fields and Metaphors: Symbolic Action in Human Society* (London and Ithaca 1974).

31 Barlow, *Thomas Becket*, 271. He also points out that Thomas's death persuaded the Bolognese masters to change canon law to reflect Thomas's views (274).

32 *Decretum magistri Gratiani*, vol. 1 of *Corpus iuris canonici*, ed. Aemilius Friedberg, 2nd ed. (Leipzig 1879, repr. Graz 1995), C.20, D.1, de cons., c.3, D.LXVIII. Under the heading 'Non debet iterum consecrari ecclesia semel consecrata':

'Ecclesiis semel Deo consecratis non debet iterum consecratio adhiberi, nisi aut ab igne exustae, aut sanguinis effusione, aut cuiuscumque semine pollutae fuerint ...'

33 Durandus, *Rationale*, 80. He notes a number of criteria to determine whether or not a church warrants reconciliation, the intent of the violators perhaps being the most central: 'Reconciliatur etiam ecclesia propter homicidium, siue cum sanguinis effusione siue sine ... Si autem absque uiolentia uel iniuria ex naso uel ore cicatrice uel in minutione ... uel menstra uel aliter naturaliter in ecclesia fluxerit aut forte ludo aut casu fortuito elicitur; aut si quodcumque animal ibi occiditur uel si quis subito per se ibi moritur, aut lapide uel ligno cadente aut fulgure occiditur, propter hec quidem et similia non reconciliatur. Nec etiam si alibi uulneratus ad ecclesia confugiens, illic sanguine multo effuso, moritur, quoniam tunc non fuit homicidium in ecclesia perpetratum.' According to Durandus, a bloodied church should be reconciled if the injury was caused by a person with ill intent. His discussion of reconsecration and reconciliation can be found on pp 74–84. The thinking of Durandus is reflected in the statutes from a synod of the churches of Quercy, La Rouerge, and Tulle held in 1289. 'Item, prohibemus ne in ecclesia consecrata sanguinis violenti aut humani feminis effusione polluta, priusquam per episcopum reconciliata fuerit, divina officia celebrentur. Si vero in ecclesia non consecrata hoc fieri contigerit, aqua per presbyterum exorcisata primo aspergatur, antequam in ea divina officia celebrentur, & quam cito commode fieri poterit consecretur.' 'Statuta synodalia Cadurcensis, Ruthenensis, et Tutelensis ecclesiarum' in *Sacrorum conciliorum nova et amplissima collectio*, ed. Giovanni Domenico Mansi, 31 vols (Florence 1759–98), 24: 1020.

34 *Materials*, 2: 321–2 (John of Salisbury): 'Ecclesia quidem, quae sacro cruore violata fuerat, vel potius consecrata, se, non tamen sine haesitatione et deliberatione multa propter metum impiorum, ad protestandam injuriam Dei, suspendere ausa est a divinis ...'

35 For accounts of the reconciliation, see *Materials*, 2: 443 (Edward Grim) and 4: 169 (Lansdowne Anonymous). Also see Ralph of Diss, *Opera historica*, 1: 349.

36 *Materials*, 2: 21. Benedict of Peterborough was a monk of Christ Church and the first custodian of the archbishop's shrine.

37 Ibid., 17: 'Cui enim proprii sanguinis unctionem procuraverat Dominus, quae erat necessitas odoris vilioris unguenti?'

38 Shirley, *Garnier's Becket*, 147: 'Blood was needed to wash this blood guilt clean; the head's head had to be offered, to raise the head up again.' *Vie*, ed. Walberg, 171:
    Icel sanc de pechié covint par sanc laver,
    Pur relever le chief, le chief del doner. (5559–60)

39 Ralph of Diss, *Opera historica*, 1: 349: 'Anno igitur integro minus novem diebus illa nobilis et excellens ecclesia cessans a divinis, archiepiscopo suo, quem per crebra miraculorum insignia glorificatum jam noverat, ad terrorem carnificum lugubres exsolvit exequias.'

Body as Champion of Church Authority and Sacred Place 211

40 Ibid. 'Ad vocationem itaque matris suae Dorobernensis ecclesiae suffraganei convenerunt in festo beati Thomae apostoli, ut ecclesiam longa suspensione consternatam, juxta mandatum summi pontificis in statum pristinum reformarent …'
41 *Vie*, ed. Walberg, 157: 'Ja mustier ne altel ne tens n'i guarderunt' (5094). In fact, Guernes gives us Edward Grim's reaction (*Vie*, ed. Walberg, 171):
   Maistre Eduvard le tint, que qu'il l'unt desachié.
   'Que volez, fait il, faire? Estes vus enragié?
   Esguardez u vus estes e quel sunt li feirié.
   Main sur vostre arcevesque metez a grant pechié!'
   Mais pur feirié ne l'unt, ne pur mustier, laissié. (5571–5)
42 *Materials*, 3: 137 (William fitzStephen): 'alii non esse timendum; "… Nativitas Domini est; pax regis nobis pacta est."'
43 *Materials*, 2: 318 (John of Salisbury): 'At iste … non tempore profano, sed die quem nativitatis Dominicae solennitas consecrabat.'
44 See n. 23 above. Benedict of Peterborough does not mince words and actually calls them parricides (*Materials*, 2: 15).
45 *Materials*, 2: 318 (John of Salisbury): 'non modo in urbe, sed intra ecclesiam …'
46 *Materials*, 2: 436 (Edward Grim): 'Igitur facto impetu manus sacrilegas injecerunt in eum, durius illum contrectantes et trahentes, ut extra fores ecclesiae aut jugularent, aut vinctum inde asportarent, sicut postmodum confessi sunt.'
47 *Materials*, 2: 141 (William of Canterbury): '… injectis manibus, eum ab ecclesia extrahere volebant; nisi timerent, quod populus eum esset erepturus de manibus eorum.'
48 Shirley, *Garnier's Becket*, 151; *Vie*, ed. Walberg, 175: 'Einsi fu sainte iglise hunie e violee' (5691). See also lines 5575 ('Mais pur feirié ne l'unt, ne pur mustier, laissié.'), 5619–20 ('Unt pur les clers cestui si fil martirizié / La u li mesfait sunt osté e esneié.'), 5657 ('Cele grant heresie dedenz le saint mustier …'), and 5709 ('De sun gré suffri mort en la maisun sacree …')
49 Thomas Aquinas, *Summa theologiae*, trans. with introduction, notes, appendices, and glossaries by the Fathers of the English Dominican Province [Latin text and English translation] (London and New York 1964), 2a2ae, q. 99, a. 4/2: 'Sed poena sacrilegii est excommunicatio: major quidem si volentia inferatur in personam sacram, vel si aliquis incendat vel frangat ecclesiam; minor autem in aliis sacrilegiis.'
50 *Materials*, 4: 78 (Anonymous I): 'Monachi vero, emissa multitudine populi de ecclesia, clauserunt ostia, colligentesque super pavimentum fusum sanguinem et cerebrum novi martyris reposuerunt in vasa … Supposuerunt autem et vasa ad susceptionem sanguinis defluentis; non ignorantes pretiosissimum esse martyris sanguinem qui pro Dei amore et ecclesiae libertate fusus fuerat.' According to Barlow, *Thomas Becket,* 7, Anonymous I is 'an unknown clerk who served Thomas in exile and was priested by him. He is sometimes identified as Roger,

monk of Pontigny ... ; but in his Life, composed 1176–7, he wrote little of Thomas's stay there and drew on several of his Canterbury predecessors.'

51 *Materials*, 2: 322 (John of Salisbury): 'in loco passionis ejus, et in quo ante majus altare pernoctavit humandus, et ubi tandem sepultus est, paralytici curantur, caeci vident, surdi audiunt, loquuntur muti, claudi ambulant, leprosi mundantur, evadunt febricitantes, a daemonio arrepti liberantur, et a variis morbis sanantur aegroti, blasphemi a daemonio arrepti confunduntur, et, quod a diebus patrum nostrorum non est auditum, mortui resurgent ...' See also Shirley, *Garnier's Becket*, 157.

52 Ronald C. Finucane, *Miracles and Pilgrims: Popular Beliefs in Medieval England* (New York 1995 [1977]), 30.

53 Barlow, *Thomas Becket*, 272.

54 Finucane, *Miracles and Pilgrims*, 163. See also Benedicta Ward, *Miracles and the Medieval Mind: Theory, Record and Event, 1000–1215*, rev. ed. (Philadelphia 1987 [1982]), 102–3.

55 *Materials*, 2: 319 (John of Salisbury): 'mortem libenter amplector, dummodo ecclesia in effusione sanguinis mei pacem consequatur et libertatem.'

56 See n. 28 above.

57 *Materials*, 2: 436–7. Grim calls the top of Thomas's head a *sacrum verticem* and a *coronam, quae ampla fuit*.

58 Ibid., 437: 'Cernens igitur martyr invictus horam imminere quae miserae mortalitati finem imponeret, paratam sibi et promissam a Domino coronam immortalitatis jam proximam fieri, inclinata in modum orantis cervice, junctis pariter et elevatis sursum manibus, Deo et sanctae Mariae et beato martyri Dionysio suam et ecclesiae causam commendavit. Vix verbum implevit ... nefandus miles ... insiliit in eum subito, et summitate coronae, quam sancti chrismatis unctio dicaverat Deo, abrasa, agnum Deo immolandum vulneravit in capite ...'

59 *Materials*, 2: 15 (Benedict of Peterborough): 'Cruor adinstar diadematis, forsitan in signum sanctitatis, capiti circumfusus jacuisset ...'

60 Ibid., 13: 'Quid enim gladii adversariorum confractio nisi potestatis adversae dejectionem veram, et triumphaturae per sanguinem martyris ecclesiae signare videtur victoriam?' Benedict is referring to Richard le Bret, who is recorded as having completely severed the crown from Becket's head, shattering his sword on the stone paving in the process.

61 *Materials*, 2: 135 (William of Canterbury): 'acie dissiliente praesignabat Dominus in sanguine martyris ecclesiam triumphare, malitiam superari.'

62 Ibid., 135–6: 'Non membra palpitabant, non rigor in corpore, non humor ab ore profluens aut naribus ... digitorum flexibilitas, compositio membrorum, hilaritas et gratia vultus, glorificatum hominem ... praedicabat.'

63 *Materials*, 2: 438 (Edward Grim): 'sed caput quod inclinaverat galdiis evaginatis immobile tenuit, donec confusus sanguine et cerebro, tanquam ad orandum pronus, in pavimento corpus, in sinum Abrahae spiritum, collocavit.'

64 Ibid.: 'ut videlicet secundum paternas traditiones et ecclesiae scita res ecclesiasticae tractarentur …'
65 *Materials*, 2: 320 (John of Salisbury): 'Denique in terram procidens recto corpore, non pedem movit aut manum, sicariis insultantibus se in strage proditoris pacem patriae reddidisse.'
66 Girard, *Violence and the Sacred*, 8: 'The purpose of the sacrifice is to restore harmony to the community, to reinforce the social fabric.'
67 *Materials*, 2: 15 (Benedict of Peterborough): 'inventa sunt sub eo malleolus ferreus et bisacuta a parricidis illis derelictis, quae corruens, quasi vindicata sibi in illos potestate …'
68 In other words, Thomas's body became the rejected stone that would serve as the cornerstone of Canterbury Cathedral. See Ps 118:22, Mt 21:42, Mk 12:10, Lk 20:17, and I Pt 2:7.
69 *Materials*, 2: 442 (Edward Grim).
70 Barlow, *Thomas Becket*, 250.
71 Hans Mol, *Identity and the Sacred: A Sketch for a New Social-Scientific Theory of Religion* (New York 1977 [1976]), 184.
72 W.L. Warren, *Henry II* (Berkeley and Los Angeles 1991 [1973]), 196.
73 As Warren states, p. 197, they wanted 'effective bishops not influential Cistercian abbots.' He notes on p. 194 that Henry's decision to conquer Ireland was most likely backed by two motivations. Drawing on Gervase of Canterbury, he writes: 'Henry … was invited both by the Irish and by Strongbow [a marcher baron who, through his support of Stephen during the civil war, lost much of his fortune when Henry became king]. The Irish "finding it impossible to prevail over soldiers who, although fewer in number than themselves, were braver and more skillful, sent envoys to the king of the English begging him to come to Ireland, and by taking over the lordship of the country preserve them from the ruthlessness of Earl Richard". Strongbow, fearing that the king's hostility might persuade him to accept, also sent messengers proffering his submission if the king would allow him to hold what he had won, as his vassal. Henry, Gervase adds, was susceptible to the invitations since he was anxious to stave off the sentence of interdict that threatened because of the murder of Archbishop Becket.' See *The Historical Works of Gervase of Canterbury*, ed. William Stubbs, 2 vols, Rolls Series 73 (London 1879–80), 1: 234–5. Barlow, *Thomas Becket*, 257, concurs: 'In 1171 the time had at last come. The political and military situation in the island required his personal attention, and an expedition aimed at establishing orderly government and reforming the Church would not only keep him incommunicado but also earn him merit. There is some evidence that one of his ambassadors to the curia in the spring had been instructed to air this matter again. A conquest of Ireland was one of the few cards Henry could play to prevent his excommunication by name.' See also the letter concerning the conquest of Ireland Pope

Alexander III wrote to Henry around 1172 in which the pontiff states that Henry undertook the expedition 'for the remission of [his] sins, so also in perfecting it [he] will be made worthy to receive an eternal crown.' *English Historical Documents, 1042–1189*, ed. David C. Douglas and George W. Greenaway, 2nd ed. (London and Oxford 1981), 832–3.

74 Barlow, *Thomas Becket*, 257.
75 *English Historical Documents*, 777–8.
76 Barlow, *Thomas Becket*, 272.
77 Ibid., 260–2 and 272–3. Henry, however, retained power over the English church's temporalities.
78 Warren, *Henry II*, 115.
79 Perrot, 'Violence et sacré,' 409–10: 'L'acte doit donc ressembler au châtiment légal et au sacrifice sans se confondre ni avec l'un ni avec l'autre: il ressemble au châtiment légal en ceci qu'il s'agit d'une réparation, d'une rétribution violente: le roi accepte de subir la violence, sous forme de flagellation infligée par les membres de l'Église, il s'impose de souffrir dans sa chair sur le lieu même du meurtre, en réparation de la souffrance qu'il avait indirectement infligée à un représentant de l'Église; l'acte ressemble au sacrifice en ceci que la victime expiatoire, tout en n'étant pas directement coupable du premier meurtre, se substitue à la communauté tout entière, prenant en charge la culpabilité collective, afin de concentrer sur elle la violence sacrificielle.'
80 Barlow, *Thomas Becket*, 270. Paul Fouracre notes that equivocation may have been part of the peace-making function of political hagiographies. E.g., in the *Passio Praejecti*, the life of a bishop of Clermont who was killed in 676, '… the hagiographer showed that Praejectus died unjustly but also indicated that those responsible for his death had earned a measure of forgiveness by recognizing their victim as a martyr …' According to the author, the executioners, rather than the respected members of society who often gave the orders to kill, were more apt to die agonizing deaths. See Paul Fouracre, 'Attitudes towards Violence in Seventh- and Eighth-Century Francia,' in *Violence and Society in the Early Medieval West*, ed. Guy Halsall (Rochester 1998), 66.
81 Barlow, *Thomas Becket*, 258.
82 Ibid.
83 Ibid., 259. Ranulf de Broc was the doorkeeper of Henry's chamber and keeper of the royal whores. He appears to have been the commander of the men who travelled to Canterbury to confront Thomas. He also was present at the pillage of the archbishop's palace as Henry's men searched for loot and any evidence of treason.
84 Ward, *Miracles*, 97. Gilbert Foliot was bishop of Hereford and later became bishop of London. Although friendly at first, Thomas and Gilbert's relationship soured soon after Gilbert was passed over for the position of archbishop of Canterbury.

85 See, e.g., Finucane, *Miracles and Pilgrims*, 121–6 and 162–6. See also Ward, *Miracles*, 89–109. The importance of Thomas's body to the sacred place of Canterbury Cathedral was again emphasized four years after his death when a fire devastated the church. On September 5, 1174, the cathedral was ravaged so badly that most of the structure had to be torn down. Southern notes: 'At any other time this would have been a disaster. But in the new atmosphere of activity and prosperity it was an opportunity which was vigorously seized. Within ten years, one of the greatest architectural splendours of the twelfth century had come into existence ... These activities are part of the great surge of energy and confidence in their future which followed, and was made possible by, Becket's murder.' See Richard W. Southern, *The Monks of Canterbury and the Murder of Archbishop Becket* (Canterbury 1985), 16–17.

86 Barlow, *Thomas Becket*, 268.

87 Ibid.: 'If the cause had remained in the hands of Louis VII of France and French bishops, the triumph of the cult might not have been so overwhelming. When the students of the University of Paris organized themselves into nations in the early thirteenth century and the host nation opted for St Thomas as its patron saint, the English had to make do with St Edmund. Henry II, however, was shrewd enough to heal the rift with his old servant posthumously and make renewed use of him, thus depriving Louis of his former spiritual advantage.' Barlow also notes, p. 273, that 'within a decade of the martyrdom most of the frictional points between two competing jurisdictions and systems of law were resolved by negotiation ... While Henry abandoned formally most customs which were repugnant to canon law as newly interpreted, he still retained the substance of power, control over "free" elections and the real lever, control over the temporalities of the church.'

Analogues to the quest to establish a popular cult in 12th-century England may be found in earlier centuries. E.g., Fouracre discusses attempts made to foster popular cults in areas that had been relatively uninfluenced by Roman martyr cults in 7th- and 8th-century Francia. In response to these efforts, traditional ecclesiastical centres also set up cults. The sources of these new cults were often church leaders who were named saints or martyrs, depending on the circumstances of their deaths. The result was that in the late 7th century at least five new martyrs had been created: Aunemund, bishop of Lyons; Germanus, abbot of Grandivalle in the Sornegau; Praejectus, bishop of Clermont; Leudegar, bishop of Autun; and Landibert, bishop of Tongres-Maastricht. Like Thomas's biographers, the hagiographers of these men interpreted the circumstances of their violent deaths in a Christian context that recalled Christ's Passion. Fouracre, 'Attitudes towards Violence,' 65.

10 Chaucer's *Clerk's Tale*: Interrogating 'Virtue' through Violence

M.C. BODDEN

A recent infamous program of torture expressed its dynamics in this way: 'Procrastination is ... one of the essential dimensions of the tragedy; in [this] torture the murder was forever imminent but forever postponed. Should the victim have begun to die under torture, there was an attending physician to "revive and resuscitate" him so that the process of his prolonged destruction could continue.'[1] This strategy describes the Argentine junta's war of torture against the *desaparecidos* (the 'disappeared'). Interestingly enough, it also describes a cultural aspect of the Christian tradition in which such patterns of violence were desirable. The site where these patterns were most sanctioned within that culture was hagiography. These sanctioned atrocities and the discourse that supports them are what Chaucer/the Clerk is both using and exposing in his presentation of the *Clerk's Tale*, a variant of a hagiographic tale.[2]

To examine Chaucer's use of violence,[3] I need to situate the *Clerk's Tale* within a larger cultural religious context, that of René Girard and the commentators Raymund Schwager, Gil Bailie, and Diane Culbertson. Girard, one of the most important theorists today in the field of religion and literature, maintains in *Violence and the Sacred* that the origins of religious rites and human concepts of the sacred are rooted in the problem of violence, first, because humans have projected upon a God their own violent tendencies,[4] and second, because within the structure of human desire, all human beings desire something which they lack but which they believe the other or some other person possesses. Desire attempts to appropriate what the other has by imitating that other.[5] But this sets up a situation of mimetic rivalry whereby the one desiring looks upon the other as both a model and a rival. Girard contends that in order to contain the disastrous tendency for mimetic rivalry and violence to intensify and perpetuate itself in a cycle of mimetic vengeance, certain controls were instituted whereby an expendable victim was provided who functioned as a scapegoat.[6] The human community, just before the moment of crisis, Girard explains, will find someone or a cluster of people – 'anyone conspicuously marginal who cannot retaliate ...' – whom they will expel or collectively murder/sacrifice. In the aftermath of the violence, the victim is held somehow responsible for the relative peace that follows or the healing effect. 'To sustain that effect, the story of the murder is retold and reenacted.'[7] Three consequences developed from this expelling or collectively murdering the victim, this institution of a scapegoat, in other words. First, it contained the violence; second, it made violence acceptable within ritual or sacrificial rites; and third, it privileged violence as a necessary protection for the peace and harmony of the community. The endowment of the scapegoat/victim with a paradoxical status was a fourth consequence: the scapegoat/victim became at once both social outcast and the community saviour, attaining a real and symbolic significance.[8] As Schwager remarks, those expelling the victim 'notice only that the expelled victim causes fear and at the same time brings salvation. They experience this as sacred and remain ignorant of the fact that their own collective transfer sanctified the victim.'[9] Oddly enough, even though the Christian gospel rejects this myth of violence, and, in fact, reverses it,[10] historical Christianity itself actually supported it through a fundamental misreading of the scriptures. Despite the explicitly nonviolent, nearly anti-sacrificial nature of Jesus' message, historical Christianity saw Jesus' crucifixion as a sacrifice. Indeed, the institutional church not only nurtured a culture of mimetic violence and sacrificial scapegoating, it further glorified this violence through its textual 'body' of hagiographic literature, classically illustrating, thereby, the feature of retelling and reenacting the murder – the characteristic stage, as Girard describes it, that follows the peace effected through a scapegoat's death.[11] The second consequence, privileging violence as a necessary protection for the peace and harmony of the community, became the dominant feature reenacted in hagiographic tales. One root metaphor in particular promoted that feature: namely, that of the purifying/testing God whose brutal trials imposed upon the (sinful) human were intended to purify that human's will and to bring it into harmony with and recognition of God's own will (e.g., Abraham's sacrifice of Isaac, the trials of Job). Eventually, within the Christian tradition, what had been authorized by humans as conduct appropriate to God in God's relationship with humans came also to authorize conduct appropriate to humans in their relationship with other humans, namely, the practice of humans purifying and testing other humans, in mimetic rivalry of the model. This activity was specifically sanctioned within relationships of unequal power, as in lords over their subjects, and men over women, within patriarchal systems. In the Christian tradition, Girard's insight finds immediate witness in hagiographic tales. Especially exemplary of mimetic 'purifying' violence were narratives of such saints as Agnes, Sebastian, Celia, Agatha, Lawrence, Barbara, Lucy, Christine of Tyre, and so forth. Tales such as these provided *the* paradigm wherein outright torture of martyrs and heroic virgins by other human beings was perceived as exemplifying the purifying will of God mediated through grosser human agency.[12]

In the *Clerk's Tale*, with its patient and obedient Griselda who is cruelly and endlessly tested for her 'steadfastness' by her husband, the marquis Walter, Chaucer/the Clerk exposes the Christian discourse that sanctioned such torture in the name of a purifying/testing God and glossed it with eschatological aims (e.g., communal peace or exemplary obedience). He accomplishes this by deconstructing the Christian discourse that legitimates the testing God as a model for human beings, and he secures this 'transformation' largely through constructing a bogus designer allegory, as well as extensive counter-discourse, furthering the bogus allegory's destabilization of the text. The counter-discourse aims high: first, it contests the eschatological goals of husbands who 'assay' their wives (Walter claims that the children must be removed ['killed'] so as to bring peace to his court and country). Second, it reveals the legend's Christian ideology as in conflict with contemporary theological doctrine: the tale promotes abandonment of Griselda's will to her husband, thereby gaining for her renown for virtue; but the fourteenth-century's fiercest theological debate about the nature of the will – a debate spanning the century – generally agreed that where there is no will there is no virtue. That is, where there is no will[13] there can be no moral act (which requires intention, full knowledge of the act undertaken, and full consent of the will), and where there is no moral act there can be no virtue.[14] Third, it erodes the viability of the legend as a contemporary model by representing Petrarch (the source of the legend) as a rhetorician (the techniques of which the Clerk knows a great deal about), and as a corpse ('he's dead and nailed in his chest').[15] Fourth, it subverts the agency seen to produce the virtue of patience in Griselda, namely, Walter. This is subtly achieved in two ways: first, by structuring our response to Walter through rhetorical techniques (syntactically sabotaging Walter's reputation through his name,[16] and exposing Walter's relationship with his thegns as one of questionable respect: 'they obeyed him more or less'). The second form of subversion is the truly brilliant technique, and it is the principle subject of this essay: by throwing into prominence the violent aspects of the testing which Walter's 'assaying' of Griselda prove to include, Chaucer/the Clerk reveals the complicity of hagiography with violence, its empowering of social oppression, and its promotion of violence by endowing it with eschatological goals. While I will touch upon the bogus allegory (allegories being dangerous paradigms, as Chaucer appears to suggest, for reasons given below), my aim in this study will be chiefly to explore this latter effect of Chaucer's counter-discourse, namely the technique wherein, by eroding the viability of Walter's violence, Chaucer exposes hagiography's complicity with violence.

The earlier arguments that saw this tale as allegorical of humankind's relationship with a God who tests them[17] ignore the significant fact that human beings in this tale are asked to participate in heart-rending fraudulent acts as part of that testing. They also overlook the Clerk's earlier profile of Walter as a lord deficient in governing and absorbed in self-entertainment. Creating analogues between humans and God invites a particular danger, both for the scholars of Chaucer's day and for those of our own: the impulse to celebrate a God ruling over us often involves a patriarchal blindness that doesn't ask whether a God would act like a human. It doesn't interrogate its own notion of domination. In this case, the analogue of a testing and tempting God/Walter overlooks the complicitous brutality expected of those participating in the testing and tempting, not to mention overlooking the Clerk's reproachful characterizing of Walter (God?) as a 'wedded [man who] ne knowe no mesure / Whan that they fynde a pacient creature' (lines 622–3).[18] That there is a *bogus* 'designer' allegory going on here is, I think, closer to the truth. By this I mean a system of classic, easily recognized, symbolic representations that have no intention of fully signifying correlated meanings – much less of pointing beyond those meanings – in a sustained way, to universal correspondences. Indeed, the Clerk's indulging in allegoresis is, I think, part of the sophyme (a misleading argument)[19] that operates throughout this entire Tale. Placing the narrative within an allegorical schema sets up an irreconcilability between the 'logic' of the allegory and the 'logic' of the narrative itself. The allegoresis elicits one kind of interpretative activity, but the narrative elicits a different kind, which actually works against the allegory's. When the allegory is interpreted, faithfulness or loyalty to God's will appears to be the motivating force behind the series of tests. However, when the narrative is interpreted, a disturbing obsession exercised by one human being towards another appears to be the motivating force. For example, when Walter tests Griselda, the allegorical interpretation appears to point to God's testing of Job; yet, at the story's level, Walter engages people to participate in cruelly deceitful acts and in the abuse of their office in order to accomplish his end. Further, there's the suggested typological relationship between Griselda and Mary; yet Griselda admits that she has no will. A third instance: the testing of Griselda appears to be about obedience, evoking, perhaps, the biblical obedience of Abraham's sacrifice of Isaac, as well as the singular obedience to which religious submit their will; yet, at the narrative's level, obedience appears not to be the primary goal of the testing: it seems to be, rather, Griselda's *chiere* in its response to Walter's ruthless commands. Indeed, true to the nature of a torturer, Walter never inquires as to Griselda's obedience; he is interested solely in the physical and psychological effect of his power upon her, a point to be discussed below.

From an intriguingly different aspect, John Grossi comes to a similar conclusion about Chaucer's use of allegorical structure: it is a strategic attack on nominalists. By 'inviting a comparison between Griselda and Mary and Job, the Clerk tacitly suggests an association, made more explicit later, between Walter and God.' However, 'the Clerk deliberately goes out of his way to particularize Walter and Griselda *badly* as a means of attacking extreme Nominalism.' Thus Walter and Griselda exist 'only as names,' and are 'incomprehensible as Realist types or standards of human conduct. The Clerk implies that no God could possibly be like Walter, and states that there are no Griseldas left today.'[20]

Patricia Cramer's allegorical reading likewise looks beyond the conventional parallels between related events and persons.[21] Walter's mistreatment of Griselda may be read as modelling 'the relationships of domination and submission characteristic of the religious and governmental institutions with which Walter's marriage to Griselda is compared.'[22] Ultimately, those behaviour patterns suggest 'connections between the oppression of women and the perpetuation of the patriarchal state.'[23] Walter's problematic and cruel behaviour makes such behaviour, perforce, unfeasible as a model of divine-human relationship. Furthermore, Cramer observes that many critics have noted in the Tale's comparison of Griselda to Job and to Mary, 'that medieval audiences would easily recognize Griselda's obedience as a paradigm of the people's relationship to God.'[24] However, I would like to suggest that the Clerk, counting upon this recognition, deliberately evoked the scriptural parallels of Job and Mary because the Clerk understood the difference between what can be asked by God of a human being and what can be asked by a human being of another human being. After all, the Clerk specifically says that, unlike Walter, who desires to know Griselda's 'wille,' God does not tempt us that God might 'know our will'; rather, God allows us to suffer adversities 'for our beste' (line 1161), i.e., for our benefit and spiritual growth. Walter has in mind no 'beste,' no benefit, for Griselda. As Jo Goyne remarks, this 'lack of appropriate explanations [in the text] for Walter's actions removes him from the allegorical and casts him as one who is unreliable, one whom we then regard and judge as insufficient, certainly as ungodlike.'[25]

Clearly, the critics' arguments point to a deliberate destabilizing of the allegorical correspondences. The Clerk cannot intend Walter as paradigmatic of God or of a God-human relationship. Rather, the deliberate destabilization seems intended to warn the audience: allegories as paradigms are dangerous, given the limitations and the hermeneutic inclinations of humans. Allegories contain, inherently, a potential for the abuse of power, and they can (and do) promote, particularly in the context of hagiographic tales, the cruel domination of one human being over another. By intensifying the tale's mildly hagiographic features, Chaucer's bogus designer allegory shows that the allegory, much as does mythology, functions as a recontextualizing agent imbuing atrocities with religious and eschatological purpose. Now Chaucer presses the point home. Through emphasizing ritualistic elements associated with torture – spectacle, pain, and ritual timespan – he throws into prominence the violent aspects of Walter's (and hagiography's) testing. (These ritualistic elements occurring in countless saints' or early Christians' narratives are what distinguish torture from testing.)

Of the three ritualistic elements in our Tale, *spectacle* is the most conspicuous: Chaucer's emphasis upon Griselda's face/facial expressions virtually makes spectacle, rather than obedience, the issue. Indeed, we saw that Walter never once, in his testings, asks whether Griselda has obeyed his brutal commands; rather, he is preoccupied with the spectacle of Griselda's reaction: what did her face, her expression, her *chiere* reveal?[26] Walter's declared goal in imposing such cruel demands (to ensure that he had Griselda's 'feith and [her] benygnytee' [line 1053] and 'knewe ... al [her] wille' [1078]) is challenged by the Clerk, who 'goes considerably beyond his sources'[27] to add references to Griselda's face and facial expressions: terms for 'obedience' occur only seven times in this Tale as compared to nineteen occurrences of the word *chiere*, twelve of which refer solely to Griselda. Even before he marries her, Walter shows a marked interest in Griselda's *chiere*. From the moment that he sights her in the woods, he spies upon her for several months – 'noght with wantown lookyng of folye' (236), but pensively 'upon hir chiere he wolde him ofte avyse' (238). In fact, her *chiere* is part of his negotiation in his conditions for marriage. His single request – that she obey his wishes – is particularized with this insistence: 'whan I sey "ye," ne sey nat "nay," / Neither by word ne frownyng contenance' (355–6). Terms for face (*countenance, chiere*, and *visage*) occur thirty-three times in the poem. He sneaks looks at her 'chiere' (598–9),[28] he has his thane describe 'point for point' (577)[29] her 'wordes and hire cheere' (576) after he has taken her daughter from her, and even though she never mentions either her daughter or her son's name after she believes that he has killed them, he continues to wait 'if by word or contenance / That she to hym was changed of corage, / but nevere koude he fynde variance' (708–10). The point of Chaucer's emphasis upon *chiere* is that it significantly shifts the putative object of the testings in Petrarch's tale – namely, Griselda's *sadnesse* or solidness and faithfulness – to that of the knowledge of the Other. *Chiere* is the liminal area where human interiority and exteriority meet. In emphasizing *chiere*, Chaucer points to the problem of human inner nature or psychological interiority, a problem always confronting the gaze or spectatorship. This is further complicated by torture's drive to objectify its power. As

Elaine Scarry notes concerning interrogations of political prisoners (although she is describing physical pain through torture): 'In the very processes [torture] uses to produce pain within the body of the prisoner, it bestows visibility on the structure and enormity of what is usually private and incommunicable, contained within the boundaries of the sufferer's body.'[30] Scarry's conclusion that 'the point here is not just that pain can be apprehended in the image of the weapon (or wound), but that it almost cannot be apprehended without it,'[31] accounts in part, I think, for Walter's surveillance of Griselda's *chiere*. He needs to see the 'wound' in order to see his power. His power, even his identity,[32] has become inordinately dependent upon having access to the thoughts and passions of the Other. This sort of testing is reminiscent of interrogatory torture whose goal has usually been characterized as the acquisition of knowledge – the discovery of 'truth.' (However, interrogatory torture is frequently shown to have knowledge of the Other as its goal rather than information or 'truth.')[33] It also links the repressive and epistemological concerns of the torturer into an intimate relationship. Walter interprets his torture as a procedure whose goal is a truth about Griselda's 'faith' or steadfastness to her oath. But Griselda's 'truth' is a condition of her soul, a spiritual self-possession in contrast to the possession of her body. Walter already recognizes that she has passed every one of his trials and has acted in harmony with his will; but it is her face, her *chiere*, that he sees as interposing between his knowledge of her loyalty and his knowledge of the Other, – her 'truth,' in other words. The rhetorical structure of interrogatory torture assumes as fact that the victim is in possession of a hidden truth which the interrogator must uncover – usually through violent means. Walter comes as close to intervention on the body of Griselda as a means of compelling the 'truth' as any actual physical torture would on the bodies of its victims.

Interestingly enough, much as with Colatyn's Lucrece, one of the subjects of Chaucer's *Man of Law's Tale*, whose domestic virtue perversely 'arouses not admiration but lust in Tarquinius and impels him to destroy this perfect wife's chastity,'[34] so, too, the spectacle of Griselda's composed *chiere* arouses Walter's desire to construct another and yet another cruel test. We could hardly seek a more forceful reminder of mimetic rivalry's and violence's tendency to 'intensify and to perpetuate itself in a cycle of mimetic vengeance.' Gil Bailie's observation also comes to mind: 'cultural violence that does not climax in *catharsis* will result in *mimesis*.' In other words, 'an unquenched appetite for violence lingers.'[35]

Along with spectacle, torture also emphasizes pain. Torture's relationship with pain is captured in Graziano's description of the ritualistic tortures of the Argentine junta: 'the derivation of pleasure from another's pain ... contributes substantially to the bond forged between eroticism and violence. Spectacles of atrocity ... aroused in the one watching a *sensual* experience redoubled in intensity by virtue of the ambivalence it generated.'[36] If the derivation of Walter's pleasure comes from Griselda's response to his violent acts, then perforce the derivation of Walter's pleasure comes from Griselda's pain. The issue of pain, introduced into the Clerk's counter-discourse, is intended to call into question the tale's hagiographic tendencies to confer eschatological goals upon acts of brutality. For example, in the Petrarchan source, after the birth of the first child, the narrator observes that Walter longed 'to tempte his wyf, hir sadnesse for to know' (line 452); yet he could not 'out of his herte throwe / This merveillous desir' (453–4) to test his wife despite frequent earlier testings in which he 'foond hire evere good' (457). Walter's purpose in testing, we are here given to believe, is to make this 'final judgment' in the final hour of truth: how resolute is Griselda's faithfulness, how fixed is her 'sadnesse,' her steadfastness? However, Chaucer counters with a judgment of his own: twice, within two stanzas, the Clerk explicitly names fear as Walter's reason for testing Griselda: 'Nedelees, God woot, he thoghte hire for t'affraye' (455), and 'But as for me, I seye that yvele it sit / To assaye a wyf whan that it is no nede, / and putten hire in angwyssh and in drede' (460–2). This is extremely significant: the sources, so far as Severs shows, do not make terrorizing Griselda the aim of the tests. Yet, not only has Chaucer's Clerk made terrorizing an explicit motive for Walter's tests, he also makes torment the explicit effect experienced by Griselda. At line 1038, where the Latin and French sources see Walter's behaviour as reprehensible but not unduly harsh,[37] Chaucer has Griselda describe Walter's behaviour as 'causing pain with tormenting' ('That ye ne prikke with no tormentynge'). And the sergeant whom Walter sends in to take the infant daughter from Griselda becomes, in Chaucer's version, a person notorious for undertaking 'thynges badde' (line 522) – a description original with Chaucer. The level of psychological pain intended for Griselda is elevated: the sergeant now 'stalks' into her chambre, and when he seizes the child, Chaucer's Clerk has him rudely make a face 'As thogh he wolde han slayn it er he wente' (536).[38] Even more emphatically identifying this scene with the hagiography's mimesis of 'purifying' violence are the following lines, original with Chaucer (italicized portions):

> *She wende he wolde han slawen it right tho.*
> ...
> *That she moste kisse hire child er that it deyde.*
> And in her barm this litel child she leyde
> *With ful sad face, and gan the child to blisse,*
> *And lulled it, and after gan it kisse.*
> ...

> 'But sith I thee have marked with the croys
> *Of thilke Fader – blessed moote he be! –*
> *That for us deyde upon a croys of tree,*
> *Thy soule, litel child, I hym bitake,*
> For this nyght shaltow dyen for my sake.' (544–60)

This is strategically brilliant recontextualization: Chaucer has deliberately added the symbolics of deification, having earlier introduced the images of Griselda falling 'doun upon hir knes' (line 292) in the 'oxes stalle' (291) to hear 'what was the lordes wille' (294), and now adding language freighted with scriptural allusions and early Christian sacrificial stances ('marked with the croys / Of thilke Fader ... / That for us deyde upon a croys of tree,' and 'this nyght shaltow dyen for my sake'), thereby transforming Griselda, the ritual victim, into a symbolic martyr and Walter, the torturer, into a symbolic deity. But this recontextualization, this drawing upon the myth of the nativity scene and the story of the incarnation, passion, and death of Christ, is, I think, Chaucer's form of courting our sympathies with the tale's ideological position, only to exploit, and thus reveal, hagiography's complicity with violence. Moreover, as Severs points out, Chaucer 'suppresses [material] which tends to humanize the sergeant' in his Petrarchan and French sources, and 'makes [Walter] seem more obstinately wilful, more heartless, more cruel than he is made out to be in Petrarch's Tale.'[39] For example, in the Latin and French originals, after the sergeant describes Griselda's poignant farewell to her daughter, Chaucer writes of Walter, '*Somwhat* this lord hadde routhe in his manere' (579, emphasis mine). However, the Latin and French sources show Walter to be excessively moved by the sergeant's account. And, 'in both the Latin and the French originals, when Walter grants the single shift in response to Griseldis's request, he cannot restrain his tears, but weeps copiously.'[40] Suppressing Walter's humanity heightens the element of pain as part of torture, and emphasizes the gratuitous violence on the part of the torturer.

Finally, torture depends on ritual timespan for its efficacy. In the torture of saints, ritual timespan was often represented as part of the means by which God tests human beings (e.g., taking away one thing after another from a person so as to ensure a 'purified' soul or will). The classic model is Job. A later and more bizarre example is the legend of St Appollonia.[41] Graziano best expresses the psychological world constructed through ritual timespan: the victim 'is constantly suspended in the time of the Other.' 'What ultimately matters is not the truth but the hour of truth.'[42] In the Argentine's 'theatre of operation' (i.e., the Argentine's torturing of the *disappeared*), the truth 'was temporally fixed in this closure of the "fruitful moment" in which the ... torturer exploited his power to dominate.'[43] Walter begins suspending Griselda in his own time when he puts her 'on notice' from the first moment of their contracting their betrothal:

> 'I seye this: be ye redy with good herte
> To al my lust, and that I frely may,
> As me best thynketh, do yow laughe or smerte,
> And nevere ye to grucche it, nyght ne day?
> And eek whan I sey "ye," ne sey nat "nay,"
> Neither by word ne frownying contenance?
> Swere this, and heere I swere oure alliance.' (351–7)

The terms 'ready,' 'never,' and 'night' and 'day' introduce a perpetual testing stance wherein Walter literally contracts Griselda's will to be wholly submitted to his, thereby guaranteeing her impotence and preempting any expression of her dissent or independence. Even when Griselda fully and unconditionally consents to Walter's brutal commands, he continues to suspend her in his time: he is 'glad ... of hire answeryng' (line 512), but he sets his face to reflect a 'drery ... cheere' (514) – implying to the reader that her 'answeryng' matters little and that he has not yet finished. And after the sergeant removes the daughter, Walter

> now gooth he ful faste ymaginyng
> If by his wyves cheere he myghte se,
> Or by hire word aperceyve, that she
> Were chaunged; but he nevere hire koude fynde
> But evere in oon ylike sad and kynde. (598–602)

The protracted period suggested by the adverbs 'nevere' and 'evere' underscore the ritual timespan whereby the hour of truth matters more than the truth. Much as with 'the victim ... whose real or mythic transgressions earn[s her] body the privilege of serving as agency of eroticized violence and as object of the sensual gaze,'[44] so, too, Griselda's *chiere* serves as Walter's spectacle of violence; her face was to be, endlessly, the 'ocular proof' of his power.

Six years later, after Griselda's new child, a son, turns two, Walter tells her that the boy must be 'servede by nyghte' (line 640) as was his sister. Despite the fact that the country was ecstatic over the birth of this son, he claims that the people's dislike of both their marriage and the 'blood of Janicle' (Griselda's father) in his children, is now 'worse than evere in al oure age' (627). His eschatological goal: he must concede to communal harmony; he must 'lyve in pees' (638). This time, the sergeant is even more explicit in his gesture of intent to kill the child as he seizes it from her. For the first time, Griselda refers to her own death; in the same breath in which she assumes, aloud, that her son, as was her daughter, would 'be slayn' (648), she tells Walter that she willingly would die for him because her love for him is so great. The point is that, regardless of her reason for dying for Walter, his torture has suggested to her that next stage of sacrifice, her own death. Nancy Chodorow observes: 'When one is in an abusive relationship, whether physical or mental/emotional violence, the violence is not only what is being done *but the perpetual threat that it can be done*. That is, the knowledge of what has been done can, as well, be unimaginably greater and unending. The intent is to render someone powerless and it succeeds.'[45] It seems to me that such a success might well account for Griselda's expressed willingness to die if it should please Walter, a willingness decried by most critics of the Tale. Yet, her extreme statement is utterly mimetic of hagiography's own dramatic mimesis of sacrificial acts. In those saints' tales, the ante on sacrifice keeps rising; here, too: for the healing effect upon the community and for the lord's peace, first the daughter must be sacrificed, then the son, and now, Griselda offers her own life.

In the five years following the phantom infanticide of his son, Walter 'wait[s] if by word or contenance' (line 709) Griselda were changed toward him. The element of procrastination, that 'essential dimension of tragedy,' is assuredly exploited here. Murder is indeed 'forever imminent, forever postponed.'[46] In fact, Walter is named a 'mordrere' (732) by the people who think that he has killed his children. Yet even though he knows of the people's suspicion,

> He of his crueel purpos nolde stente;
> To tempte his wyf was set al his entente. (734–5)

It is just this fascination with the consequences of his own appalling actions that brings to mind the 'exhilaration that lies at the basis both of sacrifice and literature because what compels and excites in sacrificial ritual and fiction is "what uses up our strength and our resources and, if necessary, places our life in danger".'[47] Walter is virtually unable to stop his torture of Griselda. He is gripped not so much by the 'truth' but by the 'hour of truth.' He even moves to pervert the world of religion itself in his quest for the knowledge of the Other: he engages the papal court in fraudulent actions,

> Comaundynge hem swiche bulles to devyse
> As to his crueel purpose may suffyse –
> How that the pope, as for his peples reste,
> Bad hym to wedde another, if hym leste. (739–42)

Note the endorsement of the fraud (the source of yet more pain for Griselda) for the eschatological aim of 'his peples reste.' Moreover, in the midst of these counterfeited documents and elaborate preparations to return the children,

> yet his wyf to tempte moore
> To the outtreste preeve of hir corage,
> Fully to han experience and loore
> If that she were as stidefast as bifoore, (786–9)

(we are back at the desire to access the victim's mind through the sentience of her body)

> He on a day in open audience
> Ful boistously hath seyd hire this sentence:
>   'Certes, Grisilde, I hadde ynogh plesance
> To han yow to my wyf for youre goodnesse,' (790–3)

and, blaming his people's desire (and the country's peace) that he take another wife, Walter tells Griselda that his new wife is on her way. Be strong of heart, he says, and vacate immediately her place. Griselda's response (italics mine),

> 'I ne heeld me *nevere* digne in no manere
> To be youre wyf, no, ne youre chamberere' (818–19)

and again

> 'I *nevere* heeld me lady ne mistresse,
> But humble servant to youre worthynesse,' (823–4)

reveals just how profoundly for twelve years she has been suspended in the time of the Other. For twelve years she has assumed that her children were slain at his command. For twelve years she has been 'redy with good herte / to al [his] lust ... to sey "ye," to his "ye".' Nor does the ritual timespan end after Griselda is expelled from their home. She is recalled later and pressed into service as the overseer of his wedding to another. At the heart of this process of prolonged destruction engineered by Walter is a radical attack on Griselda's self. It aims at emptying her of self. The emptying begins when he requires her abandonment of her will to his in the prenuptial oath; it continues when he takes away her clothes, literally having her stripped naked.[48] Of relevant interest here is Winstead's observation that 'hagiographers themselves often betray a candid fascination with their protagonists' bodies. William Paris, for example, virtually leers at his heroine's nakedness ... The same fascination is obvious in the visual arts, which often feature the saints as naked, voluptuous young women.'[49] From stripping Griselda of her clothes, Walter moves to strip her daughter from her, then, her son, and finally, her identity. This, too, may be a critique of hagiography insofar as the emptying of the self is a process which hagiography traces in imitating Christ. Because hagiography is largely a male enterprise, emptying the self of self may also be, largely, a male enterprise. Consequently, when a narrative, mimicking a hagiographic model, promotes a paradigm that requires women to empty themselves, this can become problematic, because the culture already requires women to be empty of self – to belong to others, namely, their children and their husbands. Emptying of self is indeed at the heart of the making of saints (and virtuous women), but the difference is that Christianity would expect the saint to fill her-/himself with God. What becomes evident here is that Griselda isn't filling herself with anything. The torturer is emptying her as a gesture of his power and his possession.

Nor does the triumphant procession and celebration, ending in the reinstallation of Griselda as Walter's wife, serve unconditionally as a means of reconciliation, as it often does in countless hagiographic tales. While it does indeed mimic closely the 'decisive reordering that occurs at the end of the ritual performance, normally through the mediation of sacrifice,'[50] the final celebration in our Tale functions, as well, as a facile legitimization of violence at both the textual and the contextual level. At the contextual level, the whole spectacle of the splendour and the musical accompaniment in the procession in which Walter rides to reveal his bride is original with Chaucer. So, too, is his portrayal of the triumphant procession of the two children riding into Saluces, bearing Walter's proclaimed new bride. The elevated pomp of the second procession reinforces a point being made at the textual level: since Walter is, presumably, a person of merit and power, his violence has merit, much as the scriptural models of God's heaping of sufferings and illnesses upon Job and Abraham's intended violence against Isaac have merit assigned to them. Romila Thapar has noted that in certain sacrifice rituals, 'if the ritual spectacle is impressive enough, the issue behind the violence becomes less pronounced.'[51] Thapar's conclusion has relevance for our Tale: 'Here we see an important ideological function of ritual: by displaying power in pageantry, the power is seen as legitimate. Therefore, any exercises of that power can be seen as legitimate as well.'[52] That's why the citizens appear not only to ignore their earlier condemnation of Walter's behaviour towards Griselda and his children, but they also now endorse his intention to remarry, saying that the new bride would ensure that 'fairer fruyt bitwene hem sholde falle' (line 990). In the midst of his pageantry and power, Walter himself sanctions his violence. Its 'purpose,' he claims, was to test her womanhood, thereby directly identifying womanhood with submission to another's will. We need to remember that this is the point of view of the triumphant one, the one with power. It is also a view which Chaucer deliberately sets at variance with the narrator's 'reading' of Walter's reason, namely, that, first, he was virtually unable to stop himself from testing Griselda. The effect of this reading is to shift Walter's purpose from judging another's faithfulness to desiring to experience the Other through torture. Second, the narrator further 'reads' Walter's true reason as a desire to frighten Griselda, to 'putten hire in angwyssh and in drede' (line 462).

In most saints' narratives, such celebrations in the form of triumphant processions or the violent conversion of the tyrant effectively invite the audience to murderous complicity as a means to reconciliation. With Petrarch, if this narrative was intended as a critique of persecutory violence, its service as such was undercut by the glorifying, triumphant procession, offered to violence as a means to achieve peace. *The Clerk's Tale* appears to subscribe to the usual triumphant procession as exemplified in the cult of the saints. Here, however, the procession celebrating the reinstallation of Griselda as Walter's wife and assuring the audience of a better marriage by the daughter, along with a peaceful future, is reversed with Chaucer/the Clerk's repudiation of its mimetic possibilities – it is not a desirable model to pursue. *That* is the point of the Envoy. If nothing else demonstrates that the Clerk's Envoy is integral to the Tale, the relationship between Chaucer/the Clerk's deliberate recontextualization of the Tale so as to exaggerate its aspects of violence and the explicit disavowal of violence in the Envoy ought to put that issue to rest. What we have in the Envoy, I think, is a narrative ethic. Mark Ledbetter observes:

> We as readers tend to read disruptive moments in a text by looking at the larger whole of the narrative and then forcing some consistency of pattern on to the unruly part of the text. I am suggesting that often we are called on to read the whole of narrative in relation to its part, a moment in the text that is an anomaly. Could it be that an interruption in the text, where the story line appears broken and our own expectations for the narrative are not met, is the narrative's most profound and defining moment? Could the story be calling us to a closer look at its failure to clarify, conclude or justify an issue that is simply too complex and ambiguous to be settled by simple description and narrative consistency? I am convinced that such 'problems' in narrative serve an interpretative purpose of pointing us towards a narrative ethic.[53]

The history of scholarship on the Envoy reflects exactly what Ledbetter is describing. Critics have dismissed the Envoy as ironic, even overtly antifeminist. Yet Chaucer's pronounced adjustments to his sources in order to emphasize the violence inherent in hagiography's traditional formula for pious women and saints bear out the rightness of Ledbetter's interpretation: that we need to read the whole of the Tale in relation to the Envoy; I would say, even, read it *through* the Envoy. Given Chaucer's adjustments whereby he emphasizes spectacle, pain, and torture, isn't the Envoy compelling us to take a closer look at the failure of traditional hagiographic tales or pious romances of docile women 'to clarify, conclude or justify an issue that is simply too complex and ambiguous to be settled by ... narrative consistency' (Ledbetter, above)?

In the first place, while Envoys function as postscripts, they need not be a logical conclusion to the Tale or poem.[54] The Clerk takes advantage of this latitude. With the Envoy, he can dispute the Tale. He can challenge hagiography's or semi-hagiography's ideologically charged structure that reifies patriarchal male-female relationships as constitutive of wifehood and of virtuous women. The opening stanza vigorously declares that Griselda and her patience are dead and buried. The Clerk adds: 'For which I crie in open audience' (line 1179): let no wedded man test his wife's patience in such a way. It's the Clerk's pointed reference to crying out in open audience that alerts us to the cause that he is about to advance, namely, do not let virtue silence you: 'Lat noon humylitee youre tonge naille' (1184). The next stanza grows more specific, in both a comic and a serious spirit: not only should the 'noble wyves, ful of heigh prudence' (1183) not remain silent, but they should follow Echo, who replied to every reply. Language is control, the Clerk says. Don't be cowed for your innocence, but sharply take control, he coaches, rhyming 'governaille' with 'countretaille.' Then he adds, 'for commune profit' (1194). This is no insignificant addition, considering that the increasing economic autonomy of middle-class women during this period was one of the reasons for 'the burgeoning of works voicing hostility towards [outspoken] aggressive women.'[55] Moreover, coaching women to take control of (their) language 'for commune profit,' or the welfare of all, is astonishingly bold advice given that 'in the fourteenth century, two medieval towns attempted to legislate female silence ... one of many pieces of evidence that medieval men considered women's speech habits deplorable.'[56] Even sermon anecdotes commonly and frequently criticized women as talkative and noisily contentious.[57] More important, Chaucer's advice was exceptionally farsighted and liberating when one considers that the next line in the Envoy explicitly connects the power of language to a woman's physical safety. To 'sklendre wyves' (1198), who are feeble in battle, he advises, 'clappeth as a mille' (1200), as a way of defending yourself against men who would 'yow doon offense' (1197). The latter phrase, 'yow doon offense,' clearly resists readings that see the Envoy as solely comical or ironic. And lest we doubt it, the narrator/Chaucer unambiguously adds: Neither fear men/husbands nor honour them. Rather, use the arrows of your 'crabbed eloquence' (1203) to pierce your husband's armour. From language as a defence, he moves to proposing outright rebellion against submissiveness or obeisance in any form. If you are fair, show your face and your apparel when you are with people; if you are foul, spend freely and get friends to do your work. In your *chiere* be cool, and let them 'care, and wepe, and wrynge and waille' (1212). The thesis of this Envoy is: Women, construct your own identity; construct it with language, and construct it with *chiere*.

Finally, the Envoy functions as the Clerk's concluding act of disobedience to Herry Bailly. The Clerk, supreme and impudent rhetorician to the end, ends the Tale not just with the Envoy but with *four* endings[58] within the Envoy. Every ending is a form of disavowal of what the Tale values: namely, silent women and uncritical obedience, and the arbitrary and violent exercise of husbands' power justified as a way of discerning their wives' faithfulness, or (less morally supportable) their 'wommanheede.' And the Envoy itself candidly and outrageously proposes disobedience to the Tale's more obvious moral: extreme patience and extreme obedience. The final stanza advising disingenuity as part of women's *chiere* is a linguistic triumph on the Clerk's part, considering that Walter's obsession with Griselda's *chiere* lay in his unappeasable desire to see behind it.

If Karen Winstead is right – that Middle English writers of the fourteenth century were using 'familiar conventions of saints' lives to endorse a new kind of saint,' demure, gentle, and obedient, 'differing sharply from the obstreperous heroines of contemporaneous martyr legends'[59] – then Chaucer's Envoy not only flies in the face of such a trend but appears to be critiquing this new wave of pious romances idealizing women as docile, virtuous, and wholly subjected to their husbands. Undoubtedly, as Winstead points out, 'it is surely no coincidence that all three of the *Canterbury Tales* that deal with docile female "saints" – the *Man of Law's Tale*, the *Clerk's Tale* and the *Physician's Tale* – are told by men and are warmly received by men.'[60] However, Chaucer neither accepts this pious tale's theology nor its value as part of a closed hermeneutic system. His *Clerk's Tale* is no co-opting of a saint's life to glorify the cultural domination over women. It is a cultural backlash. The trick is one of interpretation: so artfully and subtly does Chaucer 'pass along' his Petrarchan tale that one has to look hard to see that he is not replicating the tale but exploiting it, so as to expose it. The intratextual relationship between it and the Envoy confirms this. Indeed, the Envoy virtually catapults him out of any closed hermeneutic system. Outside of the system, outside of the paradigm, Chaucer/the Clerk employs the Envoy to treat, openly, the issue of violence against women, where, in the text, violence as a problem surfaces largely through hints revealed through Chaucer/the Clerk's deconstruction of the story. And the tactically brilliant opening image of the Envoy functions as a perfect link between the Tale and the Envoy: it openly addresses violence while capturing both the nature of the Tale's violence and the hagiographic literary form that conceals (and promotes) such violence: 'Lat noon humylitee youre tonge naille' (line 1184). Nailing down one's tongue is an image of brutal physical pain. Humility nailing down one's tongue sanctions the concept of virtue effected through physical force – precisely what had been privileged in the story of Griselda: psychological and physical violence (the 'slaying' of the children) as a means of producing emotional silence. Small wonder that Chaucer/the Clerk in his Envoy so outrageously proposes to women disobedience, and 'with lusty herte, fressh and grene' (1173), champions their obstreperous speech.

Notes

1. Frank Graziano, *Divine Violence: Spectacle, Psychosexuality, & Radical Christianity in the Argentine 'Dirty War'* (Boulder 1992), 186.
2. Speculation as to whether the *Clerk's Tale* was a fable or a history cannot rely upon the title commonly given as the source of the tale, Petrarch's fable, *De obedientia ac fide uxoria mythologia*, as Charlotte C. Morse demonstrates in *The Uses of Manuscripts in Literary Studies* (Kalamazoo 1992). The title comes from the 1581 Basle edition, and appears to have been based upon rubrics in the MSS. But MS rubrics (from which titles were commonly drawn) 'were often scribal in origin [and] especially subject to variation' (Morse, *Uses of Manuscripts*, 264, paraphrasing Walter Ong, *Ramus, Method, and the Decay of Dialogue* [Cambridge 1983], 311–13). As Morse points out, while *fabula* occurs in a number of MSS, 'fifty-seven manuscripts designate the tale as an *historia* before the tale's beginning' (269). In an earlier article, 'The Exemplary Griselda,' *Studies in the Age of Chaucer* 7 (1985) 51–86, Morse reminds us that 'sharp distinctions between history and fiction, common to modern thinking, were neither common nor especially meaningful in the late Middle Ages' (63). Her MS research offers strong specific support: although the *Clerk's Tale* is rarely copied apart from the *Canterbury Tales*, it 'appears once with saint's lives and three times with romances, illustrating the tendency, particularly in the English tradition, to group saints' lives and romances, suggesting a less sharp distinction' (66 n. 35). Examining the complicated early Christian and medieval attitudes toward martyrdom, she concludes, nevertheless, that 'Petrarch thought of Griselda in terms of pagan martyrs,' and implicitly Chaucer thought of her in terms 'of Christian martyrs ... ' (81). Given that Chaucer's sources were Petrarch's Latin and the anonymous French *Livre de Griseldis* (J. Burke Severs, *The Literary Relationships of Chaucer's 'Clerkes Tale'* [New Haven 1942]), the weightiest evidence supporting Morse's conclusion might well come from Eli Golenistscheff-Koutouzoff's work on the French evidence of transmission and reception of the Griselda tale in *L'Histoire de Griseldis en France au XIVe et au XVe siècle* (Paris 1933): see his p. 133. Golenistscheff-Koutouzoff 'considers the view of Griselda as a martyr to have been commonly held in France and Italy in

the 15th century' (Morse, *Uses of Manuscripts*, 81). Quite apart from the evidence drawn from historical sources and textual transmission, the *Clerk's Tale* is unquestionably hagiographic in key ways. The 'wild excesses of hagiography,' as Helen M. Jewel, *Women in Medieval England* (Manchester 1996), 10, describes the unrestrained features of the biographies of female saints, are, here, conspicuous: the repeated humiliating indignities quietly accepted, the assumed brutalities against her children silently suffered, the exultation of self-effacement, and the emphasis upon submission as the female ideal of obedience. Further, the Clerk's frank caution at the Tale's end, 'This storie is seyd nat for that wyves sholde / Folwen Grisilde as in humylitee, / for it were inportable, ...' (lines 1142–4), underscores the didactic purpose intrinsic to that 'storie of swich mervaille' (1186).

Helen Cooper, *Oxford Guides to Chaucer: The Canterbury Tales*, 2nd ed. (Oxford 1996), 188, notes that the Host describes the tale 'at the end both as a "legende", with its primary meaning of a saint's life, and a "gentil tale", the romance opposite of the "cherles tale".'

3   'We understand violence as the extreme application of social control. Usually understood as the use of physical force, it can take a psychological form when manifested through direct harassment ... By definition, gender violence is any interpersonal, organizational, or politically oriented violation perpetrated against people due to their gender identity, sexual orientation, or *location in the hierarchy of male-dominated social systems such as families, military organizations, or the labor force*' (emphasis mine): 'Preface: Conceptualizing Gender Violence,' in *Gender Violence*, ed. Laura L. O'Toole and Jessica R. Schiffman (New York 1997), xii.

4   René Girard, *Violence and the Sacred* (Baltimore 1977), 2, 81–3, 92. See also ch. 1, 'Mimesis and Violence,' in *The Girard Reader*, ed. James G. Williams (New York 1996), 9–19, esp. 9–12. Raymund Schwager, *Must There be Scapegoats?*, trans. Maria L. Assad (San Francisco 1987), 5, points out that Girard's 'insight into the blind fury of rage, coupled with [his awareness] of the social function of tribal religions, [made] Girard ask whether it was not precisely the ritual sacrifices that secretly aimed to give violence a substitute object and thus, by a controlled process, neutralize its dangerous power and protect people from mutual destruction.'

5   Girard, *Violence*, 145–9.

6   Girard, *Violence*, 14, 17, 24, 94–7, 145–9; *Girard Reader*, ed. Williams, 10–15. Gil Bailie, *Violence Unveiled* (New York 1995), 16, puts Girard's thesis succinctly: 'it was religion – archaic religion – that came into being ... with the sacralization of a spontaneous act of scapegoating violence. In other words, archaic religion is humanity's astonishing instrument for turning murder and madness into a sacralized bulwark against madness and murder.'

7   Diana Culbertson, ' "Ain't Nobody Clean": The Liturgy of Violence in *Glory*,' *Religion and Literature* 25.2 (1993) 39.

8 Girard, *Violence*, 4, 7, 8, 86–7.
9 Schwager, *Must There be Scapegoats?*, 20.
10 Girard argues that the death and crucifixion of Jesus was not at all a sacrifice, and that love – of God and of another – was explicitly taught by Jesus in opposition to sacrifices and taboos, and rituals. He cites 'I demand mercy, not sacrifice,' 'love your enemies,' and the two commandments 'love God with all your heart' and 'love your neighbour as yourself.'
11 Girard, 'The Nonsacrificial Death of Christ,' in *Girard Reader*, ed. Williams, 177–88.
12 The fact that virgin martyr legends 'dramatized ... staples of Christian teaching – for example, that one should be willing to sacrifice all for God' accounted, in part, for their popularity (Karen Winstead, *Virgin Martyrs: Legends of Sainthood in Late Medieval England* [Ithaca 1997], 5). Indeed, the fact that during the late Middle Ages 'many late collections contain more legends of virgin martyrs than of all other female saints together' attests to their 'unabated appeal' (ibid., 10, 11). And these tales' features show little change 'from legend to legend through the centuries.' The saint's ordeal often included being 'stripped and beaten before an audience of leering spectators. She is hauled to a brothel or otherwise threatened with rape. Her breasts or nipples are torn off' (ibid., 5, 6). Even by the high Middle Ages, this 'diet of licensed "body-ripping"' was the 'typical profile of the female virgin martyr saint' (Jocelyn Wogan-Browne, 'Saints' Lives and the Female Reader,' *Forum for Modern Language Studies* 27.4 [1991] 314–42, at 315). Of relevant interest is the fact that 'rarely are the perpetrators of these atrocities remote public figures. The emperor, prefect, or judge presiding over her trial is frequently her father, her suitor, or her suitor's father. In fact, sometimes the role of father and suitor coincide: in the legends of Barbara and Christine, jealous fathers immure their daughters in towers ...' (Winstead, *Virgin Martyrs*, 6).
13 The issue is not whether or not Griselda acted against her will. The issue is whether contemporaneous theological positions would have conceded a moral quality to the actions of any person abandoning her/his will to any one other than to God. As for acting against her will – given the role which Thomas Aquinas awards to the will, Helen Cooper (*Oxford Guides*, 195) would be correct when she observes that 'Griselde is not an unwilling victim. Her promise of obedience is freely given and fully intended.' Since Aquinas allows that 'even when someone acts against his choice, he may nevertheless be acting in accordance with his will,' Griselda's acts would qualify as moral acts. But inclination of the will is not in question here. Nor is the question of whether the will can act against reason's judgment: 'for on Aquinas's theory, it cannot,' asserts Bonnie Kent in her study, *Virtues of the Will: The Transformation of Ethics in the Late Thirteenth Century*

(Washington 1995), 156, citing Aquinas, *Summa theologica* 1, q.86, a.I. In the same study, Kent also discusses challenges to Aquinas's views on these issues by 14th-century theologians. See also Brian Thomas Mullady, *The Meaning of the Term 'Moral' in St Thomas Aquinas*, Studi Tomistici 27 (Vatican City 1986), ch. 2 B. 'Morals: The Question of Judgment,' 62–74. The intense discussions on reason and will in *Boece,* the *Tale of Melibee*, the *Parson's Tale*, and the *Romaunt of the Rose* (Fragment B), not to mention the descants on free will, predestination, and 'necessitee' in *Boece, Troilus and Criseyde*, the *Knight's Tale*, and the *Nun's Priest's Tale* indicate that Chaucer's familiarity with these issues would clearly have been his Clerk's as well.

14 E.g., Ockham (ca 1285–1349) 'proposed that the will was the sole determining agent in a moral act' (Vernon Bourke, *The Will in Western Thought* [New York 1964], 51); he 'made free will a prerequisite in any act of merit' (John M. Bowers, *The Crisis of Will in Piers Plowman* [Washington 1986], 52). Even Aquinas (1225–74), while 'he assigned to the will a lesser role in the operation of the soul' (Bowers, 47), nevertheless made it a 'cardinal principle ... that for an act to be moral, it must be possible to will it' (Mullady, *Meaning of 'Moral,'* 59).

15 The beginning of Chaucer's Envoy, 'Grisilde is deed, and eek hire pacience, / and bothe atones buryed in Ytaille' (lines 1177–8), seem deliberately to echo his description of Petrarch in the Prologue, line 29: 'He is now deed and nayled in his cheste.' 'Deadness' as a relationship between Petrarch and Griselda's patience seems to me to invite the audience to question the contemporary relevance of both Petrarch's stance in this tale and his tale's attempt to identify 'wommanheede' with extravagant patience.

16 The Clerk remarks that Walter was judicious enough to guide his country, save that 'in somme thynges ... he was to blame' (line 76): he lived only in the present and he allowed 'alle othere cures' (82) to slide while he hawked and hunted. The syntax in lines 76–8 reads 'blame, Walter ... name, blame,' making Walter ironically both the subject of blame and the agent of blame. *Walter* or *Waldere* means 'ruler,' and is related to *wealdan* 'to rule,' 'to control.' Waldere/Walter merits blame because he does indeed misrule, both as lord of Saluces and as husband to Griselda.

17 Among the more influential readings are Elizabeth Salter, *Chaucer: The Knight's Tale and The Clerk's Tale* (London 1962); Alfred Kellog, 'The Evolution of the *Clerk's Tale:* A Study in Connotation,' in his *Chaucer, Langland, Arthur: Essays in Middle English Literature* (New Brunswick, NJ 1972), 276–329; and John P. McCall, 'The *Clerk's Tale* and the Theme of Obedience,' *Modern Language Quarterly* 27 (1966) 260–9.

18 All Chaucer passages cited in my text are from *The Riverside Chaucer*, 3rd ed., ed. Larry D. Benson (New York 1987). McCall, 'The *Clerk's Tale*,' 268–9, construes

Griselda's action as an 'imitation of the Passion and Resurrection' of Christ, whose 'complete obedience reverses the action by which mankind fell.' Casting Griselda in this role necessarily casts Walter, whose commands Griselda is following, in the role of God. Joseph Grossi, 'The Clerk vs The Wife of Bath: Nominalism, Carnival, and Chaucer's Last Laugh,' in *Literary Nominalism and the Theory of Rereading Late Medieval Texts*, ed. Richard J. Utz, Mediaeval Studies 5 (Lewiston 1995), 147–78, convincingly argues the reason for the Clerk's allegoresis – namely, that by so deliberately overparticularizing the characters the Clerk makes it clear that such characters cannot exist as allegorical 'standards of conduct' *except as names only* (p. 156) – but goes on to observe that, within the allegoresis, 'Walter's language evokes the image of a God who tests his creatures in order that they might better know themselves, reminding us of the role of suffering in the lives of those creatures who populate the Christian universe' (155). Yet this misses the Clerk's point: Walter is not testing Griselda *that she might better know herself.* Indeed, the Clerk has called it evil 'To assaye a wyf whan that it is no nede' (line 461). Walter is testing her so that *he* can assure *himself* of her disposition; later, he rationalizes his actions as wishing to know her 'purpos' and her 'wille' (line 1078).

19 Or a disputed question of logic. The commonest sophymes (or *sophismata*) appear to be false analogies (see C.L. Hamblin, *Fallacies* [London 1970]); but see also S. Morris Engel, *With Good Reason: An Introduction to Informal Fallacies*, 3rd ed. (New York 1986), 164, who distinguishes a sophism from a fallacy. Fallacies that draw conclusions based upon a comparison of two things alike in unimportant ways but different in important ways occur throughout. Allegories obviously are ripe for this sort of sophyme. One of the more deceptive fallacies occurs at the Tale's end, when Walter defends his actions earlier condemned by his people as cruel and malicious: he declares that he had done the deeds

'For no malice, ne for no crueltee,
But for t'assaye in thee [Griselda] thy wommanheede,
And nat to sleen my children – God forbeede! –
But for to kepe hem pryvely and stille,
Til I thy purpos knewe and al thy wille.' (1074–8)

His claim is an example of the fallacy of irrelevant thesis: attacking someone else's claim, irrelevantly, or defending one's own claim, irrelevantly. Two different questions are at issue here: (1) whether his actions were cruel, and (2) what reasons motivated his actions. He has offered a conclusion about the second question, which was not at issue, and has failed to refute the first question, which was at issue. Hamblin, *Fallacies*, 166, remarks that the irrelevant fallacy is one of the most potentially deceptive.

20 Grossi, 'Clerk vs Wife of Bath,' 155–6. Although I do not agree with Grossi's assumption that the Clerk did not 'comprehend the meaning of his own Tale'

(156), I think his thesis about the attack on Nominalism offers an illuminating explanation of many of the unresolvable contradictions in the Tale's allegorical construct. Nominalism argued that 'all universal ideas, all general concepts, were mere names' (Brian Tierney and Sidney Painter, *Western Europe in the Middle Ages, 300–1425* [New York 1992], 434–5); or, as John Keble later wrote in *Sermons Academical and Occasional*, 2nd ed. (Oxford 1848), 215 (no. 8): '[By nominalism] I mean the habit of resolving the high mysteries of the faith into mere circumstances of language.'

21 Patricia Cramer, 'Lordship, Bondage, and the Erotic: The Psychological Basis of Chaucer's *Clerk's Tale*,' *Journal of English and Germanic Philology* 89 (1990) 491–511, at 492. Taking the complicated and disturbing character of Walter into consideration, she argues that Walter's marriage to Griselda, emphasized in the context of Christianity, monarchy, and family, establishes 'a parallelism between religious, governmental, and marital institutions which is that God is to man as king is to people as husband is to wife.'

22 Ibid., 492.

23 Ibid., 493.

24 Ibid., 492.

25 Jo Goyne, 'Pleasing Virtue: The Problem of Word and Will in Chaucer's *Clerk's Tale*,' in *Representations of the Feminine in the Middle Ages*, ed. Bonnie Wheeler, Feminea medievalia 1 (Dallas 1993), 139–60, at 147. Goyne further remarks that the 'Clerk's timely interjection, that in his opinion such useless testing is evil, assures that we not fall into that unfortunate group who might find Walter's behavior "a subtil wit".' We are, she adds, 'clearly admonished by the Clerk to judge Walter's behavior as capricious and unwarranted' (147).

26 The *Middle English Dictionary* includes the following definitions of *chiere*: 2. (a) 'the face as expressing emotion, attitude, or character'; 3 (a) ' a gesture or act indicative of an attitude or intention,' 3 (b) 'outward appearance or show; ... insincere show of affection'; (4) 'manner, bearing, behavior'; 5 (a) 'frame of mind, a state of feeling, spirit.'

27 Thomas H. Bestul, 'True and False *Cheere* in Chaucer's *Clerk's Tale*,' *Journal of English and Germanic Philology* 82 (1983) 500–14, at 501, writes that 'in his care to develop this emphasis [upon facial expressions], Chaucer goes considerably beyond his sources in the Latin of Petrarch and the French adaptation of it, adding references to facial expression where none exist in his originals.'

28 Also: 'He wolde have wend ... That she hadde suffred this with sad visage' (lines 691–3); 'He waiteth if by word or contenance / That she to hym was changed of corage, / But nevere koude he fynde variance' (708–10); 'And whan this Walter saugh ... Hir glade chiere ...' (1044–5).

29 In fact, the lines 'And of Grisildis wordes and hire cheere / He tolde hym point

238 M.C. Bodden

for point, in short and pleyn' (576–7) are not in Chaucer's sources; cf. Severs, *Literary Relationships*, 272–3.
30 Elaine Scarry, *The Body in Pain: The Making and Unmaking of the World* (New York 1985), 27.
31 Ibid., 16.
32 One of the Clerk's subtextual arguments challenges the sort of person who would require blind obedience. What the Clerk sees, beyond blind obedience, is the way in which blind obedience, violence, and virility all come down to the issue of identity. In its extreme form, a virility (specifically Herry Bailly's – through his attack on the Clerk's virility – and, more generally, Walter's virility) that needs to exercise power over the other bespeaks a person who lacks a sense of identity. Control over another is a way of framing one's identity; when a person can make someone else afraid of her/him, that other's fearful response affirms, even shapes, the controller's identity.
33 Elaine Scarry, *Body in Pain*, 329 n. 7, citing examples of irrelevant questions documented in interrogations of IRA, Vietnam, Ethiopian, and Chilean prisoners, asserts: 'Although there is, of course, no way to demonstrate conclusively that the need for information is a fictitious motive for the interrogation, instance after instance can be cited of irrelevant questions.' According to Lawrence Weschler, in Uruguay torture institutions 'were methodically designed to demolish the mental, emotional, and moral integrity of their inmate populations'; this coincides with the remarks of a Chilean psychologist working with ex-victims: the aim of torture, he said, was 'to destroy the person, to destroy the political activity ... When he gets out, he'll never be the same again.' Cited in Ronald D. Crelinsten, 'In Their Own Words: The World of the Torturer,' in *The Politics of Pain: Torturers and Their Masters*, ed. Crelinsten and Alex P. Schmid (Boulder 1995), 35–64, at 41 and 43. See also Mika Haritos-Fatouros, 'The Official Torturer: A Learning Model for Obedience to the Authority of Violence,' in *Politics of Pain*, 129–46, esp. 130, 141–3.
34 Margaret Hallissey, *Clean Maids, True Wives, Steadfast Widows: Chaucer's Women and the Medieval Codes of Conduct* (London 1993), 109.
35 Bailie, *Violence Unveiled*, 90–1.
36 Graziano, *Divine Violence*, 154.
37 The Latin reads 'Unum bona fide te precor ac moneo: ne hanc illis aculeis agites quibus alteram agitasti ...' and the French 'Une chose toutesfoiz te vueil prier et requerir: que tu ne la poingnes des aguillons que tu as pointe l'autre ...' (Severs, *Literary Relationships*, 284–6 and 285–7). Robinson's explanatory note to line 1037 in the *Riverside Chaucer* (p. 883) mentions a Latin gloss and translates: 'One thing I pray and advise you in all good faith: that you do not drive this woman with those goads you have driven another ...'

38 Preceding the phrase 'she thought that he would have slain the baby right there,' the line, 'Allas! Hir doghter that she loved so' (543) is original with Chaucer. Introducing the element of Griselda's naked love of her daughter emphasizes even further her pathos and fear.
39 Severs, *Literary Relationships*, 230–1. E.g., the sergeant pleads forgiveness of Griselda for what he is forced to do. Chaucer deliberately substitutes the description of the sergeant seizing the infant boy even more roughly than he had the daughter.
40 Ibid., 231. The alterations 'undoubtedly leave a far less favorable impression of Walter than one would gain from the Latin or French versions.'
41 Leslie Abend Callahan, 'The Torture of Saint Apollonia: Deconstructing Fouquet's Martyrdom Stage,' *Studies in Iconography* 16 (1994) 119–38, points to the 3rd-century letter by 'Bishop Dionysus of Alexandria' that 'describes Apollonia as an "aged virgin: whose teeth were broken out with blows on the jaws"' (119). In the 13th-century *Legenda aurea*, this 'certain admirable virgin of advanced age' is still described as having all of her teeth 'knocked out': 'primo ei omnes dentes ejus excusserunt' (119–20). However, Winstead notes in *Virgin Martyrs*, 9, that by the 14th and 15th centuries 'hagiographers, undeterred by either Dionysius's details or his omissions, transformed the "wonderful old lady" into a beautiful princess whose father tortures, and in some versions, kills her for her faith.' And now her teeth are removed one by one: 'et singulos dentes ex ore divelli ...' (Callahan, 'Torture of St Apollonia,' 121–2). Callahan continues: 'In contrast to the earlier accounts in which the torture is swift and violent, this extraction of teeth one at a time is slow' (122).
42 Graziano, *Divine Violence*, 186.
43 Ibid.
44 Ibid., 154.
45 Nancy Chodorow, *Femininities, Masculinities, Sexualities: Freud and Beyond* (Lexington 1994), 110 n. 6 (emphasis mine).
46 Graziano, *Divine Violence*, 186.
47 Edith Wyschogrod, commenting upon Georges Bataille's theory about the relationship between sacrifice and literature in 'Killing the Cat: Sacrifice and Beauty in Genet and Mishima,' *Religion and Literature* 25.2 (1993) 107–19, at 107. Wyschogrod's citation is from Bataille, *The History of Eroticism*, vol. 2 of *The Accursed Share: An Essay on General Economy*, trans. Robert Hurley (New York 1991), 105. Of interest is Wyschogrod's demonstration that Genet's and Mishima's novels 'employ sacrifice not only as a theme but as the structuring principle of an entire aesthetic' ('Killing the Cat,' 105). It strikes me that any text involved in ritual timespan and torture must inevitably employ the same sort of structuring principle.

48 Dorothy Kelly points out that disrobing/stripping another is 'a form of dispossession as a means of rendering powerless.' See her *Telling Glances: Voyeurism in the French Novel* (New Brunswick, NJ 1992), 24.
49 Winstead, *Virgin Martyrs*, 109. Winstead's example includes William Paris, who writes in his 'Christine': 'Hire paps were als rounde ywis(s)e / As an appille, thate growes in felde' (lines 441–2).
50 Girard, 'Mimesis and Violence,' in *Girard Reader*, ed. Williams, 11.
51 Romila Thapar, 'Sacrifice, Surplus, and the Soul,' *History of Religions* 33.4 (1994) 305–24, at 315.
52 Ibid., 315.
53 Mark Ledbetter, *Victims and the Postmodern Narrative, or: Doing Violence to the Body* (London 1996), 2.
54 Traditionally, the Envoy often functioned as 'a means of connecting the action to actual life, by establishing a realistic context for the abstract ideas' of the work (Benson, ed., *Riverside Chaucer*, 883, note on line 1177, citing Daniel Poirion, *Le Poète et le prince: L'Evolution du lyrisme courtois de Guillaume de Machaut à Charles d'Orléans* [Paris 1965], 373).
55 Karen Winstead, 'Saints, Wives, and Other "Hooly Thynges": Pious Laywomen in Middle English Romance,' *Chaucer Yearbook: A Journal of Late Medieval Studies* 2 (1995) 153.
56 Hallissy, *Clean Maids*, 59, 61.
57 Ibid., 61.
58 The four endings: (1) Let no man so try his wife's patience to discern in her a Griselda, 'for in certein he shal faille' (lines 1180–1); (2) let no virtue 'youre tonge naille,' and let no clerk have reason to write of you 'a storie of swich mervaille' (1184–6) and use language to control your destiny ('sharply taak on yow the governaille' [1192]); (3) do not dread husbands but use language to defend yourself; (4) show your face and your clothes to your advantage, and, if 'thou be foul' use money to secure friends, and of your 'chiere' be 'light as leef on lynde' (1211) – no 'sadnesse,' no 'sad visage' here.
59 Winstead, 'Saints, Wives,' 139: 'Far from challenging social institutions and denigrating the men who upheld them, as saints' lives so often do, pious romances sanction patriarchal authority and iterate a recurring theme in late medieval conduct books:
> What man þe wedde schall befor God with a rynge,
> Honour hym and wurschipe him, and bowe ouer all þinge.
> Mekely hym answere and noght to haterlynge,
> And so þou schalt slake his mod and be his derlynge.

Winstead's excerpt cites *The Good Wife Taught Her Daughter*, ed. Tauno F. Mustanoja (Helsinki 1948), 161, lines 26–9.
60 Winstead, 'Saints, Wives,' 150.

11 Violence, the Queen's Body, and the Medieval Body Politic[1]

JOHN CARMI PARSONS

In March 1184, a teenaged queen of France incited an outbreak of civic violence in the town of Senlis that left an indelible mark on Capetian dynastic and diplomatic history. Not yet fourteen,[2] Isabelle of Hainaut heard in that month that her husband, King Philip II, had called his barons to Senlis to announce a divorce after four years of marriage. Modern historians surmise that Philip hoped a threatened divorce would shock his father-in-law, Baldwin V of Hainaut, into readier compliance with his wishes.[3] Medieval writers, however, ignore any such diplomatic motives and focus instead on Isabelle's reactions to the announcement.

The earliest of these chroniclers was Gislebert of Mons, in 1184 Baldwin V's chancellor, who gives the fullest account of Isabelle's response: on the day fixed for the divorce, she removed her royal robes and, clad only in a penitential shift, went barefoot through the streets to every church in Senlis. At each altar, she begged God to save her from the counsel of those who sought her ruin. Seeing her plight, the town's lepers and paupers went to the royal residence and, during a meeting of the royal council, rioted in Philip's hearing, asking God to defeat Isabelle's enemies. In these menacing circumstances, Philip's paternal uncle Count Robert of Braine and his cousins, Robert's sons, were able to induce him on the spot to abandon the divorce.[4]

That Isabelle's provocation of a disturbance sufficed to dissuade Philip II from his stated course jars fiercely enough with a queen's traditional role as peaceweaver to attract our attention, and intriguingly enough we have two other, later, accounts with which to compare Gislebert's. Some twenty years after the events at Senlis, an independent Flemish chronicler added a few plausible details to his report: Isabelle carries tapers as she walks, prays especially in a church of the Virgin, gives alms to the poor, and feeds them herself. But the Flemish author mentions no riot; rather, Philip gives up the divorce when Isabelle's humility rouses his pity.[5] Our third source, a vernacular late thirteenth-century history directed by Isabelle's grandnephew Baldwin of Avesnes (1219–1295), notes the announced divorce but not Isabelle's pilgrimage, nor the popular reaction to it. In Baldwin's version, when everything is ready for Isabelle to leave court, Philip gathers his courtiers and tells her, 'Lady, I wish everyone to know that you leave not by any offence of yours, but only as it seems I may not have an heir by you. Name any baron in my realm you may wish as your lord, and you shall have him at any cost.' She tearfully replies, 'Sire, you astound God; it displeases Him that any mortal should lie in the bed you have occupied.' Philip responds, 'Well said, lady; you shall never depart hence.'[6] This dialogue may be invented, or a popular legend, or the work of another hand between 1184 and the completion of Avesnes's work ca 1278.[7] But Philip II did announce at Senlis his intent to divorce Isabelle of Hainaut in March 1184, and as Baldwin of Avesnes was Isabelle's kinsman, he may well have drawn on family lore that we should not reject outright. Sterility was often alleged to justify medieval royal divorce and, despite his wife's youth, Philip did perhaps intend to use this convenient and not readily disprovable excuse. In any event, they did not divorce; in March 1190, Isabelle died bearing twins, her fourth and fifth children. She left one son, the future Louis VIII, born in 1187, in whose name Philip II annexed to the royal domain Isabelle's dowry, the rich Artois region.[8]

These three varied accounts of a single intriguing incident, in which a queen resists her husband's wish to divorce her and compels him to keep her as his wife, touch closely upon many issues opened to scrutiny by current scholarly interest in the aristocratic consorts of medieval Europe. Documenting such women's lives casts new light on their negotiation of narratives that governed their places in society; but today, we attend as well to society's experience of a ruler's wife as a woman whose intimate relationships to centres of authority implied a unique influence on a male ruler's affairs. Consorts were thus lightning rods for prevailing ideas on gender and power, and with this realization we seek to fathom how others understood these women in light of medieval ideas on women's access to power, or how their public images could shape that of their husbands and of the hierarchies of authority they represented. Depictions of consorts could thus reflect significant tensions within political society, tensions that could, and did, extend to the kind of violent manifestation Queen Isabelle sparked at Senlis in 1184. Aristocratic consorts' potentially broad impact on political life is evident in the attention given their roles and images, and reactions to them, in a broad range of artistic, liturgical, or literary sources as well as in chronicles or letters.

Peggy McCracken, for example, has studied the image of the adulterous queen in twelfth- and thirteenth-century French romance, and sees the faithless queen's body in these works as the site of a struggle for the realm's good governance. These romances were written as Capetian kings consolidated hereditary right to the throne and extended their authority over the royal domain and beyond; McCracken sees the adulterous queen's literary image as a way to define queenship in this changing political landscape. As a queen's fertility and chastity became critical to political society, adulterous romance queens are usually barren, but their bodily integrity is equated to the integrity of their husbands' rule. Adultery charges often mask efforts to oust a queen's lover from a privileged place at court arising from prior friendship with the king. In the image of the queen who seduces a favoured vassal, McCracken discerns anxieties for bastard births and women's power to hide paternity, subvert succession, and wield illicit power by seduction. Romance queens' often spurious proof of their purity, frequently established through ordeals that threaten violence upon their persons, rehabilitates a sovereignty challenged by the adultery charges, and restores a political stability menaced by such accusations against queen and vassal.[9]

Lynn Hunt has likewise shown how pamphlet attacks on Marie Antoinette in the 1780s reveal what was held to be wrong with the governance of France. While Hunt deals with the modern state, her views and McCracken's are not discordant – stating what is wrong is, after all, to state what should be right. Hunt's queen operates only through the agency of men, whom she must subvert by dissimulation or seduction. As her intrusion into the public sphere threatens to feminize the male apparatus of state, she menaces sexual differentiation; her sexual body corrupts the body politic, threatening what the nation reveres. In the years before the French Revolution, Marie Antoinette was thus accused of adultery, lesbianism, and, at her 1793 trial, incest with her son, the heir to the throne. Scapegoated for a regime in crisis, she embodied threats that could be ended only by the ultimate act of violence upon her body.[10]

In this chapter I examine the reports of Isabelle of Hainaut's walk through Senlis, and a similar story of a fourteenth-century duchess of Gueldres, to suggest something of medieval understandings of male rulers' consorts, their relationships to government, the means (not excluding violence) by which those relationships could express themselves, the images and actions by which they manifested those connections, and how observers might interpret such actions. These contexts arise from the links McCracken and Hunt imply among a consort's body, ideal good governance, and the role of violence in arguing and establishing that ideal. A medieval queen's body perpetuated the link between realm and royal lineage, but the power implicit in her motherhood was sufficiently threatening that political society sought to curtail it. Ecclesiastical and royal ritual as well as male-authored literary works decentred consorts' physical maternity; instead, their nurturing maternal qualities were emphasized, and that nurturing behaviour was linked to the socially sanctioned role of the submissive, powerless intercessor. Familiar to all, the Marian image served as the supreme model for such maternal mediation, glorifying the queenly office even as it idealized a compliant and chaste but fertile consort whose children's legitimacy was assured.[11] But other, similarly multivalent images existed beside that of the Virgin, images that consorts could exploit in their own interests and that male writers could adapt to laud consorts' behaviour or to sanitize their contentious actions; at the same time, however, observers or readers could use these images to interpret consorts' behaviour for themselves. One result, I argue, was that a consort's ideally submissive, nurturant body could also be seen to produce conflict and even violence.

Isabelle of Hainaut was not, of course, the only medieval consort who resisted divorce. Philip II's struggle to discard his second wife, Ingeborg of Denmark, is as well known as Catherine of Aragon's defiance of Henry VIII of England, and it is tempting to think that Isabelle's successful demonstration at Senlis led Philip to imprison Ingeborg precisely to prevent her mounting a similar spectacle.[12] If neither Ingeborg nor Catherine salvaged her marriage, a third consort's tale is usefully similar to Isabelle's. Eleanor Plantagenet (1318–1355), daughter of England's Edward II by Isabelle of France, in 1332 wed Duke Rainald II of Gueldres (d. 1343); an incident from their marriage is noted as a popular tale ('als man saget') by an anonymous Dutch writer whose work is dated 1569. The duke leaves Eleanor, claiming she has an unsightly growth in one breast. At Nijmegen castle, the duchess disrobes save for a mantle over a shift whose sheerness the author emphasizes,[13] and enters the great hall with her two young sons as Rainald is dining with his knights. Mounting a table, she drops the mantle and opens her shift to expose her breasts, turns about to show everyone that she is unblemished and, in tears, faces the duke: 'My lord, I beg you look here for the growth you basely and falsely impute to me. I am as any other woman; by God's grace I have no such infirmity. Our sons stand strong and healthy before you; with God's help there will be no obstacle to our having more, lest the time come when the folk of Gueldres lament our separation, for they will have no more sons of our blood.' There were no more children who survived, but she remained the duke's wife.[14]

However terse,[15] these reports resonate with other medieval images of women in like crises – multivalent images familiar to some or all who observed Isabelle at Senlis, to the authors discussed here, and to their readers: the penitent pilgrim, Godiva, Griselda, and countless ecclesiastical or secular directives that women, especially aristocratic consorts, must behave discreetly and modestly. It is striking that themes suggested by these same images surface so similarly in chronicle reports of Queen Isabelle's passage at Senlis and in the later, popular – perhaps imaginary – tale of Duchess Eleanor at Nijmegen. These similarities imply that noble consorts were already as prominent in medieval popular tales as they are in our post-brothers Grimm world. Chaucer's Constance is perhaps the best known medieval example of a beleaguered queen, and a near relative of Duchess Eleanor's story appears in a fourteenth-century tale about Blanche of Castile: rumoured to be pregnant by a cardinal's envoy, the widowed queen stands on a table clad only in shift and mantle, drops the mantle and turns about to show the royal council that she is not with child.[16] That similar tales of such women appear in courtly romance and in sermon *exempla* – many of which contain recognizable folk elements – further implies that whether the tales originated in popular, courtly, or learned spheres, such images in association with aristocratic consorts were, in one form or another, accessible to all levels of medieval society.[17] While we cannot know to what degree such images may have directly influenced Isabelle's actions (or Eleanor's, assuming her story may rest on some lost grain of truth), I ponder here the ways in which such images could have underlain authors' choices in reporting these events – sometimes with the apparent motive of shrouding the violence the consorts could incite – and others' understandings of what they saw or read. I am concerned especially with the authors' portrayal of eminent women in these particular ways. If male narrative writers, allegedly preoccupied with matters of interest to male readers, say this much about women in crisis, we should attend to what they say, how they say it, and their reasons for doing so. In this context, the evolution of the accounts of events at Senlis is significant: the violence of Gislebert's riot vanishes in the Flemish account, while Avesnes stresses the eminently proper female virtues of piety and duty – an apparent sanitizing process that may offer insights into male writers' handling of events involving eminent women. If, historically speaking, Duchess Eleanor's story is probably less reliable than at least the earlier accounts of events at Senlis, for purposes of discussion I take all four stories as indicators of how male writers might think about consorts and depict them in such crises as Isabelle and Eleanor confront.

Shifting Roles

The rulers Baldwin of Avesnes and the Dutch writer describe infirmity imposed on female bodies in order to discard them; the consorts respond with speech (albeit male-authored) and by publicly disrobing. The words ascribed to them are not disruptive, but rather offer assurances of order. By shifting blame for Philip's actions to his advisors, as Gislebert has it, Isabelle tacitly reminds the king that he must govern with good counsel; in Baldwin's tale, Philip argues his duty to beget an heir, but Isabelle points out that he will bear responsibility for adultery if he forces a new husband on her – and, of course, if he remarries (as he must, if he is to father the heir he fears she cannot bear him). Duchess Eleanor urges that she and Rainald have more sons for his people's good. In dutiful, altruistic words, then, both women offer good counsel and help their lords see their duty; and as Louise Fradenburg has shown that royal marriage modelled loving community to the realm,[18] these royal women serve male authority by working to save that image of order. But if the words ascribed to them accord with their expected stance as diligent consorts, what is said of their actions, as expressed particularly through bodies and clothing, strongly suggests otherwise.

An *exemplum* from the widely copied *Gesta Romanorum* indicates the extent of consorts' embodiment. From her window, an empress sees two knights battling in a field. She becomes enamoured of the victor, and consequently falls ill. Her doctors realize she is dying of love but are helpless until they identify her beloved. She tells the emperor of the knight, who is killed at the doctors' orders; her body is anointed with his blood, and she enjoys better health than before. This is clearly a salvation fable; the *exemplum* moralizes as Christ the man sacrificed to save the empress, and just as plainly, her salvation is depicted not as a spiritual event, but as a recovery from bodily illness – a classic example of the gender distinctions inscribed upon female flesh.[19] Such embodiment profoundly influenced popular perceptions of noble consorts, whose bodily practices, especially of modesty and chastity, were of particular moment to their subjects. As witnessed by countless depictions of queens as sexual distractions from regal duties and by frequent ritual adjurations to chaste behaviour, a consort's body figured her desire's destructiveness: her desiring body was seen as a potential threat to her lord's fulfilment of his duties to his people.[20] Consorts were, moreover, constructed as exemplary figures to society at large and were often told to offer proper examples to their subjects by – among other aspects of their behaviour – dressing modestly and not roaming freely. As the anchorite figured this enclosed, chaste female body for the religious sphere, the aristocratic consort did for the secular, modelling female modesty's vital role in constructing and upholding male honour.[21] To manifest a ruler's dominion, then, his wife's body may *be displayed* at certain times and places, and in ways that support his dominion; but she cannot violate the tenets of modesty appropriate to her rank by *displaying herself* in such way as to contest his sovereignty.

The richly varied *exempla* that approve consorts' modesty reveal how strikingly Isabelle and Eleanor breach such limits by displaying their barely clad bodies. Most apt to discussion here is an *exemplum* about St Louis' daughter, Queen Isabelle of Navarre (1242–71), who reputedly never removed her shift, even abed with her husband; dying, she told her servants to shroud her body well, so that it would not be seen as it was boiled.[22] The image of this linen undergarment as a bastion of virtue appears clearly in the Virgin Mary's revelations to St Birgitta of Sweden: the unseen shift must be a spotless foundation, for spiritually it signifies contrition. As it is worn nearest the flesh, so contrition and confession are the first means of turning to God. This imagery's intimate association with the individual soul echoes Augustine's analogy between the relationship of attire to body and that of body to soul. Commenting on the strong woman working with wool and linen (Prov 31:10–31), Augustine noted that linen garments are worn next to the body, beneath those of wool: as the woollen garments are visible and the linen invisible, so the actions of the flesh are externally perceptible while those of the soul are not.[23]

As well as signifying proper feminine modesty, then, the unseen linen garment could figure the soul itself and the supremely personal, individual acts of contrition and penitence. The privacy and intimacy thus implied afford new overtones to Isabelle and Eleanor's actions in so openly exposing themselves in their shifts. Well before St Birgitta's day, for example, medieval moral writers had significantly problematized this intimate attire as a token of wifely delicacy. Images of concealment and revelation competed: if the Fathers insisted on modesty, maintaining that purity revealed was purity lost, later hagiographical romance made the passive stripping and physical display of virgin female martyrs' bodies an integral aspect of the martyrdoms that witnessed their sanctity.[24] Likewise, if penitential writers urged that a husband should never see his wife nude, confessional writers and canonists feared that a wife who wore even the sheerest nightgown to bed would signal aversion to the sex act and drive her spouse to seek a more willing partner. In the *Prose Lancelot* and *The Knight of the Cart*, moreover, knights keep on drawers and shirts to signify such resistance when tricked into bed with women they do not wish to seduce – and the *exemplum* that extols Isabelle of Navarre's modesty tells us that her husband kept on his shirt and hose in bed with her.[25] The historical Isabelle of Navarre conceived at least one child.[26] But her modesty – approved in the *exemplum* through the hidden shift that can conceal as well as reveal – could hint at resistance to conjugal life. It might also convey a certain tension in the image of a ruler's modest wife who covers her body (as so much implied she should do), or reveals it to attract him (as she also heard she should do, but which might imply her intent to seduce him from his duty). In working to save their marriages against their lords' will, then, Isabelle and Eleanor exploit an imagery of conjugal *honestas* that, to those aware of its contesting implications, could carry significant ambiguities of concealment and exposure, submission and resistance.

More attention is thus needed to the shift's role in establishing the image Isabelle and Eleanor offer. Jane Burns notes that while fetishized female bodies in medieval romance are often hidden and re-identified by lovingly detailed clothing, written sources rarely mention such unseen garments as the shift, echoing Augustine's reference to the shift's invisibility and the Virgin's description of its links to the potent intimacy of contrition and penitence. Burns and Jill Mann note that such undergarments surface in literature only at moments of tension or struggle, as in the *Prose Lancelot*, *The Knight of the Cart*, or the ardent contexts of the Virgin's speech to Birgitta – and, of course, the crises Isabelle and Eleanor confront. As with women's literary identification through clothing, moreover, medieval women were, in Dyan Elliott's words, social mannequins whose dress was expected to reflect or uphold male status and honour. But clad only in their shifts, Isabelle and Eleanor are no longer identifiable as aristocratic consorts. They are socially naked; the ambiguous simplicity of their attire – in Burns's view, as good as nudity for women of such high rank, whose array should reflect their lords' authority – visualizes their abruptly challenged and uncertain relationships to society.[27]

In the present context, such 'nakedness' also recalls the ritual stripping and reclothing of a foreign-born consort for entry into her new lord's domains, lest her native dress contest his dominion: bared and then re-identified by clothing (as if in courtly romance), her body was visibly subjected to her lord's control.[28] This image irresistibly calls to mind that of Griselda, a peasant girl stripped of humble garb and clothed at her wedding in rich attire befitting her new rank as a marchioness; when her lord divorces her, she compliantly puts off the lavish garb he gave her and asks to retain only a shift in recompense for her lost virginity. Unlike Isabelle and Eleanor, Griselda appears to accept dismissal patiently. But Elaine Hansen cogently argues such compliance's latent subversiveness: like Philip and Rainald, Griselda's lord ultimately loses control by unwittingly allowing her to reveal her virtue's hidden power.[29] Kristine Gilmartin, moreover, anticipates Burns in seeing Griselda's shift as signifying the maiden nakedness that was all she could bring to her marriage. Gilmartin stresses Griselda's assertion that her rich attire signified not a change within herself but rather, the new will – her husband's – she assumed at marriage: in resuming her nakedness, she thus reclaims her own will.[30] To some, then, the image of a consort in such humble garb might, as with Isabelle's appearance at Senlis, recall the shift's penitential overtones. But just as Griselda's compliance is latently subversive, that same humble image, as Isabelle and Eleanor exploit it, could also echo the shift's implications of resistance to conjugal duty – and in these cases, to a male ruler's authority. (Griselda's compliant removal of her rich attire stands between the passively stripped noble brides of history and the consorts discussed here, who actively shed regal robes to resist their lords – and to retain them, a subversive salvaging of their marriages that resonates with the shift's doubled revelation and concealment.)

Concealing and Revealing

Griselda's insistence that she has undergone no inner change, her equation of her outer attire with her husband's will and nakedness with her own will, point to gendered perceptions of women's inner spiritual impulses that decide Isabelle and Eleanor's resort to such visual displays. Echoing consorts' reclothing in the attire of their lords' realms, Dyan Elliott's remark that 'masculine authority is only truly safe when clothing symbolizes external, not internal realities' highlights medieval male distrust of women's interior life. Clerics who wrote the *vitae* of holy women they advised stressed exterior signs of the women's sanctity, not their inaccessible inner impulses; canonists censured women who honoured inner spiritual impulses by rejecting fine outer dress.[31] Isabelle and Eleanor's male-authored speeches imply that, like the undraped noble Godiva, they altruistically seek to benefit subjects and lords alike, not themselves alone. But as Leofric compels Godiva to do, Isabelle and Eleanor expose themselves to give their altruism exterior expression.[32] Women's transformative abilities to reveal – to bring forth what is concealed – were central to consorts' socially sanctioned roles. Coronation *ordines* uniformly contrasted the outer glory of a newly crowned queen's gold and jewels to the inner gold of virtue and pearls of wisdom that she must seek and then reveal in the prudent counsel she offers her lord[33] – as Eleanor advises Rainald and Isabelle Philip. Consorts thus enabled rulers to alter decisions and reveal magnanimity. But if this was a lauded act of strength (*fortitudo*) in women,[34] it could also threaten male authority. To associate with the disempowered on whose behalf they entreated their lords, consorts often crossed social limits. Stripped of outer glory, Isabelle and Eleanor's humble attire visually evokes links to those furthest from the centres of power; Isabelle's supplicatory, penitent piety, common in noble female gesture, evoked a self-abasement deemed especially suitable to women of rank. Scripture abundantly authorizes the traversal of such limits. But if these directives applied equally to men or women, the latter as strangers to male-ordered hierarchy could the more easily navigate such limits; as adepts at such behaviour, they could the more effectively exploit it. Isabelle and Eleanor's exposed and exposing performances of their abjection assertively contest the hierarchy mapped by the very boundaries they cross.[35]

The associations among shift, soul, and body, suggested by Augustine and in Birgitta's revelations, imply that if Isabelle and Eleanor's transgressive displays of the intimate, secreted shift carry part of their message, their bodies do so as well. We are familiar today with studies of torture – physical violence visited upon individual bodies, exposed to manifest a ruler's power to punish.[36] These consorts are not physically tortured, but the rulers do torment their bodies with claims of deformity or sterility. Ailing or barren bodies such as Philip and Rainald imagine, and reject, were commonly hidden in bedchambers or convents; but these women do not hide themselves, nor is it the rulers who order them exposed. Both consorts appropriate that aspect of their lords' authority and expose themselves, Isabelle as if on pilgrimage to seek a cure for sterility, Eleanor to prove her bodily health. They create spontaneously for themselves a kind of ordeal, initiated like the martyrdoms of female saints in hagiographic romance by the theatrical removal of clothing – though again, these consorts are not passively stripped, but actively remove their own raiment.[37] Both women's bodily responses also include the copious shedding of tears, another object lesson in the fields of interpretation open to medieval actors and observers alike. As a token of female power, tears were criticized as a sign of undue emotion, as in Margery Kempe's case, or of deceptive manipulation, as Chaucer's Wife of Bath admits. But women's tears were also approved by images of the Innocents' grieving mothers, or of the Virgin mourning her Son. Significantly in these contexts, Rebecca Beal links the weeping figures of Guenevere and the duchess of Metz in the Alliterative *Morte Arthure* to a feminine sense of loss, specifically related to a system of 'worship' or honour, that results from male violence. As the duchess of Metz begs Arthur's mercy on her besieged city, noblewomen's tears are, moreover, associated with the supplicant, and so with consorts' mediatory roles. Tears thus denoted women's part in the scheme of salvation as intercessors and witnesses, and invested them with spiritual authority. Isabelle and Eleanor's tears enhance their claims to moral worth; by making visible as well the hidden shifts that figure the penitent soul (likewise associated with weeping), they assert a spiritual purity that affirms the same for their tormented but healthy bodies.[38]

Eleanor's appearance at Nijmegen with her sons highlights her physical maternity in a situation that plainly involves her bodily health. By openly naming a maternity decentred in royal women, she reclaims an aspect of her life appropriated by or to the ruler, and uses it to subvert Rainald's excuse for leaving her. Her actions echo an episode in the Middle English romance *Athelston*, in which Athelston's queen enters his council chamber and displays her pregnant body to induce him to defer a hasty death sentence. In Elizabeth Rowe's words, this queen's request that parliament be consulted links her gravid body to 'the vocal throngs of Parliament and the swelling masses of rebellious subjects'; Athelston kicks her, killing their unborn son.[39] Eleanor's appeal to Rainald, her sons at her side as she pleads for his subjects' welfare before a crowd of knights who would have had a vested interest in the ducal line's survival, likewise links her body's maternal promise with those who might be expected to oppose Rainald's separation from her. In Baldwin of Avesnes's story, Isabelle claims her right to remain Philip's wife and, tacitly, to bear the heir he professes to believe she cannot.

The consort who asserts her maternity may bring forth violence. That the issue of her mouth or her womb can nonetheless assure good governance further recalls the head-abdomen inversions prominent in Mikhail Bakhtin's writings on the grotesque body – out of place, revealing what should be concealed, affronting the existing order. A consort's speech, the issue of her mouth, recalls Bakhtin's 'high,' the courtly setting in which she counsels the ruler; her womb's issue girds her appeal to popular sentiment, Bakhtin's 'low.' Thus Isabelle and Eleanor's maternally grounded appeal to the popular can be read as inversive/subversive parodies of their male-articulated and male-dominated office, which they subject, briefly, to the influence of those who do not properly wield sovereign authority.[40] Margaret Miles further argues the female body's special susceptibility to male figuration as grotesque in its perceived lack of integrity and its endless implication in Eve's sin, heralding all human iniquity. The consorts' insistence on childbearing evokes images of natural grotesqueness that contrast their bodies' perviousness with the male ruler's impermeable body, which figures and assures his realm's boundaries. The consorts' disrobed and displayed bodies thus suggest openings through which a ruler's honour may be depleted, and the indigent claim a voice in governance. The ruler's control of his wife's body signifies control of his domains; by inviting a disorder antithetical to his first duty to his subjects, these consorts compel the rulers who tried to reject their bodies to resume control over them. The consorts' nakedness thus exposes the vulnerability of their lords' rule to their desiring natural bodies and their adoptive political bodies alike. Of course, they also expose their stake in their lords' authority, without which they would not be consorts and their actions would lack the weight with which their rank invests them. And by inviting their lords to accept their bodies, they offer a concurrent remedy and again figuratively assure good governance. As implied by McCracken's linking of a queen's bodily integrity to that of a king's rule, these consorts assure the quality of their lords' rule by affirming the physical health their lords have impugned.[41]

Royal Bodies and the Body Politic

In sum, then, the submissive and altruistic words ascribed to Isabelle and Eleanor condignly remind their lords of their duty to assure their subjects the benefits of good governance. But by removing their rich robes they transform the complexly concealed and concealing shift into a revelatory offensive weapon. Shedding all signs of rank derived from marriage implies rejection of their husbands' will; their lack of clothing links them to the destitute, menacing the hierarchy male rulers generate and protect. The women's appeals are further linked to a physical maternity generally obscured to limit any power they might claim from it. However loftily grounded and expressed, the women's resistance to their lords aligns with, and may elicit, resistance from the ruler's subjects. Self-exposure, as they seek to reinscribe themselves in a patriarchal economy of marriage exchange and claim their bodies as their husbands' chattels, associates their bodies with those who may violently oppose the ruler – a potential subversion of male authority at odds with the dutiful speech male writers ascribe to both women. Given McCracken's view of the faithless romance-queen's body as the site of a struggle for good governance, we might say that Isabelle at Senlis committed a political adultery that produced its own peculiar consequences. A consort properly reveals herself to, or shares herself with, only the ruler whom she counsels and whose children she bears. By exposing herself to those not normally associated in governance, and arousing them to claim a voice in that process, Isabelle brought forth not stability in the form of heirs and counsel, but violence. Her body's promises of continued good governance excited the indigent to rise up and constrain the king, again linking her bodily to a perceived right order in the realm.

Whatever their authenticity, these accounts show that historical narrative projected significant meanings onto consorts, or deployed them to enunciate ideas on relations between subjects and rulers. To return, then, to the questions framed earlier: why did male writers depict eminent women in such ways, and what may such stories reveal about social attitudes toward rulers' wives? That a consort's body could be a signifier of ideas on statecraft, as McCracken and Hunt imply, raises questions about the forms in which such ideas were expressed. Ritual and art constructed rulers' wives as benevolent and compliant with male authority. But at the same time such expressions created a fund of images open to divergent interpretation, thanks to widely ranging commentaries found, among other sources, in confessional literature, *exempla*, and romance. I have focused here on images implied by clothing and bodies in sources other than the chronicles that record Isabelle and Eleanor's actions, but other images could be cited. As Eleanor uncovers herself, for example, the courtly setting of her actions might have led some readers to recall romance's subjection of the female to the male gaze and her objectification through the fetishizing of female body parts; to others, her gesture as she links her maternity to her people's welfare might echo the interceding Virgin's bared breast, with its overtones of the potentially subversive effects of woman's ideal compliance and transformative agency.[42] To varying extents and in varying combinations, consort, writer, and subject alike probably knew these images. Consorts and writers exploited them; readers or observers used them to interpret what they saw.

Alfred Thomas's recent study of late medieval Bohemian society and literature offers a helpful approach to medieval chroniclers' deployment of such images by positing women's bodies as metaphors for conflicts that male writers displaced onto them:

> Sexual politics were inseparable from questions of hermeneutics and truth in the Middle Ages. This connection ... is clearly evident in Czech writings of the early fifteenth century, when virtually all tenets of orthodox belief – from the veneration of images to the sacerdotal control of the Eucharist – were coming under assault from the Hussite heretics. The threat to male well-being traditionally associated with the female body as a locus of corruption, decay and sexual desire was a convenient, ready-made metaphor [for] the spiritual and political crisis of Bohemian society ... Since Christ's body as a metaphor for the sacrament and for society in general was at the heart of [this] struggle ... we might interpret the presence of the female body and the discursive conflict to define and control it ... as a displacement from the male, sacred body onto the female, secular body.[43]

In considering consorts' place in the body politic, it is natural to approach Thomas's ideas by way of their roles in diplomacy and politics. That Isabelle embodied an alliance irksome to Philip II because of her male kin's wavering loyalty[44] solicits attention to French chroniclers' silence on her actions at Senlis: the chronicles that describe those events were written in her native Hainaut or her mother's homeland, Flanders. Aware of her male kin's hopes for her marriage, Gislebert of Mons and Baldwin of Avesnes praised the loyal daughter and niece who saved it. (Did they enjoy recording that the queen and a mob of indigents had manoeuvred Philip out of an important decision?) Politically speaking, Isabelle's walk through Senlis took place at a time of noble anxieties for the strengthening of Capetian authority over the royal domain and its extension into the great fiefs of northern France.[45] By marrying Isabelle, Philip had claimed independence from his mother's powerful family, of whom the counts of Champagne and Blois and the archbishop of Reims favoured his divorce. The uncle and cousins who urged him not to divorce were agnatic Capetian kin, traditionally powerful voices in royal counsel.[46] On one level, then, Isabelle figures contention between royal and aristocratic power. More seriously, the riot she incited at Senlis gave political voice to those remote from the centres of power; by supporting a queen who – like Philip's paternal kin – asserted a traditional role as royal counsellor (and a worthier one than those who approved the divorce), the mob at Senlis endorsed a way of governing that was vanishing as trained bureaucrats and lawyers were supplanting customary royal advisors, a change as fraught for the people at large as for any baron.[47] Accounts of events at Senlis thus align the consort with a conservative nostalgia for the good old days or at least the *status quo nunc*, and the ruler with an expansive progressivism – an opposition that again inscribes the consort as potentially subversive to male authority. If Hainaudian and Flemish writers could thus praise Isabelle's actions, French authors kept discreetly silent on such ominous matters.

The boundary-crossing behaviour implicit in Isabelle and Eleanor's actions echoes what Louise Fradenburg calls the 'dangerous' communitarian work that linked consorts to those on the margins, implying both threats and benefits to male authority. Victor Turner used the term *communitas* to describe the suspended social relationships typical of (among other liminal situations) pilgrimage; such suspension can imply criticism of those structures similar to that observed in the implied social commentaries of such works as the *Canterbury Tales* – a criticism also readily associated with the petitions consorts, in intercessory guise, regularly received from suitors both wealthy and indigent. Like medieval English queens' intercessory requests from childbed, the events noted here show how the association of consort and people could involve her body, especially its maternal promise. Fradenburg argues that a ruler's domestication of his wife's strangeness – by extension, absorbing her body into the body politic and subduing any threats her communitarian labour might imply – importantly suggested his ability to control his realm. Thus a male ruler who tried to discard that female body rejected a means to manifest his political skills; by fighting to remain his wife, she preserved that means for him, salvaging her role in such processes and any power she might wield as a result. If this echoes Fradenburg's ideas on the consort's role in constructing sovereignty, it again aligns a consort with the unruly masses into which she must be absorbed, reinscribing her as a potential focus for disorder, even violence.[48] Later authors sanitized the subversion latent in Isabelle's actions by stressing her penitent humility and good counsel, a progression that cautions us to watch for other cases in which male writers may have recast contentious female behaviour in similarly compliant terms.[49]

Isabelle and Eleanor's struggles to remain dutiful wives and bear children – unlike McCracken's barren adulterous queens – reflects their need to produce heirs to secure a share in diplomacy or politics. That biogenetic function was crucial for Isabelle when French kings were working to centre loyalty on the Capetian line; to continue his line, Philip II needed a son. As found in a text from 1569, Eleanor's hopes for more sons gain wider meaning against Gueldres's later history. Its ruling line often failed; indeed, the native line ended with the deaths of Eleanor's sons in the 1370s. Only thirty years before the Dutch account was written, William V of Cleves inherited Gueldres not by descent, but by the acclamation of its estates at the testamentary urging of the childless Karl I, whose only sister had married the Catholic duke of Lorraine. Karl hoped to assure his subjects a Protestant duke, but in 1543 William was defeated by the Catholic Charles V and ceded Gueldres to him.[50] A lack of heirs had again led to a stranger's accession that, in this case, plunged the folk of Gueldres into crisis. Given Janet Nelson's stress on a realm's integrity and a people's identity as tied to the perpetuation of ruling lineages, it is no surprise that a Dutch author in 1569 ascribed such philoprogenitive sentiments to a duchess whose further childbearing might have avoided such turmoil.[51]

As Thomas's thoughts imply, then, the resisting women's bodies become metaphors for crisis and conflict. Isabelle figures noble and civic anxieties as royal power was expanded and bolstered by bureaucratic evolution – the same changing political setting in which McCracken's adulterous queens appear. Eleanor embodies fears attending the quickening separation of state and dynastic powers as bureaucratization's effects were manifest in the birth of the modern state and the loss of a people's comforting link to their native ruling lineage. As well, both consorts echo male officialdom's distrust of women's informal, maternally grounded power. A ruler's refusal to sire heirs, or claims that his wife was barren, undercut that power as effectively as adultery charges might do, but consorts could subversively reassert themselves: as mothers, they were indispensable to hereditary monarchy.[52]

Such defining tensions at rulership's heart were readily and naturally associated with contention, implying how deeply violence (or a potential therefor) was embedded even in that element of society most urgently associated with order and stability. This aspect of consorts' images contested their missions as peaceweavers or mediators. But even as sites of disorder, consorts like Isabelle and Eleanor revealed the need for a strong ruler and so invited his control of his domains, literally embodying means by which he might do so. By extension, consorts consistently attracted notice as wives, mothers, or counsellors. Male writers expressed hopes or fears for their success or failure in all these roles, which could activate effectively in political, diplomatic, or dynastic crises.

Fradenburg notes consorts' special associations with such 'times out of joint': women most easily entered official life at such junctures, often by claiming traditions arising from a trove of images familiar to themselves and to observers.[53] Given all that has come to light on such women's roles in diplomacy, patronage, or mediation, it appears that even in such allegedly gender-specific areas rulers could rarely discount their wives, who were perhaps closer to the arenas of action than has been thought. That chroniclers dealt with these women's actions by using widely familiar images implies, too, that gendered discourses of power and honour were not closely bounded systems; women might play as active a role in them as men.[54] If we have learnt anything from the study of medieval consorts it is that we should not ignore what depictions of them, in art as well as in literature or historical narrative, can tell us about the society with which they interacted in so many significant ways.

Notes

1 Versions of this material were read at the South Central Women's Studies Association March 1998 Conference at the University of Houston–Clear Lake, and the University of Toronto's Centre for Medieval Studies 1998 Annual Conference. A shorter text appears in *The Man of Many Devices Who Travelled Full Many Ways*, ed. B. Nagy and M. Sebök (Budapest 1999). Impetus was given this essay by Aline Hornaday's forthcoming 'Isabelle of Hainaut: Capetian Queen as Street Demonstrator,' in *Capetian Women*, ed. J.C. Parsons and K. Nolan (New York 2001). Bonnie Wheeler, Jeremy du Q. Adams, Peggy McCracken, Lorraine Stock, Laura Hodges, Nadia Margolis, Jo Goyne, and Oren Falk commented on its various manifestations, and members of the Friday workshops at the Centre for Reformation and Renaissance Studies at Victoria University in Toronto were generous with reactions and suggestions. I am grateful to these friends and colleagues for their valuable advice, and shift none of my errors on to them.

2 Born in April 1170 (Gislebert of Mons, *Chronicon Hanoniense*, ed. L. Vanderkindere as *La Chronique de Gislebert de Mons* [Brussels 1904], 101), Isabelle married Philip on 28 April 1180 (J.W. Baldwin, *The Government of Philip Augustus: Foundations of French Royal Power in the Middle Ages* [Berkeley and Los Angeles 1986], 15, 18).

3 There is little question that Philip's marriage to Isabelle helped him end the dominance of his mother and her Champenois relatives, and that it was of great diplomatic and political importance in the early years of his reign (see n. 43 below).

4 *Chronique de Gislebert*, 153. Chaplain to Isabelle's father from 1175, Gislebert (d. 1224) was the count's chancellor 1178–95; Vanderkindere's Introduction, viii–xxiii, suggests it was written, or at least finished, in 1195–6, just after the count died.

5 *Genealogiae comitum Flandriae*, ed. G.H. Pertz, MGH Scriptores 9 (Hanover 1851), 313–35, esp. (for the date) 313–14, and (for events at Senlis) 328.
6 With other anecdotal material, this passage is omitted from *Chronicon Hanoniense quod dicitur Balduini Avennensis*, ed. J. Heller, MGH Scriptores 25 (Hanover 1869), 411–67 (for Baldwin's kinship to Isabelle, 415 n. 5). The dialogue is given from one MS by A. Cartellieri, *Philipp II August, König von Frankreich*, 4 vols (Leipzig 1899–1922, repr. Aalen 1969), 1, beilagen: 87–8 (my translation). On the work, which Baldwin evidently commissioned and directed but almost certainly did not write, see *Dictionnaire des lettres françaises publié sous la direction du Cardinal Georges Grente: Le Moyen Age*, ed. A. Pauphilet, L. Richard, and R. Renaud de Lage (Paris 1964), 187; rev. ed. G. Hasenohr and M. Zink (Paris 1993), 290 (I owe the latter reference to Nadia Margolis).
7 Citing Cartellieri, *Philipp II*, 1: 136–9, who uses Gislebert and the Flemish Anonymous, Baldwin, *Government*, 16–19, tacitly accepts those accounts but does not cite Baldwin of Avesnes; Cartellieri (1, beilagen: 87–8) sees Avesnes's version as merely an attractive legend.
8 Baldwin, *Government*, 26. Bradbury, *Philip Augustus*, 177, says that before her son Louis was born in October 1187 Isabelle had two stillbirths; neither is dated, but the first was a daughter, buried at Notre-Dame in Paris (Cartellieri, *Philipp II*, 1, beilagen: 87). By 1184, then, Isabelle may have had one stillbirth, and Philip could well have known that Eleanor of Aquitaine was childless for years after a failed pregnancy early in her marriage to his father (*Vita Bernardi*, in *Recueil des historiens des Gaules et de la France* [henceforth *RHF*], ed. M. Bouquet et al., 24 vols [Paris 1738–1904], 14: 376). On the other hand, *Chronique de Gislebert*, 153, says that after Senlis Philip neither ate nor slept with Isabelle (perhaps until she were older; see J.C. Parsons, 'Mothers, Daughters, Marriage, Power: Some Plantagenet Evidence, 1150–1500,' in *Medieval Queenship*, ed. Parsons [New York 1993], 63–78). On manipulation of sterility claims, cf. Lothar II's assertion of Theutberga's sterility only after incest and abortion charges had failed to secure a divorce (S. Airlie, 'Private Bodies and the Body Politic in the Divorce Case of Lothar II,' *Past and Present* 161 [1998] 3–38, at 12 [an article of which I became aware when this essay was substantially complete]).
9 P. McCracken, *The Romance of Adultery: Queenship and Sexual Transgression in Old French Literature* (Philadelphia 1998).
10 L. Hunt, 'The Many Bodies of Marie Antoinette: Political Pornography and the Problem of the Feminine in the French Revolution,' in *Eroticism and the Body Politic*, ed. Hunt (Baltimore, 1991), 108–30, revised in Hunt, *The Family Romance of the French Revolution* (Berkeley 1993); cf. the slightly different but complementary reading of contemporary attacks on Marie-Antoinette in S. Schama, *Citizens: A Chronicle of the French Revolution* (New York 1989), 203–27. At least one Tudor dramatist displaced onto a medieval English queen anxieties for

loss of sexual differentiation in Elizabeth I's reign (J.C. Parsons, *Eleanor of Castile: Queen and Society in Thirteenth-Century England* [New York 1995], 233–5).

11 J.C. Parsons, 'The Queen's Intercession in Thirteenth-Century England,' in *Power of the Weak: Studies on Medieval Women*, ed. J. Carpenter and S.B. MacLean (Urbana 1995), 147–77, and 'The Pregnant Queen as Counsellor and the Medieval Construction of Motherhood,' in *Medieval Mothering*, ed. Parsons and B. Wheeler (New York 1996), 39–61.

12 On Ingeborg, see Baldwin, *Government*, 82–7; N. Damsholt, 'Medieval Women's Identity in a Postmodern Light: The Example of Queen Ingeborg,' in *The Birth of Identities: Denmark and Europe in the Middle Ages*, ed. B.P. McGuire (Copenhagen 1996), 225–41; G. Conklin, 'Ingeborg of Denmark, Queen of France, 1193–1223,' in *Queens and Queenship in Medieval Europe*, ed. A. Duggan (Woodbridge 1997), 38–52. Catharine of Aragon has had no critical biographer since G. Mattingly, *Catharine of Aragon* (London 1941); see D. Loades, *The Tudor Court* (London 1987) and *Mary Tudor: A Life* (Oxford 1990); E. Ives, *Anne Boleyn* (Oxford 1986); R. Warnicke, *The Rise and Fall of Anne Boleyn: Family Politics at the Court of Henry VIII* (Cambridge 1991).

13 C. Willett and P. Cunnington, *The History of Underclothes*, rev. ed. by A.D. and V. Mansfield (London 1981 [1951]), 25, state that by Chaucer's time some shifts were sheer to the point of transparency; the nobility's could be of silk (as the Dutch author perhaps anachronistically says Duchess Eleanor's was). I owe this reference to Lorraine Stock.

14 [Matthias Baux?], *Geldersche Kroniek berustende in het archief der Stad Erkelenz*, ed. P.N. van Doornik (Arnhem 1908), 147–214, esp. 165–6. Dr Anneke Mulder-Bakker kindly provided this reference and a photocopy of the relevant passage. The *Kroniek* implies that Eleanor's sons (b. 1333 and 1336) were young boys at the time of the incident, suggesting a date ca 1340. The text is imprecise on the growth (*mallaetzerei*) imputed to her; her denial of infirmity (*gebrech*) may suggest cancer, but that Eleanor (d. 1355) survived Rainald (d. 1343) by twelve years argues against any such illness in historical fact.

15 These brief chronicle accounts do not equal in length the accounts elicited by Philip II's efforts to discard Ingeborg, Henry VIII's divorce from Catharine of Aragon (above, n. 11), nor Lothar II's attempt in the 850s and 860s to divorce his wife and marry a concubine (Airlie, 'Private Bodies and the Body Politic,' 3–38).

16 *Récits d'un ménestrel de Reims au treizième siècle*, ed. Natalis de Wailly (Paris 1876), 98. McCracken, *Romance of Adultery*, 132, calls this anecdotal work a 'pseudo-chronicle'; on another of its doubtful tales see Parsons, 'Pregnant Queen,' 45, and cf. nn 50–1 below. On Chaucer's Constance in this chapter's contexts, see E. Clasby, 'Chaucer's Constance: Womanly Virtue and the Heroic Life,' *Chaucer Review* 13 (1979) 221–33; S. Manning, 'Chaucer's Constance:

Pale and Passive,' in *Chaucerian Problems and Perspectives: Essays Presented to Paul E. Beichner, CSC* (Notre Dame 1979), 13–23; J.S. Russell, 'Dido, Emily, and Constance: Femininity and Subversion in the Mature Chaucer,' *Medieval Perspectives* 1 (1988) 65–74; and, with reference to the tale of 'La Fille aux mains coupées' (see next note), M. Schauch, *Chaucer's Constance and Accused Queens* (New York 1927), and E. Archibald, 'The Flight from Incest: Two Late Classical Precursors of the Constance Theme,' *Chaucer Review* 20 (1986) 259–72.

17 For *exempla* versions of 'La Fille aux mains coupées,' see *La Scala Celi de Jean Gobi*, ed. M.-A. Polo de Beaulieu (Paris 1991), 235–7; and *Exempla aus Handschriften des Mittelalters*, ed. J. Klapper (Heidelberg 1911), 1–6 (resembling the modern 'Snow White'). On this tale in romance and folklore, C. Velay-Vallantin, *L'Histoire des contes* (Paris 1992), 95–139, a reference I owe Carl Lindahl; F. Suard, 'Chanson de geste et roman devant le materiau folklorique: Le Conte de la *Fille aux mains coupées* dans la *Belle Hélène de Constantinople*, *Lion de Bourges* et la *Manekine*,' in *Mittelalter aus neuer Perspektive: Diskussionsanstösse zu amour courtois, Subjectivität in der Dichtung und Strategien des Erzählens. Kolloquium Würzburg 1984*, ed. E. Ruhe and R. Behrens (Munich 1985), 364–79. On folktales in *exempla*, C. Velay-Vallentin, 'From "Little Red Riding Hood" to the "Beast of Gévaudan": The Tale in the Long Term Continuum,' in *Telling Tales: Medieval Narratives and the Folk Tradition*, ed. F.C. Sautman, D. Conchado, and G.C. DiScipio (New York 1998), 269–95 (cf. J.M. Ziolkowski, 'A Fairy Tale from before Fairy Tales: Egbert of Liège's "De puella a lupellis seruata" and the Medieval Background of "Little Red Riding Hood,"' *Speculum* 67 [1992] 549–750); Burchard of Worms, *Decretum*, in PL 140: 965 ('The Elves and the Shoemaker'); *Juan Manuel: El conde Lucanor*, ed. C. Alonso (Gerona 1978), 196–201 ('The Emperor's New Clothes'). On *exempla* and patterns of cultural exchange, with specific reference to folklore, C. Bremond, J. LeGoff, and J.-C. Schmitt, *L'Exemplum*, Typologie des sources du moyen âge occidental, fasc. 40 (Turnhout 1982), 85–107; G. Duby, 'The Diffusion of Cultural Patterns in Feudal Society,' in his *Chivalrous Society*, trans. C. Postan (Berkeley and Los Angeles 1980), 171–7.

18 L.O. Fradenburg, 'Rethinking Queenship' and 'Sovereign Love: The Wedding of Margaret Tudor and James IV of Scotland,' in *Women and Sovereignty*, ed. Fradenburg, special number of *Cosmos*, 7 (Edinburgh 1992), 1–13 and 78–100; the same themes are treated in her *City, Marriage, Tournament: Arts of Rule in Late Medieval Scotland* (Madison 1991), 67–83. On royal marriage as mediating divine models of community, J.C. Parsons, ' "Never was a body buried in England with such solemnity and honour": The Burials and Posthumous Commemorations of English Queens to 1500,' in *Queens and Queenship*, ed. Duggan, 334–5 and n. 57.

19 *Gesta Romanorum*, ed. H. Oesterley, 2 vols (Berlin 1872), 2: 685–6 (no. 281). On female flesh and gender distinctions, B. Cazelles, *The Lady as Saint: A*

Collection of French Hagiographic Romances of the Thirteenth Century (Philadelphia 1991), 48–9; and for the convergences of spiritual and physical health, J. Murray, 'Sexuality and Spirituality: The Intersection of Medieval Theology and Medicine,' *Fides et Historia* 23 (1991) 20–36.

20 Parsons, 'Queen's Intercession,' 158–9.

21 On the enclosed body, J. Wogan-Browne, 'Chaste Bodies: Frames and Experiences,' in *Framing Medieval Bodies*, ed. S. Kay and M. Rubin (Manchester 1994), 24–41; on consorts' role, J.C. Parsons, ' "Loved him – hated her": Shame and Honor at the Medieval Court,' in *Conflicted Identities and Multiple Masculinities: Constructing Men in Medieval Society*, ed. J. Murray (New York 1999). On anchorites, M.B. McInerney, ' "In the Meydens Womb": Julian of Norwich and the Poetics of Enclosure,' in *Medieval Mothering*, ed. Parsons and Wheeler, 157–82. A 1292 *exempla* collection ascribed to Sancho IV of Castile states that 'queens ... must be more virtuous than other women in all things ... for as others see them do, so shall they all do' (*Castigos e documentos del rey don Sancho*, ed. P. de Gayangos in *Escritores en prosa anteriores al siglo XV*, Biblioteca de autores españoles 51 [Madrid 1912], 217). On clerical letters, Parsons, 'Queen's Intercession,' 150–1 and, e.g., PL 207: 448–9; C. Casagrande, 'The Protected Woman,' in *Silences of the Middle Ages*, ed. C. Klapisch-Zuber, trans. A. Goldhammer, A History of Women in the West 2 (Cambridge, MA 1992), 70–104, esp. 78–9. The Bourgeois of Paris ca 1393 offered Valois queens as models to his wife: 'Since such high and honored ladies do this, lesser women ... should do so as well' (*Le Ménagier de Paris*, ed. G.E. Brereton and J.M. Ferrier [Oxford 1981], 56). See also *Ménagier*, 9, 11, 43–5 (regarding women outside the home); *The Book of the Knight of the Tower, Translated by William Caxton*, ed. M.Y. Offord, 2 vols, EETS s.s. 2 (London and New York 1971), 1: 23–5; and D. Bornstein, *The Lady in the Tower: Medieval Courtesy Literature for Women* (Hamden 1983), esp. 76–93.

22 C. Ribaucourt, '*L'Alphabet des récits:* Pour parler des dames,' in *Prêcher d'exemples: Récits de prédicateurs du moyen âge*, ed. J.-C. Schmitt (Paris 1985), 118–19 *bis*. On social conventions' controlling function, e.g., N. Elias, *Über den Prozess der Zivilisation*, 2 vols (Basel 1939); and for the human body, M. Mauss, 'Body Techniques,' in his *Sociology and Psychology: Essays* (London 1979), 97–123.

23 *The Liber celestis of St Bridget of Sweden: The Middle English Version in British Library MS. Claudius B i, together with a Life of the Saint from the Same Manuscript*, ed. R. Ellis, EETS o.s. 291 (London 1987), 14; J. Pépin, 'Saint Augustin et le symbolisme néoplatonicien de la vêture,' *Augustinus Magister: Congrès international augustinien, Paris, 21–24 septembre 1954. Communications*, 2 vols, Études augustiniennes (Paris 1954), 1: 293–306; I owe this reference to Laura Hodges. Discussion of obvious resonances here with Judith Butler, *Gender*

Trouble: Feminism and the Subversion of Identity (New York 1990), at 163–80, is outside the scope of this essay and must await further attention elsewhere.

24 On concealing the holy female body, Cazelles, *Lady as Saint*, 48–9, and R.H. Bloch, *Medieval Misogyny and the Invention of Western Romantic Love* (Chicago 1991), 99–100, though Gregory of Nyssa's *On Virginity* sees the virgin body as a mirror reflecting divine purity (P. Brown, *The Body and Society: Men, Women, and Sexual Renunciation in Early Christianity* [New York 1988], 299). Beth Crachiolo's essay in the present volume affords valuable additional insights.

25 E.J. Burns, 'Ladies Don't Wear *Braies*: Underwear and Outerwear in the French *Prose Lancelot*,' in *The Lancelot Grail Cycle: Text and Transformations*, ed. W.W. Kibler (Austin 1994), 152–74, esp. 166; J. Mann, 'Sir Gawain and the Romance Hero,' in *Heroes and Heroines in Medieval English Literature: A Festschrift Presented to André Crépin on the Occasion of His Sixty-Fifth Birthday*, ed. L. Carruthers (Woodbridge 1994), 105–17, esp. 113.

26 Isabelle married Thibaut II of Navarre (1237–70) in July 1255. No children are known to have survived the couple, but the *Libro de las generaciones*, ed. J. Ferrandis Martínez, Textos medievales 23 (Valencia 1968), 61, says they had had a child by the time that work was finished (1258 x 1270). G. Zurita's 16th-century *Anales de la corona de Aragón*, ed. A. Ubieto Arteta and L. Ballesteros Ballesteros, 3 vols in 4 (Valencia 1967–72), 3.2: 114, says Isabelle died in April 1271 'siendo preñada,' five months after Thibaut's death.

27 Burns, 'Ladies Don't Wear *Braies*,' 153–4 and 162; and *Bodytalk: When Women Speak in Old French Literature* (Philadelphia 1993), 107–11; Mann, 'Sir Gawain and the Romance Hero,' 113; D. Elliott, 'Dress as Mediator Between Inner and Outer Self: The Pious Matron of the High and Later Middle Ages,' *Mediaeval Studies* 53 (1991) 279–308, esp. 289. For one report of a physical inspection of a future queen couched in language seemingly influenced by courtly literature, D.A. Trotter, 'Walter of Stapeldon and the Premarital Inspection of Philippa of Hainault,' *French Studies Bulletin* 49 (1993) 1–4.

28 On consorts' dress and absorption into their lords' domains, D.O. Hughes, 'Regulating Women's Fashion,' in *Silences of the Middle Ages*, ed. Klapisch-Zuber, 136–58, esp. 139–40. The best-known reclothed medieval bride (1384) is Isabeau of Bavaria, wife of Charles VI of France (Jehan Froissart, *Oeuvres*, ed. J.M.B.C. Kervyn de Lettenhove, 25 vols [Brussels 1867–77], 10: 349). Cf. A. Zanger, 'Fashioning the Body Politic: Imagining the Queen in the Marriage of Louis XIV,' in *Women and Sovereignty*, ed. Fradenburg, 101–20; S. Zweig, *Marie Antoinette: Portrait of an Average Woman*, trans. E. and C. Paul (New York 1933), 13; and *Erec et Enide*, trans. D. Staines in *The Complete Romances of Chrétien de Troyes* (Bloomington 1990), 18–22: Erec – a king's son – insists that his fiancée Enide, smock-clad daughter of a 'poor vavasor,' be given rich attire not by her

uncle, a count, but by Queen Guinevere, whose ladies clothe Enide in robes from the royal closet. English reactions in 1382 to Anne of Bohemia's headgear would typify results if a consort retained native dress, but the story told by A. Strickland, *Lives of the Queens of England*, 4th ed., 8 vols [London 1851], 1: 597, lacks proof; costume historians' dating of such attire does not coincide with Anne's lifetime (Laura Hodges kindly provided decisive information on this point).

29 E.T. Hansen, 'The Powers of Silence: The Case of the Clerk's Griselda,' in *Women and Power in the Middle Ages*, ed. M. Erler and M. Kowaleski (Athens, GA 1988), 230–49, esp. 234–5 (cf. Enide, who as she is clothed in Guinevere's royal robes asks that her old smock, a sign of her past life, be given to the poor [*Erec et Enide*, trans. Staines, 22], and Griselda's reclaiming of her shift [see immediately below and next note]). Willett and Cunnington, *History of Underclothes*, 20 and n. 2, cite the penitential implications of Griselda's appearance in her shift, and reference the public penance often imposed on heretics. As Griselda compliantly removes her noble attire herself and is allowed the shift at her own request, however, the frame of reference is visibly different in her case.

30 K. Gilmartin, 'Array in the *Clerk's Tale*,' *The Chaucer Review* 13.3 (1979) 234–46, esp. 237–9. The Griselda story did not exist in its familiar guise before the mid-14th century, but the custom of clothing noble brides to signify subjection to their lords' authority, and *ex opposito* the idea that removing such attire can signify rejection of that authority, give historical weight to the Griselda image; Hughes, 'Women's Fashion,' 140, citing Griselda, sees women's fickle changes of dress as implying 'individual personae that defied [marital] authority.' The points on which Gilmartin's study of Chaucer's text rests are common to all the 14th-century Griselda texts. See Giovanni Boccaccio, *Il decameron*, ed. A. Rossi (Bologna 1977), 570; E. Golenitscheff-Koutouzoff, *L'Histoire de Griseldis en France au XIVe et XVe siècle* (Paris 1933), 153–82, esp. 173–4 (Philippe de Mézières's text), 193–213, esp. 209 (*Livre de Griseldis*), 249–70, esp. 263 (Petrarch's letter); *The Riverside Chaucer*, 3rd ed., ed. L.D. Benson (Boston 1987), 142, 148–9, and 152 (lines 372–85, 876–91, 897–8, and 1115–20); *Le Ménagier de Paris: Traité de morale et d'économie domestique composé vers 1393 par un bourgeois parisien*, ed. J. Pichon, 2 vols (Paris 1847, repr. Geneva 1967), 2: 99–124, esp. 117 (the 1981 Brereton-Ferrier critical edition of *Ménagier* omits the Griselda text, though at pp 372–5 the editors discuss the author's tailoring of the story to fit his circumstances as the elderly husband of a young wife).

31 D. Elliott, 'Dress as Mediator,' 308, and '*Dominae* or *Dominatae*? Female Mysticism and the Trauma of Textuality,' in *Women, Marriage, and Family in Medieval Christendom: Essays in Memory of Michael M. Sheehan, CSB*, ed. C.M. Rousseau and J.T. Rosenthal (Kalamazoo 1998), 47–78; J. Coakley, 'Friars as Confidants of Holy Women in Medieval Dominican Hagiography,' in *Images of*

Sainthood in Medieval Europe, ed. R. Blumenfeld-Kosinski and T. Szell (Ithaca 1991), 222–46, and 'Gender and the Authority of the Friars: The Significance of Holy Women in Medieval Dominican Hagiography,' *Church History* 60 (1991) 445–60. Conflicts inherent in medieval society's stress on the role women's bodies played in social interaction, and male writers' emphasis on women's spirituality, are briefly noted by Casagrande, 'Protected Woman,' 91–2.

32 K.L. French, 'The Legend of Lady Godiva and the Image of the Female Body,' *Journal of Medieval History* 18 (1992) 3–19; cf. Airlie, 'Private Bodies,' 26.

33 Parsons, 'Ritual and Symbol,' 60–78, and 'Queen's Intercession,' 156–7. J.-C. Schmitt, 'The Rationale of Gestures in the West: Third to Thirteenth Centuries,' in *A Cultural History of Gesture*, ed. J. Bremmer and H. Roodenburg (Ithaca 1991), 59–70, esp. 60–1, deals concisely (though without attending to gender) with *intus-foris* relationships in medieval gesture, esp. those associated with charity, penance, or piety.

34 A. Blamires, *The Case for Women in Medieval Culture* (Oxford 1997), 51–7, rather underplays plausible negative interpretations of the views on womanhood in 3 Esdras, the core of the discussion at this point in Blamires's work.

35 For noble female supplicatory piety, L.L. Huneycutt, 'Intercession and the High-Medieval Queen: The *Esther* Topos,' in *Power of the Weak*, ed. Carpenter and MacLean, 126–46; cf. Parsons, 'Queen's Intercession,' 158 n. 44, 160, and idem, 'Piety, Power, and the Reputations of Two Thirteenth-Century English Queens,' in *Queens, Regents, and Potentates*, ed. T.M. Vann, Women of Power 1 (Dallas 1993), 107–23. On performance, C. Brown, '*Muliebriter:* Doing Gender in the Letters of Heloise,' in *Gender and Text in the Later Middle Ages*, ed. J. Chance (Gainesville 1996), 25–51, noting that the 'manipulation of authoritative (and "oppressive") constructs through the artifice of performance ... can be an active, nay aggressive, means of rewriting those very constructs to the pragmatic benefit of the (re)writing subject.' The weight given male rulers' self-abasement underscores the threat of women's like actions. G. Koziol, *Begging Pardon and Favor: Ritual and Political Order in Early Medieval France* (Ithaca 1992), and M. de Jong, 'Power and Humility in Carolingian Society: The Public Penance of Louis the Pious,' *Early Medieval History* 1 (1992) 29–52, discuss male rulers' passive abasement to beg other males' pardon or to mark the rulers' political demise. Women rarely intrude on such scenes; contemporary writers graphically recount the abasement of Louis the Pious, but only obliquely note his wife's religious enclosure, which evidently was not seen to share the 'public' nature of Louis's penance. In contrast, Airlie, 'Private Bodies,' 28–30, describes Queen Theutberga's display of anguish at Aachen in 860, and the bishops' response, as 'emotional theatre.'

36 Studies of tortured bodies depend from M. Foucault, *Discipline and Punish: The Birth of the Prison*, trans. A. Sheridan (Harmondsworth 1979); for overview and

literature, see S. Lehrer, ' "Representyd now in yower syght": The Culture of Spectatorship in Late-Fifteenth-Century England,' in *Bodies and Disciplines: Intersections of Literature and History in Fifteenth-Century England*, ed. B.A. Hanawalt and D. Wallace (Minneapolis 1996), 29–62, esp. nn 7 and 13, at 56–7. Exceptional recent studies are M.B. Merback, *The Thief, the Cross, and the Wheel: Pain and the Spectacle of Punishment in Medieval and Renaissance Europe* (Chicago 1998); and L. Silverman, *Tortured Subjects: Pain, Truth, and the Body in Early Modern France* (Chicago 2001). That neither Isabelle nor Eleanor was physically tortured or maimed, though both give evidence of emotional torment, raises interesting points of contact and comparison with Elaine Scarry, *The Body in Pain: The Making and Unmaking of the World* (Oxford and New York 1985), though the present discussion cannot address them (e.g., Scarry's theme that pain resists and destroys language echoes Isabelle and Eleanor's use of their bodies to express resistance to their lords' will). René Girard, *Le Bouc émissaire* (Paris 1982), trans. Y. Freccero as *The Scapegoat* (Baltimore 1986), suggests absorbing paths for further consideration, though again Isabelle and Eleanor's active resistance differentiates them from the ideally passive scapegoat.

37 Forcible public exposure in underclothes was a common punishment for adulterers or heretics (Willett and Cunnington, *History of Underclothes*, 20), likely based on the shift's penitential associations and its figuration of the soul; but here the consorts' voluntary assumption of otherwise degrading attire alters the frame of reference. Cazelles, *Lady as Saint*, 52–3, stresses that passive stripping to initiate the ordeal is an attribute of female saints, not males; female hermits who actively remove clothing when retiring from the world (i.e., initiate their own 'ordeals') are renouncing seductive artifices. These consorts' creation of ordeals to prove their bodily health echoes G. Bührer-Thierry's view – in an excellent study of adulterous medieval queens – that the ordeal interpreted the body as an instrument for proving the truth (Bührer-Thierry, 'La Reine adultère,' *Cahiers de civilisation médiévale* 35 [1992] 299–312; and see Airlie, 'Private Bodies,' 28).

38 N.A. Jones, 'By Woman's Tears Redeemed: Female Lament in St Augustine's *Confessions* and the Correspondence of Abelard and Heloise,' in *Sex and Gender in Medieval and Renaissance Latin Texts: The Latin Tradition*, ed. B. Gold, P. Miller, and C. Platter (Albany 1997), 15–39; R.S. Beal, 'Guenevere's Tears in the Alliterative *Morte Arthure*: Doubly Wife, Doubly Mother, Doubly Damned,' in *On Arthurian Women: Essays in Memory of Maureen Fries*, ed. B. Wheeler and F. Tolhurst (Dallas 2001), 1–9. Cf. Murray, 'Sexuality and Spirituality,' 20–36, and Airlie, 'Private Bodies,' 26; see also K. Nolan, ' "Ploratus et ululatus": The Mothers in the Massacre of the Innocents at Chartres Cathedral,' *Studies in Iconography* 17 (1996) 95–141. There are important points of contact here with Butler, *Gender Trouble*, esp. 163–80, but discussion is beyond this essay's scope.

K. Lochrie, *Margery Kempe and Translations of the Flesh* (Philadelphia 1991), 177–93, offers new insight on legitimizing weeping by the models of the Virgin and Magdalene mourning Christ. For the Wife of Bath, see Geoffrey Chaucer, *The Wife of Bath*, ed. P.G. Beidler, Case Studies in Contemporary Criticism (Boston 1996), the *Wife's Prologue,* lines 400–2, at p. 58. The association there of deceit, weeping, and spinning as attributes women enjoy, by reason of their sex, as tools to manipulate men, echoes studies showing that village women's textile-related activities, while associated with relegation to a domestic sphere, can convey subversive female discourse (B. Messick, 'Subordinate Discourse: Women, Weaving, and Gender Relations in North Africa,' *American Ethnologist* 14 [1987] 210–25; F. Biscoglio, ' "Unspun" Heroes: Iconography of the Spinning Woman in the Middle Ages,' *Journal of Medieval and Renaissance Studies* 25 [1995] 163–76).

39 Parsons, 'Pregnant Queen,' 41–55; E.A. Rowe, 'The Female Body Politic and the Miscarriage of Justice in *Athelston*,' *Studies in the Age of Chaucer* 17 (1995) 79–98, esp. 97.

40 For mouth/womb, speech/childbirth inversion, M. Bakhtin, *Rabelais and His World*, trans. H. Iswolsky (Bloomington 1984), 308–9; for mouth/womb as sexual *receptacles*, McInerney, ' "In the Meydens Womb," ' 157–82, esp. 160–1. On the popular meanings of consorts' childbearing, Parsons, 'Pregnant Queen,' 44; cf. a farm labourer's 1448 blast against Margaret of Anjou, unfit to be queen 'because that sche bereth no child' (J.L. Chamberlayne, 'Crowns and Virgins: Queenmaking during the Wars of the Roses,' in *Young Medieval Women*, ed. K.J. Lewis, N.J. Menuge, and K.M. Phillips [New York 1999], 47–68, esp. 49), with the duchess of York's positive 1453 letter to Margaret (C. Rawcliffe, 'Richard, Duke of York, the King's "obeisant liegeman": A New Source for the Protectorates of 1454 and 1455,' *Bulletin of the Institute of Historical Research* 60 [1987] 232–9).

41 M.R. Miles, *Carnal Knowing: Female Nakedness and Religious Meaning in the Christian West* (Tunbridge Wells 1992), 144–68; using different sources, Fradenburg's *City, Marriage, Tournament*, 244–54, associates similar political meanings with the consort's body. J. Kristeva, *Powers of Horror: An Essay on Abjection*, trans. L.S. Roudiez (New York 1982) has also shaped my reading here; I must thank Paul Strohm for suggesting its resonances for my argument. Cf. Airlie, 'Private Bodies,' 26–8.

42 Bynum, *Holy Feast and Holy Fast*, 270–2; M. Miles, 'The Virgin's One Bare Breast: Nudity, Gender, and Religious Meaning in Tuscan Early Renaissance Culture,' in *The Female Body in Western Culture: Contemporary Perspectives*, ed. S. Suleiman (Cambridge, MA 1985), 192–208 (repr. in *The Expanding Discourse: Feminism and Art History* , ed. N. Broude and M. Garrard [New York 1992], 27–37).

43 A. Thomas, *Anne's Bohemia: Czech Literature and Society, 1310–1420*, Medieval Cultures 13 (Minneapolis 1998), 147.

44 If the 1569 story contains any grain of truth, Rainald II was not out to weaken his ties to Edward III by repudiating Edward's sister. The families were related (J.C. Parsons, *The Court and Household of Eleanor of Castile in 1290* [Toronto, 1977], 113). Edward was a brother-in-law of Emperor Louis IV, whom he had induced to create Rainald a duke in 1339 (W.J. Alberts, *Geschiedenis van Gelderland, Boek I: Tot 1492* (Zutphen 1975), 78–9. Rainald later supported Edward against Scotland and France (J.A. Ramsay, *The Genesis of Lancaster*, 2 vols [Oxford 1913], 1: 237, 264, 282).

45 G. Spiegel, '*Pseudo-Turpin*, the Crisis of the Aristocracy, and the Beginnings of Vernacular Historiography in France,' *Journal of Medieval History* 12 (1986) 207–23.

46 Respectively Count Robert of Braine (1123?–88) and his sons Robert of Dreux (1154?–1218) and bishops Philip of Beauvais (d. 1217) and Henry of Orléans (d. 1199), who got his see only in 1186 (*Chronique de Gislebert*, 153). It is worth noting that had Philip II died childless, Robert of Braine or his sons would have been the king's nearest agnatic heirs and might have reached the throne (W.K. von Isenburg-Büdingen and F. Freytag von Loringhoven, *Stammtafeln zur Geschichte der Europäische Staaten*, 3 vols in 4 [Leipzig 1953], 1.2, tables 14 and 29); their move to urge Philip not to divorce a potentially barren wife might not, then, have been entirely influenced by the immediate circumstance of the riot Isabelle had incited. Among the advocates of divorce, Gislebert includes the count of Clermont-en-Beauvaisis, an influential baron in the royal domain, but wrongly identifies the count of Champagne as the king's maternal uncle, who in fact had died in 1181; the count in 1184 was a nephew. Isabelle was first betrothed to that nephew, but her childless Flemish uncle induced her father to end that betrothal by promising him the reversion to Flanders. Philip II then wed her with Artois as her dowry to extend his influence into Picardy and, by allying with Flanders, to offset his maternal Blois-Champagne kin – to whom his marriage was thus doubly offensive (Baldwin, *Government*, 14–18; Bradbury, *Philip Augustus*, 54–6; *Chronique de Gislebert*, 101–3 and 126; *Sigeberti continuatio Aquicinctina*, ed. G.H. Pertz, MGH Scriptores 6 (Hanover 1844), 405–38, esp. 428).

47 C.W. Hollister and J.W. Baldwin, 'The Rise of Administrative Kingship: Henry I and Philip Augustus,' *American Historical Review* 88 (1978) 867–905. I suggest the impact of such administrative development on the queen's intercessory role in 'The Queen's Intercession,' 153–4.

48 Fradenburg, 'Rethinking Queenship,' 4–6, draws on Turnerian *communitas*, for which, esp. regarding pilgrimage, see V. and E. Turner, *Image and Pilgrimage in Christian Culture: Anthropological Perspectives* (Oxford 1978), 253–55, and V.

Turner, *Dramas, Fields, and Metaphors: Symbolic Action in Human Society* (Ithaca 1974), 196. Cf. Fradenburg, *City, Marriage, Tournament*, 244–64; Parsons, 'Queen's Intercession,' 159–61, 'Ritual and Symbol,' 67, and 'Pregnant Queen,' 44 and 49. On *communitas* and social criticism, V. Turner, *From Ritual to Theatre: The Human Seriousness of Play* (New York 1982), 47; on queens' intercession as critique of male behaviour, P. Strohm, 'Queens as Intercessors,' in his *Hochon's Arrow: The Social Imagination of Medieval Texts* (Princeton 1992), 95–120, esp. 103–4. Cf. J. Ferrante, 'Public Postures and Private Manoeuvers: Roles Medieval Women Play,' and Hansen, 'Powers of Silence,' in *Women and Power in the Middle Ages*, ed. Erler and Kowaleski, 213–29 and 230–49 respectively. French, 'Legend of Lady Godiva,' associates the altruistic, interceding woman's naked body with the *community*, but not in Turner's or Fradenburg's *communitarian* sense.

49 Eleanor's offer of her maternity for the good of Rainald's subjects legitimizes her actions; cf. Elizabeth of York's behaviour after her son's death in 1502 (Parsons, 'Pregnant Queen,' 45 and 51).

50 W. Juppe Alberts, *Geschiedenis van Gelderland: Boek II, 1492–1795* (Zutphen 1975), 72–8.

51 J. Nelson, 'Inauguration Rituals,' in *Early Medieval Kingship*, ed. P.H. Sawyer and I.N. Wood (Leeds 1977), 71. If the Blanche of Castile tale (above, n. 15) is a forebear of the Eleanor story, some significance must attach to its evolution from proof that Blanche was *not* pregnant into Eleanor's plea to have *more* children.

52 A point underlined by Blanche of Castile's self-exposure to prove her sexual purity (above, n. 15), and Eleanor's to incite Rainald to have more sons with her. Cf. McCracken, *Romance of Adultery*, 169–70.

53 Fradenburg, 'Rethinking Queenship,' introduction to *Women and Sovereignty*, 7; Parsons, 'Queens, Courts, and Books,' 187–8.

54 Further study is needed into the anxieties male writers' accounts of such women may betray for the patriarchal discourses of honour and hierarchy; see, e.g., J. Findon, *A Woman's Words: Emer and Female Speech in the Ulster Cycle* (Toronto 1997).

12 Violence in the Early Robin Hood Poems

RICHARD FIRTH GREEN

There are several ways in which those Robin Hood ballads that can claim to have been composed before 1500 (the *Gest of Robyn Hode, Robin Hood and the Potter, Robin Hood and the Monk, Robin Hood and Guy of Gisborne,* and *Robin Hood's Death*) are liable to frustrate the expectations of modern first-time readers.[1] Such readers will encounter barely a hint of Friar Tuck and, more importantly, no Maid Marian – indeed, hardly any women at all, apart from the treacherous Abbess of Kirklees and the cupidinous Sheriff of Nottingham's wife. (If romantic liaisons are what they're looking for they will do better to turn to Robin's fellow outlaw, the uxorious William of Cloudesly.) There is also very little taking from the rich and giving to the poor (a motif Stephen Knight associates with a later sixteenth-century gentrification of the tradition):[2] early recipients of Robin's generosity, like Sir Richard atte Lee or the Potter, are hardly to be classed with the lowest dregs of society. Finally (the feature that is be my subject here), there is in all but *Robin Hood and the Potter* a marked streak of ruthless violence (also a feature of other early outlaw poems like *Gamelyn* and *Adam Bell, Clim of the Clough, and William of Cloudesly*) that is the very antithesis of the mood of chivalrous fair play that we have come to associate with these romantic denizens of the greenwood.[3] Indeed, even a generation of students brought up on Hollywood action movies is liable to feel offended by the spirit of cold-blooded vindictiveness with which Robin dispatches his opponents in these early ballads.

Take, for instance, the end of the Sheriff of Nottingham in the comparatively restrained *Gest of Robyn Hode*. After rescuing Richard atte Lee from captivity in Nottingham,

> Robyn bent a full goode bowe,
> An arrowe he drowe at wyll;

> He hit so the proude sherife,
> Upon the grounde he lay full still.
> And or he myght up aryse,
> On his fete to stonde,
> He smote of the sherifs hede,
> With his bright bronde [i.e., sword]. (*Gest*, stanzas 347–8)

That is to say, Robin decapitates the injured sheriff while he is lying helpless on the ground – the kind of job the old Westerns assigned to the cowboys wearing the black hats. The same sheriff's end in *Robin Hood and Guy of Gisborne* at Little John's hands is, if anything, even more unsporting:

> But he cold neither soe fast goe,
> Nor away soe fast runn,
> But Litle John, with an arrow broade,
> Did cleave his heart in twinn. (*Guy* 58)

In other words, Little John shoots him in the back as he is fleeing for his life. A ballad that can be traced back only to the end of the sixteenth century but may well be earlier, *Robin Hood's Progress to Nottingham*, reveals a similar lack of good sportsmanship:[4] after Robin has killed fourteen of a band of fifteen foresters,

> He that did this quarrel first begin
> Went tripping over the plain,
> But Robin Hood he bent his noble bow,
> And hee fetch him back again.
> 'You said I was no archer,' said Robin Hood,
> 'But say so now again';
> With that he sent another arrow
> That split his head in twain. (*Progress* 13–14)

In *Robin Hood and the Monk* the manner in which Little John and Much deal with an unarmed monk and his boy, whom they waylay in Sherwood with letters announcing Robin's capture to the king, is similarly ruthless:

> John smote of the munkis hed,
> No longer wolde he dwell;
> So did Moch the litull page,
> Ffor ferd lest he wold tell. (*Monk* 52)

Though this monk, who had earlier raised the alarm when Robin had visited St Mary's Church in Nottingham and seems to have had a hand in his subsequent capture, might be thought to have in some measure deserved such rough justice, the same could hardly be said of his little boy. Like a number of other minor characters who get in the outlaws' way in these early ballads, this page is simply expendable. A bit later in the same ballad, for instance, John and Much murder a porter and a jailer in the course of rescuing Robin from Nottingham prison:

> The porter rose anon sertan,
> As sone as he herd John calle;
> Litul John was redy with a swerd,
> And bare hym to the walle. (*Monk* 70)

Another porter, this one from Carlisle, meets a similarly brutal end at the hands of Adam Bell and Clim of the Clough when they find that he is an impediment to their rescue of William of Cloudesly:

> They called the porter to counsell,
> And wronge hys necke in two,
> And caste hym in a depe dongeon,
> And toke hys keys hym fro. (*Adam Bell* 65)

The unceremonious manner in which Adam and Clim dispose of the porter's dead body is matched in other early ballads; the monk and his little boy, for instance:

> Ther thei beryed hem bothe,
> In nouther mosse nor lyng, (*Monk* 53)

which I take to mean that they didn't bury them at all. Such treatment is nothing, however, to the fate Robin Hood imagines for the decapitated corpse of the treacherous Roger of Doncaster:

> Says, 'Ly there, ly there, Red Roger
> The dogges they must thee eate;' (*Death* 22)

or to his desecration of Guy of Gisborne's dead body:

> He tooke Sir Guys head by the hayre,
> And sticked itt on his bowes end:
> 'Thou hast beene traytor all thy liffe,
> Which thing must have an ende.'
> Robin pulled forth an Irish kniffe,
> And nicked Sir Guy in the fface,
> That hee was never on a woman borne
> Cold tell who Sir Guye was. (*Guy* 41–2)

That Robin renders Sir Guy's features unrecognizable because he is planning to assume the dead bounty hunter's identity only partly justifies the poem's relish for casual violence here. In the closely related fifteenth-century play of *Robin Hood and the Sheriff*, Robin, having fought *at ottraunce* with an unnamed knight, strips the clothes from his dead body and, in a gruesome play on words, rides off with the severed head in his hood:

> 'Now I have the maystry [upper hand] here,
> Off I smyte this sory swyre.
> This knyghtys clothis wolle I were,
> And in my hode his hede woll bere.'[5]

In all these scenes there is a strong element of cynical brutality, quite at odds with what we have come to expect of these idealized heroes.

One possible explanation of the appearance of such brutality is that it is nothing other than simple, unvarnished realism. The early Robin Hood ballads were composed at a time when outlawry was still a legal and social actuality, and it is not hard to believe that the existence of those who lived outside the law might have been lawless in the most Hobbesian of senses. Yet this is not really the experience of those who read these early ballads. We are a world away from the canting rogues of writers like Greene and Dekker: the outlaws' life is characterized by a strong sense of community and conviviality and, except in very specific contexts, it is neither brutal nor lawless. Thieves' honour means that when the outlaws spar among themselves (as they do with surprising regularity) their ritual violence is contained by a set of clearly recognized rules. Only in their dealings with outsiders, and particularly with those who are implicated in some way with the legal authority of the state, are these rules suspended.

In his counter-history of punishment in western society, Michel Foucault distinguishes two distinct stages: the *spectacular* (*éclatant*), in which the state parades its political power by inflicting ritualized violence, often of a stomach-turning kind, upon the bodies of its subjects, and the *carceral*, through which the state projects a sense of omnipresent surveillance over its members' private lives.[6] The first stage belongs primarily to the early modern world (particularly that of the *Ancien Régime*), the second, heralded by Bentham's famous Panopticon, to the nineteenth and twentieth centuries. For Foucault, who shares Hobbes's and Nietzsche's obsession with the operations of power, the advantage of the carceral from the point of view of the state is that it enables it to reserve all the power to itself, whereas under a spectacular regimen it is forced to share it with its subjects: when the crowd plays as important a role as the executioner, the violence of state power must in some sense be dissipated by the violence of those who are required to witness it. By partaking with the state in an orgy of spectacular brutality, then, the people might seem to be weakening the state's monopoly of political authority. Indeed, in England (if Thomas Laqueur is to be believed), the balance tipped decisively in favour of the popular: 'the crowd,' he writes, 'was the central actor in English executions,' and 'the hangings and beheadings of seventeenth-, eighteenth-, and nineteenth-century England were unpromising vehicles for the display of power, if by this is meant the sovereign power of the state.'[7] Can this be what we are experiencing in these early Robin Hood ballads: evidence of an emergent political structure in which the violated human body becomes the site of a power struggle between state and subject? The answer, it seems to me, is both yes and no.

Foucault's interest in the Middle Ages was notoriously slim and it does not take much effort to show that his spectacular, far from representing a kind of ur-state in which power has yet to be disengaged from its intimate involvement with physical violence, is itself the successor to a still earlier penal regime. If the Panopticon replaces the public scaffold, this selfsame scaffold in turn replaces the wolf's head: the widespread propensity of traditional communities to turn to rejection, expulsion, banishment, and outlawry as a way of coping with the worst offences their members can commit.[8] This instinct is diametrically opposed to everything implied by the spectacular: it is not the exposure of guilt to the public gaze that is its object but rather the concealment of shame. We may call it, to distinguish it from Foucault's *carceral* and *spectacular*, an *occlusive* economy of punishment.

At the beginning of *Madness and Civilization* where he treats, with surprising literal-mindedness, the motif of the ship of fools, Foucault might have found an occasion to explore such an occlusive economy, but, distracted by his lifelong obsession with systems of containment, he was predictably enough preoccupied by the ship and not its voyaging.[9] In *Discipline and Punish* a discussion of the 'rituals of exclusion' that were brought to bear upon lepers in the early modern world offered him another opportunity to realize this economy, but, unable to conceive of power except in terms of authoritarian power, he relates these mechanisms to the quarantining of plague victims,[10] whereas the reality was rather different. The power to quarantine – whether manifest in the prison, the plague hospital, or the lunatic asylum – is centripetal: it flows inward to that mysterious central nexus of authority that so fascinated Foucault throughout his career. The power to expel the leper, however, is a communal power, and its direction of flow is self-evidently centrifugal.

The story of how the direction of flow in punitive systems switched from centrifugal to centripetal, of how royal authority, at one time seen as a refuge from the arbitrary exercise of power, came to be itself popularly regarded as a source of such power, is too complex to go into here, but its medieval phase has been brilliantly epitomized by F.W. Maitland. What Foucault in *The Will to Knowledge* will call the negatory power (*prélèvement*) of the absolutist monarchy[11] is shown by Maitland to have developed out of an earlier expulsive power that had resided in the community:

> Many of the pure punishments, the 'afflictive' punishments, have their roots in outlawry. They are mitigations of that comprehensive penalty. The outlaw forfeits all, life and limb, lands and goods. This, as law and kingship grow stronger, puts the fate of many criminals into the king's hands. The king may take life and choose the kind of death, or he may be content with a limb; he can insist on banishment, or the abjuration of his realm, or a forfeiture of chattels. The man who has committed one of the bad crimes which have been causes of outlawry is not regarded as having a right to just this or that punishment ... It was not for him to complain if a foot was taken instead of his eyes, or if he was hanged instead of being beheaded.[12]

Cruel as such punishments must often have been, what must have seemed far worse, from the point of view of those who witnessed them, was their very arbitrariness; by deliberately flouting jural expectations deeply rooted in communal custom they inevitably provoked suspicion and hostility.

An important stimulus to the development of spectacular punishment was clearly the emergence of something dimly foreshadowing the modern idea of an offence against the state. Here for instance is how Gervase of Canterbury describes the death of William Longbeard, who had led a tax revolt in London at the very end of the twelfth century: 'He was dragged, with his feet attached to the collar of a horse, from the aforesaid Tower through the center of the city to the elms [at Tyburn], his flesh was demolished and spread all over the pavement and, fettered with a chain, he was hanged that same day on the elms with his associates and died.'[13]

A superficial comparison of this description with Foucault's account of the execution of Damiens in Paris in 1757 might suggest that the two punishments differ only in degree, not in kind – as Maitland observed, 'the worst cruelties belong to a politer time' (2: 453) – but, however much some aspects of this Angevin justice might seem to resemble the *prélèvement* of the *Ancien Régime*, in other respects it diverged from it dramatically: in 1196 the elms of Tyburn stood well outside the city – indeed Tyburn was still a remote, even pastoral, location when London executions were removed from there to Newgate as late as 1783[14] – and while the king might have wished to make a public spectacle of William Longbeard's death, Londoners made sure that he did it well outside their city walls. Only in the late Middle Ages can we begin to detect a fully spectacular penal regime in England, and interestingly its early manifestations seem to have provoked strong popular resentment.

One of the most conspicuous exponents of such a regime was William Tiptoft, earl of Worcester and constable of England under Edward IV, described by one chronicler as 'a savage executioner and a terrible beheader of men' [*trux carnifex et hominum decollator horridus*],[15] but known to the common people simply as 'the Bowcher of England.'[16] Two aspects of his administration seem particularly to have distressed his contemporaries: his habit of turning the execution of his Lancastrian enemies into a public display, and the care he took to have their dead bodies desecrated. In 1462, for instance, according to *Warkworth's Chronicle*, the earl of Oxford and his eldest son were, 'hade to the Toure Hylle, where was made a scaffolde of viij fote hy3t, and ther was there hedes smyten of, that alle menne myght see; whereof the moste people were sory,'[17] and in 1470, after some of Warwick the Kingmaker's followers had been captured at Southampton,

> xx. persones of gentylmen and yomenne were hangede, drawne, and quartered, and hedede [beheaded]; and after that thei hanged uppe by the leggys, and a stake made scharpe at bothe endes, whereof one ende was putt in att buttokys, and the other ende ther heddes were putt uppe one; for the whiche the peple of the londe were gretely displesyd; and evere afterwarde the Erle of Worcestre was gretely behatede [hated] emonge the peple, for ther dysordinate [immoderate] dethe that he used, contrarye to the lawe of the londe.[18]

Rightly or wrongly, Tiptoft's schooling in Italy led people to suppose that he had learned such tricks abroad (he was said to have condemned the earl of Oxford 'by lawe padowe' [of Padua]), and when he himself was arrested and condemned at the time of Henry VI's readeption later in 1470 'moche people reioysed,' and so great was the press of spectators that turned up at Tower Hill to 'gaze & gawre upon hym' that his execution had to be deferred for a day.[19]

If the first appearance of a fully realized regime of spectacular punishment in England might be traced to Tiptoft's constableship, it was already implicit, as I have suggested, in William Longbeard's execution two hundred years earlier. From at least the end of the twelfth century onward, a clear gap had begun to open up between the attitude of central authority to afflictive punishment and that of the local community. It is not that local communities were necessarily more lenient than the central authority, or even more squeamish, it is just that they preserved a preference for the centrifugal over the centripetal, the occlusive over the spectacular. The best evidence for this comes from the ordinances of those boroughs that maintained a jurisdiction over major felonies to the end of the Middle Ages.[20] Three elements in their regulation of afflictive punishment stand out in marked contrast to the spectacular regimen described by Foucault.

First, the place of execution was not in the town square but at the furthest margins of the community, as if, even in death, the criminal was subject to a kind of symbolic occlusion. Clearly, the elms of Tyburn had performed such a function for Londoners from before Gervase of Canterbury's day; at Sandwich, we hear of a place called the *Thiefdounes*, located at Sandown (*Borough Customs*, ed. Bateson, 1: 79), and at Pevensey a certain place called the felons-tree

(*Wah3trew*) located at Lowey (ibid., 1: 75); the place of execution at Portsmouth was called *Cattcliff* (1: 75), and at Fordwich it was called *Thefeswells* (1: 76); at both Winchelsea and Rye, the ordinances specify that all those condemned for homicide 'must be hanged upon the salt marsh on the east side of the town, beyond the salt water of the town' (1: 76).[21] A set of regulations from Hastings, dating from the very end of the Middle Ages, recognize that the penal regime of the king's courts was of a quite different kind: 'but now of a newe and speciall grace and graunte of oure lorde the kyng Edward IIII[t] the barouns and proved men of the porte of Hastyng shal use hereafter suche execucyon as ys accordyng to the commune lawe of Inglonde, as hangyng on galowes' (1: 76).

Secondly, the traditional methods of execution were also often occlusive. For instance, Sandwich practised burial alive, Fordwich drowning in a well (Bateson, 1: 74); at Pevensey freemen were thrown from the town bridge at high tide – all others were hanged (1: 75). Throwing from cliffs is recorded from the Isle of Man, as well as at Hastings and Dover (1: 76); some other coastal towns, such as Portsmouth, employed drowning by the tide.[22] There is a well-known account of a woman drowned at London Bridge for witchcraft around 970, but as late as 1300 the London *Liber custumarum* is specifying as a penalty for treason, that 'he shall be bound to a stake, at the piles which stand in the Thames at Timberhythe where boats are fastened, for two flows and two ebbs of the tide' (1: 75). Lest we should suppose that such regulations preserve judicial archaisms no longer part of the actual lives of late medieval townspeople, we might note that there is at least one recorded case from fifteenth-century Folkestone in which someone was threatened with being thrown from a cliff.[23] Many such methods of execution imply a reluctance to employ direct human agency in order to bring about death, as if the community is unwilling to go further than to expose the felon to a situation where natural forces will hasten his or her end. Again, this is very different from Foucault's spectacular punishment, where ritualized execution is employed in a public display of state power.

Finally, there is a survival of the ancient notion that all law is essentially private law and that he who prosecutes, not some central political authority, must carry out the judgment. The ancient maxim, *ille qui sequitur faciet justiciam*, for instance, is explicitly recorded in a Preston ordinance from the twelfth century (Bateson, 1: 73). The drowning in a well described in a fifteenth-century ordinance from Fordwich is to be carried out by the suitor: *Hoc fiat per ipsum qui sequitur* (1: 76). Of the throwing from a cliff in a Dover ordinance of the same date we learn that 'yf he be atteynte [convicted] at the sute of the partye the appelour shal do execucioun, and yf it be at the kyng's sute the baylly shall doo it' (1: 76). From Romney at the very end of the fifteenth century we read that 'the bayleff shall fynde [provide] the galows and the rope, and the suter which maketh the appele shall fynde the hangman. And if he may fynde non hangman neither that he wyll noght do that same office himself, he shall dwelle in prison with the felon unto the tyme that he wyll do that office or else find an hangman' (1: 74). Again, there is a marked difference here from Foucault's spectacular displays of political power.

All this may seem to have taken us a long way from the outlaw ballads with which I began this paper, but the point I want to make is really quite simple. The cynical brutality found in the early Robin Hood ballads, as well as in *Gamelyn* and *Adam Bell*, should be read as symptomatic of a clash between two penal regimes, the older occlusive regime that underlies the very institution of outlawry itself, and the newer spectacular regime represented by the Sheriff of Nottingham and his officials. Reacting with reciprocal brutality to a system designed to brutalize him, Robin treats with particular savagery those, like Guy of Gisborne and the Monk (the bounty hunter and the turncoat), who set out to betray him to that system. Thus, while such outlaw violence can certainly be related to the political violence Foucault articulates, it remains quite distinct from it; Robin's violence, unlike the spectator's, is in no sense complicit with the power of the state. It is, indeed, openly resistant to it.

Nowhere is such resistance more evident than in the orgy of violence that accompanies William of Cloudesley's rescue from the gallows by his faithful companions, Adam and Clim:

> The kyng opened the letter anone,
> Himselfe he red it thro,
> And founde how these outlawes had slain
> Thre hundred men and mo.
>
> Fyrst the justice, and the sheryfe,
> And the mayre of Caerlal [Carlisle] towne;
> Of all the constables and the catchipolles
> Alyve were left not one:
>
> The baylyes, and the bedels both
> And the sergeaunts of the law,
> And forty fosters [foresters] of the fee [estate],
> These outlawes had yslaw [slain]. (*Adam Bell* 138–41)

Robin Hood, likewise, mounts spectacular rescues from the gallows in later ballads like *Robin Hood and the Beggar I*, *Robin Hood Rescuing Three Squires*, and *Robin Hood Rescuing Will Stutly*,[24] though in none of these do we encounter a death toll as sensational as the one in *Adam Bell*. In one version of *Robin Hood Rescuing Three Squires*, however, we do find a late survival of the traditional motif of authority turned upside down, of the sheriff hanged on his own gallows:

> They took the gallows from the slack,
> They set it in the glen,
> They hangd the proud sheriff on that,
> Released their own three men. (Child 140B, stanza 29)

That this representative of the king's law should come to so shameful an end on his own gallows, rather than meeting an honourable death in fair fight, is of course entirely fitting;[25] as the poet had remarked dryly of the death of one of the sheriff's men in *Robin Hood and Guy of Gisborne*,

> It had beene better for William a Trent
> To hang upon a gallowe
> Then for to lye in the greenwoode,
> There slaine with an arrowe. (*Guy* 18)

Both these motifs (the orgy of violence directed against representatives of the king's law, and the instruments of official correction turned against those maintained to employ them) are combined in the very early *Tale of Gamelyn*. Here the roles of outlaw and judge are conspicuously reversed, with Gamelyn holding a formal trial of the sheriff (his treacherous elder brother), the justice, and twelve jurymen:

> 'Thow hast ȝeven domes þat ben yuel dight,
> I wil sitten in þy sete and dressen hem aright.' (*Gamelyn* 847–8)

['You have passed judgments that were wickedly decided; I will sit in your seat and set them right.']

The verdict is entirely predictable:

> For to make schort tale and nouȝt to tarie longe,
> He ordeyned him a queste of his men so stronge;
> The iustice and þe scherreue boþe honged hye
> To weyuen wiþ ropes and wiþ the wynd drye.
> And þe twelue sisours – sorwe haue þat rekke! –
> Alle þey were hanged faste by þe nekke.
> Thus ended þe fals knight wiþ his treccherie,
> That euer had ilad his lyf in falsnes and folye. (*Gamelyn* 876–83)

[To keep the story brief and not delay too long, he empanelled a jury of his own strong men. The judge and the sheriff were hanged up high and left to swing on their ropes and dry out in the wind, and the twelve jurymen were all hanged by the neck (cursed be anyone who cares about them!). That was the end of the false knight and his treachery, a man who had spent his whole life in falsehood and wickedness.]

That Gamelyn should describe his actions here as a 'bourde' [jest] (line 858), raises one further aspect of this anti-judicial violence that I should like to discuss briefly. Peter Stallybrass has characterized the violent excess and role-reversals of sixteenth-century Robin Hood games and of some seventeenth-century ballads such as *Robin Hood and the Bishop* and *Robin Hood Rescuing Three Squires* as carnivalesque,[26] while Thomas Laqueur, in an article I have already mentioned, has employed the same adjective to characterize the crowds that attended public executions in early modern England. If the actions of those who were portrayed as resisting state violence and those who colluded with it can both be described as *carnivalesque*, it is plain that either Stallybrass and Laqueur are using the word in rather different senses or the distinction I have been trying to draw between the spectacular and the occlusive regimes will not hold water.

In fact, the difficulty does seem to me to be largely terminological, for even Mikhail Bakhtin's classic study *Rabelais and His World* had offered two discrete definitions of the role of carnival in medieval and early modern Europe (indeed, it is probably Bakhtin's own shifting use of the term that lies behind the quite distinct views of carnival put forward by Stallybrass and Laqueur).[27] As a folklorist, Bakhtin saw the carnival as an embodiment of the perennial struggle between crabbed winter and bounteous summer:

> In such a system the king is the clown. He is elected by all the people and mocked by all the people. He is abused and beaten when the time of his reign is over, just as the carnival dummy of winter or of the dying year is mocked, beaten, torn to pieces, burned, or drowned even in our time ... But in this system death is followed by regeneration, by the new year, new youth, and a new spring. Therefore abuse is followed by praise. They are two aspects of one world. (*Rabelais*, 197–8)

As a revolutionary, on the other hand, Bakhtin clearly wished to see the carnival as an instance of proletarian opposition to the dominant ideology (the oppressive official world to which it stands in such obvious contrast):

> Carnival with all its images, indecencies and curses affirms the people's immortal, indestructible character. In the world of carnival the awareness of the people's immortality is combined with the realization that established authority and truth are relative. Popular-festive forms look into the future. They present the victory of this future, of the golden age, over the past. This is the victory of all the people's material abundance, freedom, equality, brotherhood. (*Rabelais*, 256)

The first of these two models represents carnival as a form that, in its ritual repetitions, stands outside linear time, a form that can in fact be licensed, tolerated, even encouraged by the dominant ideology. The second, by contrast, treats carnival as a genuine threat to this ideology, a force for reform, even revolution, very much wedded to an historical, even eschatological, model of temporal progression.[28]

From this point of view, Laqueur's hanging crowd, if it is carnivalesque at all, is so only in Bakhtin's first, folkloric, sense. It was a drunken, lecherous, abusive, holiday crowd, certainly, and it was there to witness a death, symbolic as well as actual. If not all felons went to the scaffold (in Defoe's phrase) 'as neat and trim as if they were going to a wedding,'[29] enough did so to add a disturbingly theatrical inflection to these grim proceedings. Not that there was anything seasonal about such public executions, nor, more importantly, did the crowd show much interest in assisting at a rebirth. In the Middle Ages a botched execution had been taken as a sign of divine intervention and had led to an automatic reprieve for the condemned: 'It is noȝt vsed in erþe to hangen a feloun / Ofter þan ones' [it is not the custom to hang felons more than once], as William Langland remarks (*PPl.* B 18.379–80).[30] The survival of this belief into the seventeenth century probably helped save Ann Greene, who revived hours after being cut down from the gallows, from having to face a second execution in Oxford in 1649,[31] but by the eighteenth century even when the rope broke (as it did in the case of the notorious pirate Captain Kidd) the mob was still not to be balked of its prey. Similarly, last-minute reprieves were often unpopular with the mob. It is difficult not to feel some sympathy for E.P. Thompson's indignant outburst against Laqueur: 'to present the Tyburn crowd as a "carnival crowd" is both to misunderstand the crowd and to libel "carnival"... That sort of execution crowd was *an execution crowd* (and a carnival nothing). It was one of the most brutalized phenomena in history and historians ought to say so.'[32] In fairness to Laqueur, Bakhtin himself would probably have been prepared to regard Tyburn as one of those 'folk spectacles and carnival forms, which were still alive, though degenerate' in the age of Sterne.[33]

There is, by contrast, nothing either passive or voyeuristic about the dramatic gallows rescues effected by Adam and Clim or by Robin himself, and in Bakhtin's terms, they might well be taken to represent both 'an element of victory ... over supernatural awe, over the sacred, over death; [and] the defeat of power, of earthly kings, of the earthly upper classes, of all that oppresses and restricts.'[34] When Peter Stallybrass points out that 'the carnivalesque play of Robin Hood [was not] always confined to the *licensed* misrule of May,'[35] he acknowledges this second, revolutionary Bakhtinian carnival, but he also complicates the issue by associating it with the concept of *play*. Aguing persuasively that, while the ruling class found in the idea of play a way to marginalize or contain heterodox notions of legality, the oppressed themselves might see play as a vehicle for challenging or contesting the dominant ideology, he concludes that the 'plebeian "play" [of Robin Hood] was both a means of unmasking legal violence (i.e., the violence of which the state claimed a monopoly), and of producing alternative definitions of "law."'[36] It will be obvious that I find Stallybrass's reading of the carnivalesque in this context far more helpful than Laqueur's, but I still have two reservations about it. In the first place, by treating play as primarily a set of rhetorical practices (rather than as a social event), he risks associating himself with what Alan Sinfield has termed 'the entrapment model' of ideology and power, 'whereby even, or especially, manoeuvres that seem designed to challenge the system help to maintain it.'[37] Secondly, he seems to me seriously to understate the possibility of a carnivalesque element in traditional legal strategies. Some forms of carnival, in other words, do more than merely unmask or even define law; in a very real sense, they represent law.

One expression of 'carnival,' alluded to by both Bakhtin and Stallybrass but insufficiently distinguished by them from some other festive practices which it formally resembles, had an inherent potential for violence: the *charivari*. Charivari was always potentially violent because it functioned, not merely as licensed misrule, but (like the occlusive punishments we have been discussing) as the instrument of a genuine alternative form of rule, and the exercise of any mode of social control must always depend, explicitly or implicitly, upon directed violence. In fact, in a discussion of the affiliation between *Robin Hood and the Bishop* and the charivari, Stallybrass himself clearly recognizes this potential: 'the symbolic system of carnival is used then to legitimate popular justice against the official ideological and legal apparatus which claims to have a monopoly of justice. The outlaw becomes the enforcer of popular law.'[38] Even here, however, he does not quite take the final step of seeing popular law as different in kind (rather than merely in application) from the law of the state; at most the charivari is 'quasi-legal,'[39] and as an expression of 'the symbolic system of carnival' it comes to underlie his later weak elision of law with rhetorical play. However, as Natalie Zemon Davis for one has shown, the original charivari was lawless and playful in only very restricted senses;[40] one might even go so far as to see the charivari as one of the underlying procedures on which an occlusive system of punishment depended: a process designed to expel all those who refused to submit to its discipline from the community. Clearly, it had a genuine judicial role to perform in the regulation of early modern communities, and this serious purpose was reinforced by its ever-present potential to turn violent.

I should like to conclude this discussion by looking briefly at just such an instance of popular law turning to violence – a riot (in reality a series of riots) that was associated with a Robin Hood game in Edinburgh in 1561.[41] My point is not to suggest that this riot was in any sense typical of Robin Hood games generally (clearly it was not),[42] but to show how the image of the outlaw might offer far more than simply 'a means of unmasking legal violence.'[43] This riot is mentioned in passing by Stallybrass as an instance of the way in which the 'boundaries between May play and the playing out of ritual subversion were unclear,'[44] but – as I hope to show – the boundaries, at least in this instance, were relatively well drawn. Moreover, it should quickly become apparent that to call the events that culminated in the 1561 riot 'May play,' as Stallybrass does, is a little like describing an Orange parade through Newry or Londonderry in our own time as 'July play.' As we shall see, the figure of Robin Hood was quite deliberately employed to focus a dispute that had arisen between the lesser tradespeople and the city governors – the provost, the two bailies, and the town clerk (backed by the council and, ultimately, by the queen and the nobility). It was not, as Stallybrass would have it, that 'the law of carnivalesque play triumphed over statutory law';[45] rather one form of law, one form of punishment, was brought into violent conflict with another, and carnival provided an appropriate vehicle for their opposition. The argument, in other words, was over something far deeper than the mere right to play.

The trouble, according to John Knox, who was an eyewitness, had begun in June of the previous year when the city fathers had passed a law 'against fornicators and adulterers that the one and the other should be carted through the towns and so banished.'[46] In accordance with this decree, the city magistrates duly arrested and convicted a butcher called John Sanderson, but when the punishment was to be carried out, 'the rascal multitude, inflamed by some ungodly craftsmen, made insurrection, broke the cart, boisted [insulted] the officers, and took away the malefactor. This was the beginning of further evils, as we shall after hear.'[47] It is difficult, at this distance of time, to penetrate the web of political alliances that surrounded this incident; clearly the opposing forces divided partly on religious grounds (barely a month later the Scottish Parliament was to recognize Knox's reformation in law), as well as along class lines (petty tradesmen martialled against the great guilds), but one further element must surely have been the appropriation of an instrument of popular law, the charivari, by those who were seeking to impose their rule from above. Carting was, after all, a meaningless discipline unless the people as a whole collaborated in it. Resentment seems to have simmered for the best part of a year and by the following Spring was ready to flare up once more.

On Wednesday, 23 April, the city council, 'vnderstanding that the prentissis and seruandis of merchanttis and craftismen and vtheris within this burgh ar of mynd vpoun Sounday nixt to mak convocatioun and assemblie efter the auld wikit maner of Robene Hude,'[48] issued a proclamation forbidding any such assembly and threatening to punish anyone who participated, or allowed his servants to participate, in it; detailed provisions against the bearing of arms in the streets show that this was no routine attempt to suppress overenthusiastic merrymaking. For the following two Sundays the council seems to have been successful in enforcing its regulations, but on Monday, 12 May, it had to call an emergency meeting of the heads [the deacons] of nine guilds (including the wrights, smiths, tailors, and shoemakers) to get them to discipline those of their apprentices ['craft childer'] who had participated in a riot the previous day. We learn a little more about this riot from the court proceedings against ten men (two tailors, a shoemaker, a smith, a sword-sharpener, a cook, and four taborers) on 20 July, all of whom were found guilty of participating in a parade led by a tailor, 'George Durye, callit Lord of (In)obedience,' that marched under displayed banners and with an assortment of fearsome weaponry ('halbrownis, jakkis, culveringis, morriounis, twa handit swerdis, cotis of malʒe, and vþeris wapynnis invasive') from the East Gate of the city to the Castle Hill and back again, despite being confronted at the outset by the bailies and the city council and ordered to disband.[49] Records of the court proceedings against George Durye himself seem not to have survived (though we know from a later document that he and some of his companions were outlawed), but on the next day a trial was held of a man who was to become the focus for the next round of rioting, a shoemaker's servant called James Gillone.

On 21 July the provost and bailies 'causit … Gilloun, takin of befoir for playing in Edinburgh with Robene hude, to wnderly [answer to] the law and put him to the knawlege of ane assyiss, qhuilk thaj haid electit of thair favouraris, qhua with schort deliberatioun condemnit him to be hangit for the said cryme.'[50] What happened next was a scene worthy of Robin Hood himself (and indeed the chronicler's account may well be coloured by his recollections of the outlaw's exploits):

> Quhen the tyme of the said pover mans hanging approchit and that the hangman wes cumand [coming] to the jibbat with the ledder vpoun the quhilk [which] the said cordinare should haue bene hangit, ane certane and remanent craftischilder, quha [who] wes put to the horne [i.e., outlawed] with the said Gillone for the said Robene Huides playes, and vtheris thair assistaris and favouraris, past to [handed out] wappynnis: and thaj brak doun the said jibbat, and then chacit the said provest, baillies and Alexander Guthrie [the town clerk] in the said Alexanderis writting buith [booth], and held thame thairin. (*Diurnal*, 283–4)

It would be nice to be able to report that the rioters had cut James Gillone down from the gallows and marched off with him held shoulder high, but evidently he had still to be taken from his cell in the Tollbooth at this point. Accordingly, the rioters had to break into the jail before they could release him (along with all the other prisoners) and parade him through the streets. No sooner had they vacated the Tollbooth, however, than the provost and bailies took possession of it, only to find themselves under siege: 'thair was nathing but tak and slay, that is the ane pairt schotand furth and castand stanes, the vther pairt schotand hagbutis [muskets] in agane.'[51] After three hours of this, the constable of the castle managed to arrange a truce, and the city officials were constrained finally 'to give their handwrits that they should never pursue any of them that were of that tumult for any crime that was done in that behalf. And this was proclaimed at the Cross after nine hours at night. And so that trouble quieted.'[52] The council was still sufficiently nervous a year later, however, to issue a proclamation in the queen's name that 'on na wys ye permit nor suffer this yeir ony sic as Robene Hude or Litil Jhonne to be chosin, nor that ony vther vnleissum [unlawful] gammis be vseit within oure said burgh quhilk may disquiet the communitie thairof'; and that same year the town council of Aberdeen, significantly, prosecuted a bellman for proclaiming May Games 'eppeirandlie [evidently] to raiss tumult and Ingener [stir up] discord betuix the craftismen and the fre burgess[i]s of gild.'[53]

What, then, were these Edinburgh riots about? Clearly, they were not simply about official opposition to a Robin Hood Play,[54] any more than a riot provoked by an Orange parade in our time is simply about a fife and drum marching band. At root, I wish to suggest, they were about a struggle between two political orders and two systems of law. On one side, an oligarchy of rich burghers dispensing ordinances *ex cathedra* and backed by the omnipresent threat of the gallows; on the other, the community of ordinary citizens, prepared to cart and outlaw those who disturbed its peace, but quick to resist all who sought to interfere with its traditional customs from above.[55] According to Knox, when the provost and bailies appealed for help to the deacons of the rampaging craftsmen in the second of the 1561 riots, they were treated with derision: 'but they passed to their four-hours penny [i.e., their regular penny ale at four o'clock], and in their jesting said, "They will be Magistrates alone, let them rule the multitude alone."'[56] In such a setting, Robin Hood (Robin Hood the violent avenger, not the gentrified good sport of later tradition) offered the people a genuine model for resistance. In the most profound of all the carnivalesque inversions of his legend, 'the outlaw becomes the enforcer of popular law.'

Notes

1 These works are cited from *Rymes of Robyn Hood: An Introduction to the English Outlaw*, ed. R.B. Dobson and J. Taylor (Gloucester 1989), as follows: *A Gest of Robyn Hode* (pp 71–112), *Robin Hood and the Potter* (123–32), *Robin Hood and the Monk* (113–22), *Robin Hood and Guy of Gisborne* (140–5), and *Robin Hood's Death* (A version; 133–7). I have not included here a 15th-century *Ryme of Robyn Hode* (ed. George E. Morris, *Modern Language Review* 43 [1948] 507–8), as being too fragmentary to support any conclusions.

2 S. Knight, *Robin Hood: A Complete Study of the English Outlaw* (Oxford 1994), 69–70 and 88–97.

3 For *Adam Bell, Clim of the Clough, and William of Cloudesly*, see *Rymes of Robyn Hood*, ed. Dobson and Taylor, 258–73; for *Gamelyn*, see *The Complete Works of Geoffrey Chaucer*, ed. W.W. Skeat, 6 vols, 2nd ed. (Oxford 1899–1900), 4: 645–67.
4 *English and Scottish Popular Ballads*, ed. F.J. Child, 5 vols (Cambridge, MA 1882–98), 3: 175–7 (no. 139).
5 *Rymes of Robyn Hood*, ed. Dobson and Taylor, 201–7, at 206.
6 Michel Foucault, *Surveiller et punir: Naissance de la prison* (Paris 1975); trans. Alan Sheridan as *Discipline and Punish: The Birth of the Prison*, 2nd ed. (New York 1995).
7 Thomas W. Laqueur, 'Crowds, Carnival, and the State in English Executions, 1604–1868,' in *The First Modern Society: Essays in English History in Honour of Lawrence Stone*, ed. A.L. Beier, David Cannadine, and James M. Rosenheim (Cambridge 1989), 309.
8 In *Le Temps des supplices: De l'obéissance sous les rois absolus. XVe–XVIIIe siècle* (Paris 1992), 53–76, Robert Muchembled relates a tendency to replace banishment with exemplary and spectacular punishment among the Arrageois after ca 1480 to the rise of absolutism. See also Nicole Gonthier, *Le Châtiment du crime au moyen âge* (Rennes 1998), 170–2 and 190–1.
9 Michel Foucault, *Histoire de la folie à l'âge classique* (Paris 1972 [1961]), 18–24; trans. Richard Howard as *Madness and Civilization: A History of Insanity in the Age of Reason* (New York 1965), 7–17.
10 Foucault, *Surveiller et punir*, 200–1; *Discipline and Punish*, 198–200.
11 Michel Foucault, *La Volonté de savoir: Histoire de la sexualité, I* (Paris 1976), 179ff; trans. Robert Hurley as *The History of Sexuality, Volume 1: An Introduction* (New York 1990 [1978]), 135ff. (Hurley translates *prélèvement* as 'deduction,' which misses the grammatical play.)
12 Frederick Pollock and Frederic William Maitland, *The History of English Law before the Time of Edward I*, 2nd ed., rev. S.F.C. Milsom, 2 vols (Cambridge 1968), 2: 461.
13 *English Lawsuits from William I to Richard I*, ed. R.C. Van Caenegem, 2 vols, Selden Society 106–7 (London 1990–1), 2: 692.
14 Laqueur, 'Crowds, Carnival, and the State,' 311–13.
15 'A Brief Latin Chronicle,' in *Three Fifteenth-Century Chronicles*, ed. James Gairdner (London 1880), 183.
16 *Chronicles of London*, ed. Charles L. Kingsford (Oxford 1905), 182.
17 John Warkworth, *A Chronicle of the First Thirteen Years of the Reign of King Edward the Fourth*, ed. James O. Halliwell (London 1879), 5.
18 *Warkworth's Chronicle*, ed. Halliwell, 9; cf. *The Great Chronicle of London* [Fabyan's Chronicle], ed. A.H. Thomas and I.D. Thornley (London 1938), 213.
19 *Chronicles of London*, ed. Kingsford, 182; *Great Chronicle*, ed. Thomas and Thornley, 213.

20 *Borough Customs*, ed. Mary Bateson, 2 vols, Selden Society 18 and 21 (London 1904–6).
21 For a similar situation at Arras, see Muchembled, *Temps des supplices*, 47–8. The *Coutume general des pays et duché de Bourgogne* (Dijon 1698) notes: 'Chasseneuz [1517] dit, qu'on ne doit pas ériger le signe patibulaire dans les villes, mais hors de leur enceinte. ... Neanmoins parmi nous ... l'on a vu durant un grand nombre d'années le signe patibulaire dans une place publique de cette ville de Dijon' (p. 45).
22 This also seems to have been an earlier penalty at Sandwich (*Borough Customs*, ed. Bateson, 1: 74 n. 6), Fordwich (1: 75 n. 1), and Winchelsea and Rye (1: 76 n. 1).
23 Margaret E. Avery, 'The History of Equitable Jurisdiction of Chancery before 1460,' *Bulletin of the Institute of Historical Research* 42 (1969) 138.
24 *English and Scottish Popular Ballads*, ed. Child, nos 133, 140, and 141.
25 Cf. *Robin Hood Rescuing Will Stutly* (Child no. 141), stanzas 19 and 20.
26 P. Stallybrass, ' "Drunk with the cup of liberty": Robin Hood, the Carnivalesque, and the Rhetoric of Violence in Early Modern England,' *Semiotica* 54 (1985) 113–45.
27 Mikhail Bakhtin, *Rabelais and His World*, trans. Hélène Iswolsky (Bloomington 1984 [1968]).
28 For a discussion of these two positions, see Chris Humphrey, *The Politics of Carnival: Festive Misrule in Medieval England* (Manchester 2001), 11–37.
29 Laqueur, 'Crowds, Carnival, and the State,' 348.
30 *Piers Plowman: The B Version*, ed. George Kane and E. Talbot Donaldson (London 1975), 628. Cf. David J. Siepp, 'Crime in the Year Books,' in *Law Reporting in Britain*, ed. Chantal Stebbings (London 1995), 19 and 27, and *Notes and Queries* 9 (1854) 280 and 453–4; for French examples see Natalie Zemon Davis, *Fiction in the Archives: Pardon Tales and Their Tellers in Sixteenth-Century France* (Stanford 1987), 62–3 and 181 n. 89, and Gonthier, *Châtiment du crime*, 149.
31 Carl Boardman, *Oxfordshire Sinners and Villains* (Stroud 1994), 118–19.
32 E.P. Thompson, *Customs in Common: Studies in Traditional Popular Culture* (New York 1993), 48 n. 3.
33 Bakhtin, *Rabelais*, 36.
34 Ibid., 92.
35 Stallybrass, ' "Drunk with the cup of liberty," ' 115.
36 Ibid., 142.
37 Alan Sinfield, *Faultlines: Cultural Materialism and the Politics of Dissident Reading* (Berkeley 1992), 38ff.
38 Stallybrass, ' "Drunk with the cup of liberty," ' 119.
39 Ibid., 118.
40 Natalie Zemon Davis, 'Charivari, Honor, and Community in Seventeenth-Century Lyon and Geneva,' in *Rite, Drama, Festival, Spectacle*, ed. John J. MacAloon (Philadelphia 1984), 42–57.

41 There exist four sources of information on the Edinburgh riots of 1561: orders from the borough register, a record of legal proceedings against some of the rioters (printed in Anna Jean Mill, *Mediaeval Plays in Scotland*, St Andrews University Publications 24 [New York 1927], 221–2 and n. 2.), and two narrative accounts: the first, a 16th-century journal called the *Diurnal of Remarkable Occurents that have Passed within the Country of Scotland* (ed. Thomas Thomson [Edinburgh 1833]), which seems not to have been known to Stallybrass; the second, John Knox's *History of the Reformation in Scotland* (ed. William C. Dickinson, 2 vols [London 1949]), which he quotes only at second hand. These authorities do not always agree with one another and there are some surprising gaps and inconsistencies, but nevertheless the main outlines are reasonably clear. For an excellent modern account of city politics at this period see Michael Lynch, *Edinburgh and the Reformation* (Edinburgh 1981).

42 The Robin Hood May Games that are mentioned in churchwarden's accounts from various towns and villages in southern England in the late 15th and early 16th centuries were a common way of raising money for parish expenses; see W.E. Simeone, 'The May Games and the Robin Hood Legend,' *Journal of American Folklore* 64 (1951) 271–2.

43 See n. 36 above. For another example, see David Underdown, *Revel, Riot, and Rebellion* (Oxford 1985), 110.

44 Stallybrass, ' "Drunk with the cup of liberty," ' 115.

45 Ibid., 116.

46 Knox, *History of the Reformation*, 1: 355.

47 Ibid., 355–6.

48 Mill, *Mediaeval Plays in Scotland*, 221.

49 Ibid., 221–2 and n. 2. Knox suggests that the rioters were temporarily disarmed, but made such threats of violence that their weapons had to be returned to them (*History of the Reformation*, 1: 357).

50 *Diurnal of Remarkable Occurents*, ed. Thomson, 283.

51 Ibid., 66.

52 Knox, *History of the Reformation*, 1: 359.

53 Both quotations in this sentence are from Mill, *Mediaeval Plays in Scotland*, 223 and 152 respectively.

54 Cf. 'so disappointed were they at being unable to stage a Robin Hood, they rose in fury' (Simeone, 'May Games,' 273).

55 Michael Lynch points out (*Edinburgh and the Reformation*, 94–5) that fifteen of those later arrested for taking part in this disturbance (or for failing to help suppress it) were master craftsmen, not apprentices (they included the deacons of the goldsmiths, bakers, and wrights).

56 Knox, *History of the Reformation*, 1: 358.

13 Canon Laws regarding Female Military Commanders up to the Time of Gratian: Some Texts and Their Historical Contexts

DAVID HAY

> Warfare is the one human activity from which women, with the most insignificant exceptions, have always and everywhere stood apart. Women look to men to protect them from danger ... women, however, do not fight. They rarely fight among themselves and they never, in any military sense, fight men. If warfare is as old as history and as universal as mankind, we must now enter the supremely important limitation that it is an entirely masculine activity.[1]

The preceding quote, taken from the distinguished military historian John Keegan's 1993 monograph, *A History of Warfare*, serves to illustrate the extent to which gender stereotypes continue to be constructed and maintained around the issue of women's participation in warfare. In addition to the firmly entrenched masculine bias of modern military history,[2] the tendency of popular feminism to view war as a manifestation of patriarchy further hinders awareness of female combatants.[3] The underlying assumption, common to many works of military history and popular feminism alike, is that violence – especially the organized violence of warfare – is exclusively and essentially masculine and that women have never engaged in it in any significant way. The work of other scholars has shown, however, that the assumption is quite simply incorrect. In the last two decades alone, several studies of female combatants in modern warfare have documented how women could participate in warfare effectively and in large numbers, as did the Soviet women's combat battalions in the Second World War.[4] Just over one decade ago, the path was cleared for the scholarly study of medieval women by the publication of Meghan McLaughlin's groundbreaking 1990 article 'The Woman Warrior: Gender, Warfare, and Society in Medieval Europe,' in which the author provided numerous examples of medieval 'warrior' women.[5]

In surveying the history of female combatants and attempting to identify general developments, McLaughlin also attempted to prove the more problematic assertion that the number of women engaging in warfare was less in the late Middle Ages than in earlier centuries. Expanding upon the thesis first put forth by Betty Bandel,[6] McLaughlin argued that the attitude of writers towards female warriors grew sharply more negative in the high medieval period. She stated that 'from the late eleventh century on, a variety of sanctions were directed at women who participated in warfare, sanctions ranging from restrictive legislation to ridicule to charges of sexual misconduct or even witchcraft,' and she maintained that such measures, combined with the dissolution of the feudal system, accounted for the apparent decline in the number of women 'warriors' in the later Middle Ages.[7] As an example of such restrictive legislation, McLaughlin cited chapter (*capitulum*) 29 of book 7 of Bonizo de Sutri's late eleventh-century collection of canon law, the *Liber de vita Christiana*.[8]

In the following paper, I examine the text and historical context of Bonizo's chapter and other relevant canons concerning women's participation in medieval warfare during the period leading up to Gratian's authoritative *Decretum* (ca 1140). What such a contextualized analysis of the canonical sources reveals is that Bonizo's legislation was far from new. Although his chapter may have been more explicit than earlier canons, a repressive general attitude towards female sovereigns and military commanders had been firmly entrenched in canon law long before the eleventh century. Moreover, while there is indeed evidence that the canons regarding this issue were modified to a certain extent during the period of the so-called Gregorian Reform, the main direction of the change was initially not away from but rather towards a more liberal stance. To be more specific, certain reforming polemicists and canonists actually accepted and defended a woman's right to exercise military command because they recognized the crucial role played by Countess Matilda of Canossa[9] in defending the reforming papacy from its enemies. Thus, although the canonical texts of the Reform period do in some ways mark a departure from earlier approaches, as a whole they certainly must not be cited as evidence for the *birth* of repressive attitudes. On the contrary, the canons reveal that in the high Middle Ages the early medieval tension between canonical theory (which had sought to restrict women's access to public authority) and military practices (in which women sometimes did exercise command) spread for a brief time into the realm of canon law itself. Nevertheless, the very existence of conflict between opposing canons clearly does contradict the assumptions of Keegan et al. and does, in fact, support McLaughlin's most fundamental assertion: namely, that women did personally participate in medieval warfare, that their actions were socially, legally, and militarily important, and that they cannot be summarily dismissed as mere insignificant exceptions.

An understanding of both the text and the context of Bonizo's prohibitive canon is fundamental to the study of this issue. Bonizo de Sutri (ca 1045–ca 1094) completed his collection of canon law, the *Liber de vita Christiana*, in late 1089 or shortly thereafter.[10] It is the work of a radical reformer with an obvious concern for the lives of the laity, and in it Bonizo defines what he feels to be the divinely appointed roles for all members of Christian society. Book 7 is devoted to the upper ranks of the laity. In the penultimate chapter (28) Bonizo provides an outline of a code of conduct for those who would enter the military profession,[11] while in the final chapter he looks specifically at women holding positions of military and judicial authority.[12] Here he argues that, although women do have a legitimate role to play in Christian society, access to such positions must be restricted to men alone. He states that while the Roman Empire was begun by pagans, its laws nevertheless agree with those of the Lord in this respect: both command that women be subject to men.

Of course, Bonizo is then forced to confront the issue of the numerous women of sacred and secular history who served as military and political leaders. His response is to defend their historicity but to contend that they never ruled over men without causing extraordinary harm to their subjects. To bolster his argument he provides a number of biblical and historical *exempla*, such as Cleopatra, the Frankish queen Fredegund, and the Lombard queen Rosalend,[13] who brought shame, hardship, or even divine destruction down upon themselves and their subjects by daring to contradict the law and to seek military or political offices. Bonizo then discusses the lives of virgins and widows, and concludes the chapter by spelling out what he feels to be proper and improper conduct for the married woman: she should love her husband, tremble under his power, raise his children, and tend his household; she should dread wars and fear soldiers; her concern should be with the loom and the spindle, not with the leading of military expeditions.[14]

If nothing else, such a passage strongly suggests that some of Bonizo's female contemporaries were engaging in warfare. Why else would he have made such an explicit attempt to prohibit them from doing so? In fact, the chapter has long been read as a critique of a particular woman – Countess Matilda of Canossa (1046–1115) – towards whom Bonizo, at the time that he was writing the *Liber de vita Christiana*, had recently developed a bitter animosity.[15] This marks a considerable change of heart on the part of Bonizo,[16] who in an earlier work had showered the countess with praise. After being expelled from his bishopric of Sutri and captured by Emperor Henry IV in 1082,[17] Bonizo had found refuge with Matilda, under whose protection, in 1085 or 1086,[18] he composed a work known as the *Liber ad amicum*.[19] In this historical narrative, written to assure the followers of Gregory that their warfare was licit and to encourage them to fight against the antipope Clement III and his adherents,[20] the author describes the 'gran contessa' in only the most flattering of terms: *excellentissima, nobilissima, gloriosissima*.[21] In the concluding exhortation, Bonizo depicts Matilda as a soldier of God and makes an important allusion to the biblical heroine Jael, who killed Sisara, general of the Canaanites. Here Matilda is praised for having 'a virile mind,' for being a true daughter of St Peter, for being prepared to die to defend the divine law and 'to fight by every means, as long as her resources last, against the heresy which now rages in the Church.'[22]

What apparently transformed Bonizo's attitude towards Matilda was the countess's subsequent alliance with formerly schismatic or imperially invested bishops and her role in facilitating reconciliation between them and the newly consecrated pope, Urban II. In order to convert these prelates to the reform party, Matilda and Urban showed them tremendous leniency, with the pope even going so far as to reordain Daimbert of Pisa[23] and to recall and send a *pallium* to Anselm III of Milan.[24] To Bonizo and the radical Pataria faction[25] – indeed, even to some more moderate reformers – Matilda's intercession on behalf of men who had attained their positions through lay investiture or 'simony' must have represented precisely the type of secular interference in the affairs of the church against which they had fought so tenaciously.[26] To make matters worse, Bonizo appears to have received only lukewarm support from Matilda and Urban for his episcopacy in Piacenza; Bonizo's questionable election and the radical agenda of his Patarene allies apparently conflicted with the countess's and the pope's attempts at reconciliation with their former opponents. As a result, Bonizo was in effect abandoned to his enemies:[27] unable to maintain his position in Piacenza, he was brutally maimed and expelled from the city in 1089.[28] Bonizo responded by denouncing not the pope but Matilda, who, owing to the long history of canonical prohibitions on women's participation in war and politics (which I shall discuss below), provided an easy target.

If we are to read Bonizo's chapter as a thinly veiled criticism of the countess, however, we must first specify which of Matilda's military activities in particular the chapter was intended to condemn. Was Bonizo dismayed that the countess personally wore armour and fought in the ranks like the male soldiers, or was it that she assumed a position of authority over men by acting as their commander? Before scrutinizing Bonizo's canon, let us first survey the historical sources in order to determine whether or not Matilda actually performed either of these functions. The historical sources clearly show that, if nothing else, Matilda was a military leader. Throughout Gregory's reign and into that of Urban II, Matilda was by far the most consistent and important lay defender of the reforming papacy.[29] Without her near-constant campaigning on its behalf, all of Rome and the popes themselves would almost surely have fallen into Emperor Henry IV's hands. An extensive and diverse array of

Canon Laws Regarding Female Military Commanders 291

sources document her exercise of military command: her *vita* and those of her counsellor Anselm describe her issuing orders to the troops; papal letters testify to her involvement in the planning of and recruitment for campaigns;[30] diplomatic sources confirm her presence at sieges and show her building and garrisoning castles and rewarding her vassals for their services in war; and a plethora of both sympathetic and hostile contemporary chronicles detail her numerous campaigns.[31]

Despite the abundance of evidence for Matilda's generalship, however, we cannot be certain that she herself ever used weapons or even wore armour in combat.[32] Early modern authors portray Matilda wielding a lance and wading into the fray with her sword, but the medieval sources are never so explicit. No reliable source from the Middle Ages specifically states that she ever used an actual weapon (as opposed to the symbolic/allegorical 'secular sword,' which symbolized the authority to *direct* legitimate violence), and there is no solid evidence that she ever gave or received wounds on the battlefield.[33] Moreover, unlike modern soldiers, medieval generals did not necessarily have to fight their way up the ranks before being given positions of command.

When assessing the extent of women's involvement in medieval warfare we must proceed cautiously and guard against the tendency, sometimes found in the works of historians anxious to uncover examples of women's power, to elaborate on ambiguous or laconic evidence.[34] While excessive elaboration occurs less frequently than the contrary dismissive approach of Keegan and other military historians, it can nevertheless just as easily lead to historiographical fallacy, particularly in works designed for a popular audience. Thus, in a recent work on medieval women, a manuscript illumination depicting a lady using a sword to behead a man is cited as evidence of women's widespread participation in warfare; what is not mentioned is that the illumination is taken from the entirely allegorical fantasy *Roman de la rose*, wherein personified virtues and vices assume the genders of their corresponding Old French terms![35]

A careful reading of the historical sources, then, supports only the conclusion that Matilda was a 'commander' and leaves open the question of whether or not she was also a 'warrior.' In contrasting these two terms – commander and warrior – I am departing from the methodology of McLaughlin, who rejects the distinction as anachronistic and lacking in any real significance.[36] I would argue that conflating the two terms is even more anachronistic and confusing, and that it renders the task of understanding the true nature of Bonizo's criticism of the countess even more difficult. To begin with, it is certainly questionable to call women like Matilda 'warriors' when they may never have used a weapon in combat. McLaughlin responds to this by arguing that medieval male leaders could often be considered successful 'warriors' – her translation of the words *milites* and *bellatores* – without ever having delivered a blow.[37] The problem with such an argument, however, lies in the different meanings of these Latin terms. *Miles, bellator*, and similar words were indeed often applied indiscriminately to a wide range of individuals, from commanders in charge of thousands of troops to landless retainers fighting in the ranks. Nevertheless, as Guy Halsall has recently noted, when used in this sense the terms are best translated not as 'warriors' but as 'those who make war'[38] – that is to say, they refer to the members of an *ordo* that theoretically possessed a monopoly on legitimate 'public'[39] violence and therefore included both people who fought with weapons and the people who commanded them. This usage, however, does not imply that a conceptual distinction between fighting and commanding was foreign to the period, or that no vocabulary existed to express this distinction. On the contrary, we find numerous passages in which these very terms, *miles* and *bellator*, were used in another sense – the classical, specific one – to distinguish those who actually wielded weapons from the *imperatores* or *duces* who commanded them.[40] William of Malmesbury's description of Henry I of England succinctly illustrates the point: 'Disinclined towards personal combat, he [Henry] verified the saying of Scipio Africanus, 'My mother bore me to be a general [*imperatorem*], not a soldier [*bellatorem*].''[41] The *functions* of warrior and commander could be distinguished even when, as was frequently the case in medieval warfare, a single person was said to have performed both functions simultaneously:

> To Caesar it was sufficient for his glory and his interest to fight with the Britons or the Gauls by commanding; indeed he rarely fought with his own hand. This was the normal custom of the generals of the ancients ... But to William [the Conqueror] it seemed dishonourable and of little use, in that battle in which he crushed the English, to carry out the duties of a general [*officia imperatoris*] unless he also carried out those of a soldier [*officia militis*], as had been the custom in other wars. For in every battle in which he was present he was accustomed to be the first, or among the first, to fight with his sword.[42]

As the people of the Middle Ages were certainly capable of distinguishing between fighting with weapons and commanding the troops, I will hereafter use the term 'warrior' to denote only those who were known to have been trained or to have fought with weapons, and 'commander' to designate only those who are known to have issued orders.

Maintaining the medieval distinction between the *officia imperatoris* and the *officia militis* enables us to explore the effects of class and social status on the experiences of those participating in war. Divergent social pressures and obligations usually ensured that delineations of military function would correspond to pre-existing social boundaries: the uppermost classes were expected to lead, the lower to follow and to fight. Moreover, it is only by distinguishing between classes and their appropriate functions that we can fully appreciate Bonizo's *Liber de vita Christiana* 7.29. For the chapter is quite clearly directed against women of the uppermost class, the class from which commanders rather than soldiers were drawn. It begins with the statement that women should not hold offices of military or judicial authority – the terms used correspond precisely to Matilda's position as feudal overlord of her domains[43] – and the women censured in the chapter (Cleopatra, Fredegund, Deborah, etc.) are queens, rulers, or judges. Moreover, these women are condemned not for wielding weapons themselves but for daring to assume positions of power over men. Thus Mary, sister of Moses, and in her own right judge and leader of the people of Israel, is described as being carried away by feminine unruliness into the sin of pride and as a result being struck with leprosy (a disease commonly seen as God's punishment for those who assumed a role greater than that ordained for them).[44] Conscious of the way in which other reformers (and indeed he himself in his *Liber ad amicum*) have praised Matilda by comparing her to Jael, Bonizo now creates a conceptual distance between the two women by pointing out that Jael was a foreigner with a living husband (Matilda being an Italian whose first husband had died in 1076). In this new interpretation, Matilda now appears more as the type of the widow Deborah,[45] to whom the countess is also frequently compared in contemporary polemics.[46] Unlike other reforming polemicists, however, Bonizo now portrays Deborah as hubristic. In fact, he reinterprets the entire Jael-Deborah-Sisara narrative as a warning to widows against seeking out positions of authority: God denied Deborah the honour of actually killing Sisara, explains Bonizo, lest it serve as an example to widows of holding offices of military leadership [*ducatus*]. With Matilda now safely distanced from Jael, Bonizo is free to portray Jael's use of a weapon (she is said to have killed Sisara by driving a spike through his temple) as an honour conferred on her by God. Clearly, *Liber de vita Christiana* 7.29 was not directed against women who personally wielded weapons *per se*, but against women such as Deborah/Matilda,[47] who held positions of military, political, and judicial authority. Bonizo was not condemning female warriors, but female commanders.

While this repressive stance on the issue of female commanders may have been new to Bonizo,[48] it nevertheless had considerable canonical precedent. This fact is crucial to understanding the high medieval laws regarding women in war. Bonizo's stance was firmly in line with the more conservative perspective of the contemporary imperialist clergy, whose censure Matilda had incurred about fifteen years earlier on account of her service to Pope Gregory – service which, we may note, had included helping him to organize a failed military expedition against the Normans.[49] In response to Matilda's influence at the papal court, the bishops who attended the imperialist synod of Worms in 1076 wrote to Pope Gregory to complain that 'all judgements, all decrees are enacted in the apostolic seat by women, and the laws of the entire world and the Church are administered by women.'[50] Their complaint was, moreover, representative of the general attitude of both secular and canon law since late Antiquity. Thus canon 19 from the council of Nantes, held ca 896, reads:

> Although the apostle says: 'Women should be silent in church, for they are not permitted to speak; for it is shameful for a woman to speak in church'; it is astonishing to see that certain little hussies [*mulierculae*] impudently act, with little shame [*attrita fronte*], against divine and human laws, indecently attend courts and public assemblies and disturb rather than arrange the business of the realm and the republic; although it is indecent, and reprehensible even amongst barbarians, that women disrupt legal proceedings; and that those who ought to debate about weaving and the making of fabric and women's affairs as they sit in their women's workshops [*genitiarias*] publicly usurp the senatorial authority as if they were sitting in the senate. This presumption seems to be considered more disgraceful for their patrons than for the women themselves. Wherefore, since divine laws forbid this (as demonstrated above), and human laws also prohibit that women attend cases other than their own (for the Theodosian Law says that 'On no account should women have the power to prosecute cases other than their own, nor should the case of another be prosecuted by them'), for this reason we order by canonical authority that no chaste young lady [*sanctimonialis virgo*] or widow should risk attendance at court, unless summoned by the prince or by her bishop, or on account of some necessity (and this with a license from the bishop).[51]

It is true that Bonizo's chapter is somewhat more explicit than this canon. Bonizo did not simply reiterate the ancient general prohibitions on women assuming public authority, but rather expanded them in order to transform them into a more specific indictment of Matilda.[52] Thus, like Nantes 19, he cites the passage from Paul, 1 Cor. 14:34–5 (that women should be silent in church and that it is shameful for a woman to speak), but he then adds his own interpretation that it must therefore be all the more shameful for women to rule the people.[53] Nevertheless, the similarities between the two chapters are striking. Both Bonizo and Nantes state that divine and human law agree that women should not hold public power.[54] Regarding the 'divine law,' both include 1 Cor. 14: 34–5; as to the human law, the Council of Nantes specifically quotes the *Breviary of Alaric*,[55] and it is this legislation to which Bonizo is apparently referring as the 'Roman Laws' he mentions in the first sentence of his chapter 29. Both Bonizo's chapter and the Nantes canon 19 attempt to define the limits of feminine propriety by restricting women to the gendered roles of spinning and weaving, and by denying them access to public authority. Finally, both mention the shamelessness of women who refuse to abide by such restrictions: in the canon from Nantes they are described as acting *attrita fronte*, and in Bonizo *feminea licentia, feminea audatia*.

Obviously, then, repressive legislation predates the Gregorian Reform. Although the Pauline letters, the *Lex Theodosiana*, and other sources from Antiquity had not specifically named female commanders, they had prohibited women from attending assemblies and holding most public offices. These restrictions, if enforced, would have made exercising military command extremely difficult, if not impossible. The prohibitive agenda then passed from secular and scriptural sources into early medieval canon law and proved consistently popular.[56] Indeed, the Nantes canon 19 found its way into many of the subsequent major collections of the pre-Reform era, including Regino of Prüm's *Libri duo de synodalibus causis et disciplinis ecclesiasticis* (ca 906)[57] and Burchard of Worms's *Decretum* (compiled between 1008 and 1012).[58] Several other collections either included Nantes 19 or the lines from Paul or used still other material to separate women from warfare and prohibit them from holding public or 'male' offices.[59]

In the Gregorian period, however, we begin to see signs of an alternative to this tradition. Interestingly, while Nantes 19 found its way into major pre-Gregorian collections, it was not included in the works of the two most influential reforming canonists, Anselm of Lucca and Cardinal Deusdedit. Granted, these men did not display as great an interest in the lives of the laity as Bonizo did, but both were firmly within the Gregorian camp and both defended the legitimacy of Matilda's military campaigns in their polemical works.[60] Moreover, if Anselm and Deusdedit's silence on Nantes 19 merely hints at an alternative approach to the issue of women's involvement in warfare, the inclusion in their collections of another canon speaks volumes. For both Anselm of Lucca's *Collectio canonum* (completed ca 1081–6)[61] and Deusdedit's *Collectio canonum* (completed 1087)[62] contain a previously obscure passage from one of Gregory the Great's letters to the Frankish queen Brunhild, in which the pope sanctions her use of force against the violent and the wicked.[63] In the centuries leading up to the Gregorian period, this passage had been all but completely ignored by canonists, regardless of their political orientation.[64] Although the extant sources do not provide much information regarding the life and career of Deusdedit, our more precise knowledge of Anselm's life and the historical context of his collection supports the idea that Anselm interpreted the letter to Brunhild as a justification of Matilda's military activities. Like Bonizo, Anselm had been protected by the countess after being expelled from his seat in late 1080 or early 1081.[65] Until he died in 1086, Anselm served not only as Matilda's military and political ally but as her spiritual counsellor, and his collection is quite clearly an attempt to justify the Gregorians' use of force.[66] In fact, book 13 of his *Collectio canonum* is the first major systematic canonical justification of warfare in the Christian tradition, and as such was fundamentally important for later Christian approaches to organized violence.[67] It is therefore significant that, in the A recension of his collection, Gregory the Great's letter is given the rubric 'That the power to correct evildoers is granted to the queen.'[68] Although we cannot be absolutely sure that these are Anselm's own words (at least until the thorny problem of the relationship between the different recensions of his collection is definitively settled),[69] it is clear that either he or several of his recensors read the canon, not just as a general justification of the use of force (as it was later to be interpreted by Gratian), but as a specific justification of female military authority.

The Gregorian age can thus be described as one of controversy regarding not only papal authority but also the licit range of women's authority. Matilda's military career engendered a disagreement over the legitimacy of female commanders that can be traced in the collections of the period. If any canon broke with the tradition of the previous few centuries, however, it was clearly not Bonizo's but Anselm's.

If Bonizo's canon was the less original of the two, was it at least the more influential? Did it lead later canonists to issue specific condemnations of female commanders? If we trace the development of legislation regarding women's authority up to about 1140, when Gratian completed his *Decretum* (which became the authoritative and universally accepted collection of canon law), we find that in fact neither Bonizo's nor Anselm's canons had a major impact on subsequent ecclesiastical laws.

Let us begin by briefly examining the works attributed to Ivo of Chartres (ca 1040–1115), which constituted some of the most important collections compiled in the period between the Gregorians and Gratian. Ivo either ignored or was unaware of Bonizo's *Liber de vita Christiana* 7.29; likewise, he did not include Anselm's *Collectio canonum* 13.23 in any of his three collections (completed ca 1093–6).[70] What Ivo did do was return to the early medieval tradition by including Nantes 19 in his *Decretum* (7.103) and retain it as a general prohibition of women's public authority. Ivo also took a further step by including in his *Decretum* a host of other canons that echoed Nantes 19 but were derived from even more ancient sources – namely, patristic authors – whose importance as authorities for canon law was increasing at this time.[71] These chapters, namely *Decretum* 8.85, 91–2, and 94–8, are taken exclusively from the church fathers (five from Augustine, two from Ambrose, one from pseudo-Ambrose, and one from Jerome), and all are used to argue that women must be subject to men.[72] Interestingly, when writing his *Panormia* a year or two later, Ivo appears to have felt that this patristic material rendered Nantes

19 redundant; for while the *Panormia* does contain *Decretum* 8.85, 91–2, and 94–8, it does not contain Nantes 19. We can therefore conclude that, taken as a whole, the Ivonian collections marked a return not to Bonizo but to the yet more ancient misogyny of the church fathers.

The collections compiled after Ivo's works, up to and including Gratian's *Decretum*, document how subsequent canonists adopted the ancient texts and doctrine sanctioned by Ivo. To begin with, there was the enormous popularity of the *Panormia* itself, which was one of the most frequently used collections of canon law in the entire medieval period. After its publication, many lesser-known canonists used its chapters in their own works.[73] Finally, we find Gratian, in his *Decretum* or *Concord of Discordant Canons* (published ca 1140), following the approach taken by the later Ivo, excluding Nantes 19 and instead incorporating all of his *Panormia* 7.43–51 into Causa 33, quaestio 5, capitula 11–19 [C.33 q.5 cc.11–19] of the *Concord*.[74]

In fact, neither Bonizo's specific prohibition of women's military authority nor Anselm's justification of it was accepted by Gratian. The Bologna master, like most canonists of his time, ignored or was simply unaware of Bonizo's *Liber de vita Christiana* 7.29.[75] Anselm's work, as a material source for twelfth-century canonists interested in the legitimacy of organized violence, proved far more influential than that of Bonizo, and we find that Gratian himself made use of the letter from Gregory to Brunhild (C.23 q.4 c.47). Nevertheless, the presentation of this letter in the *Concord* was such as to direct it away from justifying women's military authority. Although the inscription does state that the text is excerpted from Gregory's letter to Brunhild, in the *Concord of Discordant Canons* the passage appears, not under the title 'That the power of correcting evildoers is granted to the queen,' but following the rubric 'That omnipotent God is appeased by the correction of the evil.'[76] With the fact that power to correct malefactors had been granted to a queen no longer stressed, the canon's ability to legitimize women's military authority was substantially weakened. It was then counterbalanced by the repressive Ivonian texts and rubrics, which, as noted above, Gratian reproduced in full. Some ambiguity may have remained in the fact that Gratian did not place the repressive texts alongside the letter to Brunhild in C.23 (which dealt with the legitimacy of forms of warfare), but in C.33 (which discussed rights within marriage and the conjugal debt). Nevertheless, on the whole it can be said that Gratian's thought on these issues, like that of Ivo, constituted a reiteration of the traditional repressive orthodoxy of the late antique and early medieval laws.

Obviously, the situation regarding the status of female commanders in eleventh-century canonical texts is somewhat more complex than a straightforward hardening of attitudes. In the eleventh century, gender stereotypes were constructed, developed, and maintained around the issue of the female commander, and many of the clergy held very negative views regarding women's participation in war and government. This must not, however, obscure the fact (sometimes overlooked in studies based on historical texts alone) that the laws and the attitudes sustaining them were already ancient. If one compares, as McLaughlin and Bandel do,[77] the laconic annals of the early Middle Ages to the more descriptive histories of the high Middle Ages, one may find in the latter more instances of women being criticized for engaging in warfare;[78] but does this relative abundance of high medieval criticism indicate a real change in attitudes or simply the proliferation of historical writing?[79] This is a question which the study of the canonical sources can help us to answer. Bonizo's chapter 29 may have constituted a more explicit denial of women's military authority than had hitherto been heard, but it was in fact merely an extension of more general late antique and early medieval legislation that had invoked both divine and human laws to prohibit women from assuming public office. Moreover, as we have demonstrated, it was not to Bonizo himself but to the ancient misogyny of Antiquity and the early Middle Ages that the most influential high-medieval canonists returned. The most novel aspect of the collections and the polemics of the eleventh century, then, was not Bonizo's attempt to repress women's military authority but other Gregorians' efforts, in light of Matilda's importance to the reform papacy, to provide it with a canonical basis. Surveyed as a whole, the canon laws of the Reform period do not appear so much to have inhibited Matilda's ability to command her forces as to have justified it. Even after the publication of Bonizo's *Liber de vita Christiana* the countess continued to lead armies and take an active role in politics,[80] and the authors who praised Matilda for this continued to be at least as numerous and as influential as those who condemned her for it.[81]

Whether other women were as fortunate as Matilda remains to be seen. Much work is still to be done if we are to trace the course of the canons beyond Gratian and to understand them within the context of other social and military developments. It may be that after Gratian new, more specifically restrictive, canons appeared, or that individuals and institutions grew more capable of enforcing the traditional general prohibitions, but I have not as yet found much evidence for this. We do know that a prohibition of women's involvement in war appeared in at least one later, non-canonical source,[82] but on the other hand the charges against Joan of Arc seem to have been directed more against her practice of wearing men's clothing than leading armies *per se*.[83] Without more studies of specific women like Matilda, and without studies that distinguish between women not only of different times but of different classes and military functions, it is premature to conclude that women were less inclined to participate in warfare in the late than in the high or early Middle Ages. We simply do not know much about middle- and lower-class women, but what we know of upper-class women indicates that many of them continued to take active roles in war well into the late medieval period.[84] Moreover, the numerous examples of women who disguised themselves as men in order to join modern armies suggests that the numbers of female warriors and commanders may be even greater than the sources would indicate.[85] Armed with a more precise vocabulary and methodology, however, we are now able to demonstrate that there was considerable continuity in attempts to prohibit women from serving as commanders throughout the early and high Middle Ages. We can also show how this view was repeatedly challenged not only by the activities of women like Matilda but even, for a brief period in the late eleventh century when the debate about the authenticity of ecclesiastical traditions reached a crescendo, by the polemical pamphlets and canonical treatises of certain prominent Gregorians. The question, very much alive in this period, was which to follow: the traditional, theoretical prohibitions established by St Paul, Roman law, and the early medieval canons, or the newer approach, which relied on the practices of women of sacred and secular history and the ostensible sanction of Gregory the Great's letter to Brunhild. Although ultimately Gratian's work appears to have resolved the dispute in favour of repression, the scope and virulence of the controversy, to say nothing of the remarkably successful career of Matilda herself, constitute the most telling refutation of the all-too-common assumption that warfare is the one human activity from which women 'have always and everywhere stood apart.'

Notes

1   John Keegan, *A History of Warfare* (New York 1993), 76.
2   Consider, e.g., the work of Kelly DeVries, who is one of the few prominent military historians to study a woman's military career. In his otherwise excellent *Joan of Arc: A Military Leader* (Stroud 1999), even he includes some lamentable pages on questions such as 'Was she sexually attractive?', and exaggerates the lack of other women's participation in war in order to present Joan as unprecedented and unique (pp 31–3). See also DeVries, 'A Woman as Leader of Men: Joan of Arc's Military Career,' in *Fresh Verdicts on Joan of Arc*, ed. Bonnie Wheeler and Charles T. Wood (New York 1996), 4 and n. 4, where he states that by Joan's time 'those few occasions in earlier medieval history of women leading soldiers were not well known, were thought to be mythological, or were, at best, a distant historical memory,' and that he has found 'no evidence of late-medieval women warriors other than Joan.'

Leaving aside the problematic question of the extent to which medieval authors distinguished between myth and history, one need only pick up the letters of

Margaret Paston (*The Paston Letters: A Selection in Modern Spelling*, ed. Norman Davis [London 1963], nos 7, 63, 70–1, and 87) or examine the numerous women cited in R. Archer, '"How Ladies ... who live on their manors ought to manage their households and estates": Women as Landholders and Administrators in the Later Middle Ages,' in *Woman is a Worthy Wight: Women in English Society, c. 1200–1500*, ed. P.J.P. Goldberg (Wolfeboro Falls, NH 1992), 160–1, in order to find examples of late medieval women participating in war. The common necessity of having to defend one's estates even led Christine de Pisan to advise noble ladies to familiarize themselves with all things military: 'We have also said that she ought to have the heart of a man, that is, she ought to know how to use weapons and be familiar with everything that pertains to them, so that she may be ready to command her men if the need arises. She should know how to launch an attack, or defend against one ...' Christine de Pisan, *Treasure of the City of Ladies; or, The Book of Three Virtues*, trans. Sarah Lawson (New York 1985), 129.

3 Helen Nicholson, 'Women on the Third Crusade,' *Journal of Medieval History* 23.4 (1997) 335–49, at 342.

4 Even the opponents of assigning women to combat roles in modern armies acknowledge the contributions of Soviet women: Jeff M. Tuten, 'The Argument against Female Combatants' and 'Germany and the World Wars,' in *Female Soldiers – Combatants or Noncombatants?*, ed. Nancy Loring Goldman (Westport, CT 1982). The same volume also contains several other studies of modern women combatants.

5 Megan McLaughlin, 'The Woman Warrior: Gender, Warfare, and Society in Medieval Europe,' *Women's Studies* 17 (1990) 193–209. There are, of course, a number of earlier studies of women in war, but they tend to be rather unscholarly in method. Mary Beard's *Women as Force in History* (New York 1946) and Antonia Fraser's *The Warrior Queens* (New York 1989) are perhaps the two best-known examples. After the publication of McLaughlin's paper, more scholarly studies have begun to appear, the most notable of which are Nicholson's (see n. 3 above) and Jean A. Truax's 'Anglo-Norman Women at War: Valiant Soldiers, Prudent Strategists, or Charismatic Leaders?' in *The Circle of War in the Middle Ages: Essays on Medieval Military and Naval History*, ed. Donald J. Kagay and L.J. Andrew Villalon (Woodbridge 1999), 111–25. On McLaughlin's use of the term 'warrior' to describe these women, see below.

6 Betty Bandel, 'The English Chroniclers' Attitude toward Women,' *Journal of the History of Ideas* 16 (1955) 113–18. Note, however, that Bandel's argument only extended to *English* chroniclers' attitudes.

7 McLaughlin, 'Woman Warrior,' 200; see also 201ff. Earlier in the same article (p. 195), citing Bandel, McLaughlin writes: 'From the late eleventh century on, confrontation with behavior considered unusual for women began to elicit strong reactions, in which assumptions about gender were fully expressed.'

8 Bonizo de Sutri, *Liber de vita Christiana*, ed. Ernst Perels, foreword by Walter Berschin (Hildesheim 1998).
9 Otherwise known as 'la gran contessa' or 'Matilda of Tuscany.' The latter is not a particularly accurate title, for although Matilda was indeed the countess of Tuscany, her family's most ancient possessions – and the military core of her dominions – lay in Emilia (with the lordship radiating outwards from the ancestral castle of Canossa in the Emilian Apennines). Mantua, acquired by her father Boniface and situated still further to the north on the plain of the Po, is considered by many to have been the political 'capital': see Giuseppe Sissa, 'L'azione della contessa Matilde in Mantova e nel suo contado (l'Abbazia di San Benedetto Pollirone),' in *Studi matildici: Atti e memorie del convegno di studi matildici, Modena e Reggio Emilia, 19–21 ottobre 1963* (Modena 1964), 147. For a general bibliography of Matilda see L.L. Ghirardini, *Storia critica di Matilde di Canossa* (Modena 1989), 385ff.
10 Walter Berschin, *Bonizo von Sutri: Leben und Werk* (New York 1972) 23; cf. idem, 'Bonizone da Sutri e lo stato di vita laicale: Il codice Mantova 439,' in *Sant'Anselmo, Mantova, e la lotta per le investiture: Atti del convegno internazionale di studi (Mantova 23-24-25 maggio 1986)*, ed. P. Golinelli (Bologna 1987), 281–90, at 284.
11 *Liber de vita Christiana* 7.28 (ed. Perels, 248–9). Many at the time remained unsure as to whether a Christian could legitimately take up arms, and Bonizo's earlier work, the *Liber ad amicum*, was in part a response (in the affirmative) to this question. On this work see below.
12 *Liber de vita Christiana* 7.29 (ed. Perels, 249–51).
13 Jacques Fournier, 'Bonizo de Sutri, Urbain II, et la comtesse Mathilde d'après le *Liber de vita Christiana* de Bonizo,' *Bibliothèque de l'École des chartres* 76 (1915) 265–98, at 294, notes that he probably meant Rosemond.
14 'Maritata est, diligat virum, sub eius tremescat imperio, filios nutriat, sue domus curam gerat, bella horrescat, armatos formidet, pacem diligat, pensa et colum et fusos et stamina, linum lanamque et sericum gestet in manibus; de expeditionibus vero ordinandis non magnopere curet.' Bonizo, *Liber de vita Christiana* 7.29 (ed. Perels, 251).
15 Fournier, 'Bonizo de Sutri'; cf. Berschin, *Bonizo von Sutri*, esp. 16–17 and n. 62.
16 This was in fact but one aspect of a noticeable transformation of Bonizo's mentality: see Berschin, *Bonizo von Sutri*, 15–17; H. Saur, 'Studien über Bonizo,' *Forschungen zur deutschen Geschichte* 8 (1868) 432; and Fournier, 'Bonizo de Sutri.'
17 Bernold of Constance, *Chronicon*, ed. G. Waitz, MGH Scriptores 5 (Hanover 1844), 437; see also Berschin, *Bonizo von Sutri*, 9–10.
18 Berschin, *Bonizo von Sutri*, 22–3 and n. 78.
19 On the identity of the 'amicus' – once thought to be Matilda herself – see ibid., 10 and n. 35. On the sources for Bonizo during this period see ibid., 10ff.

302 David Hay

20 'Sed cum superius a me quesisses, amice dulcissime, si licet christiano armis pro veritate certare, hystoriam petebas.' Bonizo, *Liber ad amicum*, ed. E. Dümmler, MGH LdL 1 (Hanover 1891), VIIII, p. 618.
21 Ibid., 599, 602, 605, 606, 609, 610, 612, 613.
22 'Igitur pugnent gloriosissimi Dei milites pro veritate, certent pro iustitia, pugnent vero animo adversus heresim, extollentem se adversus omne, quod dicitur vel quod colitur deus. Emulentur in bonum excellentissimam comitissam Matildam, filiam beati Petri, que virili animo, omnibus mundanis rebus posthabitis, mori parata est potius quam legem Dei infringere et contra heresim, que nunc sevit in ecclesia, prout vires suppetunt, omnibus modis impugnare; in manu cuius credimus quia tradetur Sisara, et sicut Iabin in torrente Cison disperiet ...' Bonizo, *Liber ad amicum*, 620. See also Ludovico Gatto, 'Matilde di Canossa nel *Liber ad amicum* di Bonizone da Sutri,' in *Studi matildici: Atti e memorie del II convegno di studi matildici, Modena-Reggio E., 1-2-3 maggio 1970* (Modena 1971), 307–25.
23 At Matilda's request, Urban also gave jurisdiction over Corsica to Daimbert, as we know from one of Urban's letter's (PL 151: 344–6); cf. Bernold, *Chronicon* a. 1095 (ed. Waitz, 461): 'Domnus papa Urbanus ... nativitatem Domini in Tuscia gloriosissime celebravit; in qua provincia Pisanus episcopus, nomine Dagobertus, ei studiossime servivit, quem ipse iam dudum archiepiscopali pallio et potestate sublimavit, quod eatenus Pisanae sedis episcopus habere non consuevit.' This was the same Daimbert who later became patriarch of Jerusalem.
24 Berschin, *Bonizo von Sutri*, 17 and n. 63; H.E.J. Cowdrey, 'The Papacy, the Patarines, and the Church of Milan,' *Transactions of the Royal Historical Society*, 5th ser. 18 (1968) 25–48, at 45; Carl Erdmann, *The Origin of the Idea of Crusade*, trans. Marshall W. Baldwin and Walter Goffart (Princeton 1977), 313–14. We may also note that shortly afterwards Matilda and her new husband Welf concluded an alliance with Milan and other Lombard cities against the emperor: see Bernold, *Chronicon* a. 1093 (ed. Waitz, 456).
25 On the Pataria see C. Violante, *La Pataria milanese e la riforma ecclesiastica*, I: *Le premese* (Rome 1955); P. Golinelli, *La Pataria: Lotte religiose e sociali nella Milano dell'XI secolo* (Milan 1984); Cowdrey, 'Papacy, Patarines, and the Church of Milan.'
26 Berschin, *Bonizo von Sutri*, 17 n. 63; Cowdrey, 'Papacy, Patarines, and the Church of Milan.' On reactions to the reordination of Daimbert see Fournier, 'Bonizo de Sutri,' 288.
27 Fournier, 'Bonizo de Sutri,' 273–4; Berschin, *Bonizo von Sutri*, 11–12.
28 'Bonizo piae memoriae Sutriensis episcopus, set inde pro fidelitate sancti Petri iam dudum expulsus, tandem post multas captiones, tribulationes et exilia, a Plancentinis catholicis pro episcopo redipetur; set a scismaticis eiusdem loci effosis oculis, truncatis omnibus pene menbris martirio coronatur.' Bernold,

Chronicon a. 1080 (ed. Waitz, 449). On interpreting this passage and the other sources for these events, see Fournier, 'Bonizo de Sutri,' 272ff.

29 Robert Guiscard, although perhaps more powerful than Matilda, was also much more fickle and unreliable, and he died early in the struggle (1085).

30 Unlike McLaughlin ('Woman Warrior,' 196), I consider operational planning to be an important aspect of women's participation in warfare; it is certainly an essential part of generalship.

31 I examine this issue in more depth in my doctoral dissertation, 'The Campaigns of Countess Matilda of Canossa (1046–1115): An Analysis of the History and Social Significance of a Woman's Military Leadership' (University of Toronto PhD diss., 2000). For a brief summary of her campaigns to 1092, see Valerie Eads, 'The Campaigns of Matilda of Tuscany,' *Minerva* 4 (1986) 167–81. For Matilda's involvement in the 'Crusade' of 1074 see n. 49 below. For her military activities in general see *Vita Anselmi episcopi Lucensis*, ed. R. Wilmans, MGH Scriptores 12 (Hanover 1856), 1–35, passim; Donizo, *Vita Mathildis celeberrimae princeps Italiae*, ed. Luigi Simeoni, 2nd ed., Rerum Italicarum scriptores 5.2 (Bologna 1940), passim; Rangerius of Lucca, *Vita metrica S. Anselmi Lucensis episcopi*, ed. E. Sackur et al., MGH Scriptores 30.2 (Leipzig 1926–34), 1152–1307, passim; *Chronica monasterii Casinensis* 3.69, ed. H. Hoffmann, MGH Scriptores 34 (Hanover 1980), 750. Matilda's later campaigns, perhaps lacking the glamour of the war against the emperor, have not been properly studied, but certainly do provide some very good evidence of Matilda's generalship. She was involved in organizing or leading campaigns against Ferrara (1101), Parma (1104), and Mantua (1114), for which Donizo is the best source. She also issued two diplomas testifying to her presence at the siege of Prato in 1107: *Die Urkunden und Briefe der Markgräfin Mathilde von Tuszien*, ed. Elke Goez and Werner Goez, MGH Laienfürsten und Dynastenurkunden der Kaiserzeit 2 (Hanover 1998), nos 102–3.

32 The only evidence that she wore armour is the somewhat suspect testimony of Vedriani, who claims that two suits of Matilda's armour were sold in Reggio in 1622: Pietro Vedriani, *Historia dell'antichissima citta di Modena*, 2 vols (Modena 1666), 2: 19.

33 As Jean Truax notes, the same is true of Anglo-Norman women: the sources rarely if ever portray them wielding weapons in open battles. However, she goes on to prove that 'despite the fact that Anglo-Norman women apparently did not fight in battle alongside their male contemporaries, there is no doubt that the chroniclers considered them capable of commanding the defense of besieged castles and directing the movements of armies in the field. In their minds, a woman did not need actual combat experience in order to be qualified to make strategic decisions.' Truax, 'Anglo-Norman Women at War,' 123.

34 Ibid., 111.
35 The illumination is cited in Carol Adams et al., *From Workshop to Warfare: The Lives of Medieval Women* (Cambridge 1983), 7, with the inscriptions 'A lady might have to defend herself and her household against attacks' and 'These women are defending their castle. How are the men reacting?' For a description of the MS see Otto Pacht and J. J. G. Alexander, *Illuminated Manuscripts in the Bodleian Library*, 3 vols (Oxford 1966–73), 1: 61 (MS. Douce 195).
36 In rebutting the charge that the women she describes as 'warriors' may more properly be termed 'generals,' McLaughlin argues that 'the decisive test [of a female combatant] would seem to be whether someone was present at and involved in a battle to a significant degree, not the number of blows she struck' ('Woman Warrior,' 196). Thus, for McLaughlin, all women personally 'involved in' warfare – excluding those who merely planned expeditions – are to be considered 'warriors.'
37 McLaughlin, 'Woman Warrior,' 196.
38 Halsall notes that 'to medieval people in the theorization of the *ordines* of their society, aristocrats were *bellatores:* those who fight (or, more accurately, those who make war, which is an important difference).' Guy Halsall, 'Violence and Society in the Early Medieval West: An Introductory Survey,' in *Violence and Society in the Early Medieval West*, ed. Halsall (Woodbridge 1998), 1–45, at 5.
39 Although the distinction between 'public' and 'private' violence is admittedly sometimes a murky one, I believe it is still useful to make. On this issue see Halsall, 'Violence and Society,' 9–10.
40 The term *imperator* meant, quite literally, 'commander.' *Dux* was usually synonymous, indicating military command – see, e.g., William of Poitiers, *Gesta Guillelmi* 2.40, ed. and trans. R.H.C. Davis and Marjorie Chibnall (Oxford 1998), 174, where the term is used to describe Caesar.
41 'Minus pugnacis famae, Scipionis Africani dictum repraesentabat, "Imperatorem me mea mater, non bellatorem, peperit." Quapropter sapientianulli unquam modernorum regum secundus ...' William of Malmesbury, *Gesta regum Anglorum* 5.412, ed. T.D. Hardy, 2 vols, Publications of the English Historical Society (Vaduz 1964), 2: 642.
42 'Caesari satis fuerat ad laudem vel utilitatem praelia cum Britannis, uti cum Gallis, imperando facere; equidem sua manu raro pugnavit. Haec multa ducum antiquorum consuetudo fuit ... At dedecus visum est Guillelmo, ac parum utile, in eo conflictu quo contriuit Anglos officia praestare imperatoris , nisi praestaret officia quoque militis, uti bellis aliis consueuerat: in omni enim certamine ubi praesens aderat, primus aut in primis gladio suo pugnare solitus erat.' William of Poitiers, *Gesta Guillelmi* 2.40 (ed. Davis and Chibnall, 172). The translation is that of Davis and Chibnall.
43 'ut non ducatus teneant nec iudicatus regant.' Bonizo, *Liber de vita Christiana*

7.29 (ed. Perels, 249). Fournier, 'Bonizo de Sutri,' 295, first noted that the term *ducatus* corresponds to Matilda's military and political jurisdiction as countess of Tuscany. I would add that Bonizo's use of the term *iudicatus* is just as obviously directed at Matilda, since we know that Matilda frequently presided over courts; for instances of this see Goez and Goez, *Urkunden und Briefe*, nos 21–2, 24, 30–2, 52, 58–60. Cf. Elke Goez, *Beatrix von Canossa und Tuszien: Eine Untersuchung zur Geschichte des 11. Jahrhunderts*, Vorträge und Forschungen, Sonderband 41 (Sigmaringen 1995), 91–2, who argues that Beatrice and Matilda were virtually 'the first women who regularly held their own *placita*.'

44 'Si quis vero mihi obiecerit sororem Moysi Mariam ducem fuisse populi Israel et iudicem, non abnuo; set audio eam feminea licentia in superbiam elatam. Si enim dux non esset, nec superbiret nec extra castra mansisset ad breve leprosa.' Bonizo, *Liber de vita Christiana* 7.29 (ed. Perels, 250). Other examples of leprosy as divine punishment are provided in the letter of Damian reproduced by Deusdedit in his *Collectio canonum*, ed. V.W. von Glanvell, *Die Kanonessammlung des Kardinals Deusdedit* (Paderborn 1905): 'Azarias rex quia sacerdotale usurpat officium, lepra perfunditur' (c. 246, p. 534); also '... et Ozias rex lepra percussus est, quia officium turrificandi assumpsit' (c. 247, p. 536).

45 On the perception of Deborah as a widow, see Berschin, *Bonizo von Sutri*, 16 n. 59.

46 E.g., *Vita Anselmi episcopi Lucensis* c. 11 (ed. Wilmans, 16): '... ut quasi altera Delbora populum iudicet, militiam peragat, haereticis ac schismaticis resistat'; Paul of Bernried, *Vita Gregorii VII*, in *Pontificum Romanorum ... vitae*, ed. J.B.M. Watterich, 2 vols (Aalen 1966), 1: 506. Donizo, *Vita Mathildis* 2.743–50 (ed. Simeoni, 80), compares Matilda to both Deborah and Jael.

We should note that at the time Bonizo was writing Matilda had recently remarried (on the date of her marriage to Welf see L.L. Ghirardini, *Storia critica di Matilde di Canossa* [Modena 1989] ch. 4, esp. 146ff.). She continued to be portrayed as a widow, however, in some polemical sources (e.g., Rangerius, *Vita metrica* 1292, has Matilda's enemies calling her a widow), while her biographer Donizo simply avoids mentioning her purely political and ultimately unsuccessful marriage to Welf of Bavaria in 1088. Bonizo responds to Matilda's conduct as both widow and married woman at the end of his chapter. First he states that widows must not associate with 'calamistratos vel barbatulos pueros' (Welf was 16, Matilda 42 at the time of their marriage); then he warns that if widows remarry they must refrain from leading military expeditions.

On the comparisons of Matilda to biblical figures like Jael and Deborah in general see Giampaolo Ropa, 'Studio e utilazzione ideologica della bibbia nell' ambiente Matildico (sec. XI–XII),' in *Studi matildici: Atti e memorie del III convegno di studi matildici, Reggio Emilia, 7–9 ottobre 1977* (Modena 1978).

47 Berschin, *Bonizo von Sutri*, 17 n. 62, writes that if one considers what Deborah

and Jael mean in the polemical literature, this chapter must be read as a hidden criticism of Matilda.

48 In addition to praising Matilda in the *Liber ad amicum*, Bonizo also describes how the wife of the Roman emperor Valens succeeded (where her husband had failed) in delivering Constantinople from the attacks of the barbarians (*Liber ad amicum* 575). In general, however, Bonizo's attitude towards female rulers in the *Liber ad amicum* is rather harsh. He denounces Empess Agnes's 'feminine unruliness,' describing how she 'regni tenebat gubernacula. Que multa contra ius feminea faciebat audacia' (593) and how, when the Lombard bishops sought to elect an antipope, 'animumque imperatricis utpote femineum alliciunt, figmenta quedam componentes quasi veri similia ... His et talibus machinationibus decepta imperatrix feminea licentia assensum dedit operi nefario ...' (594–5). The terms he uses here – *feminea audacia, feminea licentia* – are the same ones he employs later in his *Liber de vita Christiana*. I would suggest that his praise of Matilda in the *Liber ad amicum* is not so much indicative of his general attitude towards female rulers as it is an immediate and emotional response to the countess's generosity. On the relationship between the *Liber ad amicum* and the *Liber de vita Christiana* in general see Berschin, *Bonizo von Sutri*, 70–1.

49 Matilda intended to be one of the leaders of the campaign but, called away by other military necessities, she was prevented from linking up with the pope. On this expedition, which was also aimed at aiding Christians in the East (once the Normans were subjugated), see H.E.J. Cowdrey, 'Pope Gregory VII's "Crusading" Plans of 1074,' in *Outremer: Studies in the History of the Crusading Kingdom of Jerusalem*, ed. B.Z. Kedar, H.E. Mayer, and R.C. Smail (Jerusalem 1982); repr. in Cowdrey's *Popes, Monks, and Crusaders* (London 1984), 27–40.

50 'Quamvis hec generalis querela ubique personuerit: omnia iudicia omnia decreta per feminas in sede apostolica actitari, denique per feminas totius orbis et ecclesiae iura amministrari.' *Monumenta Bambergensia* 48, ed. Philipp Jaffé, Bibliotheca rerum Germanicarum 5 (Berlin 1869), 106. Cf. the specific criticism of Matilda in the imperialist polemic *Liber de unitate ecclesiae conservanda* 2.36, ed. W. Schwenkenbecher, MGH LdL 2 (Hanover 1892), 263, lines 14–30.

51 'Cum apostolus dicat: Mulieres in ecclesia taceant, non enim permittitur eis loqui: turpe est enim mulieri loqui in ecclesia; Mirum videtur, quod quaedam mulierculae, contra divinas humanasque leges attrita fronte impudenter agentes, placita generalia et publicos conventus indesinenter adeant, et negotia regni, utilitatesque reipublicae magis perturbent, quam disponant: cum indecens sit, et etiam inter barbaras gentes reprehensibile, mulieres virorum causas discutere; et quae de lanificiis suis, et operibus textilibus, et muliebribus, inter genitiarias suas residentes, debuerant disputare, in conventu publico, ac si in curia residentes, senatoriam sibi usurpant auctoritatem. Quae ignominiosa praesumptio fautoribus magis imputanda videtur, quam

foeminis. Unde, quia divinae leges, ut supra monstratum est, hoc contradicunt, et humanae nihilominus id ipsum prohibent, ut foeminae nihil aliud prosequantur in publico, quam suam causam: (ait enim lex Theodosiana: Nulla ratione foeminae amplius quam suas causas agendi habeant potestatum, nec alicuius causam a se noverint prosequendam;) idcirco ex auctoritate canonica interdicimus, ut nulla sanctimonialis virgo, vel vidua, conventus generales audeat, nisi a principe fuerit evocata, aut ab episcopo suo: nisi forte propriae necessitatis ratio impulerit, et hoc ipsum cum licentia episcopi sui.' *Concilia Namnetensis* c. 19, in *Sacrorum conciliorum nova et amplissima collectio*, ed. J.D. Mansi, 31 vols (Florence 1759–98), 18: 171–2. Note also that in the list of chapters this one is headed 'Ne fœminæ publicis conventibus ac placitis se immisceant.' I have translated *sanctimonialis virgo* as 'chaste young lady,' although it could perhaps also be translated as 'nun.'

52 Berschin, 'Bonizone da Sutri,' 285 (see n. 10 above), discusses how Bonizo resorted to providing his own rubrics and personal opinions (*dicta*) when canonical material was lacking. In this instance, however, Bonizo does refer to Roman and ecclesiastical law and does appear to have had an ancient canon as his model.

53 'Set hoc dico, quod apostolus dicet. Paulus mulieribus sanctis precipit silentium, dicens: "Mulieres in ecclesia taceant. Turpe est enim mulieri docere." Quodsi turpe est docere, multo turpius est populos regere.' *Liber de vita Christiana* 7.29 (ed. Perels, 250). Bonizo's interpretation echoes the words of a late antique commentary once attributed to Ambrose and Augustine: 'Nec docere enim potest nec testis esse neque fidem dicere nec iudicare: quanto magis imperare.' See *Quaestiones Veteris et Novi Testamenti* c. 45, ed. Alexander Souter, CSEL 50 (Leipzig 1908), 83.

We should note in passing the slight differences in form between the versions of Bonizo and Nantes. The Vulgate reads 'Mulieres in ecclesiis taceant, non enim permittitur eis loqui, sed subditas esse, sicut et lex dicit. Si quid autem volunt discere, domi viros suos interrogent. Turpe est enim mulieri loqui in ecclesia.' Nantes 19 reads 'Mulieres in ecclesia taceant, non enim permittitur eis loqui; turpe est enim mulieri loqui in ecclesia.' In Bonizo's version, the scriptural passage is even more truncated and *loqui* has been changed to *docere*, thus: 'Mulieres in ecclesia taceant. Turpe est enim mulieri docere.'

54 It should be noted, however, that phrases such as 'divina et humana leges' recur in the sources of this period: e.g., Petrus Crassus, *Defensio Heinrici IV. regis*, ed. L. de Heinemann, MGH LdL 1(Hanover 1891), 444; *Decretum Wiberti vel Clementis papae*, ed. E. Dümmler, MGH LdL 1 (Hanover 1891), 626, etc.

55 *Lex Romana Visigothorum* 9.1.2, ed. Gustav Haenel (Berlin 1849), 48–9.

56 Jean Chélini notes how the antifeminism of the age echoed the views of the church fathers and the authors of the Carolingian age, and Berschin acknowledges that in the chapter on women in war Bonizo follows the misogyny of late antique authors

like Jerome: Chélini, 'Les Femmes dans la société médiévale au temps de la comtesse Mathilde a travers l'oeuvre de Pierre Damien,' in *Studi matildici* [II] (see n. 22 above), 295–6; Berschin, 'Bonizone da Sutri,' 287.

In fact many ancient authors had firmly separated warfare from women's affairs. The late antique writer Vegetius, whose *Epitoma rei militaris* was by far the most popular treatise on the subject in the Middle Ages, had warned against recruiting even men who had been engaged in women's work: 'linteones, omnesque, qui aliquid tractasse videbuntur ad gynaecea pertinens, longe arbitror pellendos a castris.' *Epitoma rei militaris*, ed. Leo F. Stelten (New York 1990), 18. For some examples of classical hostility towards female commanders and conceptual distancing of the feminine from military activity see David Herlihy, *Opera muliebria: Women and Work in Medieval Europe* (New York 1990) 7–8, and Fraser, *Warrior Queens*, 33, 39–40, 51–2. According to Herodotus, even female warriors – the Amazons – refrained from women's work: Herodotus, *History* 4.114, trans. A.D. Godley, Loeb Classical Library, 4 vols (Cambridge, MA 1971) 2: 313–15.

Regarding female warriors, we know of at least one early medieval secular law that was a response to bands of women using weapons against men: see the interesting discussion of this law (an edict of the Lombard king Liutprand from 734) in Ross Balzaretti, ' "These are things that men do, not women": The Social Regulation of Female Violence in Langobard Italy,' in *Violence and Society in the Early Medieval West*, 175–92, at 186–9.

We should note in contrast that Plato had advocated allowing women greater roles in war and government, and that there do appear to have been some female wrestlers and gladiators in the Roman Empire. Both Plato and the wrestlers, however, drew severe criticism: see Herlihy, *Opera muliebria*, 7–8, and Juvenal's satire on female gladiators in his *Satires*, book 6 (as quoted in Naphtali Lewis and Meyer Reinhold, *Roman Civilization: Selected Readings*, 3rd ed., vol. 2: *The Empire* (New York 1990), 357–8.

57 Regino of Prüm, *Libri duo de synodalibus causis et disciplinis ecclesiasticis* 2.174, ed. F.G.A. Wasserschleben (Leipzig 1840), 281–2.
58 Burchard of Worms, *Decretum* 8.85 (PL 140: 808).
59 E.g., *Collectio canonum Hibernensis: Die irische Kanonensammlung*, ed. Hermann Wasserschleben (Leipzig 1885; repr. 1966), 45.18–20, 46.24–5; *Collectio IX partium* 7.132 (Vatican City, BAV, MS. Vat. Lat. 1349). *Statuta ecclesia antiqua* 37, which reads 'Mulier, quamvis docta et sancta, viros in conventu docere non praesumat,' was another one of the more common canons used to restrict women's right to public authority. It is found in numerous collections, including those of Regino and Burchard, while in the Collection in 183 Titles it is actually combined with Nantes 19 to form its own chapter. The collection was compiled ca 475: *Statuta ecclesia antiqua* 37 (99), in *Concilia Galliae, a. 314–a. 506*, ed. C. Munier,

CCSL 148 (Turnholt 1963), 172; Regino, *Libri duo de synodalibus*, App. 1.19; Burchard, *Decretum* 8.83; *Liber canonum diversorum sanctorum patrum, sive: Collectio in CLXXXIII titulos digesta* 144.1, ed. G. Motta (Vatican City 1988), 228.

60 Several contemporaries believed that Anselm's collection had been undertaken at Gregory's request, although modern historians have had reservations about this perception. On the issue of the extent to which Anselm's collection can be seen as a defence of Gregory's policies, see Giorgio Picasso, 'La "Collectio canonum" di Anselmo nella storia delle collezioni canoniche,' in *Sant'Anselmo, Mantova, e la lotta*, 314–15; and Kathleen Cushing, *Papacy and Law in the Gregorian Revolution: The Canonistic Work of Anselm of Lucca* (Oxford 1998), 104 ff. Deusdedit was also seen as a disciple of Gregory, although there were important differences between them in certain matters of doctrine and in their approach to reform (Cushing, *Papacy and Law*, 99). Politically, however, both Anselm and Deusdedit were clearly within the camp of Gregory and Matilda, as both the criticism levelled at them and their own polemics reveal: *Benonis aliorumque cardinalium schismaticorum contra Gregorium VII et Urbanum II scripta*, ed. K. Franche, MGH LdL 2 (Hanover 1892), 366–422, at 399 and 416; Anselm of Lucca, *Liber contra Wibertum*, ed. E. Bernheim, MGH LdL 1 (Hanover 1891), 527; Deusdedit, *Libellus contra invasores et symoniacos et reliquos schismaticos*, ed. E Sackur, MGH LdL 2 (Hanover 1892), 330. Note also Deusdedit's more general justification of the use of force by secular powers in the *Libellus contra invasores* (ed. Sackur, 300).

61 The only attempt at an edition of Anselm's collection was made by Friedrich Thaner: *Anselmi episcopi Lucensis collectio canonum una cum collectione minore*, 2 vols in 1 (Innsbruck 1906–15). Unfortunately, Thaner did not edit the final two books (12–13) of the collection. In lieu of a critical edition of these books I have followed Kathleen Cushing's working edition from her *Papacy and Law*, 179–200, which is preferable to the edition added by Edith Pásztor to her article 'Lotta per le investiture e "ius belli": La posizione di Anselmo di Luca,' in *Sant'Anselmo, Manova, e la lotte per le investiture*, 405–21. The letter from Gregory the Great to Brunhild is contained in bk 13, c. 23 of the collection.

Anselm's collection was not written before March 15, 1081, since he inserts the famous letter from Gregory VII to Bishop Hermann of Metz into canon 80 of bk 1 (under the rubric 'Quod Apostolico licet imperatores excommunicare ac deponere, quod etiam aliqui fecerunt episcopi'). Anselm, who died in 1086, has been justifiably described by I.S. Robinson as 'the most influential Gregorian canonist': Robinson, *The Papacy, 1073–1198* (Cambridge 1990), 317–18.

62 Deusdedit, *Collectio canonum* 4.103 (ed. von Glanvell, 445).

63 'Si quos igitur violentos, si quos adulteros, si quos fures vel aliis pravis actibus studere cognoscitis, Deum de eorum correctione placare festinate, ut per vos flagellum perfidarum gentium, quod, quantum videmus, ad multarum nationum

vindictam excitatum est, non inducat, ne, si, quod credimus, divinae ultionis iracundia sceleratorum fuerit actione commota, belli pestis interimat, quos delinquentes ad rectitudinis viam Dei praecepta non revocant.' Gregory the Great, *Registrum* 8.4, ed. D. Norberg, CCSL 140a (Turnholt 1982), 521.

Note the passage in Rangerius of Lucca's life of Anselm II of Lucca that seems to echo this: 'Adsunt vicini captantes praemia Tusci / Et fugiunt dominae iusta flagella suae,' *Vita metrica* 5865–6 (ed. Sackur et al., 1278). The *domina* in question was Matilda.

Anselm and Deusdedit appear to have been working independently, although they may have relied on one or more of the same minor or 'intermediate' collections, which remain almost completely unedited, but which contain many papal decretals (Cushing, *Papacy and Law*, 65–7). Both Anselm and Deusdedit relied, to a much greater extent than had earlier compilers, on papal letters to secular princes (Cushing, 97–9). Anselm may have found the letter in one of the MSS at S. Benedetto Polirone just south of Mantua (one of which is known to contain Gregory's letter to Brunhild – see Giuseppe Motta, 'I codici canonistici di Polirone', in *Sant'Anselmo, Mantova, e la lotta*, 360 n. 35), while Deusdedit had access to the papal archives and to Gregory's register.

64 It is not to be found in the *Pseudo-Isidorian Decretals*, ed. Paul Hinschius (Leipzig 1863); the *Capitularis Benedicti Levitae* (PL 97); the *Anselmo dedicata* (PL 56), the *Spicilegium, sive: Collectio veterum aliquot scriptorum qui in Galliae bibliothecis delituerant*, vol. 1, ed. Luc d'Achery and L.F.J. de la Barre (Paris 1723; repr. Farnborough 1967) [the 'd'Acheriana']; Regino of Prum, *Libri duo de synodalibus*; Burchard of Worms, *Decretum*; the *Collectio XII partium* (Troyes, Bibliothèque Municipale, MS. 246); or the *Collectio in CLXXXIII titulos*. The only collection composed before the 1080s in which I have been able to find it is the relatively minor *Collectio Herovalliana*, dating roughly from the 7th century, which was based mostly on the *Vetus Gallica*. J.-P. Migne has provided a list of chapter titles of the *Herovalliana* in PL 56: 307, and the incipit of c. 75 reads 'Item ejusdem [s. Gregorii] epistola ad Brunichildam reginam pro haeresi simoniaca destruenda.'

65 See Alfred Overmann, *Gräfin Mathilde von Tuscien* (Innsbruck 1895; repr. Frankfurt a. M. 1965), 147 #40b.

66 Although Anselm disagreed with Gregory (or at least with the *dictatus papae*) on a couple of issues (see Cushing, *Papacy and Law*, 216–22, esp. #2 and #24), on the whole – and especially on the issue of the right of Christians to use force against heretics and schismatics – they were certainly in agreement.

67 As Kathleen Cushing has recently noted, 'Anselm employed texts written to combat fifth-century heresies to support his condemnation of eleventh-century schismatics whom he identified as heretics. Here, Anselm can be seen almost

groping for categories to describe these 'new' heresies which were effectively the product of the need to vilify the opponents of reform. With such modifications, he created universal, and relevant canons, from what were specific and perhaps out-dated injunctions.' In doing so, Anselm extended the role of defender of the church to an ever wider circle; Cushing, *Papacy and Law*, 76–7, 124–6, and 133. On Anselm and the use of force in general see also A.M. Stickler, 'Il potere coattivo materiale della chiesa nella riforma gregoriana secondo Anselmo da Lucca,' *Studi Gregoriani* 2 (1947) 235–85; Pásztor, 'Lotta per le investiture,' 375–404; and Erdmann, *Origin of the Idea of the Crusade*, 241ff.

68 'Quod reginae corrigendi malefactores potestas datur': Anselm, *Collectio canonum* 13.23, in Cushing, *Papacy and Law*, 198. This is the rubric in two A MSS (Cambridge, Corpus Christi College, 269; Paris, BN, Lat. 12519), while in the third A MS (Vatican City, BAV, Vat. Lat. 1363) the rubrics break off at exactly this point, with a space being left for them to the end of the book. On the MSS of Anselm's collection see P. Landau, 'Erweiterte Fassungen der Kanonessammlung des Anselm von Lucca aus dem 12. Jahrhundert,' in *Sant'Anselmo, Mantova, e la lotta*; and P. Fournier, *Mélanges de droit canonique*, vol. 2 (Aalen 1983), 658–62.

69 As Berschin notes, the collections of Anselm, Bonizo, and Deusdedit are closely connected, but the precise relationship between them will probably not be solved until a better edition of Anselm appears. Berschin, *Bonizo von Sutri*, 67; cf. S. Kuttner, 'Some Roman Manuscripts of Canonical Collections,' *Bulletin of Medieval Canon Law* n.s. 1 (1971) 7–29.

Anselm's authorship of bks 8–13 has been called into question (see Pásztor, 'Lotta per le investiture,' 376 n. 5), but most scholars see the rubrics as indicative of Anselm's own views.

70 For the *Decretum*, *Panormia*, and *Tripartita* I have used the incipit–explicit editions in Linda Fowler-Magerl, *Kanones J: A Selection of Canon Law Collections Compiled between 1000 and 1140: Access with Data Processing* (CD-ROM: Piesenkofen 2003).

72 E.g., 8.85 (from pseudo-Ambrose, with the rubric 'Nulla est mulieris potestas, sed in omnibus dominio viri subject est'): 'Mulierem constat subjectam sub dominio viri, et nullam auctoritatem habere, nec docere enim potest nec testis esse, nec fidem dare, nec judicare'; 8.91 (Ambrose): 'Adam per Evam deceptus est, non Eva per Adam. Quem vocavit ad culpam mulier, justum est ut eam in gubernationem assumat, ne iterum femina sua facilitate labatur.'; 8.97: '... verbum autem Domini blasphematur ... dum contra legem fidemque naturae ea, quae Chrisitana est et ex lege Dei subjecta est viro, imperare desiderat, cum etiam gentiles feminae viris suis serviant communi lege naturali.'

I have been unable to find any of these patristic texts in any of the major collections compiled in the few centuries leading up to Ivo's *Decretum*. I have examined the *Pseudo-Isidorian Decretals,* the d'Acheriana, the *Anselmo dedicata,* Regino of Prüm, Burchard of Worms, *the Collection in 12 Parts,* the *183 Titles,* the *Collectio Britannica* (London, BL, MS. Add. 8873), the *Collection in 74 Titles* (*Diversorum patrum sententie sive collectio in LXXIV titulos digesta,* ed. J. Gilchrist, Monumenta iuris canonici series B: Corpus collectionum 1 [Vatican City 1973]), the collections of Anselm of Lucca and Deusdedit, Bonizo's *Liber de vita Christiana,* and Fowler-Magerl, *Kanones J.* Perhaps Ivo, like Anselm and other compilers of this period, was relying on intermediate collections for his versions of these patristic canons. He could have found them in the *Collectio canonum* of Paris, Bibliothèque de l'Arsenal, MS. 713, fols 162v and 163r–v.

73 E.g., the *Collectio X partium* 8.10.1.1–8.10.3 (Florence, Biblioteca Nazionale, MS. Conventi soppressi D.2.1476, fols 167r–168r) corresponds to *Panormia* 7.43–51, while the *Caesaraugustana* (version I) 5.91, 10.43–4, and 10.46–8 (Salamanca, Universidad Civil, MS. 2644, fols 42r and 90r–v) correspond to *Panormia* 7.49, 7.43, 7.50–1, and 7.45, respectively.

Canons in collections that may or may not have been influenced by the Ivonian corpus include: *Collectio IX librorum* 8.1.141 (Vatican City, Archivio di San Pietro, MS. C.118, fol. 102v), which corresponds to *Panormia* 7.45; *Collectio canonum Ambrosiana* (version I) 214 (Milan, Archivio Capitolare di S. Ambrogio, MS. M. 11, fol. 56r) and *Collectio X partium* 10.8.10 (Cologne, Historisches Archiv, MS. W. Kl. Fol. 199, fol. 174r–v), both of which correspond to *Panormia* 7.48; and *Collectio IX librorum* 8.1.142 (Vatican City, Archivio di San Pietro, MS. C.118, fol. 102v) and *Collectio Brugensis* 360 (London, BL, MS. Cotton Cleopatra C.VIII, fol. 173v), both of which correspond to *Panormia* 7.49.

74 Gratian, *Decretum,* in *Corpus iuris canonici,* ed. Ae. Friedberg, vol. 1 (Leipzig 1879), cols 1253–6. The order of the canons in Gratian's *Decretum* also follows the order of Ivo's *Panormia* more closely than that of Ivo's *Decretum.* The correspondence is as follows: Ivo's *Panormia* 7.43–51 = Ivo's *Decretum* 8.94–7, 8.98a–b, 85, 91–2 and Gratian's *Decretum* C.33 q.5 cc. 12–16, 11, 17–19, respectively. Note that *Panormia* 7.47–8 corresponds to *Decretum* 8.98a–b.

75 On the reception of Bonizo's work in the Middle Ages see Berschin, *Bonizo von Sutri,* 95ff.

76 'In correptione malorum Deus omnipotens placatur': Gratian, C.23 q.4 c.47. This rubric follows most closely that found in a 'B' recension of Anselm's *Collectio canonum* (Vatican City, BAV, MS. Vat. Lat. 6381), which reads 'Quod Dominus pacatur de vindicta malorum': Cushing, *Papacy and Law,* 198. On Gratian's use of a recension of Anselm's collection see G. Picasso, 'La *Collectio canonum* di Anselmo,' in *Sant'Anselmo, Mantova, e la lotta,* 320.

77 See for examples the comparisons between Richilde of Hainaut in the *Annales Blandiniensis* and the women in Saxo Grammaticus's *History of the Danes*

(McLaughlin, 'Woman Warrior,' 194–5 and 200 n. 33), or the contrast between the portrayal of Aethelfled in the *Anglo-Saxon Chronicle* and in Henry of Huntingdon (Bandel, 'English Chroniclers' Attitude' [see n. 6 above], 116).

78 Of course, one will also find examples of women being praised for the very same actions: see, e.g., Truax, 'Anglo-Norman Women', 117ff.

79 Pauline Stafford, 'The Portrayal of Royal Women in England, Mid-Tenth to Mid-Twelfth Centuries,' in *Medieval Queenship*, ed. John C. Parsons (New York 1993), 156–7. McLaughlin, 'Woman Warrior,' 195, notes that high medieval writers often alluded to biblical or classical models when describing 'warrior' women, but does not mention the continuing popularity of misogynistic classical texts in the early Middle Ages.

80 Although Pope Gregory VII appears to have publicly distanced himself from Matilda in order to avoid any hint of impropriety in their relationship (see H.E.J. Cowdrey, *Pope Gregory VII, 1073–85* [Oxford 1998], 167–8), he clearly approved of Matilda's military campaigns on his behalf.

81 In addition to the passages defending Matilda in the polemics of Anselm, Deusdedit, Donizo, et al., we may also note that Rangerius of Lucca contradicts Bonizo's *Liber de vita Christiana* 7.29 when he praises Matilda for overcoming her sex and fighting Henry: 'Quae sexum superet, quae fortia facta virorum / Non metuat, cuius omnia vincat amor,' *Vita metrica* 3705–6 (ed. Sackur et al., 1235).

82 In a version of the treatise attributed to Glanvill one finds the following statement regarding women: 'Quia non possent nec debent nec solent esse in servitio domini regis in exercitu nec in aliis servitiis regalibus.' F. Pollock and F. Maitland, *The History of English Law before the Time of Edward I*, 2nd ed. (Cambridge 1923), 485 n. 5.

83 Susan Schibanoff, 'True Lies: Transvestitism and Idolatry in the Trial of Joan of Arc,' in *Fresh Verdicts on Joan of Arc* (see n. 2 above), 31–60.

84 See n. 2 above. One possible difference between female commanders in the high versus the late Middle Ages is that in the earlier period women seem more likely to have engaged in offensive, *exercitus*-style expeditions; nearly all the examples I have found from the later period involve women defending castles.

85 E.g., Elizabeth Ewing, *Women in Uniform* (London 1975), 28–35. We may also note that some women may have disguised themselves in order to participate in the Crusades; see Beha ed-Din, *Life of Saladin*, trans. C.W. Wilson (New York 1971) 195–211, and the sources translated in Francesco Gabrieli, *Arab Historians of the Crusades* (Berkeley 1969), 189 and 206–7. See also the discussion of these passages in Nicholson, 'Women on the Third Crusade' (see n. 3 above).

Conclusion

MARK D. MEYERSON, DANIEL THIERY, and OREN FALK

The problem of interpreting violence is inextricably tied to the problem of evaluating it. Today, the use of force, coercive and destructive, persuasive and constructive, never appears quite straightforward, nor can it be discussed in value-neutral terms. Instances of violence – for private or public purposes, to entertain or to educate – immediately provoke debate, cause anxiety, and call for elaborate explanation, even apologetics. What contemporary society construes as violent rarely accords with what it regards as legitimate behaviour; numerous labels have been devised to recast certain forms of violence into morally unobjectionable endeavours – peacekeeping, national liberation, self defence – while stigmatizing others all the more vehemently: as terrorism, vigilantism, gang violence, and so forth.

Daniel Baraz's discussion of the high medieval invention of cruelty in Western Christendom hypothesizes a crucial shift in the evaluation and subsequent categorization of violent acts. Baraz sees a development from an undifferentiated early medieval discourse on violence, which makes little qualitative distinction among degrees of intensity, to a stricter late medieval ranking, in which intense forms of violence are perceived as different in kind and thus cruel. What medieval writers perceived as merely violent aroused little anxiety; what they perceived as cruel, however, caused a great deal of consternation. A greater degree of categorical distinction thus went hand in hand with the erection of stricter normative barriers. The authors Baraz discusses were not writing in a social vacuum, but rather were expressing attitudes growing out of real efforts to effect social and religious change in the high Middle Ages. Processes like the Peace and Truce of God, the Gregorian reform, crusading, chivalry, and state formation channelled, sanctioned, condemned, and gendered violence.

The essays by John Hill and Oren Falk ostensibly discuss societies in which differentiations like the one Baraz diagnoses have not yet occurred. In Anglo-Saxon England and in the Iceland of the sagas, violence seems to be productive of kinship and community in unproblematic ways. Even the violence of Grendel and his mother is not described as qualitatively different from that perpetrated by Beowulf and his cohorts: the monsters seem to follow the dictates of kinship and the feuding ethos – cruelty is not an issue. Nor does cruelty figure in the minds of those who observe and comment on Norse duels. By the later Middle Ages, one would expect (according to Baraz's interpretative framework) to find such forms of violence being socially proscribed. Yet, as Mark Meyerson and Debra Blumenthal's essays show, violence might still grow out of and further social cohesion. Thus, slaves in fifteenth-century Valencia could view themselves as active members of their masters' feuding faction, while Jews and *conversos* could communicate across religious lines in pursuit of a commonly defined notion of honour. As in earlier medieval societies, aggression was practised without inhibition, embarrassment, or any clear articulation of an absolute upper limit to allowable ferocity.

So, how *can* Dark Age Scandinavia and fifteenth-century Valencia be told apart? The obvious difference that comes to mind is the elaboration of late medieval royal and ecclesiastical institutions. While individuals and kin groups might still consider their acts of violence honourable and licit, church and state authorities with their judiciaries and constabularies begged to differ. For them, violence *per se* was problematic because of its potential to disrupt the divinely ordained order. Both authorities struggled to monopolize the right to exact violent retribution. However, the distinction between early medieval and late medieval violence may be more apparent than real. After all, the events Meyerson and Blumenthal discuss are only accessible to us through the filter of documents produced by the very institutions that sought to control violence. Hill and Falk, on the other hand, analyze sources whose particular authorial agenda is not as implicated in promoting institutional goals.

Richard Green's essay also takes up the theme of the late medieval conflict between popular and royal conceptions of legitimate violence. He shows how the Robin Hood poems glorify self-help and vigilantism, flouting the claims of state authorities that they alone should discipline and punish malefactors. Green's literary sources, which (like those used by Hill and Falk) are rooted in a popular model of justice, thrust into relief the methodological problem of understanding late medieval conceptions and practices of violence on the basis of institutional records alone. The implication of juxtaposing Green's essay to those of Blumenthal and Meyerson is that the documents produced by state authorities would have taken a markedly different stance on who could legitimately wield the sword. One could imagine that, in the records of the court of the King's Bench, the actions of Robin Hood would be described as sinister, even subversive.

The poems of the Robin Hood cycle postdate the discovery of cruelty, but they do not delegitimize any violence, no matter how horrific. The same cannot be said of the work of the Scottish Blind Harry or of John Gower's poetry. Anne McKim shows how differences of nationality can lead to diametrically opposed interpretations of political violence: what is heroic in a Scotsman becomes villainous when performed by an Englishman, and vice versa. Eve Salisbury addresses the same hermeneutic gap across social strata, showing how the ritually cleansing violence of a mob of commoners becomes an act of desecration in the hands of the *litteratus* Gower. For the writers McKim and Salisbury discuss, the violence of English armies and rioting peasants is excessive and undoubtedly cruel. These contributors' essential point, so basic to how the reality of violence is constructed in the late and post-medieval world, can hardly be emphasized too often in an age when wars, political protest, and acts of nihilistic desperation all play out in real time on seemingly objective television and computer screens worldwide.

One thing fourteenth- and fifteenth-century chroniclers and poets take for granted is that the practice of violence is a male prerogative; women, if present at all, can only play the part of victims. Gender categories in the early Middle Ages seem to have been more malleable, allowing women on occasion to take agent roles in violence. The eleventh-century controversies over the career of Matilda of Tuscany, which David Hay explores, demonstrate the efforts to gender military activity more strictly and to deprive women of such agency. Like cruelty, gender emerges in the high Middle Ages as an organizing principle governing the thinking about violence, delimiting spheres of propriety, and creating new kinds of anxiety.

This renewed effort to ban women from the battlefield aimed to limit their social options by underlining their gender. But confining women to a defined sphere of gendered activity was insufficient: even within that sphere, women's bodies had to be controlled, limiting their social options by underlining their sex. Such efforts did not go unopposed. In John Parsons's essay, aristocratic women use their unambiguously female bodies to make political statements; when they do, all hell breaks loose. The uncontrolled female body is both a metaphor and an instrument for violent disorder. Women, in this sense at least, seem to have been pushed farther outside the bounds of late medieval society than ever the Grendelkin had been in an earlier period.

Whereas the assertion of aristocratic women's physical independence destabilizes the body politic, the willing submission of female saints' bodies to the violent domination of men bolsters the framework of a gendered religious ideology. Beth Crachiolo's juxtaposition of male and female martyrs in the *South English Legendary* highlights this gender gap. Men, whether tormentors or tormented, exercise political and religious authority, their office assuming greater prominence than their flesh. Women, on the other hand, are always on the receiving end, their bodies both sites of struggle and the focus of the reader's gaze. Through their beatific acceptance of torment, female saints are complicit in upholding gendered notions of who should practise physical violence.

By courting torture, female martyrs seem to assign a positive value to cruelty. But even if we resist the temptation to read these martyrdom narratives quite so literally as the women's own condoning of what is done to them, certainly the hagiographers, while branding the violence against their heroines as heinous, nonetheless perceive it as productive of a greater good. Chaucer, in contrast, as M.C. Bodden's treatment of the *Clerk's Tale* shows, uses the voice of the Envoy to subvert the hagiographical trajectory of this story of wifely forbearance. Griselda is as meek and receptive to torment as any virgin martyr, yet the Envoy warns against accepting her 'pacience' as a recipe for marital bliss. According to Bodden, Chaucer posits a qualitative gulf between divinely enacted and human agents' violence as unbridgeable as the chasm, whose widening Baraz detects, between mere violence and cruelty. The stratification of genders does not automatically translate into a female meritocracy of suffering.

The Envoy's argument against the virtue of the victim's passivity is undermined by narratives describing the martyrdom of Thomas Becket. Here was an active, intransigent man, whose forceful resistance to the will of the king has been expunged from the hagiography: ideology demanded that a victimized cleric, whose ordination had rendered him (in R.N. Swanson's phrase) 'emasculine,' submit to violence like a woman. Dawn Marie Hayes elucidates the dialectic process by which the sacrilegious shedding of clerical blood paradoxically sanctifies the cleric himself and the cathedral he dies in, even boding salvation for his murderers. The violation of Becket's ordained body, intended to reduce him to the status of an enemy of the king, instead placed the crown of martyrdom upon his head. But at the same time that it elevated Becket, the violence against him reinforced the powerful coupling of saintly victimhood with passive suffering, helping to make violence against victims whose emasculinity is gendered rather than vocational more acceptable and more likely.

In all of these passion narratives, the virtue of the victims' compliance may be open to debate, but the actions of the persecutors are depicted as unequivocally tyrannical. Walter's violence is disparaged for going well beyond the bounds of rightful patriarchal correction, as is that of the pagan magistrates who send female saints to their brutal ends. Likewise, the vicious murderers of Becket are castigated for executing the commands of an intemperate monarch: *any* violence against the clergy is excessive, indeed impious. The late medieval shift towards a greater categorization and regulation of violence, evident in Baraz's chronology of the invention of cruelty, manifests itself in the efforts of canon lawyers, hagiographers, chroniclers, and poets to deny the legitimacy of targeting women and clerics and to curb the unrestrained violence of lay males. The increasingly fine distinctions made among types of violence thus came to depend exclusively on discrimination between licit and illicit victims, while assailants came under automatic and uniform censure. The same logic can be seen operating in other niches of the persecuting societies budding in the later Middle Ages: the absolute condemnation of Jews as Christ's murderers, for example, at the same time that the resulting death was celebrated as an absolute salvific gift.

A prohibition of physical aggression was inherent in the medieval construction of the female gender, affording women a notional shield against victimization while denying them the prerogative to commit violent acts themselves. The analogous removal of clerics from the arena of violence thus deconstructed their masculine identity. Full-fledged men, on the other hand, remained rooted in a world of violence, both as predators and as prey. Late medieval constructions of masculinity demanded that men of all classes use aggression in some form, whether fighting for king and country in war or defending their honour in street brawls. Because of the premium placed on masculine violence, the autumn of the Middle Ages remained an open season on men – always potential, and usually justifiable, victims.

But if all men, *qua* men, were implicated in violence, not all were created equal. Peasants and artisans were socially proscribed from crossing class lines to attack their betters, but not vice versa. State institutions sought to deny the legitimacy of lower-class agency altogether and to confine the exercise of violence to the ruling elite. Their rudimentary policing capabilities, however, limited their ability to enforce their claims. Plebeian males, while reluctant to challenge their social superiors (except when swept up in the momentum of mass rebellion), continued to shed the blood of their peers in local power struggles.

By the end of the Middle Ages, social class, gendered divisions of labour, and distinctions between secular and religious spheres were crystallizing as criteria for parsing the gamut of violent potentiality. Because they are rooted in medieval discourse, these criteria help the modern scholar interpret the violent acts of medieval people; but the meaning of medieval violence remains elusive and polyvalent. Indeed, the discourse itself impedes just as much as it facilitates interpretation. Synchronic variation in terminology and conventions across genres, as well as diachronic changes in institutional and intellectual milieux, complicate the effort to correlate phrases like 'a great effusion of blood' to any underlying reality. Modern methodological approaches provide ways of negotiating this gap between discursive practice and social fact, but – as even anthropologists and literary critics working in modern contexts acknowledge – the bridges thus built are not always secure. They are still shakier for medievalists, who, when hazarding such analyses, are compelled to rely on analogies at many centuries' remove from the medieval past. Yet, by taking into account both specific acts of violence and the institutional, social, and ideological context in which they were enmeshed, the essays in this volume vault ambitiously across the interpretative chasm. Perhaps these ventures into the past can repay the loan of modern theoretical constructs by offering their own bridgeheads into interpreting modern violence.